Ancestors

# World Anthropology

*General Editor*

SOL TAX

*Patrons*

CLAUDE LÉVI-STRAUSS
MARGARET MEAD
LAILA SHUKRY EL HAMAMSY
M. N. SRINIVAS

MOUTON PUBLISHERS · THE HAGUE · PARIS
DISTRIBUTED IN THE USA AND CANADA BY ALDINE, CHICAGO

# Ancestors

*Editor*

WILLIAM H. NEWELL

MOUTON PUBLISHERS · THE HAGUE · PARIS
DISTRIBUTED IN THE USA AND CANADA BY ALDINE, CHICAGO

# *General Editor's Preface*

Among all animal species, it is probable that only humans are aware that each living specimen is related in terms of a common origin. But even humans can usually trace their ancestry back only a short while. This book deals only with remembered and identified ancestors. Cultures vary in the way they isolate their ancestors for special treatment by the living. In this volume emphasis is directed principally at certain unilineal societies in Africa and Asia and brings up-to-date theory on a topic of traditional anthropological interest presently known as ancestor worship. It is a result of a conference preceding an international Congress that an unusually rich atmosphere for discussions on this subject was available to the editor and authors of this volume.

Like most contemporary sciences, anthropology is a product of the European tradition. Some argue that it is a product of colonialism, with one small and self-interested part of the species dominating the study of the whole. If we are to understand the species, our science needs substantial input from scholars who represent a variety of the world's cultures. It was a deliberate purpose of the IXth International Congress of Anthropological and Ethnological Sciences to provide impetus in this direction. The *World Anthropology* volumes, therefore, offer a first glimpse of a human science in which members from all societies have played an active role. Each of the books is designed to be self-contained; each is an attempt to update its particular sector of scientific knowledge and is written by specialists from all parts of the world. Each volume should be read and reviewed individually as a separate volume on its own given subject. The set as a whole will indicate what changes are in store for anthropology as scholars from the developing countries join in studying the species of which we are all a part.

The IXth Congress was planned from the beginning not only to include as many of the scholars from every part of the world as possible, but also with a view toward the eventual publication of the papers in high-quality volumes. At previous Congresses scholars were invited to bring papers which were then read out loud. They were necessarily limited in length; many were only summarized; there was little time for discussion; and the sparse discussion could only be in one language. The IXth Congress was an experiment aimed at changing this. Papers were written with the intention of exchanging them before the Congress, particularly in extensive pre-Congress sessions; they were not intended to be read aloud at the Congress, that time being devoted to discussions — discussions which were simultaneously and professionally translated into five languages. The method for eliciting the papers was structured to make as representative a sample as was allowable when scholarly creativity — hence self-selection — was critically important. Scholars were asked both to propose papers of their own and to suggest topics for sessions of the Congress which they might edit into volumes. All were then informed of the suggestions and encouraged to rethink their own papers and the topics. The process, therefore, was a continuous one of feedback and exchange and it has continued to be so even after the Congress. The some two thousand papers comprising *World Anthropology* certainly then offer a substantial sample of world anthropology. It has been said that anthropology is at a turning point; if this is so, these volumes will be the historical direction-markers.

As might have been foreseen in the first postcolonial generation, the large majority of the Congress papers (82 percent) are the work of scholars identified with the industrialized world which fathered our traditional discipline and the institution of the Congress itself: Eastern Europe (15 percent); Western Europe (16 percent); North America (47 percent); Japan, South Africa, Australia, and New Zealand (4 percent). Only 18 percent of the papers are from developing areas: Africa (4 percent); Asia-Oceania (9 percent); Latin America (5 percent). Aside from the substantial representation from the U.S.S.R. and the nations of Eastern Europe, a significant difference between this corpus of written material and that of other Congresses is the addition of the large proportion of contributions from Africa, Asia, and Latin America. "Only 18 percent" is two to four times as great a proportion as that of other Congresses; moreover, 18 percent of 2,000 papers is 360 papers, 10 times the number of Third World papers presented at previous Congresses. In fact, these

360 papers are more than the total of ALL papers published after the last International Congress of Anthropological and Ethnological Sciences which was held in the United States (Philadelphia, 1956).

The significance of the increase is not simply quantitative. The input of scholars from areas which have until recently been no more than subject matter for anthropology represents both feedback and also long-awaited theoretical contributions from the perspectives of very different cultural, social, and historical traditions. Many who attended the IXth Congress were convinced that anthropology would not be the same in the future. The fact that the next Congress (India, 1978) will be our first in the "Third World" may be symbolic of the change. Meanwhile, sober consideration of the present set of books will show how much, and just where and how, our discipline is being revolutionized.

Many other volumes in this series treat topics related both to African and Asian cultures and to historical, social and religious phenomena and cultural theory, and they will contribute to a broader understanding of the subject of this volume.

*Chicago, Illinois*                                                    SOL TAX
*April 5, 1976*

# *Preface*

The study of ancestors is a topic which is almost ideal for a congress such as the IXth ICAES in Chicago. It has a long pedigree as a subject going back to the early fathers such as Tylor, Crooke, and Junod, it overlaps with fields related to social anthropology such as prehistory and double burial, it is widely distributed with strong area characteristics on every continent, and there is a substantial body of empirical material which can be drawn upon.

In the nineteenth century, religion was sometimes explained as an extension of ancestor worship. As the theoretical postulate that the source or origin of the one institution could be found in the other was gradually abandoned, general interest in ancestor worship also gradually decreased. It is only in recent times, given an increasing emphasis on the integrity and unity of certain forms of thought, that religious studies have become important once again as a way of thinking about man.

Although ancestral forms of behavior are found on all the continents, East Asia and West Africa immediately come to mind as areas having the most continuous body of contemporary material available. (Knowledge about customs relating to Roman and Greek ancestors is today accessible only through documentary evidence.) Both areas have a strong emphasis on unilinearity; both areas have a clearly defined religious and political system, and both areas have good ethnographies. Moreover, the controversy between Fortes and Freedman over the nature of ancestral authority over the living shows how easy it is for misunderstandings to arise in the absence of a comprehensive ethnographic background (Freedman 1966: 147ff.).

Conference participants outside the *Alma Mater* memorial of the University of Illinois, Urbana. From left to right: Gary Seaman (Cornell University); Karen Kerner (Institute for the Study of Human Issues, Philadelphia); David Feingold (Columbia University); Sung-hsing Wang (Academia Sinica); David Plath (University of Illinois); Robert Smith (Cornell University); D. K. Fiawoo (University of Ghana); Shoji Yonemura (Okayama University); Stevan Harrell (Stanford University); Meyer Fortes (University of Cambridge); Herman Ooms (University of Illinois, Chicago); William Newell (University of Sydney); Choshu Takeda (Doshisha University)

The session on ancestors during the Chicago Congress thus aimed to bring together contemporary scholars who are or were working in the field with a view to producing theoretical concepts of general significance within defined limits. This session was organized in three stages. First, the limits of the subject were narrowly defined by the organizer and his advisors. For example, ancestors existing in cognatic societies were excluded from consideration. Second, certain persons were invited to a pre-Congress conference in Urbana, Illinois, with an initial emphasis on scholars from non-Western countries since it is in these societies that behavior towards ancestors is most marked. The Department of Anthropology at the University of Illinois kindly hosted this conference by providing facilities. It is the thoughts developed at the Urbana conference which form the core of this book. And, finally, the general theories and ideas produced at the conference were presented to a general audience of scholars at one of the main sessions at the Chicago Congress for critical discussion.

Because of the financial difficulties that were encountered in organizing the pre-Congress conference, and perhaps also because of the number of overseas delegates who in many cases were unable to raise the supplementary funds to attend, the conference lacked some important scholars. Yet this was offset by the interchange of ideas which started to take place immediately between the Asian, African, and Western delegates. I hope that this conference will result in another, somewhat larger, meeting in which those scholars not invited to Urbana because of the specialized definition of the theme may come together at some time in the future for a more general discussion. But the basic understanding among the delegates, because of the principle of selection in the first place, undoubtedly enabled the discussion to reach a much more advanced level than might have otherwise been the case.

The initial conference at Urbana lasted for two days and was chaired in turn by Professors D. Plath (Illinois), M. Fortes (Cambridge), R. Smith (Cornell), and myself (Sydney). Some members who were invited to submit papers were unable to be present; others who have papers included in this book were invited to contribute only after the conference; a third group contributed substantially to the conference in the form of discussions and criticisms and have articles appearing elsewhere in the *World Anthropology* series. The responsibility for inclusion in this book rests entirely on the shoulders of the editor.

It was originally intended that a summary of the daily discussions should be included in this volume. Unfortunately the tape recorder

failed to reproduce the sounds adequately. A summary of the proceedings is to be found in Japanese in the *Anthropological Quarterly*
(Kyoto University 1974).

Between the time when the papers for this book were written and
published, a number of important new books have been produced
on this theme. Not only is Smith's research (1974) now published as
a book, but Ahern's study (1973) and Wolf's papers (1974) have now
appeared, as well as Choshu Takeda's monumental work in Japanese.
This book, however, focuses on comparative studies. While we have
tried to bring together studies from all important areas, it is regrettable
that no examples are included from Korea or any traditional African
unilineal society (such as the Ashanti).

In conclusion I should like to thank all those contributors and others
who made the conference and the Congress session a success, especially Professor David Plath, the local organizer on the Urbana campus
of the University of Illinois, and the travel grant committee of the
IXth ICAES who were able to partially assist some of the overseas
delegates.

WILLIAM H. NEWELL

## REFERENCES

AHERN, EMILY M.
   1973   *The cult of the dead in a Chinese village*. Stanford: Stanford
          University Press.
FREEDMAN, MAURICE
   1966   *Chinese lineage and society: Fukien and Kwangtung*. London:
          Athlone.
KYOTO UNIVERSITY SOCIETY OF ANTHROPOLOGY
   1974   *Anthropological Quarerly* 5(1). Kodansha.
SMITH, ROBERT J.
   1974   *Ancestor worship in contemporary Japan*. Stanford: Stanford
          University Press.
WOLF, ARTHUR P., *editor*
   1974   *Religion and ritual in Chinese society*. Stanford: Stanford Univer-
          sity Press.

# Table of Contents

# An Introductory Commentary

MEYER FORTES

The papers brought together in this symposium and the conference that was devoted to them at Urbana covered so wide a range that it would take a treatise to do justice to them. I want to consider only the major themes that emerge. It is over a hundred years since Tylor (as Professor Newell reminds us), summing up the views that prevailed in his day (1871: II, 113), drew special attention to ancestor worship — or, as he preferred to say (following the Roman terminologies), *Manes* worship — in his researches on the religious beliefs and practices of mankind. Nineteenth-century scholarship on this topic is excellently reviewed in the article in the Hastings Encyclopaedia of 1911 cited by Newell, and it is interesting to note how many of the current problems that are far from resolved are adumbrated there. J. R. Goody's critical assessment of later developments in theory and in research (1962) brings the perspective up to date. In this context it is not without significance that, fully in the spirit of Tylor's analysis, all the papers in the present symposium relate to Africa and Asia. For this raises a critical question. We do not hesitate to compare together such culturally, structurally, and regionally diverse societies as the Tallensi of northern Ghana and the Ewe of eastern Ghana with the technologically and economically far more complex, intellectually sophisticated, and long literate societies of China and Japan. We must conclude that whatever may be the social and cultural sources that generate ancestor worship, they cannot be referred to in technological, economic, political or even intellectual uniformities.

This leads us to another question suggested by Tylor. Is ancestor worship to be considered as primarily a system of religious beliefs and practices, in which creed and doctrine relating to death and the after-life, to concepts of the soul and of ghostly powers, and to rituals of prayer and sacrifice are the determining features? Or is it primarily an aspect, an extension as Tylor phrased it, of the structure of social relations in each society, notably at the domestic level. And, if the latter, how is the notion of extension to be understood?

Whichever way we look at it, one thing is clear. Ancestor worship, wherever it occurs, comprises customary beliefs and practices that are directed towards dead predecessors. This is taken for granted by all students of the subject. Yet it has long been maintained, in some quarters, that the beliefs and practices do not constitute "worship" in the strict sense. Nearly 40 years ago, J. H. Driberg (1936) contended that what he proposed to describe as the *pietas* exhibited in customary reverence for ancestors in Africa was not worship in the religious sense but the extension of attitudes normally directed towards living elders. This interpretation is echoed by some African scholars (cf. Brain 1973). It has been recently reasserted by Kopytoff (1971), who argues in support of this view, that Africans use the same terms for ancestors as for living "fathers," "grandfathers," and "elders." This is an inadequate, rather than totally fallacious, interpretation of the ethnographic data as Brain (1973), and Sangree (this volume) have shown. There are distinct terms for ancestors as dead in contrast to living forebears, and, as Brain remarks (1973: 121), "gifts made to elders are not equivalent to sacrifices made to ancestors. . . ." The same is true of the respect shown to elders. But what is most important is that the conditions of existence as well as the kinds and mechanism of power attributed to ancestors are totally different from those that are perceived to hold for living elders. As my Tallensi friends used to say, one can argue with living elders but not with ancestors.

Regardless of other features of ancestor worship, certain determinants are indispensable. First there is the fact that death is a necessary — though not, as Durkheim (1915), referring primarily to such simple nonliterate and subsistence-based societies as the Australian aborigines, and Weber (1951 [1912]), writing about classical China, both pointed out, a sufficient — condition for attaining ancestorhood. This is why ancestor worship is often, though incorrectly, subsumed in the more general category of cults of the dead. And secondly there is the fact that where ancestors are worshiped, not merely commemorated or taken into account for institutionalized purposes, the medium of relationship with them takes the form of ritual. I do not want to enter into definitional discussions and will therefore content myself with stating that prayer, libation, sacrifice, and other like activities described by students of ancestor worship are distinct in quality and implication from analogous and homologous nonritual secular activities. It is this that justifies us in speaking of ancestor worship, rather than of institutionalized reverence for or piety towards ancestors. We cannot, in other words, neglect the fact that ancestor worship is, as Tylor said, a branch of religion; but we must recognize that it does not comprise the whole of any people's religious system. In Japan, ancestor worship, which has its primary focus within the family system, is integrated into the socially wider hierarchy of Buddhist and Shinto temple cults, with their scriptural basis, priesthood, and nationwide predominance. Elsewhere, ancestor worship is part of religious systems which include beliefs in a Supreme Being, nature divinities, magic and witchcraft, personifications in the shape of deities of epidemic diseases or cosmic forces, and the experience of good and evil, chance, and destiny. However, what particularly restricts the scope of ancestor worship and at the same time gives it a distinctive stamp is its location primarily in the familial domain of social life. This is why the confusion has arisen that it was no more than an extension of eldership in the mundane sense. Yet the investigations of ancestor worship, over the past 30 years or so, from the point of view thus implied, that is, in relation to the social structure into which ancestor worship fits in a particular society, have most advanced our understanding of its nature and significance.

Here we meet with the problem of precisely specifying what we mean by the term "ancestor." It stands to reason that every human community, indeed every individual, must have had ancestors in the broadest biological and social sense. So also, for that matter, must every living animal have had ancestors. But such a loose usage can be of no assistance to a student of ancestor worship. What is confusing, however, is the casual employment of the notion by anthropologists. One example must suffice. Much has been written about the mythological representation of the origin of the Australian aborigines and their natural and social universe. In one authoritative paper, Ronald Berndt writes of the "mythical beings who are believed to have been responsible . . . for creating the natural species which included man . . ." and also to "have established an Aboriginal way of life. . . ." He speaks of them also as "deities" and adds that some of them ". . . are ANCESTRAL, credited with having created the progenitors of contemporary man" (1970: 216–217; original emphasis). The implication is clear that these "progenitors" of the "Dreaming" are to living Australian aboriginal societies what Adam and Eve are to those who accept the Biblical story of human origins as literally true. There is the difference of course, as Berndt's paper confirming the general literature on the subject shows, that these "ancestral" beings are not represented as being distinctively human in the contemporary sense. Indeed it seems to be unknown for actual ancestors to be traced, by known and specified steps of filiation, farther than to Ego's great-grandparents among Australian aborigines (cf. Meggitt 1962). This is not for lack of capacity to register ancestry but simply because Australian kinship institutions and religious concepts are incompatible with the recognition of human ascendants intervening between the grandparental generation and the mythological culture-heroes. Yet in the same book as that in which Berndt's article appears (Berndt, ed. 1970), there is a long paper by Nancy D. Munn in which the term "ancestors" is indiscriminately used for Berndt's "mythical beings." It is clear that these "ancestors" — who are as often as not depicted as primordial animal species — are in no way comparable to the kind of ancestors who form a line of named, identified human progenitors such as we meet with in Chinese or Tallensi lineage and clan systems (cf. Fortes 1969: Chapter 14). The Australian so-called ancestors are not conceptualized as procreators. They are not thought of as having been capable of begetting and bearing offspring as ancestors, strictly defined, must be deemed to have been. Australian aboriginal religious beliefs and practices certainly celebrate the miraculous creation of their universe by the collectivity of mythical beings in the remote past "Dreamtime," but no modern authorities describe this as ancestor worship. Indeed it is doubtful if any of their ritual practices can be regarded as acts of "worship" seeing that they lack such distinctive features as prayer, libation, and sacrifice.

Truistic as it may sound, it is nevertheless important to state that ancestors receive recognition insofar as their descendants exist and are designated as such. This does not mean that the recognition of demonstrable ancestry invariably predicates ancestor worship. This needs to be stressed to draw attention to those components of ancestor worship that transform the mere recognition of ancestry, however it may be institutionalized, into "a branch of religion." Demonstrable ancestry, or its converse, demonstrable descent, often have a purely legal or political or symbolical significance (cf. Fortes 1969: *passim*). Queen Elizabeth II succeeded to the throne of Great Britain by right of descent from her great-great-grandmother Queen Victoria, but the Royal Family does not practice ancestor worship — though ceremonies commemorating their ancestors may well be held, and if they had belonged to the Roman Catholic faith, presumably masses for the repose of their souls might well be an institutionalized practice.

What, then, are the critical determinants of ancestor worship? Our symposium brings these to light. A starting point is the premise that death does not extinguish a person's participation in the life and activities of his family and community, but rather opens a way to a mode of participation that is different from the mundane mode of the living. At the conceptual or ideological level, this premise is reflected in theories about the origin and the survival after death of "soul" or "spirit" and about the afterlife, as is illustrated by Dr. Fiawoo's analysis of Ewe beliefs. At the structural level, it is reflected in the concern for legitimate descendants of the right sex, which so conspicuously preoccupies people of both sexes in all the communities represented in our symposium. Tautologous as it seems, it is a point of importance that the attainment of ancestorhood and the ritual services of ancestor worship necessitate legitimate descendants and that the crucial step is the achievement of parenthood. Thus ancestor worship is rooted in the cultural construction of the nuclear filio-parental relationship (cf. Fortes 1974), however elaborately it may be projected onto preparental antecendants. I shall return to this presently.

How critical it is to achieve parenthood is illustrated by the exclusion of the never-married female dead from the central field of the lineage ancestor cult in rural Taiwan (cf. Ahern 1973: 127–128). But parenthood must be legitimate, or rather (and more exactly) the offspring whose existence ensures the ancestorhood and worship of the parents and their predecessors must be jurally proper. This implies the possibility of filiation for ancestor worship being created by jural action where natural offspring are lacking, as is demonstrated in the various adoption practices described for rural Taiwan and Japan. It is of great interest that in Taiwan an inmarried spouse of either sex is absorbed into his affinal lineage only in his capacity as a parent of future members, and that it is this that severs the spouse's membership in his natal lineage. For the function of marriage in all communities of the kind we are considering is fundamentally to produce offspring. But so great is the requirement to ensure the continuity of the family and the lineage that parents in Taiwan are given the right to assign children to the patrilineage of either partner to ensure continuity of succession and inheritance within the lineage to this end. Natural filiation is thus jurally manipulated to ensure what is essentially the jural continuity and identity of the lineage. As in the corresponding adoption practices followed in Japan, it is evident that the basic motive is the need that is felt for descendants to perform the ritual services of ancestor worship for the adopting lineage. It is true that birth to natural parents in legal wedlock is the preferred filiative credential, but unlike the rule in most African societies (where birth in legal wedlock, even if the father is not the true begetter, is likely to be required, and where demographic failure may extinguish a descent line leaving its ancestors to receive worship only at the collective level), there is in the Chinese and Japanese cases acute anxiety lest this breaking of the chain of descendants should occur. This has to do with their belief that the dead cannot rest in peace if there is no one to care for their worship after death.

This brings up a point of great, and perhaps universal, importance. What these devices imply is that there is a deeply felt abhorrence of the possibility of a person's total extinction by death. This holds fundamentally for the individual person, but it is extended to the corporate group viewed as a collective person by jural and ritual definition (cf. Fortes 1969: Chapter 16). In the communities we are concerned with here, this follows logically from the rule that the corporate groups, the African or Chinese lineages and the domestic groups in Japan, are kept in existence by mobilizing the succession of generations regulated by the principle of filiation. This attitude is reflected in beliefs about the soul, the spirit, and the afterlife. Though it may not stem directly from it, it is undoubtedly connected with the feeling I have previously alluded to as one reason for the recognition of ancestry, that is to say that a person's death does not extinguish the contribution he made by his life to the existence of his society — above all of course, through the offspring he has contributed to its continuity. The dead are thus thought of as having a stake in the continuity, i.e. in the future persistence of the society to which they belonged in life. In ancestor worship this is accepted as just and natural; it is this that, paradoxical as it may sound, gives ancestor worship a future orientation, rather than, as might superficially be thought to be the case, a fixation on the past.

But alternatives are possible. There is the possibility of blotting out recognition of ancestral participation in the community, for instance by way of a belief in a perpetual cycle of reincarnation as among the Australian aborigines. Similarly, as Tambiah has noticed (1970: 190–191), ancestor worship is incompatible with Thai Buddhism. The point I wish to stress is that in ancestor worship the perpetual stake which the dead are assumed to have in the society of the living is recognized by the fixing on defined persons of obligations to give ritual attention to the dead in prescribed ways. And the rule is that these obligations devolve with succession to the status of an immediate predecessor with the obligations. This amounts in effect, in the communities we are here concerned with, to succession to parental status in the filio-parental relationship. Paradigmatically, the obligations of ancestor worship thus fall on sons who succeed deceased fathers or, in the Japanese case, apparently on female household heads who succeed deceased mothers-in-law. This has to do with the fact that in the societies we are concerned with a person in a filial status cannot be jurally nor, consequently, ritually autonomous. Such a person is technically speaking a jural minor under the authority of a parent. Among other things, he or she can have no direct dealings with ancestors; if ancestors affect their lives it is only as appendages to their parents. When by the death of the significant parent the son- or daughter-in-law gains jural autonomy and succeeds to the parental status, he or she can deal directly with the ancestors through the mediation of the parent who is now among them. What is here in question is the problem of coming to terms with the tragic dilemma presented by the inevitability of the succession of the generations. Parents need and want children to ensure not only the continuity of society but their own immortality; they must in due course die to make way for these very children who must inevitably oust and displace the parents; here lie the roots of the affective and structural ambivalence which ancestor worship resolves (cf. Fortes 1974).

But before I consider this more fully let me return to the observation that death by itself does not confer ancestorhood. The best evidence for this is the occurrence of elaborate mortuary and funeral ceremonies by which the deceased is expunged from the world of the living in his human embodiment and eventually reincorporated among them in his ancestral and spiritual capacity. It is of the greatest significance that the reincorporation of the dead is made tangible in precise material terms. They are figuratively reimbodied in such material vehicles of their presence as memorial tablets or shrines and altars, which are appropriately enough placed in the home — be it ancestral hall or lineage home or the *ie* in Japan — which is in its turn the material embodiment of the group within which the deceased are reinstated. It is of course those who will be responsible for the ritual duties of caring for the dead upon whom fall the main duties of arranging their reinstatement. So it seems almost as if the living are unable or unwilling to give up their dead parents and forebears. The likely reasons for this will be considered presently.

The Japanese data are particularly instructive in this connection. For they show that far from being a consequence of death itself, full ancestorhood is conferred by the worshipers in stages over a stretch of years and by cumulative rituals that simulate the ideal life cycle of the living (cf. Ooms, this volume). It is as if the dead are nurtured into full ancestorhood by stages that mirror the normal maturation process of the living, through childhood to reproductive adulthood and finally to a second symbolic death when they are deified and removed from the domestic environment to be placed among the remote communal dead, who no longer require daily ritual attention but are acknowledged in periodical community rites.

The Japanese data suggest another important aspect of their pattern of ancestor worship. Though tablets dedicated to lineal ancestors, male and female, predominate in the domestic shrines, deceased collaterals and children of the family are also thus commemorated and ritually cared for. One is tempted to surmise that the corporate existence of the *ie* is deemed to be vested in all of its members and therefore none of them must be allowed to be wholly extinguished by death. And this is reinforced when we consider that the daily ritual feeding of the dead is the duty of the mistress of the household and not of a filial relative of a lineal deceased. Since it is the mistress of the household who is often responsible for preparing the food for all its living members, these ritual duties show clearly that the dead are felt to be present as if they were still within the family. In the African and Chinese cases it seems that the corporate existence of the lineage is deemed to be vested in its reproductive members, hence the anxiety to ensure succession by adoption and consequential postmortem ritual care for adults who die childless but who could have become parents. And this is consistent with the rule that the ritual tendance of ancestors is primarily a filial duty with the parents conjoined in their ancestral status.

Critical as it is to have descendants of the right class for ancestors to receive worship, there are additional factors to be taken into account. Thus it is commonly required that the deceased should die in accordance with what is culturally defined in his community as a normal death. In many African as well as Oriental societies people who die catastrophically, for instance of smallpox or by drowning or suicide, are excluded. If it seems odd and unjust so to penalize people for death which is often not wilfully incurred, this is understandable from two angles. On the one hand such a death is ritually polluting because it is anomalous, on the other it is wrong because it defies the ancestors. A normal death should take place either at the will of the ancestors as in African societies (even if, as among the southern Bantu, the actual killer is believed to be a witch or a sorcerer) or at least in their presence and, as it were, by their leave, as in Taiwan when the dying are removed to the ancestral hall.

In contrast, it is striking to find that a person's moral character does not determine his chances of ancestorhood. If he leaves the right descendants he must be worshiped even if he is lacking in moral virtue, though he will be more desultorily attended perhaps than an upright person would be. This is an inviolable rule among African peoples as I have explained elsewhere (Fortes 1965). But it is interesting to have evidence for it also from Taiwan and from an investigator who particularly emphasizes economic motivation in ancestor worship. Emily Ahern repeatedly adduces the acquisition of rights to land, whether by inheritance or gift or other forms of assignment, as the essential guarantor of ritual care for ancestors. The impression is conveyed, though with qualifications, that ancestors are established and given ritual care only insofar as they have left land or property to their heirs and successors. But we learn in one case that "curiously, the men who actually lost the ancestral land — most lineage members believe that second and third generation Lis gambled it away — have tablets" (1973: 142). Then there is the case (1973: 130) of the man of foreign surname who had made substantial contributions to the corporate funds of the lineage but who could only be given an incense pot rather than a whole tablet. And last, there is the interesting case of the Iap family worshiping only the Ong woman who bore children to their founding ancestor, much to the indignation of the Ong lineage who claim that they "must worship ALL Ong ancestors because they were given Ong land." Incidentally, Dr. Ahern sums up excellently the basic credentials for ancestorhood not only in Taiwan but, *mutatis mutandis*, in all ancestor-worshiping societies. She writes, "an adult man who is a direct descendant of the lineage ancestors and who has married, sired male children and handed down property to his sons is a paradigm of the person with a right to have his tablet placed in the hall" (Ahern 1973: 121). I would add only that in my opinion, the handing down of property is a desirable but not a necessary consideration.

This brings up another point of great interest. If we compare the African with the Chinese and Japanese data a significant contrast in attitude is apparent. African ancestors are for the most part offered sacrifice and prayer mainly to expiate offences or to atone for ritual neglect. Theirs is primarily a piacular form of ancestor worship. With the Chinese and Japanese, it appears that the primary purpose of the rituals of worship is to keep the ancestors — or, in Japan, all the family dead — content and at peace in the afterlife. African ancestor worship, we might say, is geared more to the protection of the living, Chinese

and Japanese to the consolation of the dead. Hence, perhaps, it is easy
for Chinese and Japanese to relegate remote ancestors to a relatively
impersonal communal status in the ancestral hierarchy while Africans
must, in most cases, take equal cognizance of all grades of ancestors.
A possible structural correlate to this distinction is the great difference
in generation depth and time span between the normal African descent
group, which rarely exceeds fourteen generations, and the equivalent
Asian group, with its documented and much deeper genealogies in the
dominant line. A much closer integration of ancestor worship at the
domestic level and at the level of the lineage, the clan, or even the
state, as among Edo (cf. Bradbury 1965) is thus possible in African
systems by contrast with the Chinese and Japanese. But the difference
also reflects different theories about the components of the living personality that are believed to endure after death and about the mode of
existence of the ancestors in the afterlife.

Given then that the critical credential for becoming a worshiped
ancestor is having descendants rather than conferring material or social
benefits on society, what is it that ensures the conscientious observance
of their ritual duties by the descendants, and what essentially are these
duties?

Ancestors, like deities, are addressed commonly in prayer, both in
African and in Asiatic societies, being invoked by name and descent
rank. They are approached as if they have a personal identity and not
just an anonymous generality. This accords with their identification
individually by name or title in the tablets or shrines and in their
graves, at any rate for the immediately preceding three or four generations. Prayer, whatever may be its intent — whether it solicits help,
offers thanks, makes apologies, admits guilt, promises reform, or what
you will — brings the ancestors into the equivalent of face-to-face confrontation with the worshipers, but it must inevitably be one-sided and
inconclusive, since unlike a similar transaction with living superiors
there can be no dialogue and no appeal to reality. It is partly for this
reason that sacrifice and libation form a major part of the ritual services of ancestor worship. This is often spoken of as "feeding" the
ancestors and it is common for the offering to be partaken of by the
worshipers, hence the description of such occasions as sacraments or
communion rites. This is not the place to discuss the symbolical implications of the variations in food offerings that range from the blood
sacrifices common in Africa to the cooked foods of normal home meals
among the Japanese and Chinese. It is enough to note that giving food,
be it cooked or merely in the form of the raw material for food, is the

most distinctive act of caring for others, keeping them alive, so to speak, and thus binding them to oneself. Food dependence is from the moment of birth the vital bond that unites child to parent. To share a meal is, as is well known, an expression of amity and trust, but what is important about it is that it presupposes the copresence of all those who share it. It is at the moment of the sacrificial offering that the presence of the ancestors is most immediately felt.

It must not be overlooked that these food offerings are not left to the free choice of the worshipers. Their form and the times and places for the offering are either prescribed or fixed by *ad hoc* demands on the part of the ancestors. On the one hand food offerings dramatize the dependence of the ancestors on the continual care of the descendants; on the other they symbolize the coercive power and authority attributed to the ancestors by the descendants.

This brings us to what is perhaps the crux of our investigation. How is the conscientious observance of the duties of ancestor worship ensured? The short answer is that failure to perform these duties is believed to anger the ancestors, so that they inflict trouble and misfortune on their delinquent descendants and thus bring them to heel again. To put it the other way round, in ancestor-worshiping societies the troubles and misfortunes that inevitably occur in the course of human life — be they economic loss, career failure, or above all the ultimate and inescapable afflictions of sickness and death — are often attributed to the ancestors. Conscientious ritual service may thus be thought of as a way of keeping the ancestors happy and thus preventing or mitigating their anger. This implies an attitude of submission to power that is capable of being arbitrarily exercised, rather than one of trust and affection. It suggests apprehension of possible retribution rather than expectation of benevolence. And the papers in this symposium, in line with the general literature on this subject, suggest that this is broadly true.

But this is only one part of the story. The issue is much more complicated. For one thing, the ancestors are not outside the moral and social universe of their descendants. They are integrally part of it, committed to it, though not in a human sense. Thus many calendrically and other fixed ritual activities directed towards them, especially in the case of the remotest communal ancestors, appear to be much more concerned with regularly reaffirming their participation in the moral and social universe, and with declaring that the well-being of the living is secured by the stability of the cosmic order this represents, than with individual conduct. For another, there is evidence that when things are going well, credit for this may be ascribed to ancestral benevolence. And last, there are often alternative explanations of the sources of affliction and of evil. Witches and sorcerers, demons and offended divinities, the devil or an evil predestiny, rather than ancestors, may be blamed.

Here it is worth looking again at the requirement that death should be normal for ancestorhood to be achieved. The abnormal, or (from the point of view of the people themselves) the sinful or illicit dead, are often, by contrast to the ancestors, conceived of as dangerous ghosts either in this world or in the other, outcasts seeking to gain admission to the family fold by causing them trouble. The question as to whether ancestors are visualized primarily as punitive or as benevolent is therefore part of a more general theodicy. In contrast to the fear of punishment as a sanction for the conscientious performance of the ritual duties of ancestor worship, it might be a sense of gratitude which entails the obligation to make a return for the gift of life if for nothing else. And indeed this is sometimes stated as the reason for the conscientious performance of the ritual. The implication of this is the premise that the ancestors are the ultimate source of life both for the individual and, much more obviously of course, for the descent group which would not exist if there had been no ancestors. But this implies the converse: that ancestors have the sole right and power to terminate the life of an individual or of a corporate group, phrased often in terms of summoning the deceased as if before a judicial tribunal.

To follow this up, let us consider again the Japanese case. Consistent with their practice of including all the household dead in the domestic cult of ancestors, they are apt to attribute misfortune to deceased kinsfolk of all generations, lineal, collateral, cognatic, and even marital, as Kerner notes. Indeed, aborted foetuses may even be blamed. Interestingly enough, there are parallels to this pattern in New Guinea among peoples like the Mae-Enga (cf. Meggitt 1965) and the Melpa (cf. Strathern 1972), who do not appear to have ancestor cults.

These cases suggest that it is simply because they are dead that all deceased kin are supposed to be capable of malevolence — as if in resentment for having been abandoned to death. It is worth noting though (e.g. for the Mae-Enga) that deceased kin of the parental generation tend to be the main targets for blame.

It could be argued, then, that it is not on account of their ancestral status but simply because of the fact of death that, like the dead everywhere, ancestors are believed to be capable of malevolence. This is a problem that needs a great deal of further study. It is important then to bear in mind that the malevolence imputed to the dead is normally taken to be limited to their relatives by kinship or marriage. We are left with the problem as to why nonrelatives are not at risk. If ghostly malevolence is simply due to the state of death, or from the observer's point of view, the fears of the living projected onto the dead, why do they not strike indiscriminately?

This is a consideration of special importance in relation to ancestor worship. Ancestors are believed to intervene only, and strictly only, in the lives of their descendants, however these are culturally defined. It is, we must therefore conclude, in the distinctive features of kinship relations for the general case, and the nuclear relationships of successive generations for ancestor worship, that we must look for answers.

This inference is confirmed when we consider the range of ancestor worship. Whatever may be its range at the maximum level, embracing perhaps not only the remotest lineage or clan ancestors but politically central ancestors such as those enshrined in Ewe clan or tribal "stools," ancestor worship at the minimum level may be reduced to the ritual tendance of dead fathers by their sons as Harrell reports. Here again, Ahern's testimony is to the point. "A parent," she writes (1973: 154), "must receive minimal rites of care in the afterlife from someone; if there is but one descendant he or she is obligated to provide them." And elaborating on this she states that though a son "was justified in not making offerings to his father if he is left no property," he still "risks his father's anger; and an angry deceased father could easily bring sickness or misfortune on him" (1973: 155). Similar observations are scattered throughout the papers of our symposium.

And here, in my view, lies the key to our inquiry. Ancestors are not believed to afflict their descendants indiscriminately or even capriciously. They are believed to punish particular descendants for such wrongdoings as ritual neglect (e.g. not "feeding" them) or moral transgressions. In other words ancestors are supposed to exact the services they are ENTITLED to from identified responsible descendants, and to adjudicate on their moral and ritual conduct. First in line come the sons of the latest generation of fathers to join them. Thus they are conceived of as acting in a mystically omnipotent, quasi-judicial capacity, enforcing their rights and authority rather than merely showing their power. For if their authority is acquiesced to, and their rights are duly honored, they may be expected, in theory at least and certainly among the Taiwanese and many African peoples, to be benevolent. It is worth noting, in passing, that these recent data from Taiwan throw doubt on the contention that ancestors among the Chinese are normally conceived of as benevolent. They cast doubt also on the thesis that the punitive character attributed to ancestors is a reflex of the struggle between holder and heir over the inheritance of property (cf. Goody 1962).

How ancestors are believed to act is, of course, an actor's or emic view of reality. From the anthropologist's point of view, the actions attributed to ancestors must be understood as representation of human experience in the social relations of successive generations as I have already several times emphasized. The hypothesis that seems most plausible to me to explain this is the following: ancestor worship provides a resolution, albeit one fraught with uncertainty, of the tragic dilemma that, as I mentioned earlier, is presented to parents and offspring by the inevitability of the succession of the generation. Being cast in terms of eschatological beliefs given expression in ritual prescriptions, it offers an emotionally and morally reassuring symbolic resolution to a dilemma that is not resolvable in terms of mundane reality. For parents must die, though they cannot but resist and fear this fate, so that children may continue the life they owe to their parents, and children must replace parents though they dare not consciously wish them out of the way. Ancestor worship achieves the goal at the same time of submitting to the reality of the death of the parents, which removes them physically, and keeping them symbolically alive and at home among the displacing offspring. It is evident that beliefs in the survival of the soul and the rituals of feeding and caring for the ancestors almost as if they are infants, dependent on their children now as these were at one time on them, are essential for these ends to be achieved.

But this is not all. It is a striking thing that ancestors are projected as figures of authority to whom powers of life and death are attributed — judicial figures as I have already suggested, rather than bountiful deities. This is not an image of the whole man or woman in his or her all-round personal character and in the capacity of the tender and loving parent who has devoted a lifetime to caring for, bringing up, and providing for the future of his or her children. The aspect selected is the other side of the parent as the inescapable source of discipline and frustration in the tasks of socializing the offspring to conform to custom and to take their proper place in society. In societies with developed structures of authority, based on legal or quasi-legal institutions, the parental authority exercised in this role has jural sanction superadded to the sanctions derived from superiority of generation and from the command over knowledge, skill, and resources. Offspring have no freedom of action in such systems, no status in society except as appendages of their parents.

The upshot is to evoke in both parents and offspring complexes of conflicting attitudes, emotions, and dispositions built up on the elementary core of the ambivalence that is established in the first months of infancy but suppressed and kept in check by customarily imposed rules of conduct and of right and duty. The death of parents, inevitable as it is, evokes feelings of guilt and anxiety, perhaps obscurely felt as due to the wishes if not the actual actions of the offspring who benefit by it.

Funeral rituals to some extent express and assuage these attitudes. But promoting parents to the mystically, that is symbolically, omnipotent status of ancestors who must be perpetually served and obeyed is even more effective; and if the responsibility for the parents' death can be fixed by religious assumption on the eternal parental status represented by the projection of parenthood into a line of ancestors — which means, in effect on themselves — the burden of the ambivalence can be completely removed.

This constellation of ultimately in-built, socially deployed, and culturally accoutered dispositions and attitudes is to my mind the key to ancestor worship.

# REFERENCES

AHERN, EMILY M.
1973 *The cult of the dead in a Chinese village.* Stanford: Stanford University Press.
BERNDT, RONALD M.
1970 "Traditional morality as expressed through the medium of an Australian Aboriginal religion," in *Australian aboriginal anthropology.* Edited by R. M. Berndt. University of West Australia Press.
BERNDT, RONALD M., *editor*
1970 *Australian aboriginal anthropology.* University of West Australia Press.
BRADBURY, R. E.
1965 "Father and senior son in Edo mortuary ritual," in *African systems of thought.* Edited by M. Fortes and G. Dieterlen. London: Oxford University Press.
BRAIN, JAMES
1973 Ancestors and elders in Africa — further thoughts. *Africa* 43(2): 122–133.

DRIBERG, J. H.

1936   The secular aspect of ancestor worship in Africa. *Journal of the Royal African Society* 35(138) (supplement).

DURKHEIM, E.

1915   *The elementary forms of the religious life: a study in religious sociology.* Translated by J. W. Swain. New York: Macmillan.

FORTES, MEYER

1965   "Some reflections on ancestor worship in Africa," in *African systems of thought.* Edited by M. Fortes and G. Dieterlen. London: Oxford University Press.

1969   *Kinship and the social order.* Chicago: Aldine.

1974   The first born. *Journal of Child Psychology and Psychiatry* 15: 81–104.

FORTES, MEYER, G. DIETERLEN, *editors*

1965   *African systems of thought.* London: Oxford University Press.

GOODY, J. R.

1962   *Death, property and the ancestors.* London: Tavistock.

KOPYTOFF, IGOR

1971   Ancestors and elders in Africa. *Africa* 42(2):129–142.

MEGGITT, MERVYN

1962   *Desert People.* Sydney: Angus Robertson.

1965   *The lineage system of the Mae-Enga of New Guinea.* Edinburgh: Oliver and Boyd.

MUNN, NANCY D.

1970   "The transformation of subjects into objects in Walbiri and Pitjintjara myth," in *Australian aboriginal anthropology.* Edited by R. M. Berndt. University of West Australia Press.

STRATHERN, ANDREW

1972   *One father, one blood.* London: Tavistock.

TAMBIAH, S. J.

1970   *Buddhism and spirit cults in north-east Thailand.* Cambridge: Cambridge University Press.

TYLOR, E. B.

1871   *Primitive culture.* London: Murray.

WEBER, MAX

1951 [1912]   *The religion of China.* Translated by H. Gerth. Glencoe, Ill.: Free Press.

# Good and Bad Ancestors

WILLIAM H. NEWELL

In the book, *Death, property and the ancestors* (Goody 1962), there is an excellent chapter dealing with the history of research on ancestors. The title of the chapter is, however, "Approaches to the study of mortuary institutions" and it is clear that Goody regards the social process by which one becomes dead as essentially the same as that by which one becomes an ancestor. In the *Encyclopedia of religion and ethics*, the heading under ancestors is "Ancestor worship and the cult of the dead" and after the introduction there are headings under Aryans, Babylonians, Greeks, Hebrews, Tasmanians, Indians, etc., a queer mixture which puts under the one heading extremely diverse forms of behavior. The author of this article, William Crooke, a distinguished Indian scholar, starts his article by quoting from Tylor (1891) and I cannot do better than by doing so myself. The worship of the Manes "is one of the great branches of the religion of mankind. Its principles are not difficult to understand, for they plainly keep up the social relations of the living world. The dead ancestor now passed into a deity, simply goes on protecting his own family and receiving suit and service from them as of old; the dead chief still watches over his own tribe, still holds his authority by helping friends and harming enemies, still rewards the right and sharply punishes the wrong."

Most of the difficulties in dealing with ancestors can be seen in this passage. (1) Ancestors keep up the social relations of the living world. But only certain selected ones do. What is the principle of selection? (2) Can one really talk about a dead person having social relations with the living? Materialistically this can only be done through a medium of some sort. The humanity of ancestors is a hindrance and the dead ancestor only behaves in certain prescribed ways. The medium either defines in what respect the dead can influence the living or else the dead person's behavior is prescribed. Even if one is concerned only with ancestors in the strict sense, one has four to choose from. Which one is relevant to the problem at hand? (3) The dead ancestor still goes on protecting his own family as of old. But quarrels between fathers and sons are not unknown even in primitive societies, and in many societies such as the Chinese and Japanese, the overwhelming proportion of bad ancestors become good after successfully crossing the Rubicon or its equivalent. Moreover there are bad ancestors who harm their descendants in some societies. Crooke tries to avoid this problem by arguing that the conflicting feelings of love and hate depend in some way on the "death aspect" of the ceremony. In our society we talk about a soul and ghost as though they were opposites. An enemy or stranger becomes a ghost; a loved one after death becomes a soul. This distinction is impossible to hold in all societies or rather, in some societies, this distinction is made but it is not of a universal type. It is rather like the magic/religion controversy which seems to be now buried once and for all as a universal distinction.

To approach this problem we must separate the study of mortuary institutions from the study of ancestors, drawing only enough information from the first to throw light on the second. The study of mortuary institutions is reasonably part of the study of *rites de passage*. But once having passed through such a rite the subsequent behavior of the one-way spirit must be dealt with in a different manner. What the dead can do to the living is important to us. What we living can do to the dead is of only minor importance to us except insofar as it redounds from the affection we have for an individual who is now dead. However there is one important common feature of death ceremonies and the creation of ancestors. An unsuccessful *rite de passage* precludes an ancestor's being created. Lepers and children are buried without ceremony in China. The Gaddis in India, if they suffer from certain skin diseases, have to be cleansed in Muttra in Kashmir, after death and cannot have their *pinds* (ashes of certain bones of the cremated dead, which represent ancestors) thrown into the Ganges at Hardwar. A suicide in England was formerly buried at a crossroad with a stake through his heart. At the time of Mariner in Tonga, slaves had no burial service and no afterlife. Only Tongan chiefs could become ancestors.

The relationship between mortuary customs and becoming an ancestor is like the relationship between marriage and divorce. The first documentary evidence you must produce in court if you wish to be divorced is proof of your marriage. The first ritual proof you must produce if you wish to become an ancestor is that you are properly buried. No matter how many children you may have begotten without a marriage certificate, the divorce courts are not interested. No matter how many terrible things you may have done as a *preta* [hungry ghost], in China, you cannot become an ancestor without the formal qualifications of burial and a tomb. This is why you are a *preta*. Thus death in itself is no admission to the ranks of the blessed. Only a minority of the dead are chosen.

Moreover as an ancestor, there must be some continuity with your former life. The Hindu *shraddha* was originally merely a rite of throwing food to the dead, all the dead. In modern times this rite applies only to named ancestors when the father (f), father's father (ff) and father's father's father (fff) are all mentioned by name. The Buddhist Feast of Orphan Spirits has nothing to do with ancestors because there is no continuity.

In traditional arguments this continuity between ancestors and their descendants has been based on the family. As a person moves gradually through the family cycle he approaches the point where he will lose the controlled use of his body. As the father is superior to the son, so will the last ancestor be hierarchically superior to the father. There are two main arguments against this: (a) All elementary families have at least three relationships: between siblings, spouses, and parents and children. Leaving aside the first two as they will possibly die close together, we have father/son, father/daughter, mother/son, mother/daughter plus extensions such as mother's siblings/sister's children and father's siblings/brother's children plus others. Logically, all these relationships should be expressed between dead and living generations; yet at the most only two are selected. (b) Moreover, the family is the cognatic unit *par excellence* and alone of all kinship institutions has as its aim self-destruction (Lévi-Strauss 1960). Thus the family and ancestors are not connected by the logical arguments put forward by Tylor and some of his successors.

It must be admitted that up to now the standard studies of ancestor worship have been in unilineal societies. It does not follow, however, that in such societies as the Maori, ancestor worship cannot be found. It can be asserted that in such societies the actual worship of identified ancestors is very shallow, rarely more than one or two generations, but this is as yet an unexplored field.

In contrast to the family, there are various institutions of a kinship-based type whose aim is permanence; a genealogy or a pedigree usually has as its aims (Fortes 1965: 123) "the assignment of rights, duties and status in relation to property, office and rank, or for ritual purposes such as liability to death, birth or caste pollution; or for establishing titles to membership of a corporate group." Yet we can have such a system without ancestor worship (such as the Nuer or Tiv). It is clear that genealogies and ancestors need not be tied together.

But it is also true that we cannot have an ancestor who is dead without having someone living to identify and to worship him. Moreover, such ancestors are exclusive to the worshiping group, and in societies of a segmentary type "distinguish that group unequivocally from collateral and co-ordinate groups of a like sort, who have remote ascendants in common with them, and worship jointly with them in situations of common concern" (Fortes 1965).

Ancestors cannot, under this rubric, be classified exclusively as a group because there must be a position where a distinction is made between differing cult groups. And that point presupposes GENEONYMY, the commemoration of ancestors by name. On some Chinese altars one might find a tablet: "To all ancestors of the Chang family." This, to my way of thinking, does not make a valid ancestor, unless it is accompanied by recent tablets with names, whose exact connection to the worshiper is made clear.

Fortes (1965: 124) goes even further than I. He gives the following definition: "An ancestor is a named dead forebear who has living descendants of a designated genealogical class representing his continued structural relevance. In ancestor worship such an ancestor receives ritual service and tendance directed specifically to him by the proper class of his descendants. Being identified by name means that he is invested with attributes distinctive of a kind of person."

Fortes, it seems to me, has gone too far in his definition. While rejecting the common study of ancestor worship and the cult of the dead, he has reduced ancestor worship to almost purely structural significance. Yet the actual structure of ancestors worship is similar to the pattern laid down by Mauss (Hubert and Mauss 1964) of a sacrificer and a place, a cult marked by a sacrifice, a subject or group who benefits, and a cult leader. To neglect any one of these aspects is to miss the point. In the Chinese ancestral cult it is not absolutely essential that the most senior male ascendant is the sacrificer. In the domestic cult it may be anyone. This differs from the domestic ritual of ancient Rome described by Fustel de Coulanges (1885): "Le père, seul interprète et seul pontife de sa religion, avait seul le pouvoir de l'enseigner, et ne pouvait l'enseigner qu'à son fils." [The father, sole interpreter and sole head of his religion, alone had the power to teach it, and could teach it only to his son.] Whether Fustel de Coulanges is too extreme or not, the exclusive nature of the father as the sole officiant of the rite may be true of both Rome and West Africa but it is certainly untrue of the Far East. It is significant that the jural authority of the senior lineage head is common both to Africa and Rome, but as Freedman (1966: 151) points out, this is NOT true of China. Fortes is too extreme.

But we must emphasize the religious nature of ancestor worship. It is true that it is a sort of secular religion where the emphasis is on relationships between some or all of the former and present members of the cult group. For the link to be maintained, however, certain ritual performances have to be carried through. Veneration, worship, or commemoration are the alternatives. Even in the case of Fortes' definition, "ritual service and tendance" must be offered to the ancestor.

What exactly is being connected with what? We have already dealt with the ideas of naming and continuity. I wish now to deal with a third point especially emphasized by Goody (1962), the body-soul dichotomy. Both Tylor and Spencer (and many of their contemporaries) were especially concerned with emphasizing the existence of Beings separate from the natural world. In fact, one of Tylor's definitions of animistic religion was a belief in Spiritual Beings: "The doctrines of the lower races fully justify us in classing the spiritual beings in general as similar in nature to the souls of Men." Spencer similarly traced all supernatural beings as coming from a belief in the soul. The soul/body dichotomy seems to be almost universal. Various explanations have been put forward for this dichotomy. Freud argued in *Totem and taboo* that it was a reaction against close relations in life which bred a hostile reaction after death. Fortes (1965) argues that ancestors are a projection of jural ties from the past to the present. Frazer tended to see the problem as merely a fear of the dead. Hertz put forward the following explanation (Goody 1962: 27 ff.): "Beliefs in an afterlife appear to be related to the basic contradiction that exists between the continuity of the social system — the relative perpetuity of the constituent groups and of their *corpus* of norms — and the impermanence of the personnel. This conflict between the mortality of the human body and the immortality of the body politic is resolved in part at least by the belief in an afterlife. A future existence is postulated as a supplement to man's earthly span, a Land of the Dead as a counterpart to the Land of the Living."

Here again we have the same difficulty we looked at earlier, having to do with ancestors and the cult of the dead. We can freely grant the existence of eternal spirit, spirits, or souls as a means of resolving the conflict between the permanent and temporary in social life. We can also see clearly that there can be no ancestors unless there is some part of the personality which is totally separate from the physical body.

But whereas in the case of eternal life it is your actual deeds which are important, one cannot but be struck, in the case of ancestral spirits, with the absence of interest in the characteristics possessed by the dead while they were alive. This absence of personal characteristics is especially noticeable in the case of the Japanese and Chinese but it seems to be widespread and it needs to be explained. In an important essay by J. D. McKnight (1967), dealing with various African societies studied by Radcliffe-Brown, Fortes, Middleton, and others, the author shows that if the patrilineal ancestors in a patrilineal society (and matrilineal in a matrilineal society) acquire their punitive harassing characteristics by virtue of their supporting the authority of the eldest lineage head, then where extradescent group ancestors are recognized (and where they also have no jural rights over the living or the dead), their characteristics should be different. But, taking our example from McKnight's comments on the Tallensi, "the mother's spirit is held to be extremely aggressive and Fortes stresses that her spirit is as important to a man as is his father's spirit. . . . Even death may be attributed to the mother's spirit. . . . The spirits of female ancestors are believed to be especially hard, cruel and capricious. This is remarkable when we consider the love and devotion a mother shows to her child throughout his life" (1967: 9). If we were to accept Radcliffe-Brown's hypothesis derived from his famous "Mother's Brother in South Africa" essay, then the mother's ancestors should be kind and gentle (as the mother is). But this is not so. If we accept Fortes' argument that the retributive ancestor is part and parcel of the jural authority of the society, then where the mother has no jural authority over the child, the ancestor also should not be punitive.

This brings us back to my earlier point, that ancestors behave not as they did when living, but as a class; and that their behavior is apparently unrelated, except by accident, to any general or specific characteristics they might have had as a member of the elementary family. In the extreme Chinese example, it just happens to be where they are buried (Freedman 1966).

What are the features of ancestors external to their former character before they became dead?

a.   There is a clear distinction between those individually named ancestors connected with the authority or continuity of the domestic group and those ancestors who are not. In Japan the distinction between these two classes takes place BEFORE they become dead, at the time of marriage, to found a new *ie* [household]. Ooms (1967) makes a distinction between *ihai* [ancestral tablets] and mortuary tablets. Only those who are in the direct line of the *ie* become ancestors; others become *muenbotoke* (those ancestors to whom descendants owe no direct "relationships"), although both are worshiped on the *butsudan* [Buddhist altar]. In China, the distinction between the family tablets and the ancestral hall tablets marks a change also in the nature of the cult group. In the domestic family, all members of the household can, if they wish, worship the tablets. In the ancestral hall only certain specified agnates, in order of seniority, worship.

b.   As the ancestors become less and less personal by virtue of genealogical distance, their characters become either less dangerous or more beneficent. They also become less powerful to influence the local cult group.

c.   Each group or class of ancestral dead has a different cult group, organized on different principles. In China, the domestic family emphasizes the principle of memorialism (and hence cognation where memory of the dead counts) with all members of the household members of the cult group, whereas at the higher level, the ancestral worship is strictly patrilineal (and hence positional), although there may be an element of memorialism in the higher cult also. In Japan, the *bunke* [side stem in a stem family system] is excluded from worshiping at the *honke*'s [main stem's] *butsudan* as soon as they acquire an ancestor for themselves by the death of the founder of the *bunke*. Thus the criterion for becoming an ancestor is *ie* membership. But any Japanese may worship at the Imperial shrine at Ise by virtue of belonging to the Japanese nation. The criterion here is not *ie* membership (to which only the Emperor belongs) but common descent, albeit through cadet lines.

d.   The character of the ancestor is quite independent of the character of the dead person when he was alive, being determined only by the class of ancestor which he joins. This rule does not apply, however, when the individually identifiable dead is not the only member of the class. For example, in some societies, such as the Tallensi, both a father and a mother may become an ancestor on death, joining the living to the father's father's lineage or to the mother's father's lineage. Here the two parents will both be in different classes and can be used to offset each other or to be prayed to in differing circumstances. But in other societies (such as the Chinese) the mother only becomes an ancestor by virtue of becoming married to the father (or more accurately, being enshrined by virtue of giving birth to the father's children). Where this occurs both mothers and fathers are usually buried in the same grave or inscribed on the same tablet. (Some recent discoveries in Japan in Chiba prefecture have shown different burials in the past for father and mother in contrast to the present (Noguchi 1966). Both China and Japan have a very strong unilineal principle for creating ancestors and one can only become a genuine ancestor through one form of filiation. Those excluded are in some way defective. In Japan they become *muenbotoke* although continuing to be worshiped by the *ie*. In China and Japan, therefore, one would expect the "class" content of the ancestor to be strong. But where there is more than one class of ancestor (as in bilateral societies or where there are more than two different classifications), ancestors that fall outside the main class are likely either to become more harmful or to acquire a personal characteristic derived from their character when alive.

In the early anthropological literature dealing with China, F. L. K. Hsu and Lin Yueh-hua among others (Hsu 1949; Lin 1948) claimed that ancestors are always beneficent or at least neutral towards their descendants. Yanagita Kunio, among others, has also asserted that ancestors in Japan are invariably beneficent to their direct descendants (Yanagita 1926). Since these articles were written, further fieldwork has substantially modified these earlier statements. As an example of new research concerning East Asia, I cite Freedman, who in his later work cites Wolf's doctoral thesis to show that in Taiwan, "the illness of a small child was ascribed to his father's deceased parents who were said to be angry because their son had made a matrilocal marriage." Evidence in Japan has also been collected by Yoshida (1968) where individual dead ascendants harmed the living.

I will not deal here with problems arising from the Chinese, but will take a Japanese example where regular rituals are performed in the presence of the ancestors. The most important ritual is that known as *Obon* (also *bon* — a family festival in which ancestors of the household are welcomed back for a visit), which usually, in the Tokyo area, takes place about the middle of August for three to four days. During this period, the *ie* welcomes all the *hotoke* [ancestors] in a direct line from the first ancestor. The first ancestor, although known to some members of the *ie*, is not worshiped separately, unlike the Chinese situation. In order to become an ancestor, one needs to have a group in which one is venerated (the *ie*), to have a death name conferred on one by a priest and to be perpetuated in an ancestral tablet. Ooms (1967) distinguishes between ancestral tablets and mortuary tablets; at death, each dead person will have a *kaimyō* [an announcement of death distributed to certain related but not close kin, such as the wife's relatives], an *ihai* [ancestral tablet] and two *tōba* [mortuary tablets], one of which will be left on the grave. New *tōba* will be made for the seventh, forty-ninth, and hundredth day, and the first, third, seventh, twenty-third, and thirty-third year of death. Unmarried children cannot have *ihai* and married children who leave the *ie* will also not have *ihai* on their father's altar but will form a new *bunke* if they have children, real or adopted. These latter group are termed *muenbotoke*, that is without *en* [obligation]. In addition, if one has died within forty-nine days of *Obon* one does not return at this time but comes the subsequent year. Thus on an altar there are the following objects at *Obon*: (1) ancestral *ihai*; (2) *muenbotoke* mortuary tablets; (3) those slips which commemorate those who have died within forty-nine days; and (4) certain slips called *kaimyō*, received from close relatives to announce deaths in related families.

These four categories are personal to the *ie* concerned. The *ihai* will remain permanently on the altar, the *muenbotoke* mortuary tablets will often be forgotten or thrown away after a few years and the slips will disappear as soon as their purpose is completed. But these *muenbotoke* are not *gakki* [wandering souls] because they are specifically identified with a particular household. While *gakki* can be harmful, *muenbotoke* are not. On the other hand there is no procedure of any sort by which they can become *muenbotoke*. But *hotoke* would lapse into *muenbotoke* immediately if the household disappeared.

There are three points to make about this system:

i.   There is a close parallel between the living from birth to marriage, and the ancestors from consecration at death to the 33rd memorial service.

ii.   At death, the main arrangements for the funeral are in the hands of neighbors of the dead person and the priest. Gradually, the community becomes less involved, and at the end even the priest, after he has performed the last memorial service, moves off leaving the ancestor's family as the sole protection against the ancestor's becoming an anonymous *muenbotoke*.

iii.   There is only ONE way of becoming an ancestor and only one sort of ancestor. Among the villagers of Ooms' village, it seemed to be uncertain as to what the actual effect of performing veneration for the ancestors was, but it was clear that ancestors could not harm the living.

Even domestic *muenbotoke* would not do this but once outside the domestic cult group, the dead may be harmful. Thus within the cult group as an object of worship, ancestors are beneficent or harmless. Outside the cult group, the dead may be harmful.

Now let us have a look at some of Yoshida's material from southwest Shikoku. The area he describes is rather strange from a Japanese point of view. There are no strong unilineal descent groups and there is no Buddhist household system. Funeral services are performed by a *tayuu* [Shintō priest]. The *tayuu* or a female exorcist also plays an active part in analyzing the cause of illness. This is of two sorts, *tatari* [retribution] and *tsuki* [possession]. This is not a medical distinction. *Tatari* is a form of impiety towards the gods or the dead. Out of eighty-three cases of both illnesses, fifteen were regarded as caused by dead ancestors. There were nine female victims and six male victims. The harmful ancestors were mostly patrilateral females although there was one case of a dead stepmother and a sibling hurting the living. In none of these fifteen cases did Yoshida discover a case of a father or father's father or mother directly harming the heir or main line of descent. Unfortunately, I have no information for this village on whether there is on the Shintō "spirit-shelf" an equivalent of the *ihai* (known in Shintō as *mitama*) (Yanagita 1926: 122). However it is clear that the local households are not linked together in a hierarchical *dōzoku* order (an association of *ie* with some corporate features based on kinship or economics), although they are called *ikke* as well as *dōzoku* and the eldest son inherits most of the property. Yet nonunilineal *kumi* [neighborhood units] are also important. Yoshida states, "Each *kumi* also has *kumi*-owned land and *kumi* funds, worships an *ujigami* [tutelary deity], performs joint praying for curing a serious illness of a member of the same *kumi*, and undertakes various other activities on a *kumi* basis" (1967: 244). In short, what I am trying to argue is that we have in this anomalous village dead ancestors connected with the living on two different principles, the traditional strict patriline, and as progenitors of the living members of a *kumi*, a bilateral neighborhood group. Certain ancestors can be detached from the strict patriline (in modern Buddhist Japan they would be *muenbotoke*, never capable of becoming *hotoke*) and given a character closer to their former village membership rather than as a member of the class of perfect beneficent ancestors. Thus harmful ancestors in the Far East are found only where bilateral links are emphasized in addition to strict unilinearity.

We are in the fortunate position of being able to verify this with material from the Ryukyus. Within the household in some parts of

Okinawa, we have three (and sometimes more) ritual centers: (1) the *buchidang*, which has *ihee* [ancestral tablets]; (2) the *fii no kang* [the kitchen hearth to the fire god represented by three stones] and (3) the *yasiki* [the god of the house] (Watanabe 1971). Each has a separate cult group with overlapping membership among the household members. In different parts of the islands and sometimes in the same area, there are also two larger principles of organization which are termed the *hiki*, a cognatic group similar in membership in Amami-Oshima to the Maori *hapu* (Nakane 1964), and a *munchū*, sometimes a patrilineal unilineal descent group (Nakane 1970). There are also two terms for ancestors in most of Okinawa. One such term is *futuki* (after the Japanese Buddhist term *hotoke*). This represents only agnates and their wives. Another such term is *fafuji*, which refers to all ancestors. The *futuki* are today commemorated by tablets placed on the *buchidang*, provided that two siblings are not placed equal to each other on the same altar.

The Okinawan cosmology is an extremely complex one (Mabuchi 1968). There are close connections between the arrangement of the Okinawan house, the behavior of the various cult groups of which it is composed, the rituals which take place outside the house by the sea and mountains, and the organization of the graves. Ancestors are, however, regarded as deeply affecting the lives of their descendants, just as those living now will affect the lives of their descendants in turn. In the case of illness and misfortune, a medium is consulted in order to identify the specific ancestors who are responsible for the illness. "When an ancestor of a certain kinship status is offensive to the *kami* (which here refers to ancestors), subsequent occupants of that status may be subject to punishment in the form of misfortune: thus if a second son in a given household commits a crime, succeeding second sons in that household may be penalised" (Lebra 1966).

Thus ancestors are not fixed clearly to a particular descendant. They are ancestors of a group (whether the *hiki* or the *munchū*), and not so representative of a "class" as in the case of the Chinese and Japanese. In the example of a *munchū* (a union of household groups, organized agnatically) put forward by Nakane (1970: 129), we have a main stem called by various names such as *modisi*, *mutu*, *soka*, etc. The heir is the eldest son who takes over the worship of the tablets and the *yashiki* god. The second and other sons may form subordinate *bunke*. But the *honke* and *bunke* are not hierarchically organized as in Japan and, in the absence of suitable heirs, the various lines may move back. That is to say, rather than start new, permanent *bunke* themselves, the object is to continue to support already established lines provided that (a) no two brothers are ever worshiped on the same *buchidang*, and (b) the adoptee comes from the same generation within the large *munchū*. Sons may move into and out of main stems at the medium's behest. Whether the adoptee is married or not is unimportant provided that he is over seven years old. The most common form of explanation of illness "caused" by ancestors is that the ill person neglected to worship them properly, yet while one's immediate ancestors will always be a member of one's *munchu* organization, they will frequently not be one's direct ascendants. Adoption is common but marrying the daughter of a line is uncommon. The *munchu* is not exogamous. The tablets which one has on one's *buchidang* do not remain the continuing responsibility of the Buddhist temple but are bought and made, when required, for cash.

I hope I have made it clear that the Ryukyuan system is not a copy of either the Japanese or Chinese system but has its own particular ethos. I submit that this independence of Okinawan ancestors is a result of the bilateral nature of Okinawan society where ancestors are merely a collective group of forebears of the *hiki* or *munchū* and not representative of a "class."

It is my hope to discover that, where ancestors behave badly and punish the living, it is because they are not so closely connected with one living cult group that their behavior will terminate their being worshiped. It is, I think, significant that cases are rarely found in East Asia of fathers actually punishing their eldest sons in the patriline. Yet in Japanese society, at least, the relationship between father and son is usually somewhat restrained and not very easy.

## REFERENCES

FORTES, M.
    1965   "Some reflections on ancestor worship in Africa," in *African systems of thought*. Edited by M. Fortes and G. Dieterlen. London: Oxford University Press.
FREEDMAN, MAURICE
    1966   *Chinese lineage and society*. London: Athlone.
FUSTEL DE COULANGES
    1885   *La cité antique*. Paris: Hachette.
GOODY, JACK
    1962   *Death, property and the ancestors, a study of the mortuary cus-*

*toms of the Lodagaa of West Africa.* London: Tavistock.
HSU, F. L. K.
1949    *Under the ancestors' shadow.* London: Routledge.
HUBERT, HENRI, MARCEL MAUSS
1964    *Sacrifice: its nature and function.* Translated by W. D. Halls.
London: Cohen and West.
LEBRA, WILLIAM P.
1966    *Okinawan religion.* Honolulu: University of Hawaii Press.
LÉVI-STRAUSS, CLAUDE
1960    "The family," in *Man, culture and society.* Edited by Harry L.
Shapiro, 261–285. New York: Galaxy
LIN, YUEH-HUA
1948    *The golden wing.* London: Routledge.
MABUCHI, TOICHI
1968    "Towards the reconstruction of Ryukyuan cosmology," in *Folk
religion and the world view in the southwestern Pacific.* Tokyo:
Keio.
MC KNIGHT, J. D.
1967    Extra-descent group ancestor cults in African societies. *Africa*
37: lff.
NAKANE, CHIE
1964    Analysis of a hiki. *Tōyō Bunka kenkyūsho kiyō* 33:119–156.
1970    Munchu and buraku. *Tōyō Bunka* 48:109–131.
NOGUCHI, TAKENORI
1966    Mortuary customs and the family-kinship system in Japan and
Ryūkyū. *Monumenta Nipponica,* Monograph 25:16–36.
OOMS, HERMAN
1967    The religion of the household: a case study of ancestor worship
in Japan. *Contemporary Religions in Japan* 8:201–334.
SUDO, KENICHI
1970    The agnatic aspects of the Hiki in Kikai Island, Amami. *Sha* 3:7–8.
TYLOR, EDWARD B.
1891    *Primiive culture,* volume two (third edition). London: Murray.
WATANABE, YOSHIO
1971    Social organisation and cosmology in an Okinawan folk village.
*Minzokugaku Kenkyu* 36:85–108.
YANAGITA, KUNIO
1926    *Senzo no hanashi.* Tokyo: Chikuma Shobo.
YOSHIDA, TEIGO
1967    Mystical retribution, spirit possession and social structure in a
Japanese village. *Ethnology* 6:237–262.
1968    "Mystical retribution and possession by ancestral spirits in Unami,
Kōchi prefecture, Shikoku." Unpublished manuscript from a
seminar on ancestors, Tokyo.

# SECTION ONE

*Note.* Japanese and Chinese names appear in traditional order (i.e. surname first) within the text of each article; in all other cases the names are in Western order.

# Who Are the "Ancestors" in Japan? A 1963 Census of Memorial Tablets

ROBERT J. SMITH

It is my purpose here to set out the results of a study conducted in 1963. The goals of the original research were quite broad but for present purposes I shall restrict my comments largely to the results of a census of memorial tablets in Japan. The unique data derived from the study answer at last a question which arose in 1962 in discussions at Berkeley with Harumi Befu and David W. Plath: "Who are the people represented by the tablets in the household Buddhist altar?"

First a brief word about the procedures used. We prepared a questionnaire/interview consisting of two parts: (1) household and family characteristics, and (2) information on each memorial tablet. For each household we asked about:
1. age and sex of head,
2. composition of family (residents only),
3. place of residence,
4. whether head identifies himself as successor (*ato-tori*) or not,
5. religion of household
6. whether household possesses *butsudan* [Buddhist altar], *kamidana* [Shintō altar], or other altars (*senzo-dana, mitama-dana*, etc.),
7. whether or not there are any memorial tablets in the house,
8. occasions on which the memorial tablets are venerated, and
9. which member(s) of the household bear primary responsibility for the care of the tablets

For each memorial tablet we asked about:
1. relationship of person represented to the present head of the household,
2. date of death,

3.  age at death, and
4.  reason for its being in this altar ("Why do you have this particular tablet?").

Part of the survey was conducted in three rural communities which account for 166 of the 595 households. Yasuhara in Kagawa Prefecture on the island of Shikoku was studied by me in 1951–1952, Sone in Mie Prefecture was studied by Bernard Bernier in 1967–1968, Takane in Iwata Prefecture was studied by Keith Brown in 1961–1963. Yasuhara (Kurusu is the name of the hamlet used in most of my publications on the place) is a largely agricultural community in which every house has a different surname. Sone is a *miyaza* community whose residents derive their income largely from lumbering, cultured pearls, and fishing. Takane, also agricultural, is a *dōzoku* community. In the discussion which follows, these three places are referred to as "rural communities." The remaining "urban" households (429 of the 595) are heavily concentrated in Tokyo and Osaka, with some from Kyoto, Nara, the Hanshin area (lying between Osaka and Kobe) and other scattered cities (see Table 3).

As can be seen in Table 1 there seems to be nothing particularly noteworthy about the character of the households surveyed. The age distribution is quite predictable; about three-quarters of all househeads are between thirty and sixty-nine years of age. Just under 10 percent of the househeads are female.

Table 1.   Age and sex of household heads (n = 595)

| Age | Sex | | | | | | | | |
|---|---|---|---|---|---|---|---|---|---|
| | Male | | Female | | No answer | | Total | |
| | Nr | Pct | Nr | Pct | Nr | Pct | Nr | Pct |
| 20–29 | 18 | 3.4 | – | – | – | – | 18 | 3.0 |
| 30–39 | 73 | 13.7 | 5 | 8.6 | – | – | 78 | 13.1 |
| 40–49 | 149 | 27.9 | 23 | 39.7 | 2 | 100.0 | 174 | 29.3 |
| 50–59 | 180 | 33.6 | 14 | 24.1 | – | – | 194 | 32.6 |
| 60–69 | 82 | 15.3 | 7 | 12.1 | – | – | 89 | 15.0 |
| 70–79 | 24 | 4.5 | 6 | 10.3 | – | – | 30 | 5.0 |
| 80–89 | 5 | 0.9 | 1 | 1.7 | – | – | 6 | 1.0 |
| No answer | 4 | 0.7 | 2 | 3.5 | – | – | 6 | 1.0 |
| Totals | 535 | 100.0 | 58 | 100.0 | 2 | 100.0 | 595 | 100.0 |

Nr = Number.    Pct = Percent.

As for household composition, shown in Table 2, the heavily predominant form is the conjugal family, accounting for about 70 percent of the total, almost all the rest being complete or broken two- and three-generation stem families. In no case did we find two married couples in the same generation living in one household.

Table 2.  Possession of memorial tablets and household type (n = 595)

| Do you have memorial tablets? | Household type | | | | | | | | | |
|---|---|---|---|---|---|---|---|---|---|---|
| | Head unmarried | | Conjugal | | Two-generation stem | | Three-generation stem | | Totals | |
| | Nr | Pct | Nr | Pct | Nr | Pct | Nr | Pct | Nr | Pct |
| Yes | 8 | 80.0 | 324 | 76.2 | 146 | 94.2 | 5 | 100.0 | 483 | 81.2 |
| No | 2 | 20.0 | 101 | 23.8 | 9 | 5.8 | – | – | 112 | 18.8 |
| Total | 10 | 100.0 | 425 | 100.0 | 155 | 100.0 | 5 | 100.0 | 595 | 100.0 |

Nr = Number.    Pct = Percent.

Of particular significance for this study are the figures in Table 2 which show that while only about three-quarters of the conjugal families have memorial tablets, almost 95 percent of the two-generation and all of the three-generation stem families have tablets. Overall, 81 percent of the households have tablets; 19 percent have none.

Table 3 presents a breakdown by place of residence of the number of tablets per household. It is at once apparent that the highest proportion (32 percent) of those without tablets is found among the Tokyo households, which also have the highest proportion of households headed by nonsuccessors. It is precisely in such neolocal households, where no death has yet occurred, that one would have found no tablets in "traditional" times as well. The Tokyo figure cannot, then, be taken to show a decline in ancestor worship. As those interviewed regularly said, when asked why they had no tablets, "No one has yet died in this house." It is also apparent from Table 3 that the urban households generally have fewer tablets, indicating shallowness of generational depth, than is the case with rural households. Such depth is most marked in Yasuhara, where most households have been resident for a great many years, but where there are no branch households of any description. In Sone and Takane, where far fewer surnames are represented, generational depth is nonetheless marked, if slightly less so in Takane.

Table 4 shows the range of religious affiliation of the families surveyed. Although Buddhist sectarian membership appears to have no clear relationship to any feature of ancestor worship discussed below, the information is presented here in the interest of completeness of background. It does serve to confirm the common observation that the emphasis on ancestor worship has long since overwhelmed all doctrinal and sectarian diversity among the Buddhists. The one Christian house-

Table 3.   Number of memorial tablets per household and place of residence (n = 595)

| Number of tablets | Place of residence | | | | | | | | | | | | | | | | | | Totals | |
|---|---|---|---|---|---|---|---|---|---|---|---|---|---|---|---|---|---|---|---|---|
| | Tokyo | | Osaka | | Kyoto | | Hanshin | | Nara | | Urban misc. | | Sone | | Yasuhara | | Takane | | | |
| | Nr | Pct | Nr | Pct | Nr | Pct | Nr | Pct | Nr | Pct | Nr | Pct | Nr | Pct | Nr | Pct | Nr | Pct | Nr | Pct |
| None | 59 | 32.2 | 19 | 18.3 | 12 | 18.2 | 3 | 18.7 | 9 | 30.0 | 3 | 10.0 | 3 | 2.7 | – | – | 4 | 12.1 | 112 | 18.8 |
| 1 | 34 | 18.6 | 15 | 14.4 | 15 | 22.7 | 2 | 12.5 | 5 | 16.7 | 2 | 6.7 | 10 | 8.8 | 1 | 5.0 | 2 | 6.1 | 86 | 14.5 |
| 2 | 28 | 15.3 | 15 | 14.4 | 15 | 22.7 | 2 | 12.5 | 1 | 3.3 | 2 | 6.7 | 9 | 8.0 | 1 | 5.0 | 2 | 6.1 | 75 | 12.6 |
| 3 | 20 | 10.9 | 18 | 17.3 | 4 | 6.1 | 2 | 12.5 | 5 | 16.7 | 7 | 23.3 | 5 | 4.4 | 1 | 5.0 | 1 | 3.0 | 63 | 10.6 |
| 4 | 13 | 7.1 | 14 | 13.5 | 3 | 4.5 | 2 | 12.5 | 1 | 3.3 | 2 | 6.7 | 8 | 7.1 | 1 | 5.0 | 1 | 3.0 | 45 | 7.6 |
| 5 | 8 | 4.4 | 10 | 9.6 | 5 | 7.6 | 1 | 6.3 | 1 | 3.3 | 3 | 10.0 | 8 | 7.1 | – | – | 4 | 12.1 | 40 | 6.7 |
| 6 | 5 | 2.7 | 1 | 1.0 | 2 | 3.0 | – | – | 2 | 6.7 | – | – | 3 | 2.7 | – | – | 2 | 6.1 | 15 | 2.5 |
| 7 | 2 | 1.1 | 2 | 1.9 | 2 | 3.0 | 1 | 6.3 | – | – | 2 | 6.7 | 9 | 8.0 | 2 | 10.0 | 4 | 12.1 | 24 | 4.0 |
| 8 | 3 | 1.6 | 2 | 1.9 | 2 | 3.0 | 1 | 6.3 | 1 | 3.3 | – | – | 11 | 9.7 | 1 | 5.0 | 1 | 3.0 | 22 | 3.7 |
| 9 | 2 | 1.1 | 2 | 1.9 | 2 | 3.0 | – | – | 1 | 3.3 | – | – | 4 | 3.5 | 2 | 10.0 | 3 | 9.1 | 16 | 2.7 |
| 10 | 2 | 1.1 | – | – | – | – | – | – | 1 | 3.3 | 1 | 3.3 | 6 | 5.3 | – | – | – | – | 10 | 1.7 |
| 11–19 | 5 | 2.7 | 5 | 4.8 | 4 | 6.1 | 1 | 6.3 | 3 | 10.0 | 6 | 20.0 | 30 | 26.5 | 1 | 5.0 | 7 | 21.2 | 62 | 10.4 |
| 20–29 | 2 | 1.1 | 1 | 1.0 | – | – | – | – | – | – | 2 | 6.7 | 6 | 5.3 | 5 | 25.0 | 2 | 6.1 | 18 | 3.0 |
| 30–39 | – | – | – | – | – | – | 1 | 6.3 | – | – | – | – | 1 | .9 | 3 | 15.0 | – | – | 5 | .8 |
| 40–57 | – | – | – | – | – | – | – | – | – | – | – | – | – | – | 2 | 10.0 | – | – | 2 | .3 |
| Total households | 183 | 100 | 104 | 100 | 66 | 100 | 16 | 100 | 30 | 100 | 30 | 100 | 113 | 100 | 20 | 100 | 33 | 100 | 595 | 100 |

Nr = Number.        Pct = Percent.

hold has tablets because "our ancestors were Buddhists and it is only proper that they be venerated in this way."

Over the years there has been some discussion of the identity of the

Table 4.  Religion of household (n = 595)

| Religious affiliation | Households | | |
|---|---|---|---|
| | Number | | Percent |
| *Buddhist* | 563 | | 94.6 |
| Jōdo shin shū | | 170 | 28.6 |
| Zen shū | | 155 | 26.1 |
| Jōdo shū | | 98[a] | 16.5 |
| Shingon shū | | 49 | 8.2 |
| Bukkyō [Buddhism] | | 39[b] | 6.6 |
| Nichiren-shū | | 31 | 5.2 |
| Nichiren shōshū | | 18 | 3.2 |
| Tendai shū | | 3 | 0.5 |
| *Other* | 8 | | 1.3 |
| Shintō | | 3 | 0.5 |
| Tenri | | 3 | 0.5 |
| Seichō no ie | | 1 | 0.2 |
| Christian | | 1 | 0.2 |
| *None* | 23 | | 3.9 |
| *No answer* | 1 | | 0.2 |
| *Total* | 595 | | 100.0 |

[a]  Includes two responses "Jōdo shū and Seichō no ie."
[b]  Includes one response "Bukkyō [Buddhism] and Shintō."

person accorded primary responsibility for caring for the memorial tablets — offering food and drink, flowers and incense. It is routinely argued that it is usually the women of the house who undertake the daily or periodic tasks of caring for the altar. Our data reveal no such unambiguous situation. In Table 5 are given tabulations of 460 responses to the question. Women ("wife," "mother," "wife and mother") are reported to be responsible for the care of tablets in almost exactly one-half of the households:

| | Households | Percent |
|---|---|---|
| Wife | 176 | 75.9 |
| Mother | 45 | 19.4 |
| Wife and mother | 11 | 4.7 |
| | 232 | 100.0 |

In another forty-four cases (about 10 percent of the total) a woman

("wife" or "mother") is said to hold joint responsibility with the male
household. Another refinement of the analysis is possible — these 276
cases account for two-thirds of the 413 households WITH MALE HEADS.
To this number should be added those (exact count as yet undetermined)
of the forty-four "other" cases who are females ("grandmother," "daughter," "son's wife," etc.). My guess is that women figure in the care of the
memorial tablets in at least 70 percent of the households answering the
question.

Table 5.    Person responsible for care of memorial tablets and household type (n = 460)

| Person(s) responsible | Household type | | | | | | | |
|---|---|---|---|---|---|---|---|---|
| | Head unmarried | | Conjugal | | Two- and three-genera-tion stem | | Totals | |
| | Nr | Pct | Nr | Pct | Nr | Pct | Nr | Pct |
| Head (male) | 3 | 42.9 | 28 | 8.8 | 8 | 5.9 | 39 | 8.5 |
| Head (female) | 2 | 28.5 | 31 | 9.8 | 7 | 5.2 | 40 | 8.7 |
| Wife | – | – | 154 | 48.4 | 22 | 16.3 | 176 | 38.3 |
| Mother | – | – | 3 | 0.9 | 42 | 31.1 | 45[a] | 9.8 |
| Head and wife | – | – | 38 | 12.0 | 3 | 2.2 | 41 | 8.9 |
| Male head and mother | 1 | 14.3 | – | – | 2 | 1.5 | 3 | 0.7 |
| Female head and mother | 1 | 14.3 | – | – | 1 | 0.7 | 2 | 0.4 |
| Wife and mother | – | – | 1 | 0.3 | 10 | 7.4 | 11 | 2.3 |
| Not fixed | – | – | 44 | 13.8 | 15 | 11.1 | 59[b] | 12.8 |
| Other | – | – | 19 | 6.0 | 25 | 18.5 | 44 | 9.6 |
| Totals | 7 | 100.0 | 318 | 100.0 | 135 | 100.0 | 460 | 100.0 |

[a]   Includes two households with female head.
[b]   Includes five households with female head.
Nr = Number.      Pct = Percent.

The final issue relating to the household's treatment of the ancestors
remains to be considered before moving to the data on the tablets themselves. We asked on what occasions offerings are made or rites performed
at the ancestral altar. Tables 6, 7, and 8 are difficult to understand without
some explanation. There are eight kinds of occasions on which the
ancestors may be venerated, leaving aside special occasions which are not
periodic in character (sharing gifts from visitors with the ancestors by
placing a portion on the altar, reporting events of importance in the lives
of the household members to the ancestors, etc.). These repetitive occasions
are listed in Table 6, with the percentage of households reporting observances of each.

Of the 483 households with tablets, 457 answered this question. Leading
the list are two occasions on which the collectivity of ancestors is honored:

(1) *bon* (also *obon*), the great midsummer's Festival of the Dead and (2) the daily morning offering of newly cooked food to the dead. Very close behind are the periodic celebrations of the anniversary of the death of an individual, usually the first, third, etc., up to the thirty-third, fiftieth, or one-hundredth. Only seven households with tablets report that they pay no attention to them at all.

Table 6.    Number of households observing given occasions of worship (n = 457[a])

| Occasion of worship in descending order of frequency | Households observing | |
|---|---|---|
| | Number | Percent |
| *bon* [Festival of the Dead] | 287 | 62.8 |
| *mai asa* [every morning] | 282 | 61.7 |
| *nenki* [periodic anniversaries of death] | 275 | 60.2 |
| *mai tsuki meinichi* [monthly on date of death] | 255 | 55.8 |
| *higan* [vernal and autumnal equinoxes] | 243 | 53.2 |
| *mai ban* [every evening] | 204 | 44.6 |
| *shō gatsu* [New Year] | 197 | 43.1 |
| *shō tsuki meinichi* [annually on date of death] | 191 | 41.8 |
| "When we think of it" | 57 | 12.5 |
| "Never" | 7 | 1.5 |

[a]    No answer: 26 households.  No tablets: 112 households.

As Table 7 shows, however, the simple listing of frequencies does not tell the whole story. Here I have set out the fourteen most common PATTERNS OF WORSHIP, i.e. those reported by nine or more households. These patterns account for only 216 of the 457 households with tablets responding to this question, meaning that the remaining 241 households report other patterns of worship, none of which is found in as many as nine households. Taking the four most common patterns in Table 7, two major types emerge:
1.   One hundred eleven households report observance of the daily morning offering (patterns 1, 2, 3, and 4); of these, sixty-four make the daily evening offering as well (patterns 1, 2, and 4).
2.   Another fifty-four households (patterns 5, 7, 10, 12, and 14) report that they make the daily morning offering in addition to *nenki* and *mai tsuki meinichi*.
   One final comment on Table 7 has to do with the bottom line, which shows the number of times a given occasion of worship occurs in the fourteen patterns, irrespective of pattern composition. There are three such occasions which appear in ten of the fourteen patterns — *nenki, mai tsuki meinichi*, and *mai asa*. The first and second are ceremonies directed primarily to an individual ancestor. The last offers comfort to the collectivity of the household's dead by including them in the family's morning meal, first portions of which are set on the ancestral altar.

Table 7.  Most common patterns of worship: occasions on which offerings are made to the memorial tablets (n = 216)

| Pattern number | Number of households reporting pattern | Periodic anniversaries of death (nenki) | Annually on date of death (shō tsuki meinichi) | Festival of the Dead (bon) | Vernal and autumnal equinoxes (higan) | New Year (shō gatsu) | Monthly on date of death (mai tsuki meinichi) | Every morning (mai asa) | Every evening (mai ban) |
|---|---|---|---|---|---|---|---|---|---|
| 1 | 35 | − | − | − | − | − | − | + | + |
| 2 | 29 | + | + | + | + | + | + | + | + |
| 3 | 24 | − | − | − | − | − | − | + | − |
| 4 | 23 | + | + | + | + | + | + | + | + |
| 5 | 16 | + | + | + | − | + | + | + | − |
| 6 | 13 | + | − | + | + | − | − | − | − |
| 7 | 11 | − | + | − | − | + | + | + | + |
| 8 | 11 | + | + | + | + | + | + | + | − |
| 9 | 9 | + | + | + | + | − | + | − | − |
| 10 | 9 | + | − | − | − | + | + | + | − |
| 11 | 9 | + | − | − | − | − | − | − | − |
| 12 | 9 | + | − | − | − | − | + | + | + |
| 13 | 9 | − | − | − | − | − | + | − | − |
| 14 | 9 | + | + | + | + | − | + | + | + |
| Number of times occasion appears in patterns | | 10 | 6 | 7 | 6 | 6 | 10 | 10 | 6 |

Finally, let us turn to Table 8 where the fourteen most common patterns of worship are shown by place of residence. Some of the patterns are heavily urban, but the figures are so small as to make positive conclusions impossible. The one genuinely curious aspect of the results shown in this table is the outcome of Sone. Patterns 4, 6, 7, 11, and 12, five of the fourteen, are accounted for in their entirety by households in this one community. The peculiarity of Sone is further highlighted by its participation in only one other pattern, 2, the one inclusive of all possible occasions of worship. The diversity and exclusivity of patterns in Sone cannot be explained by diversity of Buddhist sects for almost all of the households belong to the Zen sect and are parishioners of the local Zen temple. (I have appealed to Bernard Bernier, University of Montreal, for help in trying to understand this feature of the community he knows so well.)

Now to the census of tablets itself. Table 9 contains several kinds of information. The line headings must be explained before the table can be understood at all, for I have adopted some unusual conventions of classification of kin:

A. LINEALS: All persons related in any way to the descent line, whether through the male househead (whose wife has "married in" as is the usual case) or the female who has taken an adopted husband (who then functions as male househead although he has "married in") or an adopted child who has taken the family name. Thus, Lineals are those whose names have appeared at one time, or still do, in the household register at the time of

Table 8. Most common patterns of worship: place of residence of households (n = 216)

| Pattern number[a] | Tokyo | Osaka | Kyoto | Hanshin | Nara | Misc. Urban | Sone | Yasuhara | Takane | Total |
|---|---|---|---|---|---|---|---|---|---|---|
| 1 | 11 | 11 | 5 | – | 3 | 3 | – | 2 | – | 35 |
| 2 | 3 | 4 | 7 | 3 | 1 | 4 | 7 | – | – | 29 |
| 3 | 12 | 2 | 3 | 1 | – | – | – | 3 | 3 | 24 |
| 4 | – | – | – | – | – | – | 23 | – | – | 23 |
| 5 | 10 | 3 | – | – | 2 | 1 | – | – | – | 16 |
| 6 | – | – | – | – | – | – | 13 | – | – | 13 |
| 7 | – | – | – | – | – | – | 11 | – | – | 11 |
| 8 | 1 | 1 | 2 | – | – | – | – | 7 | – | 11 |
| 9 | 2 | 4 | 1 | 2 | – | – | – | – | – | 9 |
| 10 | 5 | 3 | 1 | – | – | – | – | – | – | 9 |
| 11 | – | – | – | – | – | – | 9 | – | – | 9 |
| 12 | – | – | – | – | – | – | 9 | – | – | 9 |
| 13 | 2 | 2 | 2 | – | 1 | – | – | 2 | – | 9 |
| 14 | – | 7 | 1 | – | 1 | – | – | – | – | 9 |

[a] See Table 7 for details of patterns of worship.

their death (with a very few very few very special exceptions). To anticipate slightly, the category of Lineals EXCLUDES all persons who are the kin of an in-marrying wife, an in-marrying adopted husband, or an adopted child.

1.   UNIDENTIFIED:   A person not identifiable by any living member of the house, but presumably Lineal.

2.   PROGENITORS:   All previous householods and their wives of all ascending generations. In the ordinary case, these will be the father and mother of the present householod. Where he is an in-marrying, adopted husband, they will of course be the father and mother of his wife. Where he or his wife are adopted children, they would in Ego-centered terminology be the present male head's foster father and mother or his wife's foster father and mother if he is the adopted husband of an adopted female. In a real sense none of this variation is of any moment, for in Japanese reckoning the deceased householod and his wife are the nearest ancestral generation *vis-à-vis* the direct line of descent and succession. Collectively, then, all the ascending generations of the householod and his wife are progenitors. Each couple commonly shares a single tablet, but for purposes of enumeration here and elsewhere I have taken each individual's name as representing one tablet.

3.   SPOUSES OF PROGENITORS:   Husbands and wives of progenitors who died before or after the marriage which produced or secured the succession to the present generation. Each commonly has a single tablet. If one's father's father was married early and his young wife died, there will be a tablet for her alone; if he remarried and his second wife bore one's father (the successor) and other children before she died, then her name will appear on the same tablet with that of the father's father; if he married a third time, whether other children were born or not, his last wife will have a single tablet.

4.   SPOUSE OF HEAD:   Husband or wife of present head, often found even when present head has remarried.

5.   SPOUSE OF SPOUSE:   Husband or wife of spouse of present head. These include male head's first wife, adopted husband's wife, first adopted husband, etc.

6.   DESCENDANTS:   Children of present householod by all marriages.

7.   SIBLINGS, THEIR SPOUSES AND CHILDREN:   Siblings of the present male householod and of the wife of an in-marrying adopted husband are clearly Lineals in my sense. These persons usually died before marrying (as we shall see below) or married out and returned to their natal house; or, where there is a whole family represented by tablets, they are a neolocal house which has died out (such a house is called *zekke*) and its tablets

reverted to the natal house of the head of the *zekke*. The tablets for siblings' spouses and their children in such families are one of the very rare, very special exceptions to the rule given in "A" above that Lineals are usually people who have at some time been listed in the household register.

8.   FATHER'S SIBLINGS, THEIR SPOUSES AND CHILDREN:   "Father" here refers to the next ascendant male hous  ehead, irrespective of the derivation of succession in the direct line.

9.   FATHER'S FATHER'S SIBLINGS, THEIR SPOUSES AND CHILDREN:   See 8 above; "father's father" is the second ascendant male househead.

10.   FATHER'S FATHER'S FATHER'S SIBLINGS, THEIR SPOUSES AND CHILDREN: See 8 above; "father's father's father" is the third ascendant male househead.

11.   OTHER:   Unclassifiable, presumably Lineal kinsmen ("uncle," "aunt," "cousin," etc.).

B.   NON-LINEALS:   Persons not in the house's register or entirely unrelated to the direct line of succession. There are three categories: (a) kin of an adopted child or adopted husband, (b) kin of the mother of the present househead where she married in, and (c) kin of the wife of the present househead where she married in. In short, these are the kin of those who have either been adopted in or who have married in. All Non-Lineals come from the natal house of an adoptee, mother or wife.

12.   UNIDENTIFIED:   See 1 above; these are all known to be Non-Lineals.

a.   *Yōshi*'s kin [adopted child or adopted husband]:

13.   PROGENITORS:   See 2 above; ascendants of adoptee's natal house.

14.   FATHER'S AND MOTHER'S SIBLINGS, THEIR SPOUSES AND CHILDREN: See 7 above; adoptee's father's or mother's (if she took an adopted husband) siblings, their spouses and children.

15.   SIBLINGS:   See 7 above; adoptee's own siblings from natal house.

b.   Mother's kin:

16.   PROGENITORS:   See 2 above; ascendants of the present househead's mother, where she is married in, from her natal house.

17.   MISCELLANEOUS:   Other kinsmen of mother from her natal house.

18.   SIBLINGS, THEIR SPOUSES AND CHILDREN:   See 7 above; mother's siblings, their spouses and children from her natal house.

c.   Wife's kin:

19.   PROGENITORS:   See 2 above; ascendants of present househead's wife, where she is married in, from her natal house.

20.   FATHER'S AND MOTHER'S SIBLINGS, THEIR SPOUSES AND CHILDREN: See 14 above; from wife's natal house.

21.   SIBLINGS:   See 15 above; from wife's natal house.

Table 9. Type of tablets held (relationship to househead) and number of tablets in each category by locality (n = 3...

| Type of tablet; relation to househead | Tokyo | | Osaka | | Kyoto | | Hanshin | |
|---|---|---|---|---|---|---|---|---|
| | Nr | Percent | Nr | Percent | Nr | Percent | Nr | Percer |
| **A.  *Lineal*** | | | | | | | | |
| 1.  Unidentified | 43 | 9.2 ( 5) | 26 | 7.4 ( 6) | 18 | 8.3 ( 2) | 12 | 13.5 |
| 2.  Progenitors | 208 | 55.9 (92) | 205 | 69.0 (78) | 102 | 58.0 (44) | 46 | 69.7 |
| 3.  Spouses of progenitors | 4 | 1.1 ( 3) | 6 | 2.0 ( 5) | 2 | 1.1 ( 2) | 2 | 3.0 |
| 4.  Spouse of head | 17 | 4.6 (17) | 12 | 4.0 (11) | 13 | 7.4 (11) | 1 | 1.5 |
| 5.  Spouse of spouse | – | – | – | – | – | – | – | – |
| 6.  Descendants | 52 | 14.0 (39) | 18 | 6.0 (13) | 20 | 11.4 (12) | 3 | 4.5 |
| 7.  Siblings, their spouses and children | 56 | 15.1 (32) | 47 | 15.8 (28) | 31 | 17.6 (13) | 14 | 21.2 |
| 8.  Fa's sibs, spouses, children | 27 | 7.3 (11) | 4 | 1.3 ( 3) | 7 | 4.0 ( 4) | – | – |
| 9.  FaFa's, sibs, spouses, children | 2 | .5 ( 2) | 2 | .7 ( 2) | 1 | .6 ( 1) | – | – |
| 10.  FaFaFa's, sibs, spouses, children | – | – | – | – | – | – | – | – |
| 11.  Other | 6 | 1.6 ( 3) | 3 | 1.0 ( 3) | – | – | – | – |
| Subtotal 2–11 | 372 | 79.5 | 297 | 84.9 | 176 | 81.1 | 66 | 74.2 |
| **B.  *Non-Lineal*** | | | | | | | | |
| 12.  Unidentified | – | – | – | – | – | – | – | – |
| a.  *Yōshi's Kin* | | | | | | | | |
| 13.  Progenitors | 11 | 21.2 ( 6) | 8 | 30.8 ( 3) | 3 | 13.0 ( 2) | 2 | 22.2 |
| 14.  Fa and Mo Siblings, spouse and children | – | – | – | – | 4 | 17.4 ( 1) | – | – |
| 15.  Siblings | 2 | 3.8 ( 1) | – | – | – | – | – | – |
| b.  *Mother's Kin* | | | | | | | | |
| 16.  Progenitors | 4 | 7.7 ( 3) | 6 | 23.1 ( 4) | 3 | 13.0 ( 3) | – | – |
| 17.  Miscellaneous | 2 | 3.8 ( 1) | 2 | 7.7 ( 1) | – | – | – | – |
| 18.  Siblings, their spouses and children | 5 | 9.6 ( 1) | 1 | 3.8 ( 1) | – | – | – | – |
| c.  *Wife's Kin* | | | | | | | | |
| 19.  Progenitors | 21 | 40.4 (14) | 7 | 26.9 ( 4) | 8 | 34.8 ( 3) | 7 | 77.8 |
| 20.  Fa and Mo Siblings, spouses and children | – | – | – | – | 4 | 17.4 ( 1) | – | – |
| 21.  Siblings | 7 | 13.5 ( 5) | 2 | 7.7 ( 1) | 1 | 4.3 ( 1) | – | – |
| Subtotal 13–21 | 52 | 11.1 | 26 | 7.4 | 23 | 10.6 | 9 | 10.1 |
| **C.  *Non-Kin*** | 1 | .2 ( 1) | 1 | .3 ( 1) | – | – | 2 | 2.2 |
| Totals | 468 | 100.0 | 350 | 100.0 | 217 | 100.0 | 89 | 100.0 |

The numbers in parentheses are the numbers of households having at least one tablet in each category (n = 4...

C.  NON-KIN:  Persons entirely unrelated in any way to any past or present member of the household either "Lineally" or "Non-Lineally"; includes teacher, stranger, lover, etc.

With no apologies for the complexity of the categorization, let us now consider some of the outstanding findings. Once again, as with Sone and the patterns of worship, we have a unique case: only in the community of Takane do we find no tablets at all for Non-Lineals and Non-Kin. Much can be made of the implications of the exclusively Lineal character of the tablets of this *dōzoku* community.

During our interviews there, we were asked why we were undertaking this extraordinary census, and when we said that we were trying to see how much diversity there is in holdings of tablets, we were not understood.

| a Percent | Miscellaneous Nr | Percent | Sone Nr | Percent | Yasuhara Nr | Percent | Takane Nr | Percent | Total Nr | Percent |
|---|---|---|---|---|---|---|---|---|---|---|
| 14.8 ( 5) | 16 | 7.6 ( 3) | 249 | 26.0 (42) | 188 | 47.4 (12) | 27 | 10.7 ( 7) | 595 | 19.5 ( 83) |
| 74.1 (19) | 122 | 72.6 (26) | 334 | 50.8 (89) | 73 | 38.4 (20) | 128 | 56.9 (26) | 1,284 | 57.3 (406) |
| 2.2 ( 2) | 7 | 4.2 ( 5) | 10 | 1.5 (10) | 3 | 1.6 ( 3) | 14 | 6.2 ( 9) | 50 | 2.2 ( 41) |
| 4.5 ( 4) | 4 | 2.4 ( 4) | 32 | 4.9 (31) | 4 | 2.1 ( 4) | 4 | 1.8 ( 4) | 91 | 4.1 ( 87) |
| – – | – | – – | 6 | .9 ( 6) | 1 | .5 ( 1) | – | – – | 7 | .3 ( 7) |
| 9.0 ( 5) | 4 | 2.4 ( 3) | 93 | 14.1 (53) | 29 | 15.3 (13) | 29 | 12.9 (13) | 256 | 11.4 (154) |
| 3.4 ( 3) | 21 | 12.5 (10) | 117 | 17.8 (56) | 43 | 22.6 (13) | 26 | 11.6 (15) | 358 | 16.0 (174) |
| 4.5 ( 2) | 5 | 3.0 ( 4) | 53 | 8.1 (29) | 25 | 13.2 ( 9) | 22 | 9.8 (11) | 147 | 6.6 ( 73) |
| 2.2 ( 2) | 1 | .6 ( 1) | 8 | 1.2 ( 5) | 11 | 5.8 ( 4) | 2 | .9 ( 2) | 29 | 1.3 ( 19) |
| – – | 4 | 2.4 ( 1) | 5 | .8 ( 3) | 1 | .5 ( 1) | – | – – | 10 | .4 ( 5) |
| – – | – | – – | – | – – | – | – – | – | – – | 9 | .4 ( 6) |
| 82.4 | 168 | 79.6 | 658 | 68.7 | 190 | 47.8 | 225 | 89.3 | 2,241 | 73.5 |
| – – | – | – – | 9 | .9 ( 4) | – | – – | – | – – | 9 | .3 ( 4) |
| – – | 8 | 29.6 ( 3) | 8 | 21.1 ( 6) | – | – – | – | – – | 40 | 22.2 ( 21) |
| – – | – | – – | 3 | 7.9 ( 2) | – | – – | – | – – | 7 | 3.9 ( 3) |
| – – | 1 | 3.7 ( 1) | 1 | 2.6 ( 1) | – | – – | – | – – | 4 | 2.2 ( 3) |
| 100.0 ( 1) | 7 | 25.9 ( 4) | 9 | 23.7 ( 5) | 1 | 33.3 ( 1) | – | – – | 32 | 17.8 ( 21) |
| – – | – | – – | 2 | 5.3 ( 2) | – | – – | – | – – | 6 | 3.3 ( 4) |
| – – | 1 | 3.7 ( 1) | 7 | 18.4 ( 3) | 1 | 33.3 ( 1) | – | – – | 15 | 8.3 ( 7) |
| – – | 6 | 4.4 ( 3) | 3 | 7.9 ( 2) | 1 | 33.3 ( 1) | – | – – | 53 | 29.4 ( 32) |
| – – | 1 | 3.7 ( 1) | 3 | 7.9 ( 1) | – | – – | – | – – | 8 | 4.4 ( 3) |
| – – | 3 | 11.1 ( 1) | 2 | 5.3 ( 1) | – | – – | – | – – | 15 | 8.3 ( 9) |
| 1.9 | 27 | 12.8 | 38 | 4.0 | 3 | .8 | – | – – | 180 | 5.9 |
| .9 ( 1) | – | – – | 4 | .4 ( 4) | 16 | 4.0 ( 1) | | | 25 | .8 |
| 100.0 | 211 | 100.0 | 958 | 100.0 | 397 | 100.0 | 252 | 100.0 | 3,050 | 100.0 |

= Number.

We then explained that in Shikoku and the cities we found many tablets for Non-Lineals and Non-Kin in the household altars. This statement was politely but firmly rejected as reflecting some misunderstanding on our part. The universal opinion was that we had to be mistaken because "no household would have tablets for such people in its altar — they belong somewhere else." My own conclusion is that in Takane the principle of lineality is so strongly held and has such crucial implications for interhousehold relations and orderly community structure that dilution of the lineal character of the tablets is simply inconceivable. Indeed, we unintentionally uncovered an irregularity in tablet possession which was at once rectified. It turned out that a branch household (*bunke*) actually had some older tablets of senior generations than were held by its main house (*honke*). They had apparently been left with the branch house for safekeeping when the main house emigrated. But the main house had returned and somehow neglected to recover the senior tablets; when the discrepancy came out in our interviews, the main house demanded the tablets back. It was clear where they properly belonged.

The Non-Lineal tablets are, of course, of special interest because they do in many ways represent an anomaly. There is absolutely nothing in the rationale for ancestor worship or in the principles which most people invoke in explaining what tablets people ought to have in their altars and why they should be there which explains the presence of the Non-Lineals. To be sure, there are only 189 such tablets, 6.2 percent of the 3,050 total. *Yōshi* kin account for 28.3 percent of them (and these are almost entirely the kin of *muko-yōshi* [in-marrying adopted husbands]; mother's kin account for 19.4 percent; wife's kin for 42.1 percent; unidentified Non-Lineals (0.3 percent) are all from Sone. What can we conclude from this distribution? Tentatively I would suggest that the practice of placing Non-Lineal tablets in a household altar may be a fairly recent practice and one that is perhaps becoming more common. It will be recalled that we are dealing with a very large population of conjugal families and that wife's kin occur far more frequently than do mother's or *yōshi*'s kin. We may have here the opening wedge of FAMILY-centered as opposed to HOUSEHOLD-centered ancestor worship.

Those who have known Japanese society for a long time will be struck by the implications of one interview we conducted. This young couple, in their thirties, had no tablets, but they did have photographs (with black bands across the corners) of the husband's mother and the wife's father and mother. When we asked why they had these photographs, the husband replied, "Why, because they are our ancestors." This is quite right; they are all the ancestors of family members, but in the traditional meaning of the term in Japan they are not all the ancestors of the house.

A final word on the tablets for Non-Lineals. Again we have the very interesting exception of Sone, where there are forty-seven (including nine unidentified) such tablets; they are rare in Yasuhara and absent in Takane. Indeed, it turns out that almost three-quarters of all Non-Lineal tablets are found in the urban areas (139 of 189), and that the most common are tablets for progenitors of the wife of the househead (thirty-two such households as against twenty-one households, each holding tablets for the progenitors of adoptees and mothers).

As for the Lineal tablets, the materials in Table 9 are largely self-explanatory, but the last column deserves special attention and has been extracted and placed in Table 10. Everywhere more households have tablets for progenitors than for any other category of kin (406 households of the 483 having any tablets). The next most commonly reported are tablets for siblings, their spouses and children (174 households) followed closely by tablets for children of the househead (154 households).

Table 10. Analysis of types of tablets (categorized according to the relationship of individual represented to present househead) among households holding at least one tablet (n = 483)

| Type of tablet | Number of households holding at least one tablet of this type | Percent of total households |
|---|---|---|
| *Lineal* | | |
| unidentified tablet | 83 | 17.2 |
| progenitor | 406 | 84.1 |
| spouse of progenitor | 41 | 8.5 |
| spouse | 87 | 18.0 |
| spouse of spouse | 7 | 1.5 |
| descendant | 154 | 31.9 |
| siblings, their spouses and children | 174 | 36.0 |
| father's siblings, their spouses and children | 73 | 15.1 |
| father's father's siblings, their spouses and children | 19 | 3.9 |
| father's father's father's siblings, their spouses and children | 5 | 1.0 |
| other | 6 | 1.2 |
| *Non-Lineal* | | |
| unidentified tablet | 4 | 0.8 |
| *Yōshi's kin* | | |
| progenitor | 21 | 4.3 |
| father's and mother's siblings, their spouses and children | 3 | 0.6 |
| siblings | 3 | 0.6 |
| Mother's kin | | |
| progenitor | 21 | 4.3 |
| miscellaneous | 4 | 0.8 |
| siblings, their spouses and children | 7 | 1.5 |
| Wife's kin | | |
| progenitor | 32 | 6.6 |
| father's and mother's siblings, their spouses and children | 3 | 0.6 |
| siblings | 9 | 1.9 |
| *Non-Kin* | | |
| miscellaneous | 9 | 1.9 |

Again we have one rural community that presents us with an unusual situation. In the households of Yasuhara is found the lowest percentage (38.4 percent) of the total of Lineal tablets for progenitors. Everywhere else, such tablets account for 50.8 percent to 72.5 percent of the total. There can be little doubt of the reason for this situation, for in Yasuhara almost half of all tablets are unidentified and virtually all are Lineals. As we have remarked, this is a community in which every household has a different surname, and where interhousehold relations depend on proximity, shared responsibility, and mutual aid. There are a great many very old tablets here, so shallow generational depth is not characteristic of these households. It is rather, I think, a place where lineality as such is simply not an issue to the extent that it is in Takane's *dōzoku* or Sone's *miyaza*. The houses are not bound by ties of kinship and each venerates its own ancestors without regard to genealogical concerns other than its own.

For the moment, let us shift our attention from the tablets to the households once more. We have seen in Table 10 the number of households having at least one tablet of each category of relationship to the househead. It is now time to look at the larger question of the number of households having Lineal, Non-Lineal, and Non-Kin tablets. Of the 595 households, we know that 112 (18.8 percent) have no tablets. It is the remaining 483 that concern us here. Of these 483,

409 (68.7 percent) have tablets for only LINEALS;

57 (9.6 percent) have tablets for both LINEALS and NON-LINEALS (see A below);

8 (1.3 percent) have tablets for only NON-LINEALS (see B below);

7 (1.2 percent) have tablets for LINEALS, NON-LINEALS, and NON-KIN (see C below);

2 (0.4 percent) have tablets for both LINEALS and NON-KIN (see D below).

A.  These fifty-seven households with both Lineals and Non-Lineals are distributed as follows:

| | | |
|---|---|---|
| Tokyo | 15 ( 8.2 percent) of 183 households |
| Osaka | 7 ( 6.7 percent) of 104 households |
| Kyoto | 6 ( 9.1 percent) of  66 households |
| Hanshin | 5 (31.3 percent) of  16 households |
| Nara | 1 ( 3.3 percent) of  30 households |
| Miscellaneous | 8 (26.7 percent) of  30 households |
| Sone | 13 (11.5 percent) of 113 households |
| Yasuhara | 2 (10.0 percent) of  20 households |

B.  These eight households with tablets for Non-Lineals only are distributed as follows:

| | | |
|---|---|---|
| Tokyo | 6 (3.3 percent) of 183 households |
| Osaka | 1 (0.9 percent) of 104 households |
| Kyoto | 1 (1.5 percent) of  66 households |

C.  These seven households with Lineals, Non-Lineals and Non-Kin are distributed as follows:

Tokyo      1 (0.5 percent) of 183 households
Osaka      1 (0.9 percent) of 104 households
Hanshin    1 (6.3 percent) of  16 households
Sone       3 (2.7 percent) of 113 households
Yasuhara   1 (5.0 percent) of  20 households

D.  These two households having both Lineals and Non-Kin are distributed as follows:

Nara       1 (3.3 percent) of  30 households
Sone       1 (0.9 percent) of 113 households

Among the 409 households having tablets for Lineals only, there are some extremely interesting cases:

30 (7.3 percent) have tablets for DESCENDANTS only
15 (3.7 percent) have tablets for SPOUSES OF HEAD only
2  (0.5 percent) have tablets for SIBLINGS only

Thus forty-seven households (11.5 percent of the 409 having Lineals only) have altars in which there are no tablets for any ascendants.

Table 11 addresses itself to yet another kind of issue. It is commonly observed that memorial services (*nenki*) for the individual deceased end at the thirty-third or fiftieth or hundredth anniversary of death, when his tablet will be taken to the temple for safekeeping, thrown into a stream or into the sea, burned, or abandoned at the grave. There is obviously some attrition of tablets, but it is apparent that a great many very old tablets are kept by the household, long after the last formal *nenki* observances for them. Taking all 3,050 tablets, only about one-half are for persons who died since 1914, fifty years before the data were collected. About 15 percent of the total died more than 100 years ago. Another comment about the data in this table is in order — there turn out to be a few persons, dead for less than fifty years, whose tablets cannot be identified by anyone in the household. In all cases, which I cannot detail here, some extraordinary turn in family fortune (such as a husband's death at an early age) had left an altar in the care of a person who knew very little about the people represented by the tablets, but who nevertheless continued to perform acts of veneration before them.

In Table 12 the preceding information is broken down by category of relationship to the present househead. The picture is a very consistent one. Of particular interest are the figures for Non-Lineals. Of the identified

Table 11.  Year of death of identifiable and unidentifiable persons represented by memorial tablets (n = 3,050)

| Year of death | Identity known | | Identity unknown | | Totals | |
|---|---|---|---|---|---|---|
| | Nr | Pct | Nr | Pct | Nr | Pct |
| Date unknown | 168 | 6.9 | 102 | 16.9 | 270 | 8.9 |
| 1600–1863 (more than 100 years ago) | 138 | 5.6 | 344 | 56.9 | 482 | 15.8 |
| 1864–1913 (51–100 years ago) | 594 | 24.3 | 133 | 22.0 | 727 | 23.8 |
| 1914–1930 (34–50 years ago) | 464 | 19.0 | 18 | 3.0 | 482 | 15.8 |
| 1931–1963 (within past 33 years) | 1,082 | 44.2 | 7 | 1.2 | 1,809 | 35.7 |
| Totals | 2,446 | 100.0 | 604 | 100.0 | 3,050 | 100.0 |

Cumulative totals for persons for whom date of death is known

| Date of death | Nr of persons | Pct | Cumulative total | Pct |
|---|---|---|---|---|
| 1931–1963 (33 years) | 1,089 | 39.2 | 1,089 | 39.2 |
| 1914–1930 (34–50 years) | 482 | 17.3 | 1,571 | 56.5 |
| 1864–1913 (51–100 years) | 727 | 16.2 | 2,298 | 82.7 |
| 1600–1863 (over 100 years) | 482 | 17.3 | 2,780 | 100.0 |

Cumulative totals for identified persons only whose date of death is known

| 1931–1963 (33 years) | 1,082 | 47.5 | 1,082 | 47.5 |
|---|---|---|---|---|
| 1914–1930 (34–50 years) | 464 | 20.4 | 1,546 | 67.9 |
| 1864–1913 (51–100 years) | 594 | 16.0 | 2,140 | 93.9 |
| 1600–1863 (over 100 years) | 138 | 6.1 | 2,278 | 100.0 |

Nr = Number.    Pct = Percent.

Table 12.  Year of death of persons represented by memorial tablets: category of relationship head of household (n = 3,050)

| Category of relationship to head of household | Year of death | | | | | | | | | | | |
| | Date unkn. | | 1600–1863 | | 1864–1913 | | 1914–1930 | | 1931–1963 | | Total | |
|---|---|---|---|---|---|---|---|---|---|---|---|---|
| | Nr | Pct | Nr | Pct | Nr | Pct | Nr | Pct | Nr | Pct | Nr | Pc |
| *Unidentified* | | | | | | | | | | | | |
| Lineal | 100 | 98.0 | 339 | 98.5 | 131 | 98.5 | 18 | 100.0 | 7 | 100.0 | 595 | 9 |
| Non-Lineal | 2 | 2.0 | 5 | 1.5 | 2 | 1.5 | – | – | – | – | 9 | |
| Non-Kin | – | – | – | – | – | – | – | – | – | – | – | |
| Subtotal | 102 | 100.0 | 344 | 100.0 | 133 | 100.0 | 18 | 100.0 | 7 | 100.0 | 604 | 10 |
| *Identified* | | | | | | | | | | | | |
| Lineal | 151 | 89.9 | 128 | 92.8 | 529 | 89.1 | 439 | 94.6 | 994 | 91.9 | 2,241 | 9 |
| Non-Lineal | 15 | 8.9 | 7 | 5.1 | 58 | 9.8 | 22 | 4.7 | 78 | 7.2 | 180 | |
| Non-Kin | 2 | 1.2 | 3 | 2.1 | 7 | 1.1 | 3 | .7 | 10 | .9 | 25 | |
| Subtotal | 168 | 100.0 | 138 | 100.0 | 594 | 100.0 | 464 | 100.0 | 1,082 | 100.0 | 2,446 | 10 |
| *Total* | 270 | 8.9 | 482 | 15.8 | 727 | 23.8 | 482 | 15.8 | 1,089 | 35.7 | 3,050 | 10 |

Nr = Number.    Pct = Percent.

persons who died within the past thirty-three years, 7.2 percent are Non-Lineals; of those who died between thirty-four and fifty years ago, 4.7 percent are Non-Lineals; of those who died between fifty-one and 100 years ago, 9.8 percent are Non-Lineals. It would be tempting, and incorrect, to conclude that there has been little change over the past 100 years in the practice of placing such tablets in the household altar. But alas, we know only the date of death of the person; we do not know for most cases when any given tablet was introduced into the altar. This obviously crucial point is one which must be got at, and in the fuller analysis I intend to explore more intensively the cases for which I can date the moving of the tablets to their present location.

Table 13 may at first glance appear to be wholly gratuitous, but in fact it presents some extremely useful information. In Table 9 we have categorized relationships of the deceased to the present househead, and we observed that there were more tablets for siblings than for children

Table 13.  Age at death and category of relationship to present head of household (n = 3,050)

| Age at death | Category of relationship to head of household | | | | | | | |
|---|---|---|---|---|---|---|---|---|
| | Lineals | | Non-Lineals | | Non-Kin | | Totals | |
| Unknown | 1,138 | 40.1 | 68 | 36.0 | 22 | 88.0 | 1,228 | 40.3 |
| – 9 | 433 | 15.3 | 5 | 2.6 | – | – | 438 | 14.4 |
| 10–19 | 67 | 2.4 | 5 | 2.6 | – | – | 72 | 2.4 |
| 20–29 | 158 | 5.6 | 8 | 4.2 | 1 | 4.0 | 167 | 5.5 |
| 30–39 | 86 | 3.0 | 8 | 4.2 | – | – | 94 | 3.1 |
| 40–49 | 134 | 4.7 | 13 | 6.9 | – | – | 147 | 4.8 |
| 50–59 | 196 | 6.9 | 16 | 8.5 | – | – | 212 | 7.0 |
| 60–69 | 235 | 8.3 | 28 | 14.8 | 1 | 4.0 | 264 | 8.7 |
| 70–79 | 244 | 8.6 | 26 | 13.8 | – | – | 270 | 8.9 |
| 80–103 | 145 | 5.1 | 12 | 6.3 | 1 | 4.0 | 158 | 5.2 |
| Totals | 2,836 | 100.0 | 189 | 100.0 | 25 | 100.0 | 3,050 | 100.0 |

Recalculated, omitting those whose age at death is unknown:

| | | | | | | | | |
|---|---|---|---|---|---|---|---|---|
| – 9 | 433 | 25.5 | 5 | 4.1 | – | – | 438 | 24.0 |
| 10–19 | 67 | 4.0 | 5 | 4.1 | – | – | 72 | 4.0 |
| 20–29 | 158 | 9.3 | 8 | 6.6 | 1 | 33.3 | 167 | 9.2 |
| 30–39 | 86 | 5.1 | 8 | 6.6 | – | – | 94 | 5.2 |
| 40–49 | 134 | 7.9 | 13 | 10.7 | – | – | 147 | 8.1 |
| 50–59 | 196 | 11.5 | 16 | 13.2 | – | – | 212 | 11.6 |
| 60–69 | 235 | 13.8 | 28 | 23.1 | 1 | 33.3 | 264 | 14.5 |
| 70–79 | 244 | 14.4 | 26 | 21.5 | – | – | 270 | 14.8 |
| 80–103 | 145 | 8.5 | 12 | 9.9 | 1 | 33.3 | 158 | 8.6 |
| Totals | 1,698 | 100.0 | 121 | 100.0 | 3 | 100.0 | 1,822 | 100.0 |

of the househead. We did not face the implications of the domestic cycle and the timing of placement of these tablets in the altar. It is obvious that siblings of the present househead are the children of the preceding househead and that their tablets may very well have been placed there by him while the present househead was himself still a child. That this was indeed the case is borne out by Table 13, which shows age at death of persons represented by tablets. Of the 1,698 Lineals whose age at death is known, 25 percent died before they were ten years old. In point of fact, this is far and away the most commonly represented age group, the next most frequently found being persons in their seventies (14.4 percent). It is impossible to say what the effect on this distribution might be if we knew the age at death of the very large number (40 percent) of Lineals for whom the information was not available. For Non-Lineals whose age at death is known, the picture is a very different one. The young are underrepresented and about half are persons who died after they had reached the age of sixty.

Table 14 addresses itself to yet another issue of recurrent concern in the study of ancestor worship — that of duplicate tablets. Many people we interviewed expressed the feeling that there should be only one tablet for an individual, "lest he become confused and not know where to go at *bon*." There is, by the way, no practice comparable to the Chinese "dotting" of the tablet with red, so there is no "real" tablet as opposed to a lifeless copy. Others reported that in the area where they were born each son, and in some cases each child, received a copy of a parent's tablet. Still others had, for reasons of sentiment and affection, asked to have a copy made of a tablet from their natal house's altar, "to bring here

Table 14.   Duplicate tablets and category of relationship to present head of household (n = 167)

| Category of relationship to head of household | Original tablet, copy known to exist elsewhere | | Copy of original known to exist elsewhere | | Duplicate, uncertain whether copy or original | | Totals | |
|---|---|---|---|---|---|---|---|---|
| | Nr | Pct | Nr | Pct | Nr | Pct | Nr | Pct |
| Lineals | 25 | 96.2 | 72 | 67.3 | 17 | 50.0 | 114 | 68.3 |
| Non-Lineals | 1 | 3.8 | 30 | 28.0 | 17 | 50.0 | 48 | 28.7 |
| Non-Kin | – | – | 5 | 4.7 | – | – | 5 | 3.0 |
| Totals | 26 | 100.0 | 107 | 100.0 | 34 | 100.0 | 167 | 100.0 |

Of 2,836 tablets for Lineals, 114 (4.0 percent) are duplicates.
Of   189 tablets for Non-Lineals, 48 (25.4 percent) are duplicates.
Of    25 tablets for Non-Kin, 5 (25 percent) are duplicates.
Of 3,050 tablets for all categories, 167 (5.5 percent) are duplicates.
Nr = Number.     Pct = Percent.

so that I could take care of the person, too." One man had asked a friend to copy the Buddhist posthumous name from the tablet of his mistress kept in the altar of her natal house, which he then wrote on a piece of wood and placed in his own house's altar.

It is, of course, difficult to determine for every tablet whether there is a duplicate somewhere else; we are certain only that there are 167 tablets (5.5 percent) in our 3,050 of which duplicates exist. The distribution among categories of kin is instructive, even though I am now convinced that a great many duplicated tablets are not reported as such. For both Non-Lineals and Non-Kin, one-fourth of all tablets are duplicates; for Lineals only 4 percent. Even more interesting, of the 167 duplicates, just over two-thirds are tablets of Lineal kin. It is my guess that these are for the most part tablets which have been copied for reasons of affection by children of the deceased to take with them to their neolocal house. One man put it succinctly when he said, "I asked my eldest brother if I could make copies of our parents' tablets and he said it would be all right. So I brought them here after I got married because I didn't want to be the head of a house without any ancestors in it."

Table 15 is largely an unaggregated data resource where the curious reader can find details on the holdings of tablets by kin relationship to househead. I have broken down the entire list by sex, and it is of passing interest that there is a preponderance of males (53.4 percent) over females (45.1 percent), but that there are no differences for Non-Lineals. One word of caution to users of this table: while terms like "father's father" should be understood to represent great genealogical variety, all the persons so listed occupy a single household-centric status (male househead in the second ascending generation). Genealogically, "father's father" may be, with respect to the present househead: father's father, father's mother's adopted husband, foster father's father, foster father's foster father, foster father's mother's adopted husband, mother's adopted husband's foster father, etc. But in every case "father's father" is the male head of the household two generations above the present head. Consanguinity is not at issue.

The Non-Kin listed at the end of Table 15 deserve some comment, if only because they are a genuinely exotic company. One of them was a teacher of the househead, probably classifiable with the three *onjin* — persons to whom Ego or an earlier househead "owes an unrepayable debt." There is one nurse, who came with the present househead's father's father's mother when she married into the house and lived out her life here. One man already has his own tablet in the altar: "Can't be too careful these days," he said, "because young people don't care much about

Table 15.   Number of tablets of Lineals, Non-Lineals, and Non-Kin: sex and relationship of individual represented to present head of household (n = 3,050)

| Kin relationship to household head | Number of tablets | Male | Female | Sex unknown |
|---|---|---|---|---|
| Lineals (totals exclude unidentified) | 2,241 | 1,198 | 1,010 | 33 |
| *Unidentified* | (595) | – | – | – |
| *Progenitors* | 1,284: | 700: | 584: | – |
| father | 351 | 351 | – | – |
| mother | 264 | – | 264 | – |
| father's father | 204 | 204 | – | – |
| father's mother | 184 | – | 184 | – |
| father's father's father | 79 | 79 | – | – |
| father's father's mother | 73 | – | 73 | – |
| 4 father | 33 | 33 | – | – |
| 4 mother | 32 | – | 32 | – |
| 5 father | 10 | 10 | – | – |
| 5 mother | 10 | – | 10 | – |
| 6 father | 5 | 5 | – | – |
| 6 mother | 5 | – | 5 | – |
| 7 father | 5 | 5 | – | – |
| 7 mother | 5 | – | 5 | – |
| 8 father | 4 | 4 | – | – |
| 8 mother | 4 | – | 4 | – |
| 9 father | 2 | 2 | – | – |
| 9 mother | 2 | – | 2 | – |
| 10 father | 2 | 2 | – | – |
| 10 mother | 2 | – | 2 | – |
| 11 father | 1 | 1 | – | – |
| 11 mother | 1 | – | 1 | – |
| 12 father | 2 | 2 | – | – |
| 12 mother (missing) | | | | |
| 13 father | 1 | 1 | – | – |
| 13 mother | 1 | – | 1 | – |
| 14 father | 1 | 1 | – | – |
| 14 mother | 1 | – | 1 | – |
| *Spouses of progenitors* | 50: | 3: | 47: | – |
| father's wife | 21 | – | 21 | |
| mother's husband | 1 | 1 | – | – |
| father's father's wife | 14 | – | 14 | – |
| father's mother's husband | 2 | 2 | – | – |
| father's father's father's wife | 11 | – | 11 | – |
| 4 father's wife | 1 | – | 1 | – |
| *Spouses of head* | 91: | 47: | 44: | – |
| wife | 44 | – | 44 | – |
| husband | 47 | 47 | – | – |
| *Spouses of spouse* | 7: | 2: | 5: | – |
| husband's wife | 5 | – | 5 | – |
| wife's husband | 2 | 2 | – | |
| *Descendants* | 256: | 132: | 98: | 26: |
| son | 127 | 127 | – | – |
| daughter | 93 | – | 93 | – |
| child | 22 | – | – | 22 |
| son's son | 4 | 4 | – | – |

| Kin relationship to household head | Number of tablets | Male | Female | Sex unknown |
|---|---|---|---|---|
| son's daughter | 5 | – | 5 | – |
| son's child | 3 | – | – | 3 |
| child's child | 1 | – | – | 1 |
| daughter's son | 1 | 1 | – | – |
| *Siblings, their spouses and children* | 358: | 212: | 144: | 2: |
| elder brother | 105 | 105 | – | – |
| elder brother's wife | 7 | – | 7 | – |
| elder brother's son | 5 | 5 | – | – |
| elder brother's daughter | 5 | – | 5 | – |
| elder brother's child | 1 | – | – | 1 |
| younger brother | 85 | 85 | – | – |
| younger brother's son | 3 | 3 | – | – |
| brother | 9 | 9 | – | – |
| elder sister | 46 | – | 46 | – |
| elder sister's husband | 1 | 1 | – | – |
| elder sister's son | 2 | 2 | – | – |
| elder sister's child | 1 | – | – | 1 |
| younger sister | 76 | – | 76 | – |
| younger sister's husband | 1 | 1 | – | – |
| sister | 10 | – | 10 | – |
| nephew | 1 | 1 | – | – |
| *Father's siblings, their spouses and children* | 147: | 77: | 659: | 5: |
| father's elder brother | 18 | 18 | – | – |
| father's elder brother's wife | 3 | – | 3 | – |
| father's elder brother's son | 3 | 3 | – | – |
| father's younger brother | 30 | 30 | – | – |
| father's younger brother's wife | 4 | – | 4 | – |
| father's younger brother's son | 1 | 1 | – | – |
| father's younger brother's daughter | 1 | – | 1 | – |
| father's younger brother's child | 4 | – | – | 4 |
| father's brother | 23 | 23 | – | – |
| father's elder sister | 10 | – | 10 | – |
| father's elder sister's son | 1 | 1 | – | – |
| father's younger sister | 24 | – | 24 | – |
| father's younger sister's son | 1 | 1 | – | – |
| father's younger sister's child | 1 | – | – | 1 |
| father's sister | 23 | – | 23 | – |
| *Father's father's siblings, their spouses and children* | 29: | 14: | 15: | – |
| father's father's elder brother | 5 | 5 | – | – |
| father's father's younger brother | 1 | 1 | – | – |
| father's father's brother | 7 | 7 | – | – |
| father's father's brother's son | 1 | 1 | – | – |
| father's father's brother's daughter | 1 | – | 1 | – |
| father's father's elder sister | 7 | – | 7 | – |
| father's father's younger sister | 3 | – | 3 | – |
| father's father's sister | 4 | – | 4 | – |
| *Father's father's father's siblings, their spouses and children* | 10: | 7: | 3: | – |
| father's father's father's brother | 7 | 7 | – | – |

Table 15. (Continued)

| Kin relationship to household head | Number of tablets | Male | Female | Sex unknown |
|---|---|---|---|---|
| father's father's father's brother's wife | 1 | – | 1 | – |
| father's father's father's sister | 2 | – | 2 | – |
| *Other* | 9: | 4: | 5: | – |
| cousin | 1 | – | 1 | – |
| aunt | 3 | – | 3 | – |
| uncle | 3 | 3 | – | – |
| aunt's father | 1 | 1 | – | – |
| aunt's mother | 1 | – | 1 | – |
| Non-Lineals (totals exclude unidentified) | 180 | 89 | 88 | 3 |
| *Unidentified* | (9) | – | – | – |
| *Yōshi's kin* | 51 | 25 | 24 | 2 |
| *Progenitors* | 40: | 20: | 20: | – |
| father | 9 | 9 | – | – |
| mother | 8 | – | 8 | – |
| father's father | 3 | 3 | – | – |
| father's mother | 6 | – | 6 | – |
| father's father's father | 2 | 2 | – | – |
| father's father's mother | 1 | – | 1 | – |
| father's mother's father | 5 | 5 | – | – |
| father's mother's mother | 4 | – | 4 | – |
| father's mother's father's father | 1 | 1 | – | – |
| father's mother's father's mother | 1 | – | 1 | – |
| *Father's and mother's siblings,* | | | | |
| *their spouses and children* | 7: | 2: | 3: | 2: |
| father's elder sister | 1 | – | 1 | – |
| father's elder sister's child | 2 | – | – | 2 |
| father's younger sister | 1 | – | 1 | – |
| father's brother | 1 | 1 | – | – |
| father's mother's brother | 1 | 1 | – | – |
| father's mother's brother's wife | 1 | – | 1 | – |
| *Siblings* | 4: | 3: | 1: | – |
| elder brother | 3 | 3 | – | – |
| elder sister | 1 | – | 1 | – |
| *Mother's kin* | 53 | 25 | 27 | 1 |
| *Progenitors* | 32: | 15: | 17: | – |
| mother's father | 13 | 13 | – | – |
| mother's mother | 15 | – | 15 | – |
| mother's father's father | 1 | 1 | – | – |
| mother's father's mother | 2 | – | 2 | – |
| mother's father's mother's father | 1 | 1 | – | – |
| *Miscellaneous* | 6: | 3: | 2: | 1: |
| mother's husband | 2 | 2 | – | – |
| mother's daughter | 1 | – | 1 | – |
| mother's uncle | 1 | 1 | – | – |
| mother's niece | 1 | – | 1 | – |
| mother's child | 1 | – | – | 1 |
| *Siblings, their spouses and children* | 15: | 7: | 8: | – |
| mother's elder brother | 2 | 2 | – | – |
| mother's younger brother | 3 | 3 | – | – |

Table 15. (Continued)

| Kin relationship to household head | Number of tablets | Male | Female | Sex unknown |
|---|---|---|---|---|
| mother's elder sister | 3 | – | 3 | – |
| mother's elder sister's husband | 1 | 1 | – | – |
| mother's younger sister | 5 | – | 5 | – |
| mother's younger sister's husband | 1 | 1 | – | – |
| *Wife's kin*                            76 | 39 | 37 | – | |
| *Progenitors* | 53: | 28: | 25: | – |
| wife's father | 24 | 24 | – | – |
| wife's mother | 21 | – | 21 | – |
| wife's father's father | 2 | 2 | – | – |
| wife's father's mother | 2 | – | 2 | – |
| wife's mother's father | 2 | 2 | – | – |
| wife's mother's mother | 2 | – | 2 | – |
| *Father's and mother's siblings,* | | | | |
| *their spouses and children* | 8: | 4: | 4: | – |
| wife's father's younger brother | 1 | 1 | – | – |
| wife's father's younger brother's wife | 1 | – | 1 | – |
| wife's father's younger sister | 1 | – | 1 | – |
| wife's father's sister | 1 | – | 1 | – |
| wife's father's father's younger brother | 1 | 1 | – | – |
| wife's mother's elder sister | 1 | – | 1 | – |
| wife's mother's elder sister's husband | 1 | 1 | – | – |
| wife's mother's elder sister's son | 1 | 1 | – | – |
| *Siblings* | 15: | 7: | 8: | – |
| wife's elder brother | 3 | 3 | – | – |
| wife's younger brother | 4 | 4 | – | – |
| wife's elder sister | 3 | – | 3 | – |
| wife's younger sister | 3 | – | 3 | – |
| wife's sister | 2 | – | 2 | – |
| Non-Kin | 25: | | | |
| teacher | 1 | | | |
| *onjin* | 3 | | | |
| father's father's mother's nurse | 1 | | | |
| Ego | 1 | | | |
| wife's mother's "husband" | 1 | | | |
| father's lover | 1 | | | |
| family into which daughter married | 16 | | | |
| *tanin* — stranger | 1 | | | |

the ancestors any more." Properly, of course, this tablet is, or will become, that of a Lineal; I have put it here only for convenience. The "wife's mother's 'husband'" is a fine example of the skeleton in the family altar, as is "father's lover."

The sixteen tablets in a single altar in a Yasuhara household greatly inflate the total of Non-Kin, and they are a rather special case. A daughter of this house who married out subsequently emigrated to Paraguay with her husband and their two children. These are all the tablets of her husband's household, left here in the place where the young couple assumed they would most likely be cared for properly. The husband's unmarried younger brother refused to take them on the grounds that there is no place for the altar in his small room in the city. It is assumed that one day he will marry and come to claim them, or that the young couple will come back and once again care for them. Why were they not taken to Paraguay? The reason is one we met with frequently where emigration had been only as far as a nearby city — the tablets would then be too far from the graves of the people they represent. And, finally, there is one *tanin* — a stranger. This tablet is in an altar in Sone, and the househead told us that he had found it on the beach after a great tidal wave had struck the Ise Peninsula and washed away many houses. We asked why he had kept it rather than turning it over to the temple to

Table 16.  Summary of Table 15 (n = 3,050)

| Kin relationship to household head | Number of tablets | Male | Female | Sex unknown |
|---|---|---|---|---|
| Lineals (excluding unidentified) | 2,241 | 1,198 | 1,010 | 33 |
| *Unidentified* | (595) | | | |
| *Progenitors* | 1,284 | 700 | 584 | – |
| *Spouses of Progenitors* | 50 | 3 | 47 | – |
| *Spouses of Head* | 91 | 47 | 44 | – |
| *Spouses of Spouses* | 7 | 2 | 5 | – |
| *Descendants* | 256 | 132 | 98 | 26 |
| *Siblings, their spouses and children* | 358 | 212 | 144 | 2 |
| *Father's siblings, their spouses and children* | 147 | 77 | 65 | 5 |
| *Father's father's siblings, their spouses and children* | 29 | 14 | 15 | – |
| *Father's father's father's siblings, their spouses and children* | 10 | 7 | 3 | – |
| *Other* | 9 | 4 | 5 | – |
| Non-Lineals (excluding unidentified) | 180 | 89 | 88 | 3 |
| *Unidentified* | (9) | | | |
| *Yōshi's kin* | 51 | 25 | 24 | 2 |
| *Progenitors* | 40 | 20 | 20 | – |
| *Father's and mother's siblings, their spouses and children* | 7 | 2 | 3 | 2 |
| *Siblings* | 4 | 3 | 1 | – |
| *Mother's kin* | 53 | 25 | 27 | 1 |
| *Progenitors* | 32 | 15 | 17 | – |
| *Miscellaneous* | 6 | 3 | 2 | 1 |
| *Siblings, their spouses and children* | 15 | 7 | 8 | – |
| *Wife's kin* | 76 | 39 | 37 | – |
| *Progenitors* | 53 | 28 | 25 | – |
| *Father's and mother's siblings, their spouses and children* | 8 | 4 | 4 | – |
| *Siblings* | 15 | 7 | 8 | – |
| Non-Kin | 25 | | | |

look after, he said, "Because I found it, I felt that I was meant to care for it."

For the convenience of reference, Table 16 extracts and summarizes certain data from Table 15.

Table 17 also presents material from Table 15, of a somewhat different character, listing the twenty-two most common kin relations represented among the Lineal tablets. In all there are ninety-three separate kin relations listed in the larger table; the twenty-two shown in Table 17 account for 88.6 percent of all identifiable Lineals. The first four in terms of frequency (father, mother, father's father, father's mother, e.g. the first two ascending generations from the present househead), account for 44.8 percent of all identifiable Lineals.

Table 17.  Tablets for Lineals: kinship relation to head of household in descending frequency of occurrence, using more than twenty occurrences and only identifiable Lineals (n = 2,241)

| Rank | Kin relation | Number | Percent |
|------|--------------|--------|---------|
| 1 | father | 351 | 15.7 |
| 2 | mother | 264 | 11.8 |
| 3 | father's father | 204 | 9.1 |
| 4 | father's mother | 184 | 8.2 |
| 5 | son | 127 | 5.7 |
| 6 | elder brother | 105 | 4.7 |
| 7 | daughter | 93 | 4.1 |
| 8 | younger brother | 85 | 3.8 |
| 9 | father's father's father | 79 | 3.5 |
| 10 | younger sister | 76 | 3.4 |
| 11 | father's father's mother | 73 | 3.3 |
| 12 | husband | 47 | 2.1 |
| 13 | elder sister | 46 | 2.1 |
| 14 | wife | 44 | 2.0 |
| 15 | father's father's father's father | 33 | 1.5 |
| 16 | father's father's father's mother | 32 | 1.4 |
| 17 | father's younger brother | 30 | 1.3 |
| 18 | father's younger sister | 24 | 1.1 |
| 19 | father's brother | 23 | 1.0 |
| 20 | father's sister | 23 | 1.0 |
| 21 | child | 22 | 1.0 |
| 22 | father's wife | 21 | 0.9 |
| | Total | 1,986 | 88.6 |

Of a total of ninety-three separate kin relations represented by the tablets, these 22 account for 88.6 percent of all Lineal tablets.
The first four in this list (father, mother, father's father, father's mother) account for 44.8 percent of all Lineal tablets.

There is scarcely a single issue raised in the foregoing pages which does not deserve lengthy elaboration. What I have tried to do is establish the ranges of several phenomena and to show diversity and commonality where they exist. In conclusion, let me emphasize one or two points about the larger issues raised by these findings.

The memorial tablets found in household altars do in part represent individuals who are ancestors in the strictest sense. But as we have seen, fully 25 percent of all the tablets were made for young children, ancestral to no one. Many others — about one-half — are for persons not in the direct line of descent; that is, they are not heads and their wives in each ascending generation. It follows that there is reported a fairly clear distinction among those memorialized in terms of strictness and duration of the special memorial observances of individual death anniversaries, the chief emphasis being on those who have contributed directly to the maintenance of the direct descent line. Nevertheless, all those represented by memorial tablets are the object of the general rites of *bon*, the equinoxes, and New Year's.

It is further apparent that while some of the spirits of the dead — the ancestral spirits — are prayed to for guidance and assistance, others are not so solicited, for they died young, or without issue, or are in the altar only because it was literally the resting place of last resort and they had no place else to go when they died. These people are cared for and comforted, but if they have any role in the ongoing life of the household, it is a generalized tutelary one. For example, a man may well ask his father's spirit for help in a venture, thank him if he succeeds, apologize to him if he fails. He would engage in no such relationship with his father's father's younger brother who died as a child. Quite the contrary, he thinks of himself as caring for the spirits of such unfortunates.

Yet for all this, the memorialized dead are everywhere referred to as *senzo* [ancestors], and all share to varying degrees in the rites before the altar. One of the myriad problems that remain to be investigated is whether, as I think is the case, differential treatment of the spirits of the dead can best be understood in terms of their closeness to the direct descent line AND in terms of the amount of time that has elapsed since their death. The axis of differentiation may well turn out to be *sosen sūhai* [worship of/reverence for ancestors] on the one hand, and *sosen kuyō* [consolation/comforting of the "ancestors"] on the other.

# A Structural Analysis of Japanese
# Ancestral Rites and Beliefs

HERMAN OOMS

Japanese ancestor worship, as Robert J. Smith wrote, has attracted much attention but little research (Smith 1966: 83). At most, the attention it received has been of a general and rather superficial nature in the form of references in general works on Japan to a phenomenon that is supposed to be commonly understood. The research devoted to Japanese ancestor worship in Western languages has been extremely limited, and has concentrated mostly on its sociological underpinnings, especially with regard to the *dōzoku* or extended family (Kitano 1962, Plath 1964).

Japanese folklorists, on the other hand, meticulously recording overt rites and practices, have produced a considerable amount of small case studies of customs related to ancestor worship, especially the *Obon* (also *bon*) festival (*Nihon minzokugaku taikei* 1958 — 1960: III, 277–278). Aside from a few monographs, however — one legal study, one ethnographic work, and one sociological inquiry (Hozumi 1901; Yanagita 1964; Takeda 1957) — the phenomenon of ancestor worship as such has enjoyed little more attention in Japan than it has in the West.

My own assumption in my fieldwork was that an anthropological study of a phenomenon such as ancestor worship, which has a religious dimension, should not be limited to a mere analysis of its social elements or its legal aspects, both of which have lost much if not all of their importance in a modern society like Japan. In my opinion, our understanding of ancestor worship, which, after all, is a form of religion, has to benefit much from a structural analysis of its symbol system, and from a behavioral approach to the examination of its belief component. This will help discard, it is hoped, unwarranted assumptions made in the minds of Western readers about the identity of ancestors, and the nature of worship.

With this in mind, I studied ancestor worship as a religious phenomenon, and I approached the subject in the above way, concentrating on the symbol system, the experience of the worshiper, his motivation and religious consciousness. What follows is a summary of the findings of my fieldwork of 1965–1967, which have already been published elsewhere (Ooms 1967). My interpretations are based on observations, casual conversations, and intensive and repetitive interviews, conducted during twenty-five visits, some of which lasted several days, over a time span of fifteen months.

The community I surveyed did not have the extreme features either of a remote mountain hamlet or of a modern city environment, and is therefore hopefully representative of a large section of the population. It was a rural community of some ninety farming households where tradition was still alive, but it was also a community on the verge of rapid change. The community in question, Nagasawa, is located just outside Tokyo in the eastern, hilly, and rural end of the industrial city of Kawasaki. The outskirts of the hamlet and the ridge of the hills were gradually, and at a quickening pace, being transformed by land developers, while the shallow valley that formed the center of the hamlet remained relatively untouched.

The great majority of the farmers possess plots of land the size of which varies between 1.2 and 3.6 acres, which include paddy fields and dry fields. Each family owns and works its own plot, although there are some remnants of *dōzoku* or extended family consciousness. More than seventy of the eighty-nine farming households have one of only six family names. Many sons of farmers commute to the metropolitan area to find work. Statistics on yearly workdays spent on farmwork give the following picture: twenty-six households put in less than sixty workdays a year, thirty-six households more than 150 days, with the rest in between. In general, the village gives an impression of prosperity and modernity.

The *dōzoku* groups have lost all economic significance. They still have, however, a certain territorial and occupational unity, which is expressed once a year at a festival at each *dōzoku*'s *inari* [fox] shrine. Close members of the extended families, living outside the hamlet, or those living within its boundaries but not involved in farming, are not considered members of the *ikke* (the local name for *dōzoku*). Furthermore one *dōzoku*, or a great part of it, very often dominates one *ku* [neighborhood subdivision of the hamlet]. While the main yearly festival at the village Shintō shrine was discontinued in 1965 due to lack of interest, and while less elaborate yearly celebrations still linger on at reduced intensity, the yearly *dōzoku* gatherings for simple offerings at their *inari* shrines, followed by a merry banquet at the house of each stem family, seem to continue undiminished. There is, however, no ancestor worship at the level of the *dōzoku*. Each household venerates its own ancestors in Japanese customary fashion: through daily offerings at the ancestral shelf in the home, a visit at the family graveyard at the spring and autumn *higan* festival, and above all in midsummer at the *Obon* festival. Ancestor worship is truly the religion of the single household. Through it the dead members of the household are venerated, which, however, involves more than simply the worship of its ancestors.

As other scholars in the past and present, Japanese as well as Westerners, have already pointed out, the subject of worship in the ancestor cult contains several categories: the ancestors proper, the recently departed forebears and relatives, and "outsiders" (Plath 1964; Hirata in Kirby 1910; Yanagita 1964; Ariga 1965).

Although stem-branch family consciousness within the *dōzoku* framework is still very pronounced, the range of worshiped ancestors is narrower than the range of reckoned ancestors. Each household venerates the successive ancestors, male and female, up to the founder of the household but never beyond. In other words, newly established branch families where the founding generation is still alive have no ancestors to pay ritual respect to. Hence the ancestor cult rather than integrating the clan, partitions it in clearly independent cultic units, the various households.

Ideally, a deceased forebear obtains ancestral status after the last memorial service, which customarily takes place at the thirty-third anniversary of the death, although there was no consensus as to the length of this road to ancestorhood. Until they reach that point ancestors are not distinguished from other deceased members of the family or other collateral relatives. Family booklets (*kakochō*) where the deceased are recorded on the particular day of the year that they have to be remembered, were first of all rare, often outdated, and moreover showed often perfectly bilateral lists of deceased (for similar findings see Smith 1966: 89).

The last category, the *muenbotoke* [outsiders or wandering souls], needs special attention. Interpretations as to who belongs to this category varied considerably. Some interviewers ascribed a general maleficent influence to a general category of uncared-for souls. Others specified that deceased children or unmarried members of the household became *muenbotoke*. As a minor but integral, yet less positive, part of the ancestor cult, the *muenbotoke* form a negative image of ancestral souls proper. Although referred to only occasionally in various ethnographic writings (Yanagita 1964: 45, 72; *Seigō Minzoku* 1960) this category of dead souls is thus of great importance for the understanding of the symbol system of ancestor worship.

## THE SYMBOL SYSTEM OF THE ANCESTOR CULT

In treating the symbol system of ancestor worship, a triple division almost naturally imposes itself. There exists a clear distinction between symbols which express the road the soul has to travel in order to reach the state of ancestorhood, those which express the final state, and those which symbolize the situation of the souls who never reach that stage.

These are the three main divisions of the analysis. For each of these three situations of the soul, the framework of analysis consists not only of the SYMBOLS and the ACTION with the symbol but includes considerations about the STATUS of the soul and the ROLES performed both by the souls and by the worshipers.

The souls of dead members of the family are still considered as members of the *ie* [household]. However, each soul does not, in this community of the living and the dead, occupy a specific individual position: the soul of the great-grandfather does not differ in its relation to the household from the soul of the grandmother, for example, or from other souls some ten generations back. Each soul belongs to one of the three main groups of souls, and within each group there is no further differentiation.

Neither is there in the living half of the household a differentiation of attitudes according to the position of each member in the household. The housewife, for instance, is not bound by other rules toward the ancestors as the siblings or the head of the household: as far as ancestor worship is concerned, each family member acts as an equal member of the household. Therefore, in this community of the living and the dead, there are only two actors when the rites are performed: the living as a group, and the dead as a group (ancestors, souls in transition, or *muenbotoke*). Generally the position of an actor is referred to as his status. For the soul, this status will change with the three different situations in which it can find itself, while the status of the living half of the *ie* remains fundamentally the same. Furthermore, the two halves of the *ie* act in a certain prescribed way to each other: certain actions are expected to occur; they are institutionalized. When an actor acts in this status, he is said to be acting out a ROLE. Thus both halves of the *ie* perform some roles toward each other. There flows a crisscross of role expectations and role performances between the two actors. Their crossing point, the place where they meet, is the rites.

Rites performed by the living half are thus representative of the role performance of that half and, at the same time, of the role expectation of the dead half towards them. Conversely, the living who perform the rites do this with a certain state of mind: they have expectations or fears toward the dead souls, which at the same time reflect the role performance of the ancestors toward the living members of the *ie*.

Since, however, role performances and role expectations are vertically complementary to each other, we will limit ourselves, for the sake of clarity, to a discussion of the role performances in both halves of the *ie*.

First we will discuss the symbols that express the process of becoming an ancestor. Life in this world is growth to full adulthood. Life in the other world is growth to full ancestorhood. Any human being who starts this earthly journey receives a new name at his birth. In the same way, every soul who starts the other journey at his death, a new starting point, also receives a new name. He receives his first name (*zokumyō* [common name]) when his body leaves his mother's womb and starts an independent existence: this revelation of a "new power" is consecrated by the new name. He receives his second name (*kaimyō* [posthumous name]) when his soul leaves his body and starts an independent existence (although like the child, he will be still highly dependent for some time upon the care of others). This new revelation of again a "new power" is symbolized by a new name. The soul receives a new name at the moment of death and not when it is supposed to reach ancestorhood, just as a man receives a name at birth and not when he reaches adulthood.

This is because a name signifies, to the point of being identical with it, a self-contained entity: the name is the symbol for the continuity of the person and its constancy in form. Thus the transition of mere soul to ancestor soul does not involve the acquisition of a new identity. On the contrary, it signifies a loss of identity because upon becoming an ancestor, the name marking the individual soul is abandoned and forgotten, and at the same time the soul loses its individuality.

The posthumous name is written on two objects: the *ihai* [tablets] and the *tōba* [memorial slats placed on the grave].

At the funeral two *ihai* are always made: one will finally find its place on the family shelf and the other is brought to the grave at the time of the burial. This latter *ihai* seems to be exposed to the elements on purpose and is left there until it disintegrates, symbolizing in a very concrete way the process which takes place underground. However non-Oriental a clear distinction of body and soul may be, the *ihai* on the grave seems to symbolize the corpse and the one on the family shelf the soul.

The *ihai* which stays in the home is very often placed together with a photograph of the deceased on a low scaffold under the family shelf. On the 49th day, it is raised to the family shelf; from then on it will receive no differential treatment, except on memorial days. At the *tomurai age* [the last memorial service], the *ihai* should ideally be brought to the temple, but this never seems to happen. Ideally the *ie no senzodaidai ihai* [ancestral tablet inscribed with all generations of the ancestors of this house] should replace the individual *ihai* from then on.

According to Yanagita Kunio's theory the individual soul is then taken up into the anonymous world of the ancestors (Yanagita 1964: 95). However, it is customary in some houses to engrave the post-humous name of the deceased on the tombstone precisely at that moment.

The *tōba* manifests in a more precise way than the ancestral tablet the change occurring in the soul. In some areas of Japan, this change is indicated by a steady increase in the size of each new *tōba*, from a *sanjaku tōba* (0.90 meters) to a *kyūshakutōba* (2.70 meters), placed on the grave on the occasion of each commemorative anniversary. In Nagasawa all *tōbas* are of the same size (only a price difference results in big or small *tōbas*), but with each commemorative anniversary the inscription on it changes. On the last memorial service (normally the 33rd year), however, some families purchase a square *tōba* which is more resistant to rain and wind and seems to symbolize that the dead soul after a period of time, corresponding in this world to the time needed to reach full adulthood, is no longer subject to change.

Let us now turn to an examination of the status of the souls. From the customs surrounding the burial, it seems that the dead are treated with caution. It is hard to determine whether it is the corpse or the wandering soul which is the object of the precautionary measures; answers from the informants about this matter are uncertain and ambiguous. If we rely only on the observation of the customs, we must conclude that most of the practices are rather inspired by a fear of material pollution resulting from contact with the corpse (the custom of putting in the coffin those small objects which were most dear to the deceased — they may be a kindness to the deceased but also a way of disposing of objects which he had often touched, thereby obviating the danger of pollution; also the customs of closing the coffin with stones, the straw sandals, the fire at the grave, and the sprinkling of the clothes of the deceased with water). But some seem more connected with the soul of the deceased: the throwing of the salt, the turning of the coffin, the continuous burning of incense, and the daily offering of water during the first 49 days after the burial. These customs, although concerned with the same soul, may lack logical consistency: the former two seem to be motivated by a fear that the dead spirit may return, whereas the latter two suppose the spirit to be at home, where he must undergo some kind of purification and be placated. At any rate the first stage of purification seems to be reached on the first seventh day when the second *tōba* is provided and the purification of the clothes comes to a close. However, during the first 49 days, the status of the soul seems to be one of uncertainty: it wanders around the house or resides on the rooftop; distant relatives are in mourning until the soul settles down in the grave (close relatives who strictly follow the rules will observe mourning until the 100th day).

We can consider the funeral as the *rite de passage* which frees the soul from the body, and the ensuing period as one of uncertainty following the release of "power;" then we can recognize the service on the 49th day as bringing under control the new power: the soul leaves for the grave. The atmosphere of uncertainty disappears. If everything is done as prescribed, nothing will go wrong from now on. The soul will still be the individual object of all memorial services; it will keep its individuality but it will be subject to change in the course of time.

The mental process evolving from the memorial services contains something more than merely keeping the memory of the deceased alive. It is as much one of remembering as of forgetting. Forgetting, as Hertz remarks, is not a simple and purely negative process: it entails a whole reconstruction (1960: 150). While the personal ties (*en*) with the living members of the *ie* are weakening, the impersonal ties with the dead members, the ancestors of the *ie*, grow stronger.

Once the memory of the deceased is abolished, his individuality will have disappeared, but he will be a full member of the ancestor half of the *ie* and no more subject to change. This transition, however, moves smoothly and does not involve such an abrupt change as the one which occurs at the funeral or on the 49th day. That there is a marked difference between the status of the soul before and after the 49th day is clear from the following. Although the soul in a certain sense is believed to be in the house all the time (on the family shelf), the household members experience two periods of intense presence: the time until the 49th day and during *Obon*. But the former is marked by a state of uncertainty and uneasiness while the latter is definitely one of joy, and a cautious attitude is completely missing — notice that the 49th day and the first *Obon* may follow each other closely. Both relate to the same soul but at a different time and at a different stage of development.

With the gradual change in the soul goes a shift in the attitude of the living members of the house. The rites until the 49th day seem concerned with readjusting the household to the new situation created by the "birth" of a new soul. The vague assumption seems to be that this soul, if not made the object of frequent rites from the beginning, might be potentially malicious, which might cause harm to the family and to the soul itself. The role of the soul seems thus to be, in extreme cases, one of threatening the house and in lesser ones, one of wandering. The members of the house have to counter this threat by purification ceremonies which will result in the final separation ceremony when the soul sets out for its new abode.

Once this is done, the living have the responsibility, which they cannot delegate to anybody else, of making the soul rest in peace (*ukabareru* [to float]) through memorial services and visits to the grave. This common expression like the *en* of *muenbotoke* uses a spatial symbol: the soul has to be set afloat from its former ties. *Muenbotoke* are also souls who have severed their ties with the *ie*, but they have done so in the wrong way: the negative side of the severing of the ties does not have its positive counterpart of *jōbutsu* [becoming a Buddha], establishing the *en* with the *ie* on a higher level, namely as ancestors. It is hard to define the role played at this stage by the soul. It might be a mixture of anticipated protection, a role eminently played by the ancestors, and of a lingering threat of *tataru* [sending a curse], as was the soul's dominant characteristic before the 49th day when there was no connotation whatsoever of a protective role.

The influence of the ritual behavior of the household members upon the soul of the deceased virtually ceases once the soul reaches ancestor-hood. However, the ancestors on their part now seem to increase their beneficent activity towards the *ie*, while the rites now take on more the character of gratefulness, generally aiming to keep in contact with the ancestors lest they lapse into *muenbotoke*.

The symbols, status and roles of the *muenbotoke* contrast sharply with those of the ancestors. When individual souls are considered to be *muenbotoke*, as is the case with deceased children, they may have their posthumous name written on a full-fledged wooden *ihai*. The posthumous name may also be recorded on a paper *ihai*. At the graveyard one sometimes finds a common stone *tōba* for the anonymous *muenbotoke*, or the names of the children may be recorded on a separate marble plate. Generally speaking, children are not as frequently honored with memorial services as other souls are.

It is hard to say what exactly the effect of the services or offerings for the *muenbotoke* is. Do they have the power of changing this unhappy state of the *muenbotoke* and turning them into *uenbotoke* ("*hotoke* with *en*," namely, regular ancestors)? The general impression is that they do not. It seems that the status of the *muenbotoke* is unchangeable and intrinsically linked with the position they had, while still alive, in the *ie:* they are the souls of those members who were unable to join some line of ancestors or to start their own. From the moment of their death, these souls cannot change their position within the *ie*. If at this time they were still members of their family of orientation and had never established their family of procreation, they are condemned to become *muenbotoke*.

Because rites seem to be unable to change the state of nonfulfillment (*ukabarenai* [not floating]) of the *muenbotoke*, their meaning must be found somewhere else. They are performed in a spirit of compassion or fear, and aim thus at bringing consolation to these souls in their miserable state; in the first case no activity seems to be assumed, no role seems to be ascribed to them. When fear is the prevailing feeling, the *muenbotoke* are thought of as active; this activity is always a negative one, contrary to the one exercised by the ancestors. In this aspect they do not seem to differ much from the souls in the first stage before the 49th day on their way to ancestorhood.

## THE WORLD VIEW OF ANCESTOR WORSHIP

Ancestor worship, like any particular religion, affirms something about life in general. It carries with it a *Weltanschauung* (the cognitive aspect of the values inherent in ancestor worship). To use Geertz's expression, it is a system of symbols, which formulates conceptions of a general order of existence (1965: 209).

According to Geertz, there are three issues which religions, however "primitive," must cope with: ignorance in the face of anomalous events (death, volcanic eruptions, etc.), pain or suffering, and the problem of evil. Within this triple domain the following findings were made. From the range of anomalous events, natural calamities are not ascribed to the ancestors nor to the *muenbotoke* as punishment from a wrathful god. For this reason the villagers will not address themselves to their ancestors for protection against drought, or flood, or earthquakes.

Death is dealt with in the framework of ancestor worship, but only at its fringes. Ancestor worship in the strict sense starts only when the situation of emotional stress, resulting from death, has been overcome. Veneration of an ancestor who died three generations ago cannot be motivated by the upheaval his death caused in the house and by the ensuing readjustment process. However, the living might be comforted to know they will some day become ancestors and they will live on in the rites throughout the ensuing generation. Indeed the oldest informant said: "I also hope to leave this house, having received such a tablet, but one with golden letters, not just a plain wooden one."

The problem of suffering is dealt with only occasionally, but when suffering becomes severe, it is dealt with almost always in the framework of ancestor worship. Conversions to a new religion are mostly motivated because these new religions claim to have a deeper insight in the causal relationship which links the ancestors with the occurring evil.

As can readily be seen, ancestor worship is rather faulty in its formulation of a "general order of existence," and it might be somehow misleading to use such a cosmic terminology for a religious phenomenon which has more modest ambitions. Because what is characteristic of ancestor worship is that its first and last preoccupation is the *ie*. It is only within the confines of the existence of the *ie* that it touches upon the problem of death.

From the analysis of the symbol system, it is clear that the main concern of ancestor worship is the *ie* and afterlife. Through ancestor worship the membership of the *ie* is enhanced to such an extent that true membership is never lost: it transcends death and lasts forever. The importance of the *ie* is even such that it is one's position in it that determines one's fate after death: it is one's position in relation to one's future line of descendants (thus to one's family of procreation) that decides if the individual joins the *uenbotoke* and later the ancestors, or the *muenbotoke*. It is therefore possible that the belief in an afterlife — which Occidentals so naturally consider a necessary condition for ancestor worship — is only secondary to and highly dependent upon this consciousness of *ie* membership.

The tripartite division of the other world in Japanese ancestor worship seems to correspond rather closely to a tripartite composition of the family of this world. The position enjoying the highest esteem and incurring the greatest responsibility in the management of the house is the office of the household head and his wife. The highest position in the other world is no doubt held by the ancestors and it is their role to protect the household. Second in importance is the successor: the one who is on his way to becoming head of the household. In the ranking of the souls, it is also the *uenbotoke* in the process of becoming ancestors who occupy the second position. Both these important roles in the household, together with the retired older generation, form the direct line of succession. The siblings, except the successor, belong to the sideline and form a third category. All are ideally destined to leave the house and start their own way to ancestorhood through marriage. If they fail to do so, they might be, as they were in earlier days, a real burden because the property of the house may not be large enough to utilize and sustain such a labor force. At any rate, it is clear that such members of the family do not have a proper structural place in the household and are relegated to the lowest position in the household. In death these members join the *muenbotoke*, which is indeed the least enjoyable state in the world beyond.

Thus the *ie* is a spiritual community, and ancestor worship is its religion. This, however, requires one more qualification. After all, the death of a household member produces a real break in his family relations, and the household must find a way to restore and rebuild the contact with its lost member. In this sense the process of becoming an ancestor can be looked upon as a ritual socialization process of the soul. This socialization process is indeed not without its parallels to the socialization process — at least on the level of ritual action — of the child and youth.

We have already drawn attention to the parallel name giving ceremony and need not return to it. A further detail in connection with the name is that the posthumous name finds, after fourteen days, its place on the family shelf (*butsudan*), while the birth name is put on the Shintō shelf (*kamidana*). A second point is that both ritual periods (socialization process of the young family member and the process of becoming an ancestor) are by and large of the same length: 23 or 33 years.

Thirdly, the two cycles start with an intensive short time span of almost one month with roughly the same characteristics. The keynote of this period is pollution, resulting from the newly released and unsettled "force." This new presence seems somehow to escape the control of man: the baby's first month of existence is probably the most perilous of his life, and man can really do little about it. The birth caused pollution to the child and to the mother. The soul's first 49 days of existence are certainly very precarious; the soul as well as the "womb" from which it freed itself — the *ie* — are negatively affected by them. At the end of this period, both new beings (the newborn child and the soul of the deceased) are purified, but not those who gave birth to them, the mother and the bereaved family. For the newborn, there follows the first visit to the village shrine (*shomiyamairi*), which is probably more significant religiously than subsequent visits such as *shichigosan* [an annual festival in November that beseeches the gods to bless children at the age of three, five and seven years]. Smilarly, the 49th day for the soul of the deceased commemorates a more significant change than subsequent memorial days.

Fourthly, within this period of one month, the seventh day seems an intermediary step of purification for the soul (the purification of the clothes ceases). Continuing the comparison, the mother on the seventh day after having given birth is permitted to approach the fire again; on the eleventh day she can ladle water. Fifthly, both the mother and the bereaved family are freed from pollution on the 100th day. Subsequent memorial days show only weak parallels to other *rites de passage* in the life of the child (*shichigosan*), but if we trace the parallel further, then the *tomurai age* [last memorial service] would somehow find its equivalent in marriage. Both ceremonies lack the purification motive and, in the latter case, are aimed at establishing the transition of the individual into its new community or *ie*, while the former one means the entrance of a new soul into the world of ancestors.

Thus a man's existence seems to consist of two cycles, by and large parallel to each other. Moreover, if the first cycle is brought successfully to its end, namely through marriage, this *ipso facto* opens the door to a successful completion of the second cycle because unmarried persons never join the ancestors. The intermediary period between marriage and death will be unable to change this pattern as long as marriage itself is not in danger (if, for instance, divorce occurs, and the wife goes back to her native home and does not remarry, then she will die as a *muenbotoke* in her native home). If the doctrine of rebirth were extant, the end of the second cycle (becoming an ancestor) would mean again the starting point of the first. However, the pattern is not perfect in this regard, and it is also difficult to see how an ancestor, once reincarnated, could still keep his character of ancestor. The two cycles can be represented graphically as shown in Figure 1.

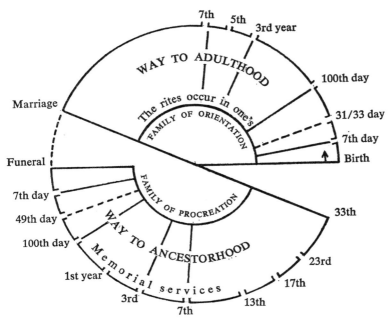

Figure 1.  The double domestic life cycle

We should notice that the center around which the two life cycles spin is the *ie*. The first cycle, meant to ritualize the growth of a human being into full manhood, occurs for him in his family of orientation. The second cycle revolves around his family of procreation: as a dead member of the family, he is subject to the *rites de passage* which make him become an ancestor.

## THE RELIGIOUS EXPERIENCE OF THE WORSHIPER

The analysis of the symbol system thus far has disclosed to us the world view of ancestor worship. It has shown us how life within the perspective of the worshiper is imagined. However, symbols have besides a conceptual aspect a dispositional one; they induce action. In other words, the values enhanced by the symbols have a so-called "emotional charge" which makes them promote and guide conduct (Firth 1964: 221): they give shape to the ethos of people.

One of the main channels through which the values inherent in the religious symbol system are interiorized is religious experience. Religious experience, however, may cover an exceedingly disparate array of events: "from the vaguest glimmerings of something sacred to rapturous mystical unions with the divine" (Stark 1965). In this context religious experience does not mean an exceptional psychological state, the privilege of some religious "virtuosi;" it points to religious experience as an institutionalized, widespread and commonly accepted phenomenon.

Thus we have first of all to specify the quality of the most common religious experience of the community if we want to understand which dispositions are induced in the worshiper and how these dispositions affect his activity.

Furthermore, the religious experience is always accompanied by some conviction or belief, with varying degrees of intensity. We will, therefore, have to determine the place that belief occupies in the overall religious life of the worshiper, if we want to understand the nature and strength of the influence that religious practices may have upon behavior.

Finally then, after having assessed the religious experience and after having situated the seriousness of the attention paid to it, we will be able to evaluate what Charles Y. Glock calls "the consequential dimension of religion." By this we mean the bearing ancestor worship has upon the profane world outside of ritual.

In analyzing the ritual symbol system of ancestor worship, the two-actor scheme proved to be a useful device. The validity of such a scheme is founded upon the fact that the ancestors, or more generally the dead souls, are *de facto* considered as members of the *ie*, and still active in their own way. Thus religious experience will take the form of an encounter with them. It seems therefore appropriate and not too farfetched to describe this experience in terms of human encounter.[1]

The axis along which social encounter can be diversified is the axis of the degree of intimacy. For our purpose we can distinguish three levels of encounter along the line of an increase in intimacy. The first one is the one brought about by official contact. The contact established between two partners by the performance of some role is of a very official nature. The focus of such an encounter is less upon the partner; the meeting is much more conditioned by the nature of the relationship set by the role definition than by the person at the end of the relationship. No real meeting takes place. The experience is one of official contact. With regard to ancestor worship, the experience of the worshiper is limited to a feeling of fulfillment of duty.[2]

---

[1]   The framework for analysis of religious experience is inspired by Stark's taxonomy (1965).

[2]   Firth (1964) urges differentiations between levels of religious contact and levels

A second level of encounter is the experience of the awareness of the partner's presence. Here, in contrast with the former case, the partner is the focus of the encounter; in the case of the ancestors, they are concretely experienced as "here" or "there." Third, the encounter may be one of mutual awareness of each other's presence; one experiences the partner noticing one's presence. The worshiper here is both aware or conscious of the existence of the ancestors and at the same time conscious that they notice and care about him. This experience may be of a general or of a particular nature and have positive or negative value. If the experience is a particular one, it might be the experience either of what the other does or of what the other says: an experience of some action or of a message. Schematically, we can represent these different possibilities as follows:

1.  A RELATIONSHIP OF DUTY TOWARD THE ANCESTORS: the relationship itself is more important than its object, the ancestors.
2.  EXPERIENCE OF THE ANCESTOR'S PRESENCE: a sense of the presence of the ancestors.
3.  EXPERIENCE OF THE ANCESTOR'S ATTENTIVE PRESENCE:
a.  General   beneficent: general feeling of protection
             maleficent: general feeling of threat
b.  Specific  beneficent: through interventions
             maleficent: through messages

These three types of possible encounter with the ancestors are not completely and adequately distinguished from each other. The latter stages include the former ones but add some elements to them; all of the stages therefore maintain a continuity. For instance, it is impossible to experience the ancestors as a responding, reacting "other" without being aware of the contact that links one with them. Thus we speak only of a first and second category insofar as they lack elements present respectively in states two and three. The material we categorize thus consists of the testimonies of the informants.

Different authors have already drawn attention to the importance of the *giri-ninjō* for a proper understanding of the relations between the Japanese and their gods or ancestors. Although this *giri-ninjō* may be present in all the relations with the divine, we reserve it here for the attitudes in which a *giri* relation seems prevalent without a concomitant awareness of the presence of the ancestors. In other words, one feels in debt towards one's ancestors without experiencing them particularly as "here" or "there."

---

of religious experience: "In using a symbol carrier, people do not necessarily use the symbol."

A woman, who was thirty-three years old, when asked if she would continue the daily offerings once the mother-in-law died, answered: "It is a bother and does not have any special meaning, but I probably will make the offerings. Doesn't one do these things naturally?" She admitted also that neither good nor bad effects result from the performance or negligence of the memorial services. A seventy-year-old woman described her experience with the words, "My mind is not at peace when I do not make the offerings." When asked about the eventual unfortunate results if the rites are neglected, she said that there is no real obligation to make the offerings and that curses (*tatari*) don't exist. A man of forty-five expressed the same feeling by saying that it was merely a question of custom: "We are deeply bound by custom; the meaning escapes us and neither good nor bad results follow from the veneration or neglect of the ancestors."

The practice of the ancestor cult is justified by the long-term link which binds the people with their ancestors or by a feeling of *giri* [indebtedness] for received *on* [obligation]. "We do this out of a feeling of gratitude because the ancestors have worked and cared for us," a fifty-six-year-old woman said. Two other informants, after a lengthy deliberation, came to the conclusion that their attitude towards the ancestors was the same as the one towards their parents and brothers. "It is close to *on*; one could say that it is thanks to the ancestors that we are able to make a living today," a sixty-nine-year-old woman and a fifty-four-year-old man agreed. Thus the thankfulness that is expressed here is not because of supernatural blessings and protection from the ancestors but because of their past endeavors and contributions to the family property when they were alive.

What is remarkable in these answers are the following two points. First, a clear set of principles or system of belief which would give a precise meaning to the practice of the ancestor cult is lacking. There is, however, a feeling (not exactly a conviction) that it is only natural that one's gratitude extends back to several generations of ancestors. Secondly, some of the informants give the impression that, after all, it does not matter that much if one worships or not. This seems in contradiction with the rather severe way some people are regarded because they are thought to be neglecting the ancestors, for example, if they profess some nontraditional belief. Clear reasons for venerating the ancestors apparently are absent, but generally nobody seems to reject worship out of some principle, and the few who are thought to do so are stigmatized by the rest of the community.

Thus in the above testimonies, an experience of the ancestors in whatever form it might be, is absent. The received benefits for which gratitude is expressed are solely accomplishments of the ancestors during their lifetime.

The Japanese usually experience the presence of the ancestors through a strong consciousness that they are here.

We asked the question if the ancestors somehow, under one form or another, still lived on somewhere. The sixty-seven-year-old head of a first-rank stem family, told us that he lived constantly in their presence.

The feeling of togetherness with the ancestors is generally preserved for the *Obon*. For some people, the performance of memorial services offers the occasion for a similar experience. A woman of sixty-three, asked if the dead soul was coming back on such a day, gave the rather blunt but clear answer, "They might come or not come, but in any case I feel as if they were here." To the question if there were also days that she did not offer rice and tea, the prompt answer of the same informant was, "People need food every day, don't they? So I offer every day and ring the little bell to notify the ancestors that everything is ready."

As soon as the feeling of their presence transcends the mere feeling of "they are there," we confront a new kind of experience: the ancestors are felt to take specific notice of the individual's existence and are thus one step closer to him. In general the experience is one of protection or of threat.

An old man of seventy-six expressed this idea of general protection clearly in his own words. Asked if he made any requests to them in times of trouble, he said, "I do not ask them to do this or to do that, but still my attitude is one of supplication." Some respondents rejected the idea completely, "All this talk about the ancestors protecting us are but nice lies." A straight rejection of the idea of protection is rare, but its wholehearted acceptance seems equally rare. The idea that the ancestors are merely interested in what is going on in the household (without extending protection) is not the object of strong belief either. A young mother who had given birth to her first son some five months ago said that she had been told by her mother before her marriage to report the birth of the first son to the ancestors of her husband's family. She had, however, neglected to do so.

Two older informants recalled that during their youth they were told: "The *hotoke* are watching over you, don't be mischievous!" Today, however, the ancestors seem no more to play the general role of moral arbiters in the educational process of the children.

A general negative feeling towards the ancestors as distinguished from the *muenbotoke* was expressed only once. A woman reported that as a child she was afraid of the *hotoke* on the family shelf and that her own daughter of six years showed the same feelings.

Specific awareness of the activity of the ancestors (be it a beneficent or a maleficent one) can take the form of special interventions or special revelations. Never did we meet with the latter, although one adherent of the Nichiren-shū and his daughter (in separate interviews) admitted the possibility of communication with the spirits of the ancestors. However, they did not speak about their own experiences, but about those of some people they knew. A very specific intervention was ascribed to the ancestors by a seventy-nine-year-old woman when she held them responsible for the safe return of her four sons from the Second World War.

A rather sophisticated view of received benefits was expressed by the reflection of a middle-aged woman who commented on the offerings of food: "The ancestors don't really eat food, but when one offers something, it is as if one were receiving." She considered the fact of giving as a kind of favor, so that she, while offering and feeling enriched by it, was really the beneficiary of the offerings.

Another astonishing benefit was reported in several places. The normal purpose of memorial services or visits to the grave is to acquire *kudoku* [merits] for the sake of the ancestors or, even better, for the dead souls. But the common view is that the recipients of the *kudoku* are the performers of the rite, not the souls. This view contrasted strongly with the conviction of the followers of Nichiren-shōshū that the recitation of their sutra is all-powerful for making the deceased rest in peace. Specific maleficent experiences with the ancestors were never reported. Several rejected the idea of a curse (*tatari*) or punishment from the ancestors or *muenbotoke* as a superstitious belief.

From the above testimonies, we can come to some conclusions as to which values are fostered and enforced by the practice of ancestor worship.

In general we can say that the people we met really did not expect either blessings or punishments from their ancestors. The main *leitmotiv* in their attitude was thankfulness and a feeling of obligation. This feeling extends as far as their consciousness of dependence upon the ancestors, mainly until the first generation of the house. In Japan the borderline of a man's dependencies extends beyond the living members of the family to include the dead ancestors, and it is only there that one's independence starts.

Those we depend upon are those who bestow *on* upon us; it is thus very important to be conscious of the web of vital *giri* relations; one has to try to pay them back. But the *on* towards the ancestors cannot really be paid back. This might explain the impression the observer receives that the ancestors really do not need these offerings, but that nevertheless it is the right thing to make them, and that it does not matter too much what the immediate meaning or effect of the actions is because the main thing is the act itself. This act shows namely that the actor is not forgetful of the ties that bind him with his ancestors, and that he is conscious of his indebtedness to them and attentive to and appreciative of what they have done for him. This disposition is also instilled in the child, even before he knows what he is in debt for to the ancestors when he is persuaded by his mother to share his gifts with them. The instilled disposition is such that the actor finds himself always in a low position at the lower end of the vertical relationship which links him with "the others." Although one can easily argue that people MUST not depend upon ancestors who died four, five, or more generations ago — especially ancestors who maladministered the property as was the case in a stem family some 120 years ago — yet the value which is selectively acted out and stressed in the rites is not the independence from them, the reliance upon oneself, but the dependence upon the ancestors. The disposition thus instilled is really a mood: it permeates and colors the whole character of the person.

## ANCESTOR BELIEF

In the testimonies of the interviewees we noticed several times apparent contradictions between their experience and meanings that seem to an observer to be necessarily inherent in the rites. Indeed the deceased do not seem to be in need of the merits of the religious services, the ancestors do not seem to be conceived of as the protectors of the *ie*, and their existence does not seem to be taken too seriously. What does this encounter with the ancestors then finally mean? Do people believe in them or not? What does belief mean in the context of ancestor worship?

Only on three occasions did we really feel some positive belief reflected in the answers. One person so keenly aware of them at the time of the rites and even in everyday life, told us, "You cannot see them with your eyes, but they do exist." The other two cases where we met with a real conviction and not a mere feeling were the testimonies of the members of the Nichiren-shū and Nichiren-shōshū. In all the other cases the author met with a polite smile or a hesitant answer at the suggestion of the eventual survival of the soul in some way after death. After a thoughtful pause they usually replied, "Well, they might be alive, but. . . ." If asked, for instance, about the soul leaving the house on the 49th day, very often the villagers responded, "Well, yes, that is the reason why we hold a service on that day, but we don't really know what happens."

Do we have then to conclude with Malinowski's words that "belief is ignored, though apparently expressed in an institution" (1955: 11)? As a broad generalization this might well characterize the situation, but it does not lead very far to its real understanding. Two important corrections should be made, it seems to me, in order to bring this statement into its proper perspective.

First of all, it might be that religious belief in the midst of ritual and religious belief as the remembered reflection of that experience in the midst of everyday life are quite different realities (Geertz 1965: 214). Geertz argues that the two worlds of ritual and everyday life are not continuous, and that a real gap separates the two outlooks on life, that is the religious one and the common-sense one. Still there is only one way to obtain a glance at belief in the midst of ritual: asking people about it afterwards. The general attitude toward belief in everyday life is one of skepticism: the content of ritual action is not taken seriously. This leads us to presume that belief during the rites is very low.

But the rites must be performed with some conviction. That is the second correction we want to make. This conviction does not bear upon the content or objective effect of the rites, but upon the necessity or the property of the performance of the rites. The conviction exists that they must be performed but not in order to prevent eventual bad consequences for the deceased. The bad consequences are connected with the worshiper and are very this-worldly. Namely, he would by completely neglecting the cult stand out in the community as a reproachable person. Therefore, the meaning of the rites is a highly subjective one: it is a question of *kimochi* [feeling]. This word came up very often in conversation: "It really comes to feeling; on days that we don't make the offerings, the mind is not at peace." A similar comment was given by two middle-aged women about rebirth, interpreting it as a mere desire: "I can understand that someone who dies in the midst of misery desires to be reborn under better conditions." The author had the impression that the whole village knew about Malinowski's emotional adjustment theory of a ritual. (Dore reports a similar reflection after considering the statements of one informant [1965: 308]).

Then, what happens in the rites, given the meaning designated by the people, if these people give another interpretation to the rites than the one which seems the most obvious to an observer? Isn't the performer of the cult taking an "as-if" attitude, isn't he only pretending to accept the values embodied in the cult? Are the rites, then, to a great extent not a kind of play?

That ritual is but a higher form of play has been demonstrated brilliantly by Johan Huizinga (1964). Structurally they bear the same formal characteristics. They show for instance the same mixture of pretense and seriousness: "Every child knows perfectly well that it is 'only pretending' but it proceeds with the utmost seriousness" (1964: 8). And: "the unity and indivisibility of belief and unbelief, the indissoluble connection between sacred earnest and 'make-believe' . . . are best understood in the concept of play itself . . . in play as we conceive it, the distinction between belief and 'make-believe' breaks down; archaic ritual is sacred play. . . . This precarious balance between seriousness and pretense is an unmistakable and integral part of culture as such, and the play-factor lies at the heart of all ritual and religion" (1964: 25, 191; see also Caillois 1950: 213).

Yet, play cannot be the last word on ritual. Because this would not recognize the difference between simple play and sacred play, Jensen and Caillois criticize and complete Huizinga's insights in this respect. Jensen says that two points distinguish the sacred play from other forms of play:

1. In sacred play, an EXPERIENCE and a COGNITION of a deeper and more fundamental relationship to reality occur; quoting Karl Kerenyi, Jensen says, "From something present, something still more present has arisen, from a reality, an even higher reality" (Jensen 1963: 52–53). Caillois also stresses the point that, although sacred play and simple play are both opposed to life, they are in a different way: sacred play is more serious than life, and life more serious than play (1950: 217, 221).

2. Sacred play or cult is an expression, the reenactment of the above-mentioned deeper cognition: the cult reenacts the true order, the order under which man lives and which shapes his image of reality; and as long as that world view retains its validity, later repetitions will reverberate with a residuum of the original creativity; it is this residuum which marks the sacred play, which distinguishes it from "mere play" (Jensen 1963: 53, 58).

Now we will take up the different theoretical points made by the above three scholars and see how they help us in the further understanding of our subject. The insight of Huizinga about the correspondence of play and ritual in their formal characteristics has become common place. A memorial service or *Obon* marks a standstill in ordinary life. As we have seen people do not exactly expect material profit from their ancestors, and services and *Obon* proceed within their own proper boundaries of time and space. Huizinga's remarks about that particular combination of seriousness and make-believe are more pertinent. During the performance of the ritual, indeed, everything happens as if it were all very true, as if the ancestors were still existing. But then, in the interviews, very few informants seem really to take the belief part of the ritual seriously. According to Huizinga we really do not have to choose either one: "We must always fall back on this lasting ambiguity" (1964: 191).

Jensen's first correction is a corroboration of what we called different levels of intensified presence. If the rites are accompanied by any experience, this is always the experience: "From something present, something more present has arisen." During the daily offering, the ancestors, although present on the shelf, become more present for the worshiper. The same holds true for the services and still more for *Obon*. This might be one of the meanings of the ambiguous *kimochi*, which we met so often in the interviews. The ancestors are felt as if they were present but they are rationally known as not existing. In everyday life this intense feeling is absent; thus in an interview we might be left with only the rational part of the ritual. We will examine Jensen's second correction later since our analysis now confronts a new problem.

By presenting an indicator to distinguish between secular play and sacred play (when does secular play become sacred play?), Jensen and Caillois have opened a path for interpreting the phenomenon of secularization (when and how does sacred ritual become mere play?).

In Huizinga's theory, the mere presence of an element of disbelief in the religious system is not *ipso facto* an indication of secularization, since disbelief is to a certain extent a built-in factor in ritual behavior. However, secularization may be a matter of proportion of belief and disbelief. If disbelief is the prevalent attitude, then folk belief has become folklore. We might come to some clarity on this subject by proceeding from the two poles existing almost in their pure state: complete belief and utter disbelief accompanying the performance of the ancestor cult. This sketch will serve, then, as a scale for measuring religious belief in Nagasawa. The scale we will establish is not foreign to the culture under investigation but taken from Japan's religious tradition itself. We will take as representative of the first pole Hirata Atsutane; the second pole will be represented by the Confucianist stream of thought, which Hirata violently attacked.

Hirata Atsutane (1776–1843) professed in unambiguous language his belief in the real existence of the ancestors.

The soul of mankind . . . is never ending through all of the ages of eternity. . . . As there are boundaries between the seen and unseen, we cannot see their [the souls'] forms — though we cannot usually see them, they have not become extinct. After death a person becomes a soul . . . there is not any doubt that souls exist. And as they are without any doubt in the shrine shelves of every house, it is best to treat them carefully and not carelessly (Kirby 1910: 236, 252–253).

He attacks the wavering attitude of Confucianists in this matter:

Confucianists and such like say there is no such thing as the soul and that after death everything is dispersed and lost like wind and fire, and cannot be known. Such sayings are spread and people's minds become steeped in such false sayings. As they are not sure whether the soul exists or not though they make offerings before the souls, it is done in a careless way (Kirby 1910: 251).

According to Hirata Atsutane, the Confucianists' misconception stems from a wrong interpretation of the attitude of Confucius, who really believed.

In his Analects it is written how he worshipped as if his ancestors were actually present. "In worshipping gods, he worshipped as if the gods were present." This shows that Confucius, whether he worshipped the gods of heaven and earth, or worshipped the souls of his ancestors, behaved just as if the bodily presence of these gods was visible, showing thus that in the wise heart of Confucius there was sure knowledge that the gods existed, and he acted accordingly. With regard to this matter, some Confucians misunderstand Confucius and say that his doctrine was "worship as if the gods are present," since he said "In worshopping the gods, act as if they are present." But this is not so (he acted as if the gods were really present) (Kirby 1910: 239–240).

We set aside the question of the validity of Hirata's interpretation of Confucius' attitude. However, it is interesting to note that Hirata's interpretation and the Confucianists' interpretation of symbolic behavior coincide respectively with what Tillich calls the positive and negative interpretation of symbols (1961: 78–81).

If a shift occurs within the first position — one theological explanation taking the place of another within the realm of positive interpretations — this is a phenomenon of religious change. Converts to Nichiren-shū, Nichiren-shōshū and the Risshōkōseikai are examples. For all of them, the reality of the ancestors has become loaded with more precise meanings. The Nichiren-shōshū followers, for instance, strongly believe that the ancestors cannot rest in peace as long as they suffer the evil influences of the "evil" religions to which they adhered during their lifetimes.

However, when the change takes place from the positive to the negative position, when belief is followed by disbelief, the religious change takes the form of secularization. To locate this phenomenon and, still more, to measure it are difficult because religious change is usually a latent process, carried on beneath symbols of nonchange.[3]

Theoretically, the conditions of the process can be spelled out even in the case of folk religion. Let us return for that to Caillois' triple division of life: sacred/profane/play.

The sacred and the play dimension both are outside the realm of daily life.... Play, however, is free activity in its purest form, it does not have a content and does not have effects on another plane besides its own. In relation to life, play is pleasure and entertainment. But life, on the contrary, in its relation to the sacred is itself but vanity and diversion.... Play must avoid real life: categories of real life brought into the realm of play destroy life on first impact. Life, on the contrary, is depending upon, suspended at the sacred (1950: 221).

Graphically this may be expressed as in Figure 2.

Figure 2.   Spheres of human activity

The relation of irreconcilability between the play sphere and real life is clear. But related to ancestor worship, what is meant by stating that the sacred is such a necessity and so indispensable for normal life? Jensen gives the answer in his first point, where he speaks about experience and cognition. We will simply apply it to our case. Ancestor worship in its cognitive aspect is an answer to a fundamental human problem: death. It gives a meaning to mortality which in itself is merely disruptive and meaningless. Therefore profane life depends upon the

---

[3]   Yinger (1963: 70). Whitehead (1961: 233, 235) notes: "symbolic elements in life have a tendency to run wild, like the vegetation in a tropical forest.... It seems probable that in any ceremonial which has lasted through many epochs, the symbolic interpretation, so far as we can obtain it, varies much more rapidly than does the actual ceremonial. Also in its flux, a symbol will have different meanings for different people."

sacred for a meaningful answer to this problem. By this a deeper and more fundamental relationship to the reality of death is established. Thus ancestor worship in its religious aspect provides man with a frame through which he is able to face a mortal existence. This insight (that is the myth) then finds a more or less exhaustive representation in rite or ceremony (Jensen 1963: 37). With its repetition the rite becomes custom, and thus can this insight be communicated and transmitted: through participation in the rites, everyone is able to partake and make the myth his own. But "like all other cultural phenomena, customs relentlessly move from the 'expressive' stage into that of an 'application.' According to an inescapable law, anything that culture has created must grow more distant from the content of the creative idea; finally it will be only a pale reflection of this original 'expression' " (Jensen 1963: 193). This process is a process of semantic depletion — namely, of the waning of the original meaning, a kind of spiritual entropy.

When the meaning of the insight expressed in the myth has thus passed away, the myth loses its relevance, its importance for daily life. The rite also loses its relevance: "Without the myth, the rite becomes a mere ineffective action, empty gestures, a powerless reproduction of the ceremony, a mere play. And myth without rite becomes a mere play of words, without content or import, just empty words" (Caillois 1950: 221–222). We can represent this graphically as shown in Figure 3.

What has happened is that the play element, the nonserious element

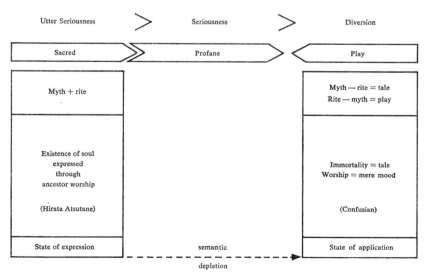

Figure 3. Myths, rites and their depleted meaning

and the formal element, present from the beginning in the rite (since the rite is only an INADEQUATE acting out of the original insight), has taken the upper hand at the expense of the serious, the belief element, the original insight, the experience.

Once arrived at its final stage of semantic depletion, the cultural phenomenon might not fit very well any more in the overall cultural system. Then the cultural phenomenon has become a survival. "Survivals," says Jensen, "having their origin in earlier culture strata, make statements about reality which are no longer experienced as true. Even where they are still comprehensible, they often contradict the central idea of the newer world view" (Jensen 1963: 37). However, no cultural phenomenon, however much it may be drained from its semantic content, dies a natural death. The strengthened play element in itself may be of significance for its continuance, or the fact simply that "our fathers did so" might be a sufficient reason for the respectful observance of it. Moreover, without a special stimulus, man does not think of jolting that which is established or of re-examining its intellectual foundation. If the custom does not gain new life by acquiring a new meaning, or if it is not eliminated by opposing forces — it will continue to exist in spite of its semantic deficiency (1963: 77).

Before a cultural phenomenon reaches this final state, it will have passed through different stages of semantic depletion. It is therefore necessary to examine any cultural configuration in order to see the extent to which it has maintained contact with its original and proper meaning.

What we could call the Hirata-type of believers is definitely a small minority in the community we surveyed. From the twenty families we investigated more closely, some five might approach this belief. For these people the ancestors are active and alive and maintain particular relationships with the living. This group corresponds to the third variety of religious experience.

Most of the other informants would find themselves somewhere along the road of the process of semantic depletion. Ancestor worship seems for this group — mostly older people and traditional Buddhists — to have been stripped from its other-worldly supernatural aspects. For them belief in the intervening power of the ancestors is on the way out. It seems to me that Hirata Atsutane would have considered many of the villagers as victims of the pernicious influence of Confucianism.

We have the impression that the myth of the ancestors is not sacred any more, and definitely a language of the past for traditional Buddhists in the village. The rite, on the contrary, is still considered sacred in a certain sense and is not given up: not even the rather elaborate rites of the building of the temporary altar, or of the welcome and sending-off fires during *Obon*. The new family shelves and the new boxes for the ancestral tablets are another proof of this. By the younger generation, this might be looked upon as mere play and doomed to disappear very soon, like the yearly autumn festival of the village. But still, when the young grow up, the motive that "our fathers did so" might be strong enough to prevent the custom from falling into disuse.

The strongest dissociation from the practice of ancestor worship we met was the opinion of the woman in her thirties who made it clear that it was all meaningless and rather a burden, but one she would eventually have to take over at the proper time. In this case the evidence indicates that we are dealing with a mere survival, and that the survival will indeed persist, if no stronger forces will act upon it in the future.

CONCLUSION

Finally, we have to address ourselves to the larger question of the meaning of the most general characteristics of a religious system to major issues of the social life and individual participation (Firth 1964: 231–232).

The relationship between ancestor worship and society is complex: ancestor worship reflects the society, is determined by it, and at the same time shapes it. Thus we do not think it possible to come to any conclusive statements about specific correlations between certain ritual acts and particular social ties (Geertz 1965: 215). We would rather concentrate upon what Tillich calls the "style" of a whole culture (1961: 81), insofar as it corresponds to the values present in a part of that culture, in the present case, ancestor worship. It is thus on a rather abstract level that we want to indicate, in concluding, the congruence of those values of the part with the whole.

The ancestor cult creates order in the passing of time as experienced in the household. It gives order to the inevitable fact of death and by the same token orders life: everybody is destined to become an ancestor. The order is structured as a process where the stages leading to this final purpose of life are clearly outlined (memorial services, steps on the path to ancestorhood). Everybody finds himself in due time on the appropriate stage. The shift from one stage to the next and the acquisition of this new status are not the result of individual endeavor or personal achievement of the subject himself. The outsiders have a certain power over him, because it is thanks to their loyalty that one can become an ancestor. But their power of intervention is limited; the order is fixed, and only when the time is ripe will the change occur almost as the result of a natural growth.

Life, however, is capricious and cannot but incompletely be brought into an ideal order; provisions for anomalies have to be made (*muenbotoke*); disorder resulting from irregularities is allotted a special place (*tatari*), *en marge* of the main body of order. This localized disorder, however, entertains only dim relations with the main body of order. It does not stand in a dialectical tension with it, is not a threat to it, and is not of equal importance.

The order thus created is but the inner order of one group (the *ie*), not between two or more such groups. Within this group, however, there reigns not an order of unchangeable objects; it is one of a living organism, and its main purpose is to provide for orderly change, development and normal growth.

A newcomer into the group will be only gradually introduced: a certain assimilation period is necessary (in the world of ritual this period will be provided for a child, a bride, or a dead soul). The process of assimilation is smoothed by a third party (for the soul, the priest at the funeral), whose role will lessen gradually but whose influence won't disappear completely. Inside the group every member is dependent upon the others so that the main theme of relationship is acknowledging one's dependency. This feeling of dependency extends even to the new member who will thus spontaneously be welcomed in such a way that the others seem to be dependent upon him. However, the more the new member becomes assimilated, the more he will grow dependent upon the others.

It is not always possible to even out the *giri*, resulting from the dependency upon the others; besides, it is not necessary. The symbolic effort, however, is necessary to manifest that one is aware of one's indebtedness. Gifts or offerings are thus important. However, the giving itself is what counts more than the gift. This might seem pure formalism if one misses the point that what matters is not the content of the act, but the dependence and gratitude expressed by it, the acknowledgement of a link.

Any new member of a group has to sever his links (*en*) with the former group of his allegiance, but this also happens gradually and in an established way (ancestors come back home, brides pay regular visits to their native homes). Because the ties with the group are so important, any breaking of them causes loneliness. Thus any remedy to this isolation is cast in forms that take away this loneliness within the framework of ancestor worship (the victory over death is a victory over the loneliness caused by the breaking of the ties).[4] Finally, the one who severs his ties with the established order in an undue manner stands really alone, and this is really death (*muenbotoke* and outcasts).

## REFERENCES

ARIGA KIZAEMON
1965   "Senzo no Kannen [Ancestor concepts]," in *Nihon no Kazoku* [The family in Japan]. Shibundo.

CAILLOIS, ROGER
1950   *L'homme et le sacré* (third edition). Paris: Gallimard. (Reprinted from 1939.)

DORE, RONALD P.
1965   *City life in Japan, a study of a Tokyo ward.* Berkeley: University of California Press. (Reprinted from 1958.)

FIRTH, RAYMOND
1964   "Study of values by social anthropologists," in *Essays on social organization and values.* Edited by R. Firth. London School of Economics Monographs on Social Anthropology. London: Athlone.

GEERTZ, CLIFFORD
1965   "Religion as a cultural system," in *Reader in comparative religion, an anthropological approach* (second edition). Edited by W. A. Lessa and E. Z. Vogt. New York: Harper and Row.

HERTZ, ROBERT
1960   *Death and the right hand.* Glencoe, Illinois: Free Press. (Reprinted from 1907.)

HOZUMI, NOBUSHIGE
1901   *Ancestor worship and Japanese law.* Tokyo: Maruzen.

HUIZINGA, JOHAN
1964   Homo ludens, *a study of the play element in culture.* London: Beacon Press. (Reprinted from 1938.)

JENSEN, ADOLF E.
1963   *Myth and cult among primitive peoples.* Chicago: University of Chicago Press.

KIRBY, R. J.
1910   "Ancestral worship in Japan," in *The Transactions of the Asiatic Society in Japan* 38.

---

[4]   Cf. Hirata Atsutane (in Kirby 1910: 239): "The descendants are the staves they can lean upon, and if these descendants are absent, we know their ancestors' souls must be lonely."

KITANO, SEIICHI
1962   " 'Dōzuku' and 'ie' in Japan: the meaning of family genealogical relationship," in *Japanese culture: its development and characteristics*. Edited by Robert J. Smith and Richard K. Beardsley. Viking Fund Publications in Anthropology 34.

MALINOWKSI, BRONISLAW
1955   *Magic, science and religion*. New York: Doubleday Anchor Books.

*Nihon minzokugaku taikei*
1958–1960   [Monographs on Japanese Folklore], volume three 227–278. Tokyo: Heibon-sha.

OOMS, HERMAN
1967   The religion of the household: a case study of ancestor worship in Japan. *Contemporary Religions in Japan* 8(3–4):201–334.

PLATH, DAVID W.
1964   Where the family of God is he family: the role of the dead in Japanese households. *American Anthropologist* 66(2):300–317.

*Seigō Minzoku*
1960   Muenbotoke. *Seigō Minzoku* 13.

SMITH, ROBERT J.
1966   Ihai: mortuary tablets, the household and kin in Japanese ancestor worship. *Transactions of the Asiatic Society of Japan*, third series, 9:83–102.

STARK, RODNEY
1965   A taxonomy of religious experience. *Journal for the Scientific Study of Religion* 5(1):97–116.

TAKEDA CHOSHU
1957   *Sosen suhai: Minzoku to Rekishi* [Ancestor worship: its folklore and history]. Kyoto: Heirakujishoten.

TILLICH, PAUL
1961   "The religious symbol," in *Symbolism in religion and literature*. Edited by Rollo May. New York: George Braziller.

WHITEHEAD, A. N.
1961   "Uses of symbolism," in *Symbolism in religion and literature*. Edited by Rollo May. New York: George Braziller.

YANAGITA KUNIO
1964   *Senzo no hanashi: Yanagita Kunio Shu*, volume ten. Chikuma Shobo. (Translated in 1970 as *About our ancestors: the Japanese family system*. Japan Society for the Promotion of Science.)

YINGER, MILTON J.
1963   *Sociology looks at religion*. New York: Macmillan.

# Optional Cult Group Affiliation Among the Puyuma and the Miyako Islanders

TOICHI MABUCHI

The term "affiliation" here implies "belongingness" as distinct from "filiation," which means "relatedness" as conceived by the present writer. This term may refer to both the process and the result of recruiting the members of a given group. The reason for preferring "affiliation" to "descent" is rather simple. The cult group as dealt with in this paper greatly deviates, at least seemingly, from the descent group in the ordinary sense; while such deviation would be subject to a series of discussions, this could perhaps lead eventually to a reinspection of the concept of descent.

In connection with this is the term "optional," involving here a somewhat wider range than that of the "ambilineal" ("ambilateral"), which refers primarily to an alternative in each generation, i.e. either patrilineal or matrilineal. In the optional affiliation as implied here, one may select — or may be led to select — one of the groups with which one's parents, grandparents, or even great-grandparents were affiliated. It may be possible to employ the term "ambilineal" to cover such a wider range as that implied here by the term "optional." However, the present writer is more concerned with the contrast as well as the interrelation between the "one-of-the-two" situation and the "one-of-them" situation in group affiliation.

Ryukyuan culture abounds in variation, especially in matters of ritual,

The writer acknowledges his indebtedness to the Wenner-Gren Foundation for their financial aid enabling him to carry out field research mainly on the central tribes of Formosa and partially on the Puyuma in the summer of 1970 on the one hand, and on various islands of the Ryukyus in 1960 and at intervals, in 1964–1965 on the other. This paper presents a part of the results concerned.

not only between localities but even between adjacent villages.[1] Here, we shall deal with a few villages on the southern coast of Miyako, an island in the northern part of the southern Ryukyus. Before doing this, however, it is desirable to obtain a bird's-eye view of the socioreligious organization of the Ryukyus as a whole so that the particular features of the southerly Miyako can be brought into relief.

Somewhat in contrast with the southern Ryukyus, where the formation of well-defined kin groups is far less manifest, the organization of an agamous patriclan or patrilineage is prevalent on the main island of Okinawa. While such patrilineal grouping relates mainly to the ancestor cult, other rituals, e.g. agrarian or fishing, are usually conducted by the village as a whole, with a sacred grove or shrine as the pivotal point of religious activities.

In the southern Ryukyus, on the other hand, the village settlement, consisting of roughly 100 to 300 households, contains several cult groups, each with its sacred grove or shrine. It is not rare that the cult group claims descent — perhaps better termed "derivation" — from some mythological or semihistorical figure whose direct line of descent, usually along the male line of primogeniture, is represented by the *mutu,* i.e. "the house of the stem family." This term literally implies "origin," "center," or "foundation." The same term can also denote the sacred grove or shrine in another context. However, the people are occasionally cognizant of the fusion of those representing other derivations into the cult group. Moreover, even siblings are often affiliated with different cult groups. These circumstances tend presumably to weaken the consciousness of a common ancestor among members of the same cult group. A series of such shifts could be traced by carrying out a comparative study involving several villages adjacent to each other. Nevertheless, in many localities the priestess-in-chief and the male manager presiding over the cult group are succeeded ideally, if not necessarily, by the eldest daughter and the eldest son born into the stem family, thus, from the father's eldest sister to her brother's daughter on the one hand and from the father to the eldest son on the other. In the Ryukyus as a whole, marriage is usually patrilocal and important property is inherited along the male line, with a considerable emphasis being laid on the eldest son.

The situation in the southern part of Miyako is peculiar in that the number of cult groups is unusually large, especially in the villages of the central south, where there are some fifteen to twenty cult groups in a

---

[1]   The term "village" as employed here is equivalent to the hamlet in the administrative classification in which a single village consists of a number of such hamlets.

single village whose size corresponds approximately to the average for all of Miyako Island as well as for most of the southern Ryukyus. Here the cult group members are classified into two categories: those who may be called the "adherents" to a given cult group and those simply affiliated with it. In a word, the latter contribute to the expenses of the rituals of the cult group, while the former participate in and carry out the rituals.

A few days after its birth, a baby is subjected to divination by lots, which will select for it membership in a certain cult group among those to which its parents, grandparents, and sometimes even great-grandparents belonged — more exactly speaking, "among those to which they adhered" and otherwise, "among those with which they were affiliated," because some people remain simply affiliated with a certain cult group, without adhering to it for life, as will be explained below. Meanwhile, the actual range of the selection concerned varies according to the circumstances of respective families — sometimes either the father's or the mother's cult group is selected for the baby. The raffle is operated by some old man who is skilled in this. Relatives or friends are eligible for selection.

In any case, such a way of determining the baby's affiliation with a given cult group indicates that in this divinatory selection, one takes into consideration a certain range of ancestors ascending as far as two or three generations along both the male and the female line. Fairly conspicuous here is the trend that the sons, above all the eldest sons, are far more frequently affiliated with the father's cult group than the daughters who are often "dragged into" the mother's cult group.

Such a result is surely incompatible with the theory of probability. While admitting that the problem remains largely unresolved, we shall have to take into account the fact that in a number of families the eldest son is not subject to the divinatory raffle on the ground that such a son will certainly be affiliated with the father's cult group after all. Some people, however, still insist that even the eldest son should be subject to the raffle, and that his resulting affiliation does reveal the will of the deities of the cult group concerned and is not the outcome of an artificial manipulation.

It may be added that it is not rare to select a secondary affiliation for the baby in the course of manipulating the divinatory raffle. This leads to a situation in which the baby, when grown up, will be qualified to appeal also to the deities of a cult group other than the one with which it has a primary affiliation, while rendering some services to those deities too.

Toward middle age (and usually after having married), both men and women often feel various kinds of anxiety and suffer from illness, often of some neurotic nature. They are now more and more inclined piously to appeal to and rely on the deities of some cult group. They try to reexamine whether or not they have been affiliated with a cult group appropriate to them by having recourse again to divinatory raffle or, more often in the case of disease, by requesting advice from professional shamans or shamanesses.[2] The disease is often supposed to be a revelation of the deities of a given cult group who are urging the person concerned to join that group. As a result, one may either remain in the same group with which one is already affiliated or transfer one's membership to another cult group. Here too, the eldest son usually remains in his father's cult group.

In any case, such an individual is now elevated to the status of the adherents, higher than those simply affiliated with a given cult group, at least as far as ritual affairs are concerned. Such adherents, either male or female, are the active members of the cult group: they perform rituals related to the main crops and to welcoming the overseas deities to secure both the fertility of farming crops and the prosperity of the people (Mabuchi i.p.). As in other areas of the Ryukyus where the female predominates over the male in ritual affairs, the adherents play an important role in the rituals of the cult group. But, one can hardly talk here about such a hereditary priestess as is often found in other areas of the Ryukyus. Here, the sooner one becomes an adherent, the higher one's position in the cult group, regardless of relative age among the adherents. This is also the case with the male managers or performers of the rituals.

The figures in Table 1, obtained from the village of Urukawa in November 1960, illustrate the above discussion, with regard to both adherence and affiliation. One may remark that quite a few men and women have failed to become adherents of any of the cult groups. Frequently, such people are those who are not troubled by the anxieties of life, always remain healthy, and never cease to enjoy native liquor, regardless of their age.

The tendency for the eldest son usually to be affiliated with or to be an adherent to his father's cult group is effective in continuing the stem family along the male line. The eldest son of a branch family may start a "family line," also along the male line, but the cult group affiliation may or may not coincide with that of the original family line. As viewed from the cult group itself, the stem always remains straight and solid,

---

[2]   Most of such professionals dwell in the towns or cities of the island, though the "village shamans or shamanesses," regarded as less efficient, sometimes seem to give advice in this regard.

Table 1. Adherence and affiliation to cult groups in Urukawa

**Male**

| age | Adherence | | Primary affiliation | | | | | | Secondary affiliation | | | | | | | Total |
|---|---|---|---|---|---|---|---|---|---|---|---|---|---|---|---|---|
| | fa | mo | fa | mo | fa-mo | mo-fa | mo-mo | fa-mo-mo | fa | mo | fa-mo | mo-fa | mo-mo | fa-mo-mo | * | |
| 1–20 | – | – | 151(56) | 23(2) | 10(3) | – | 1 | – | 2 | 11(5) | 19(5) | 1 | 4 | 2 | 3 | 188 |
| 21–30 | 5(2) | – | 27(15) | 3 | – | – | 1 | – | 3 | 4(1) | 7(6) | – | 1 | – | 1 | 37 |
| 31–40 | 18(12) | – | 12(3) | 2 | – | – | – | – | – | 8(5) | 1(1) | – | – | – | – | 32 |
| 41–50 | 22(11) | 3 | 4(3) | 1 | – | – | – | – | 3 | 9(5) | – | – | – | – | 1 | 31 |
| 51–60 | 23(10) | – | 4(1) | – | – | – | – | – | – | 9(5) | 1(1) | – | – | – | 1 | 28 |
| 61– | 16(8) | 3 | 4(1) | – | – | – | – | – | – | 9(4) | – | – | – | – | 1 | 24 |
| Total | 84(43) | 6 | 202(79) | 29(2) | 10(3) | – | 2 | – | 8 | 50(25) | 28(13) | 1 | 5 | 2 | 7 | 340 |

**Female**

| age | Adherence | | Primary affiliation | | | | | | Secondary affiliation | | | | | | | Total |
|---|---|---|---|---|---|---|---|---|---|---|---|---|---|---|---|---|
| | fa | mo | fa | mo | fa-mo | mo-fa | mo-mo | fa-mo-mo | fa | mo | fa-mo | mo-fa | mo-mo | fa-mo-mo | * | |
| 1–20 | – | – | 83 | 70 | 9 | 2 | 3 | 1 | 2 | 4 | 4 | 5 | 5 | 3 | 14 | 182 |
| 21–30 | 1 | – | 9 | 6 | – | – | – | – | 1 | 2 | – | – | – | – | 12 | 28 |
| 31–40 | 12 | 2 | 10 | 3 | – | – | – | – | 5 | 5 | – | – | – | – | 10 | 37 |
| 41–50 | 15 | 4 | 4 | 1 | – | – | – | – | 2 | 5 | – | – | – | – | 10 | 34 |
| 51–60 | 11 | 3 | 3 | – | – | – | – | – | 1 | 4 | – | – | – | – | 1 | 18 |
| 61– | 16 | 10 | 4 | – | – | – | – | – | 5 | 9 | – | – | – | – | 6 | 36 |
| Total | 55 | 19 | 113 | 80 | 9 | 2 | 3 | 1 | 16 | 29 | 4 | 5 | 5 | 3 | 53 | 335 |

Notes:

1. Abbreviations such as "fa" (father) and "mo-fa" (mother's father) refer to cult groups.
2. The asterisk indicates those from other villages or those whose adherence or affiliation remains uninvestigated.
3. The figures in the parentheses indicate the number of eldest sons included.
4. The figures in the columns headed by "Total" exclude the secondary affiliation which represents a double membership.

while its branches perpetually fluctuate, as it were. The result resembles the "stem lineage," a term coined by Marshall D. Sahlins (Sahlins 1957: 298).

In the Ryukyus as a whole, the thirteenth, fourteenth, and fifteenth days of the seventh month of the lunar calendar are the days for the so-called *bon* (also *Obon*) ritual, when the souls of the dead and of some ancestors are invited to partake of the dishes served by each household. At some stem houses of the cult groups in Urukawa, however, an extended form of the *bon* ritual has been performed until recently. In the night they performed the *bon* ritual in the same way as in other households, but in the daytime they performed a special ritual for the remote ancestors, already deified long since, to whom they offered wine specially brewed of millet or rice and sang a ritual song with rhythmic clapping of hands. Such offerings and singing are usually for the deities at the sacred grove or shrine, not for the dead. Members of the same cult group attend these rituals. The atmosphere is quite reminiscent of the ritual of a kinship group centering around a common ancestor or ancestors. Meanwhile, it should be noted that the ritual possibly excludes some of those of the same derivation as the stem household, traced along the male line, and includes others of heterogeneous derivation, all depending on the affiliation as well as the adherence relevant to the cult group concerned.

In the village Miyaguni, a few miles to the west of Urukawa, the situation is very different from that described above. Here the village officials levy a definite amount of contribution, usually in cash (replacing grains of millet or such former levy) and this contribution is divided among the representatives of all the five shrines in order to cover the expenses for rituals. While the villagers are expected not to offend against the ritual regulations or taboos on these days, especially when a joint ritual of these shrines is held, the majority of the people have no particular relation to a specific shrine as far as ritual activities are concerned. On the other hand, a considerable number of people come in order to become adherents of a certain shrine among the five selected in approximately the same way as in the village of Urukawa mentioned above. Table 2 shows the result of an investigation made in November 1960.[3]

The figures of Table 2, comparable to those in Table 1, show that the men more frequently than the women — the eldest sons always — ad-

[3] The figures in both Tables 1 and 2 were made available in part through the aid of Miss Kamata Hisako, now an associate professor of folklore at Seijo University, Tokyo. The present writer is grateful for her collaboration.

Table 2. Adherence and affiliation to cult groups in Miyaguni

*Male*

| age | fa | mo | fa-mo | mo-mo | wife's fa | wife's mo | ** | * | Total |
|---|---|---|---|---|---|---|---|---|---|
| 1–20 | – | – | – | – | – | – | 266 | – | 266 |
| 21–30 | – | – | – | – | – | – | 44 | – | 44 |
| 31–40 | 4(3) | – | – | – | – | – | 49 | – | 53 |
| 41–50 | 5(2) | – | – | – | – | – | 33 | – | 38 |
| 51–60 | 9(1) | 1 | – | – | 2 | 2 | 18 | – | 32 |
| 61– | 14(5) | 4 | – | 1 | 2 | – | 18 | 1 | 40 |
| Total | 32(11) | 5 | – | 1 | 4 | 2 | 428 | 1 | 473 |

*Female*

| age | fa | mo | fa-mo | mo-mo | husband's fa | husband's mo | ** | * | Total |
|---|---|---|---|---|---|---|---|---|---|
| 1–20 | – | – | – | – | – | – | 244 | – | 244 |
| 21–30 | – | – | – | – | – | – | 48 | – | 48 |
| 31–40 | – | 1 | – | – | 1 | – | 65 | – | 67 |
| 41–50 | 4 | 4 | – | – | 1 | 4 | 35 | – | 48 |
| 51–60 | 11 | 6 | – | – | 4 | 3 | 4 | 1 | 29 |
| 61– | 24 | 12 | 1 | – | 13 | 4 | 10 | 3 | 67 |
| Total | 39 | 23 | 1 | – | 19 | 11 | 406 | 4 | 503 |

Notes:
1. The asterisk indicates those from other villages or those whose adherence remains uninvestigated.
2. The double asterisk indicates those who have not yet become adherents of any shrine.

here to the father's shrine. Moreover, it should be noted that a number of woman adhere to the shrine of either parent of their husbands and, in a similar way, some men to that of either parent of their wives. Such adherences occasionally occur when some of the spouses' parents happened to adhere to a certain shrine.

At this point, we shall have to talk about the "family line" as distinct from the so-called "descent line," the latter being among those that may be called "consanguineal lines," that is, multilineal. A family, once started, continues to exist through a son, usually the eldest son, generation after generation, while the younger sons start branch families. But all these families, centering around the original family as a stem, may or may not bring forth a sort of patrilineage organized on the hierarchic order of families. In any case, such a concept of the "patrilineal family line" prevails in both the Ryukyus and mainland Japan, irrespective of whether or not the kinship institutions as a whole incline more to the patrilineal or the bilateral.

Such a concept is highly relevant to the people's view of marriage. John and Mary marry "each other" to start a sweet home, that is, a neolocal family, but the situation here is very different. The woman "marries into" the family of her husband. When there is no son to continue the family, a man is adopted and he marries a daughter, if any, born into the family concerned. These circumstances involve something more than the problem of marital residence.

Sooner or later after death, a person thus married into a family falls into the category of an ancestor in the family of the spouse, not in the natal family. Because patrilocal residence is customary, the ancestors of a family consist in principle of two kinds of deceased, namely, those men natal to this family and those women natal to other families, while excluding those women natal to this family who are now the ancestresses in other families. In this regard, the situation of the adopted man mentioned is similar to that of the married-in woman. In accordance with the marriage situation and the kinship ideology, the woman is separated at least institutionally from her natal family on the one hand and is incorporated into her husband's family on the other.

Certainly, the villagers of Urukawa share such a concept of family line with those of Miyaguni. On the other hand, the way of selecting both the affiliation and the adherence in Urukawa takes only the consanguineal lines into consideration, whereas the way of determining the shrine adherence in Miyaguni refers to both the consanguineal and family lines. Though the family and consanguineal lines intersect or cut across one another variously in the field of kinship relations, the figures from Miyaguni reveal that both concepts concerned are simultaneously in operation and even supplementary to each other, thus leading to a different trend in statistics from those of Urukawa. In any case, the similarity as well as dissimilarity between Urukawa and Miyaguni is highly illuminating in the investigation of the Puyuma people.

The Puyuma inhabit the southeastern plain of Formosa. While they once exerted influence both politically and culturally on the neighboring peoples in this part of aboriginal Formosa in both the plains and the mountains, they have been in direct contact with the growing population of the Chinese immigrants for a few centuries. The Puyuma population has remained rather stable, ranging roughly between 6,000 and 7,000 for several decades, while their culture has undergone an increasing change through external influences. The rapid propagation of Christianity has accelerated this change in the postwar period.

Puyuma society often has been labeled "matrilineal" chiefly on the ground that the immovable properties are mainly inherited by the daughters and that marital residence is more frequently matrilocal. However, not only are important properties, even including immovable ones, often inherited patrilineally, but patrilocal marriage is also not rare. We have not yet obtained the statistics relevant to the marital residence, but the frequency of patrilocal marriage may have been approximately one-third of the total cases of marriage in the prewar period, if we rely on the impressions of various informants. Meanwhile, the growing trend toward patrilocal residence seemed to be manifest even in the prewar period. It may be added here that, when the people talk about "relatives," it is usually in the bilateral sense of the word, and they seem to be devoid of any concept of lineage as such (Mabuchi 1960: 127–142; Suenari 1970: 87–123).

The present writer visited the Puyuma several times in the prewar period, but the length of stay was always too short to obtain sufficient information. The figures of Table 3 are mostly the result of a random survey in 1970, though some cases investigated in the earlier period are added. Of course, all these figures cover only partially the cases of the Puyuma as a whole. Moreover, a fair number of people included in these figures had already abandoned the native religion.

Each village of the Puyuma contains a number of shrines, greater or lesser, all of which are called *karumahan* or *karuma'an* according to dialect, literally "real house", notwithstanding that these are merely huts, roughly built in most cases. Especially in the greater shrines, important rituals are the ones relating to agriculture. There were lesser shrines that specialized in the hunting and headhunting rituals, the members being exclusively men. But, most of such shrines seem to have already disappeared. The leader of the shrine is generally a priest, not a priestess. In some lesser shrines that specialize in healing diseases, however, the leader is female and she plays the role of a shamaness in addition to that of a priestess.

In general, the Puyuma seem to avoid the strict discrimination between adherence and affiliation which is mentioned above. For convenience of discussion, we shall employ here a subsidiary term, "shrine membership," to include both adherence and affiliation. There seem to be roughly two major ways to determine the shrine membership: social-familial and shamanistic-diagnostic. The first refers to what may be called the "discretion of the parents" (and possibly also of the grandparents, if any) and the second to the "will of deities or ancestors." These two major ways might parallel somewhat the affiliation and the adherence of the Miyako islanders, but we shall not enter here into a further discussion of this.

When the discretion of the parents leads a child to a shrine membership, the child is simply introduced to the deities of the shrine by some procedure so that these deities will be the guardians for the child. This takes place rather early in childhood, the age fluctuating considerably. In the event that a child suffers seriously from some disease at a later time, the parents or the child by himself or herself, if grown up, will consult with a shamaness [4] about whether or not the shrine membership is appropriate to the child.

As a result of such shamanistic diagnosis, the child may either continue to retain the membership of the original shrine or transfer the membership to another shrine. In the latter case, the people often say that the deified ancestors who once belonged there have "dragged" one of their descendants into that shrine by giving the alarm in the form of disease. Such ancestors may be grandparents, great-grandparents, or even remoter ones whom it is often hard to identify, according to what some informants say. While skipping a generation or more, one can trace back to such ancestors along a certain line through blood connections. Irrespective of whether the ties are real or fictitious, some kind of kinship ideology seems to linger here.

The discretion of the parents mentioned seems to be multidirectional to the extent that it varies according to the family or the narrow circle of relatives, even within a single village. The shrine membership was very relevant to the future life of the children in former days when such membership was of considerable sociopolitical as well as magico-religious value because of some personal link with a "great man or woman" who happened to be a copartner in the shrine rituals.

In determining shrine membership for the children, some people still tend to take into consideration the distribution of economic prestige, political power, and magico-religious authority among close relatives, notwithstanding that these are largely of a vestigial nature. They seem to do this laying differing emphasis on various items, presumably leading to more variation and more confusion. On the other hand, other people tend to become more careless and even more indifferent with regard to

[4] Among the Puyuma all shamanistic performances are monopolized by women and there are no shamans but only shamanesses. An exception to this are a few "feminized shamans" among the prewar Puyuma, representing the northern extremity of the distribution of the bisexual shamans among the Indonesian-speaking peoples.

the shrine membership of their children. However, we should note that several — if not many — informants insist that the people often tend intentionally to let the sons belong to the father's shrine and the daughters to the mother's, a situation comparable with the Miyako trend mentioned.

In the village of Puyuma, from which appellation the name of the ethnic group is derived, the villagers say that they have recourse far more rarely to the "will of deities" in determining the shrine membership as compared with people of other villages. In contrast with this, shrine membership is usually determined by a shamanistic-diagnostic procedure in the village of Murivurivuk, located in the northernmost tip of the distribution area of the Puyuma. Consequently, the majority of the villagers have no membership in any of the shrines, a situation reminiscent of the village Miyaguni, on Miyako Island.

In each village of the Puyuma, there are usually several "great shrines" attached to each of the chiefly families who collaborate with each other in the village administration which in the past had a considerable magico-religious nature. The names of such shrines are simultaneously the "house-names" of the chiefly families. While the shrine continues to be operated by its members, recruited usually in the two ways mentioned, the remaining question is how the chiefly family continue to exist, along with the house-name, though the chief is chosen among the close relatives of the ex-chief, traced along both the male and the female line. Nevertheless, the chiefly family still continues to exist, as a pivotal point of the chiefly succession as it were. Marital residence in the chiefly family is ambilocal as is also the case with the families of the common people.

It is said that the children of a chiefly family tend more to belong to the shrine attached to that family. In such a case, the affiliation, too, tends to be either matrilineal or patrilineal, depending on the marital residence of the parents, insofar as the discretion of the parents predominates over the "will of the deities" as mentioned. It might be possible here to talk about the "ambilineal family line" or at least a trend toward the formation of such a family line in the case of chiefly families. If so, the chiefly family of the Puyuma may be somewhat comparable with the stem family in Miyako Island or the Ryukyus in general.

Table 3, when elaborated in detail and subjected to a close analysis, could provide us with a clue by which to reveal some hidden aspects of the Puyuma culture and society. For the moment, however, we may point out that the marital residence of the parents has relatively little to do with the determination of the shrine membership, even though such a

Table 3.   Adherence and affiliation to cult groups among the Puyuma

| village | Male | | | | | | | | Female | | | | | | | | | | | Total |
|---|---|---|---|---|---|---|---|---|---|---|---|---|---|---|---|---|---|---|---|---|
| | matrilocal | | | | | patrilocal | | | matrilocal | | | | patrilocal | | | | | | | |
| | fa | mo | both | mo-fa | mo-mo | fa | mo | fa-mo | fa | mo | mo-fa | mo-mo | fa | mo | both | fa-mo | mo-fa | mo-mo | fa-mo-mo | |
| Katatipul | 6 | 4 | – | – | – | 8 | – | – | 5 | 3 | – | – | – | 2 | – | – | 1 | 1 | – | 30 |
| Kasavakan | 1* | 5 | 1 | – | – | 3 | 1 | – | 2 | – | – | – | 4* | 6 | – | – | – | – | – | 23 |
| Rikavong | 5 | 6 | 1 | – | – | 6 | 3 | – | 2 | 10 | – | – | 17 | 2 | 1 | 1 | – | – | 1 | 55 |
| Murivurivuk | 6 | 3 | – | 1 | 2 | 2 | – | 5 | 5 | 4 | 4 | 1 | 1 | – | – | – | – | – | – | 34 |
| Puyuma | – | 4 | – | – | – | 8 | – | – | – | – | – | – | – | 7 | – | – | – | – | – | 19 |
| Total | 18 | 22 | 2 | 1 | 2 | 27 | 4 | 5 | 14 | 17 | 4 | 1 | 22 | 17 | 1 | 1 | 1 | 1 | 1 | 161 |

Notes:
1. The terms "matrilocal" and "patrilocal" indicate the marital residence of one's parents.
2. The "1*" in the case of Kasavakan village is the result of transfering the membership from the mother's cult group to the father's, and the "4*" of the same village includes a case that resulted from such transference.

correlation might be found concealed in the figures of the table. The latter trend seems to be somewhat evident in the case of the males whose fathers married patrilocally.

This paper does not intend to present a conclusive statement but to arouse a series of discussions around and about some problems which seem to be resolved most effectively by a collaboration of both religious and anthropological studies. While it is true that anthropologists have greatly contributed to the study of kinship systems as such, a wider perspective would be made available by developing this kind of collaboration. Topics such as the stem family and the family line, which we have discussed above, still remain rather marginal to anthropological discussions. However, the ethnographic representation concerned seems inevitably to involve both kinds of study as mentioned. It is hoped that the present paper may contribute to stimulating such a collaboration.

## REFERENCES

MABUCHI, TOICHI
   1960   "The aboriginal peoples of Formosa," in *Social structure in Southeast Asia*. Edited by George P. Murdock, 127–142. Chicago: Quadrangle Books.
   i.p.    "Space and time in Ryukyuan cosmology," in *Folklore in the modern world*. Edited by Richard M. Dorson. World Anthropology. The Hague: Mouton.
SAHLINS, MARSHALL D.
   1957   Differentiation by adaptation in Polynesian societies. *The Journal of the Polynesian Society* 66(3):291–300.
SUENARI, MICHIO
   1970   Taiwan Puyuma-zoku no Shinzoku-soshiki no Shikōsei [Cognatic kinship system among the Puyuma in Taiwan]. *Minzoku-gaku Kenkyū* 35(2):87–123. Tokyo.

# A Note on Ancestor Worship in "Cognatic" Societies

TOICHI MABUCHI

The term "cognatic" as employed here roughly corresponds to Murdock's "cognatic social organization" of which the "principal structural features ... differentiate three basic subtypes": bilateral or Eskimo, quasi-unilineal or Carib, and ambilineal or Polynesian (Murdock 1960: 13–14). Seemingly the prominent feature common to all three subtypes would be that institutional manipulation of kinship relations is made on a bilateral — eventually multilineal — basis. In other aspects, however, these three subtypes differ from each other in various ways, as indicated in Murdock's tabular form. Leaving aside the quasi-unilineal subtype for the moment, the most important difference between the bilateral and the ambilineal subtype seems to be that it is hard for the former to bring forth any kind of lineage, whereas the latter can lead to the formation of an ambilineage. This feature is so fundamental that one may class ambilineal and unilineal together in contrast with the bilateral, by asking whether the formation of well-defined kin group

This paper intends to be a sort of appendix to another paper "Optional cult group affiliation among the Puyuma and the Miyako Islanders" submitted last year primarily to the symposium "Ritual, Cult, and Shamanism," but afterward incorporated into the newly organized symposium "Ancestors." For these months the present writer has had no time to revise the paper already submitted or to prepare a quite independent paper to fit in with the new symposium. Accordingly, he simply adds here a brief paper which outlines the kinship framework of ancestor worship in both areas respectively of aboriginal Formosa and the Ryukyus he dealt with in the first paper — May 1974.

The writer acknowledges his indebtedness to the Wenner-Gren Foundation for their financial aid for field research mainly on the central tribes of Formosa and partially on the Puyuma in the summer of 1970, and on various islands of the Ryukyus in 1960 and at intervals in 1964–1965. This paper represents a part of the results of those investigations.

would be possible under either system. In any case, all such classifications are only relative in nature, and this paper aims to contain both the ambilineal and the bilateral in Murdock's subtypes.

Another paper of the present writer compares an optional way of obtaining cult group membership in a part of Miyako Island, southern Ryukyus, with an analogous one among the Puyuma, southeastern Formosa. Here the term "optional" is employed to cover somewhat a wider range of application than the term "ambilineal" in the ordinary sense, as discussed in another paper. Apart from the problem as to whether or not such a cult group is a descent group, the way of affiliation is rather peculiar in the southern Ryukyus or even in Miyako Island. But the way of affiliation must be seen against the background of serial shifts in the cult group organization of the southern Ryukyus. Meanwhile the Puyuma are unique as an ethnic group in southeast Formosa, displaying much more distinctiveness in the features of their culture and society as compared with other ethnic groups surrounding them.

FRAMEWORK FOR CULT ACTIVITIES

Throughout the Ryukyus, both the inheritance of property and the succession to social status are normally regulated by the patrilineal principle, with an emphasis on primogeniture. Marital residence is usually virilocal. In other aspects of kinship, a bilateral trend is generally dominant in the southern Ryukyus, in sharp contrast to the main island called Okinawa in the proper sense where the agamous patri-sib or patrilineage prevails. Such patrilineal groups, the so-called *munchū*, are concerned mainly with the ancestor cult, while other cult activities, particularly rituals relevant to the fertility of crops or human beings, are mostly conducted by the village as a whole, with a sacred grove or shrine as the focus of such activities. In the southern Ryukyus, on the other hand, a village contains several cult groups of similar function, each with a sacred grove or shrine.

The *munchū* is not localized and a village contains several *munchū*, the members of each *munchū* being often scattered in various localities. There is found a trend toward a partially systematized segmentation of the larger *munchū*. At several levels of segmentation, the segment has its own "house of stem family" (*mutu-ya*), literally implying the "origin-house," whose family line is continued usually along the primogenital male line.

As is usually found throughout the Ryukyus, ancestral tablets are placed on the altar in the ordinary house, but the tablet is removed at the thirty-third anniversary of the death of the person concerned, when the "soul" of the dead is said to be deified to unite with a mass of ancestor deities, by losing its personal identity. At the *mutu-ya* of various levels, on the other hand, a specific altar is installed for the apical ancestors of the segment who represent the remote ancestors. Such an altar is placed on the right side, that is, roughly to the east, of the family altar. At the highest level of the patri-kin group, a special hall is often built in the southeastern part of the houseyard to worship the deified founder of the group.[1] The ancestor cult operates at various levels of these patri-kin groups under the leadership of a priestess called *ukudi* who is often a shamaness as well and eligible among the patri-kin group concerned. Ideally, if not always, there are two kinds of priestesses: "male *ukudi*" and "female *ukudi*," the former dealing with male ancestors and the latter with female ancestors of the group.

Apart from ancestor worship, the *munchū* factor is not negligible in other cult activities which are conducted by the village as a whole. Certain *munchū* seem often to have been regarded as the descendants of the first settler of the village. It seems to have been fairly prevalent in former days that the direct line of descent from the village founder was represented by the stem family of the leading *munchū* and that the eldest son of the stem family succeeded to the status of village chief from his father and preferably the eldest daughter succeeded to the status of the priestess-in-chief from her father's sister. The pattern that the brother manages secular affairs and the sister the religious ones, irrespective of whether or not she married out of her natal family, was widespread in the Ryukyus, often in connection with the belief in the spiritual predominance of the sister. Moreover, this pattern was found consistently at various levels of the sociopolitical organization, from the family through the village and district up to the kingdom (Mabuchi 1964). Since that time, there have ensued a series of political changes and the male head of the stem family has lost long since his privilege in village administration, but the way of succeeding to the status of the priestess-in-chief still remains almost unchanged. A belief in the spiritual predominance of the sister survives more in the Yaeyama Archipelago (the southern part of the southern Ryukyus) than in the main island Okinawa, while it is hard to find even the vestige thereof in Miyako Island (the northern part of the southern Ryukyus).

In the southern Ryukyus as a whole, several cult groups composing

[1] With regard to the ritual implication of the cardinal points in connection with the plan of house and houseyard, see Mabuchi (1968: 121–127).

a village are independent from each other in performing their various rituals, even though they occasionally collaborate with each other in some way or other. Each cult group has its stem family house called *mutu-ya* or simply *mutu* of which the implication is the same as in the main island Okinawa. The stewardship of the cult group is usually retained by the eldest son of the stem family and the office of the priestess-in-chief is ideally, if not always, held by the eldest daughter. In this regard, the cult group of the southern Ryukyus seemingly resembles the patri-kin group of the main island Okinawa, but the *mutu-ya* in the former is not the place especially to perform the rituals for remote ancestors. The cult group members are often sceptical about whether they are of common ancestry. In correlation with this, the cult group has usually very little to do with ancestor worship, thus displaying a dissimilarity to the patri-kin group of the main island Okinawa in which ancestor worship is well systematized as mentioned above. As far as the nature of the rituals performed is concerned, the cult group of the southern Ryukyus is rather in parallel with the village of the main island Okinawa in that both are mainly charged with performing the rituals relevant to the fertility of crops and human beings.

Here we shall have to take into consideration the fact that in the southern Ryukyus the people lack any sort of mechanism by which remote ancestors ascending along the male line are worshiped in a systematic way as occurs in the *munchū* organization. In the southern Ryukyus, the people's way of inheritance, succession, and marital residence is fundamentally the same as in the main island Okinawa, and this is partially effective in creating among the people of a narrow circle a consciousness of their representing patrilineally related persons and families. The ritual superiority of their stem family is slightly manifest in contrast to the branch families in whose houses only the tablets of the relatively recent dead are placed on the altar: on some ritual occasions, the people of branch families should visit the altar of the stem family where old tablets are kept. However, the outcome is at best a quasi-patrilineage of a few generations' depth, with a boundary always fluctuating. Such a stem family is not comparable with that of the *munchū* or cult group as mentioned. It would be only natural that after the lapse of a few generations the deified ancestors tend easily to be forgotten in the people's memory and to be assimilated with other deities of "nonhuman derivation," a situation very different from that found in the main island Okinawa.

## SOUL, SPIRIT, AND DEITY

The practice of removing the ancestral tablets at the thirty-third anniversary after the death is found not only in both the areas of the Ryukyus mentioned, but also here and there in the rural localities of mainland Japan. This is usually accompanied by the theory that the soul of the dead undergoes deification at this anniversary. Such a theory seems to be more deeply rooted in the folk religion of the main island Okinawa than in the southern Ryukyus. Within the latter, on the other hand, removal of the ancestral tablet seems to be less clearly associated with the deification in Miyako Island than in the Yaeyama Archipelago which has been subject for about four centuries to "Okinawanization" encouraged by the Ryukyuan kingdom: in 1500 a local revolt was suppressed by the royal troops dispatched from the main island Okinawa. Moreover, the altar for ancestral tablets is called the "shelf for deities" in Miyako Island and indeed people often say "one has become a deity" when somebody has died. In a few villages situated in the northern extremity of Miyako Island, the people had neither ancestral tablets nor a "shelf for deities" until recently, though they have their own ritual of annually celebrating their ancestors. All this would suggest cultural diffusion from the main island Okinawa. Meanwhile, it is to be added here that the main island Okinawa, in turn, had been under the cultural influence from both mainland Japan and China, but the people seem to have largely integrated and reinterpreted these cultural traits to fit in with their own culture.

It is theoretically important to distinguish ancestor worship from the worship of the dead, but in the Ryukyus the real situation is too subtle to draw a clear line of demarcation between these two. We shall first have to note two terms in the Ryukyus dialect: "soul" of both the living and the dead on the one hand and "deities" of both human and non-human derivation on the other. Such a concept as ancestral "spirits," if present, would fall terminologically into the category of either the "soul" or the "deities" according to the context of the situation. The above mentioned theory concerning the deification of the souls of the dead at thirty-third anniversary would have been originally too artificial for the local people. The extent to which such a theory has penetrated into the folk beliefs would be fairly variable according to the island or the locality, possibly causing more or less discrepancy between the practice and belief among the local people.

Ancestral tablets of the family altar are not to be regarded simply and exclusively as representing the "souls of the dead" on whom ancestorhood has not yet been conferred. Apart from those who died an unnatural death or at an early age and are disqualified to acquire ancestorhood, a couple who died childless cannot become full-fledged ancestors, unless they adopt a male who will render service to their tablets after their death. When a male adult dies unmarried, one of his brother's sons, other than the eldest one, "inherit" the tablet of his father's brother when he starts a branch family. This may imply that a nephew "adopts" his dead uncle as a sort of father, so that the latter can acquire a stable status as an ancestor of this branch family. However, no such possibility is reserved for the adult woman who dies unmarried or returns to die at her natal family after the divorce, simply because of the social dogma that a single woman cannot be an ancestor in the true sense. Their status is unstable and this kind of woman tends to be malicious to the family members, notably in the main island Okinawa.

It deserves notice that it is the bilateral-multilineal — rather than agnatic — relatives of the deceased who are invited to participate in the serial anniversaries, namely, the first, third, seventh, thirteenth, twenty-fifth and thirty-third one, of the death. No strict distinction is made here between the male line or other ones in the kindred circle concerned, more emphasis being laid seemingly on the age and generation factor when the host deals with the participants. Meanwhile it is hard to ascertain the boundary where — or the procedure by which — the worship of the dead ends and the ancestor worship begins, with regard to those represented by the ancestral tablets on the family altar. It is said that the deification of the deceased partially starts at the twenty-fifth anniversary when the food tinged with red is offered, though the deceased are not completely deified until the thirty-third anniversary. However, we must remember that the deification does not demarcate the line by which to divide ancestors from the dead: those represented by the ancestral tablets function either simply as the dead or as ancestors according to the situation. Ancestors are moral supervisors not only of the family members but also of all the descendants reckoned multilineally, though with a trend more or less to lay an emphasis on those along the male line — presumably more so in the main island Okinawa. In any case, this would imply also that the living are supervised by all ancestors traced back multilineally, perhaps for a few generations. These ancestors are indeed bestowed with "regulative" power "for social relations and activities" (Fortes 1965:129), and may be invoked by their descendants to help or protect them as far as the worshipers conform with social norm or morality. And as is also the case with the "worship of the dead," ancestors may express their resentment against cold treatment by their descendants to whom they may bring some disaster. In this case, however, those who bear the disaster are more frequently the members of the family in whose household the ancestral tablets are placed on the altar than the wider circle of the descendants.

## CULT GROUP AND DESCENT GROUP

As mentioned above, the "tablet ancestors" are said to lose their personal identity at the thirty-third anniversary and henceforth they cease to be regularly worshiped at the family altar. Nevertheless, this does not necessarily imply that each ancestral figure suddenly disappears from the mind of the lving. It seems still possible for the people to communicate with such an individual ancestor, often by the help of a shaman, either male or female. Of course, such a figure is destined sooner or later to disappear, surviving at best for a few generations. But it sometimes looms large at some serious issue. A certain disaster is ascribed to it and the people try to appease its resentment in some way or other. Here too, the range of the "descendants" involved tends to be multilineal, perhaps representing an afterimage still surviving in spite of the formal theory relevant to the thirty-third anniversary. Such a situation is presumably more important in the southern Ryukyus where one's cult group affiliation is often determined by the interference of certain ancestors, irrespective of whether their tablets are still placed on the family altar or already removed. Here the people are not concerned with whether such ancestors are deified or not.

It is true that in many localities of the southern Ryukyus the cult group affiliation is patrilineal in the sense that the patrilineal framework of the family is fixed and extended to include branch families. Those married into the family or adopted are automatically enrolled in this framework, disregarding the cult group membership natal to them. Tentatively we shall call this PATRILINEAL AFFILIATION: the framework of the family is continued along the male line. In other localities, however, such a framework fluctuates in various ways, indicating serial shifts which seem to be rather multidirectional. Leaving aside some minor divergences for the moment, it would be possible to classify these shifts into several types.[2]

[2] At the Tenth Pacific Science Congress held in 1961, at the University of Hawaii, the writer read a paper on "Optional Descent in the Southern Ryukyus" (Mabuchi

1. FLUCTUATING PATRILINEAL AFFILIATION.   Here and there in the Yaeyama Archipelago, it occasionally happens that some children, more often daughters, do belong to a cult group other than that of the father, such as that of the mother, mother's mother or father's mother: ancestors of the cult group concerned bring certain disease or disaster to some persons among their descendants descending bilaterally (multilineally), on the ground that they neglected those ancestors by exclusively participating in the rituals of their father's cult group. Here the oracle or lot is frequently referred to.

2. PARALLEL AFFILIATION.   In the northeastern part of Miyako Island, the dominant trend is to affiliate the sons with the father's cult group and the daughters with the mother's.

3. DISTRIBUTIVE AFFILIATION.   In a few islets of Yaeyama, there are found a number of cases in which the children, irrespective of the sex or birth order, are rather irregularly allotted to either the father's cult group or the mother's, the choice being made intentionally by taking into account some populational balance between the two cult groups concerned and occasionally by referring to an oracle or lot for confirmation. In these islets, however, distributive affiliation coexists with the patrilineal affiliation, and the latter is statistically more dominant.

4. DIVINATORY AFFILIATION.   This was discussed in another paper (Mabuchi, this volume), and a brief description will suffice here. In the southern part of Miyako, the cult group affiliation is determined usually by lot which selects a certain cult group from those to which one's parents, grandparents, and sometimes great-grandparents belonged. Apart from the possibility of manipulating the lot to a certain extent, the conspicuous trend is that the sons, especially the eldest sons, are more often affiliated with the father's cult group than the daughters who are not infrequently "dragged into" the mother's. It is noteworthy that in a village where the cult group affiliation is determined relatively later in life, the women often belong to the cult group of their husband's father or mother and the "married-in" men to that of their wife's father or mother.

In all these cases, one may talk about the optional affiliation, containing here both the "partially optional" and the "completely optional" in the statistical sense. With regard to the way in which the option is

---

1961). The relevant ethnological data have greatly increased then, but only a summary of that paper is provided here to show some noteworthy trends in local variation. Though some cult groups of smaller size resemble an ambilineage, there remains an unresolved problem of whether the cult group is really a descent group. For this reason, the term "affiliation" is employed here in place of "descent."

exercised, there are found two kinds of option: intentional option made by the people themselves and the option made indirectly by "ancestors" whose will is revealed through some divination or disaster.

It is not rare in the southern Ryukyus that the cult group claims descent — perhaps better called "derivation" — from some mythological or legendary figure whose direct line of "descent," along the primo-genital male line, is thought of as represented by the stem family of the cult group. However, this is not clear enough among most of the people who simply regard the stem family as the "origin-house," without be-ing informed of the details of its derivation. Sometimes it is told that such and such a deity or deities migrated from an overseas island or came down from heaven to start a village or a hamlet. Nevertheless, this kind of deity seems to have been so "elevated" that the cult group members are rather sceptical about whether these deities are really their ancestors. When some historical or semihistorical figures are named, the situation tends to be more realistic. Even in this case, the people seem to be not very much concerned with genealogical links connecting such figures with the cult group members.

Such a trend is found equally in both the area where the patrilineal affiliation prevails and the "optional area." Another noteworthy trend common to both areas is that remote ancestors fall sooner into oblivion and negligence than in the main island Okinawa where these ancestors are worshiped individually by the stem family on various levels of patri-kin organization, even though they have lost their personal identity after the thirty-third anniversary as mentioned. Because an institutional mechanism by which to systematize ancestor worship is lacking, remote ancestors in the southern Ryukyus tend more easily to intermingle with the deities of the sacred grove or shrine of the cult group for instance.

In this connection, it would be interesting to note here a rather ex-ceptional way of performing the so-called *bon* ritual at the stem families of some cult groups in the village Urukawa, in the southern part of Miyako Island. In the Ryukyus as in mainland Japan, the thirteenth, fourteenth and fifteenth day of the seventh month in the lunar calendar (approximately in August in the solar calendar) are the days when "tablet ancestors" and some remote ones are invited to partake of dishes offered at each household. Some stem families in Urukawa, however, performed two kinds of the *bon* ritual until recently, one in the same way as in the ordinary household and another in a way similar to the rituals for the deities at the sacred grove or shrine of the cult group. The former was held in the night and the latter in the daytime when the remote ancestors of the cult group are supposed to come and the cult group members attend the ritual and the feast (Mabuchi, this volume, and i.p.).

The atmosphere of the ritual concerned would be certainly reminiscent of the ancestor worship held at the stem family of the patri-kin group in the main island Okinawa. This might suggest that some sort of kinship ideology lingers even sporadically in some other cult groups in the southern Ryukyus. Though we are still far from recognizing such a cult group definitely as a kinship or descent group, the example of Urukawa would suggest a trend toward the formation of ambilineage hand in hand with the systematization of ancestor worship.

Space does not permit us to enter into the details of the situation observed among the Puyuma, southeastern Formosa (see Mabuchi, this volume). As far as general features are concerned, the Puyuman cases resemble those found in the southern part of Miyako Island, above all in some villages where the divinatory affiliation predominates. Institutionally and ideologically, it may be said, the Puyuma incline more to matriliny in contrast with the Miyakoans among whom the trend is more toward patriliny. To a considerable extent, this seems to be reflected in the statistical figures as indicated in the paper mentioned.

## ANCESTOR WORSHIP AND MARITAL RESIDENCE

Leaving aside such an exceptional case as that of a woman who dies unmarried, for instance, the ancestral tablets of the family altar usually represent the deceased in two categories: the males natal to the family and the females married into it. On the other hand, the females natal to the family are expected normally to "marry out" to be worshiped as ancestors in other families. The marital situation in this world is continued in the afterworld, as it were. Accordingly, the husband's parents are worshiped at his family altar, while this is not the case with the wife's parents. In the Ryukyus, the primary locus of ancestor worship is the altar of the "patrilineal family" (Mabuchi, this volume) in which the father-son link is institutionally emphasized from generation to generation and the marital residence is regularly virilocal. The extent to which the "married-in" woman is institutionally assimilated with the husband's family and separated from her natal family seems to be reflected in various ways in local variations. After her death, however, the "married-in" woman is invariably an ancestor of her husband's family, not of her natal family.

It would be interesting to compare such a situation with that of the exogamous patrilineage or patri-clan in which the marital residence is normally virilocal. Here at least theoretically, all the male ancestors are natal to the lineage and all the female ones are those "married into" this lineage from other ones, whereas all the females natal to it are destined to be ancestors of other ones, as illustrated in the diagram just below (Figure 1). Such a situation — perhaps to be called the "paradox of ancestor worship" — is common to both the patrilineal family and the patrilineage.

The patrilineage or patri-clan is agamous in the main island Okinawa where second cousins are permitted to marry each other. Because intermarriage is not rare among the people of the same patri-kin group,

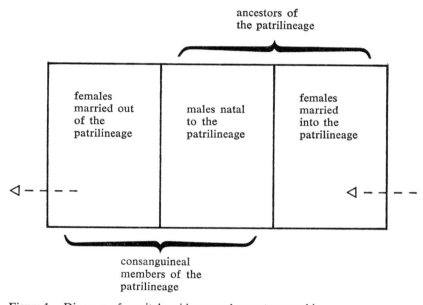

Figure 1.   Diagram of marital residence and ancestor worship

it is impossible to draw straight vertical lines as in the diagram illustrating the situation inherent to the exogamous patrilineage. However, this does not necessarily result in confusion of the "lineality." Even when both the father and the mother belong to the same patri-kin group, it is from the father's side, not from the mother's, that the task of ancestor worship is transmitted to the son who continues the family line along with the obligation of performing the rituals for ancestors.

It is hard to find a purely bilateral system, that is, eventually multilineal. The so-called bilateral system tends often to gravitate more or less toward either the patriliny or the matriliny. On the other hand, it is hardly possible to develop ancestor worship beyond a few generations in a purely bilateral system, because one cannot orient oneself to many kinds of ancestors along many lines. As far as the present writer understands, the term "cognatic" refers to a situation somewhat reminiscent of a pendulum swaying in various degrees between the patriliny and the matriliny. There would be a number of factors which give an impetus to the formation of the patrilineal family. We shall be able here to enumerate some institutional factors relevant to inheritance, succession, and marital residence, along with the obligation of performing ancestor worship which is transmitted successively between generations.

However, something ambivalent seems to be contained in the "patrilineality" of the family concerned. This is derived particularly from the subtle situation of the "married-in" as well as "married-out" women. In the folk religion of the Ryukyus, the sister is believed to have spiritual power mainly to bless or protect her brother and brother's children, irrespective of whether or not she has married out of her natal family (Mabuchi 1964). She seems to exert her spiritual influence not only during her life. After her death, she will be usually one of the "tablet ancestors" at her husband's family and her brother, brother's children and even grandchildren will participate in the rituals celebrating her anniversaries. But, if she dies unmarried or returns to die at her natal house after divorce, she will be often malicious to the family members, as mentioned above. Apart from some local variations with regard to the extent to which the married woman is institutionally assimilated with her husband's family, she seems still to retain certain ritual ties with her natal family. It may be said that her assimilation concerned is completed only after her being deified at the thirty-third anniversary when she loses her personal identity, at least theoretically.

As mentioned above, the ritual relations connecting the "tablet ancestors" and their "descendants" are extended to cover not only the members of the family concerned but also other relatives collateral — thus bilaterally multilineally linked — to the family line, notwithstanding the family's responsibility for the regular rituals for the "tablet ancestors." Beyond this range, however, ancestor worship is extended quite patrilineally, at least in the main island Okinawa.

It is not the place here to trace the process by which ancestor worship in the main island Okinawa came to include the remote ancestors along the male line beyond the ancestral tablet level, side by side with the systematization of patri-kin organization. In its general features, the kinship system in the main island Okinawa seems to indicate an advance from the bilateral to the patrilineal, not only in the field of ancestor worship but also with regard to the trends observed in the way of cohesion in social activities. On the other hand, the kinship system in the southern Ryukyus largely remains bilateral, though the "patrilineality" of the family may possibly provide a basis on which to develop a patrilineage organization. Indeed an approximation to such an organization is observable sporadically in the southern Ryukyus, too, and would suggest some earlier aspects of the patrilineage formation in the main island Okinawa. Meanwhile, the example of the Urukawa village would offer another possibility of an ambilineage formation against the background of ancestor worship.

## REFERENCES

FORTES, MEYER
    1965   "Some reflections on ancestor worship in Africa," in *African systems of thought.* Edited by M. Fortes and G. Dieterlen, 122–144. London: Oxford University Press.

MABUCHI, TOICHI
    1961   "Optional descent in the southern Ryukyus." Paper presented at the Tenth Pacific Science Congress, Honolulu, Hawaii.
    1964   "Spiritual predominance of the sister," in *Ryukyuan culture and society.* Edited by Allan H. Smith, 79–91. Honolulu: University of Hawaii Press.
    1968   "Toward the reconstruction of Ryukyuan cosmology," in *Folk religion and the worldview in the southwestern Pacific.* Edited by N. Matsumoto and T. Mabuchi, 119–140. Tokyo: Keio Institute of Cultural and Linguistic Studies.
    i.p.   "Space and time in Ryukyuan cosmolog," in *Folklore in the modern world.* Edited by Richard M. Dorson. World Anthropology. The Hague: Mouton.

MURDOCK, GEORGE P.
    1960   "Cognatic form of social organization," in *Social structure in Southeast Asia.* Edited by G. P. Murdock, 1–14. Chicago: Quadrangle Books.

# *"Family Religion" in Japan:* Ie *and Its Religious Faith*

C. TAKEDA

The life of the Japanese family has been based religiously and socially upon ancestor worship. This is so because of the unique characteristics of the family system and of the form of ancestor worship that has existed in Japan. The family system, which is generally called *ie*, is the basic unit of Japanese society, and ancestor worship as a traditional and socioreligious institution has developed in close connection with the *ie* system.

*Ie* is a social system based upon one idea of a family. The word *ie* has three meanings: (1) a house or dwelling place, (2) family or home, and (3) lineal kinship or lineage originating from an ancestor and maintained generation after generation by a succession of patriarchs. These three meanings are in fact closely related as shown by the fact that a family — or ANY family — is supposed to have a genealogy of its own and also by the fact that a family LIVES in a house.

A conjugal family normally consists of a husband and a wife and their children. In Figure 1 (ab[cd]), (gh) and (cdef) are three families: they are independent or "nuclear." However, in Japan a family is inconceivable without or apart from some lineage. A family is usually considered as a "dependent" member of a larger entity called an *ie*.

*Ie* may be then best understood as a vertical lineage consisting of member families, living and dead, which are all related by blood lineally and collaterally. Moreover, it is generally believed that *ie* as such exists above and beyond all the members of a family of each generation. One instance of the *ie* lineage is *abcdefgh* in Figure 1. According to the Japanese concept the members together as a whole constitute a certain lineage. They may or may not be living in the same household, but it is possible theoretically for any number of persons or families of the same *ie* lineage to live together. For example, there has been found a case of as many as five generations of a family living in the same household (Figure 2).

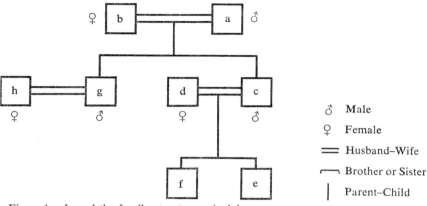

Figure 1.   *Ie* and the family structure principle

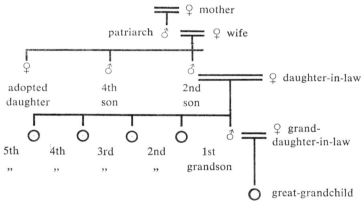

Figure 2.   Example of family structure with many generations (taken from Toda 1937: 478)

The rule of descent that prevails in the *ie* lineage is patrilineal. But exceptions to this rule have been admitted, supposedly to maintain generational continuity and ensure the succession of *ie* without break. This will show that the Japanese *ie* is a matter of lineage itself rather than of blood connection and that the social consideration is always given priority over the biological in maintaining the *ie* lineage.

One example of such exceptions is the custom of bringing in a person who is a total stranger biologically but who will as an heir assume the patriarchal position so that the lineage may not become extinct. In another case, a widow or sometimes a widower who has no children is allowed to assume the patriarchal position, although she (or he) does not constitute a family by herself (or by himself).

In still another case, that is, when all the adult members die and there is no one living to succeed to the patriarchal seat, an infant orphan will be placed temporarily under the care of a different *ie* household. The rationale behind such an arrangement is that this infant orphan will some day, upon reaching the age of maturity, revive his native *ie*.

In a fourth instance, when there is no direct descendant surviving, the possession of the *ie* title, properties, ceremonial tools and the family tomb will be placed under the custody of some trustworthy person who is expected to find a suitable heir in the manner described above.

As the life of a Japanese is inconceivable apart from and without an *ie* — he can prove his place in society only by identifying himself with a certain *ie* lineage — the eternal continuity or eternity of *ie* is a rule or norm for Japanese in general. Once established, an *ie* is supposed to last forever and never to become extinct. It exists even as an immanent entity as the last two examples cited above show.

Lastly, the ancestor is the genesis of this vertical *ie* lineage and the notion of an ancestor worship which is uniquely Japanese has emerged out of this presupposition. It is often pointed out by scholars that it is really the *ie* which is the basis of the ancestor cult in Japan. We shall next turn to the question of ancestor worship in Japan.

In every *ie* there is supposed to be an ancestor or one who founded the lineage. The implication of such a concept of the ancestor for each member family of the *ie* and each person is twofold: ethical and religious. Ethically, everyone of an *ie* is obliged to act in a way worthy of a distinguished lineage. In other words he is never to bring disgrace to the great names of his ancestors. Religiously, it is required of everyone in the *ie* to pay tribute to, and show his respect for, the ancestor. It is important to respect and worship the ancestor not only because he is the founder but also because he is ever concerned about the happiness and welfare of his descendants and has already given them enough protection and security.

Thus the concept of the ancestor as the genesis of the vertical *ie* lineage has existed in the general mentality of the Japanese as a postulate rather than as a fact. There are two other things to be said about ancestor worship in connection with the institution of the *ie*. First, it is not a matter of the individual's choice to accept or reject it. As a member of an *ie* he is bound by the obligations to worship his ancestor. Second, ancestor worship is a matter that concerns a family as a whole; that is, it is a family matter to hold the rites for the ancestors and observe various ceremonies dedicated to them. The concept of the ancestor serves as a postulate for the family as well as the individual.

This is perhaps a good place to discuss the nature of ancestor worship in Japan with a special emphasis on the religious meanings of the Japanese concept of the ancestor.

1.   The ancestor is a spiritual being or exists in spirit. Therefore it is not thought important that he should have human qualities or appear in a human form.

2.   The ancestor is a conglomerate being or a spiritual whole. In other words, it is supposed there is not ONE ancestor but MANY ancestors whose spirits merge into one or conglomerate indistinguishably to form a spiritual whole.

3.   The ancestor exists as a postulate or his existence is presupposed. It is deemed not necessary to have biological data for all the forebears now dead including the one who is supposed to have founded the *ie*. In fact, except in a few cases like the Imperial Family or families of some especially aristocratic lineages, the identity of the founder is not usually known. But this is not considered a serious defect. The important thing is to conceptualize the existence of some being who may be regarded as the founder.

4.   The ancestor is a sacred being. However, as a nameless being, he should be distinguished from the various deities who appear in classical Japanese mythology. The ancestor is nevertheless to be revered; otherwise divine retribution is sure to follow.

There are two more important observations to be made. The first is that the ancestor was often identified with the guardian god of a village or a province, the Rice Spirit, or some other agricultural deity. The reason is not difficult to find. As rice was the staple crop in Japan and as they were devoted agriculturalists, the best thing that the Japanese could expect was a good harvest — of rice in particular. A rich harvest was the sign that the *ie* was in a happy and prosperous state, and it was widely believed that the hands of the benevolent and affectionate ancestors were at work here.

The second observation is that Buddhism, a foreign religion, had greatly influenced the form of ancestor worship. However, this is not so much the influence of Buddhism on the Japanese ancestor worship as the metamorphosis of Buddhism in the course of its interaction with the indigenous folk faith. What really happened was the transformation of Buddhist deities into the ancestors of Japanese families.

Such a transformation was made possible by two factors: the Japanese concept of the ancestor as a sacred being and the latitudinarian nature of Buddhist doctrines. In the course of centuries more and more Buddhist deities were provided with ancestral significance and became a substitute for the ancestors. But this was not the transformation of Buddhism alone. It may be safe to assume that the form of ancestor worship we see today is very different from what it was in ancient times. With so much interaction having taken place between Buddhism and ancestor worship, one cannot conceive the transformation of one without thinking of that of the other.

One instance of the influence of Buddhism is that the ancestor is today constantly referred to as *hotoke*, or Buddha. In the most strict sense of the word *hotoke* means the person who has attained the spiritual awakening (*Nirvana*), but as a general term it means anyone who is dead and his or her spirit. It was natural that the Japanese ancestor, a sacred and spiritual being, was in the course of time identified as a *hotoke*. He was now regarded as the spirit of the dead or an ancestral spirit.

Another instance is the *Bon* (also *Obon*) Festival or the Festival of Lanterns for the Dead. Recent studies have shown that in olden times, before the introduction into Japan of Buddhism and the Chinese calendar, it was a widely held belief that the spirits of the ancestors would return to the family twice a year, once at the night of the full moon at the beginning of spring and the second time at the night of the full moon at the beginning of the fall. Each time special rites were held for the visiting ancestors. It has been pointed out by several scholars that the fall rites have survived in the form of the *Bon* Festival, originally a Buddhist ritual for the souls of the dead; and that the spring rites have survived in the form of the New Year's Festival.

The religious life of the Japanese family is manifest even in the structure of its dwelling place. In other words the Japanese house is built to be best suited for the purposes of observing the rites for the ancestors.

There are five places which are designated as holy and have a special meaning for the members of an *ie* religiously: (1) the family tomb (Plate 1); (2) the *kamidana* Shintoist 'divine shelf' (Plate 2); (3) the *butsudan* Buddhist 'altar' (Plate 3); (4) the *irori* 'heart' (Plate 4); *kamado* or stove (Plate 5). The family tomb is built outdoors; the rest are inside the house (see Figure 3).

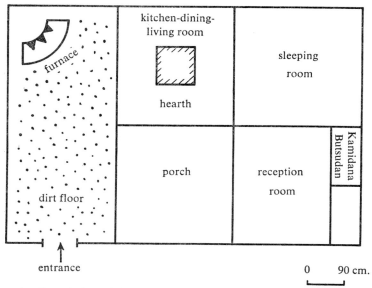

Figure 3.   Sacred places in the Japanese house: a model plan (scale: 1 to 90)

## THE FAMILY TOMB

This is the symbol of *ie* and marks the eternal presence of the spirits of the ancestors. It is not customary to erect a new tomb whenever some-one dies. In most cases there is just one tomb, a family tomb, in which the souls of all the dead members of the family are deified and under which their bodies or cremated bones are buried. In some cases, how-ever, a special tomb will be erected to commemorate the founder or some prominent forebears of the family.

The custom of erecting a family tomb did not become popular until the period 1600 to 1800. Before that time the custom had been either to use the clan or village temple, or to designate some natural object — a rock or tree — as the symbol of ancestral spirits. The mater-ial used is stone; hence the name *sekitō* 'stone tower' given to a typical Japanese family tomb. The *sekitō* is another instance of the Buddhist influence. It has been modeled after the Indian mound or tower (*stupa*) artificially constructed of earth, brick, or stone and containing the sacred relics.

It is interesting to note that on the occasion of the rites for the an-cestor a wooden *stupa* is made and placed beside the stone tower (Plate 6). The wooden *stupa* also marks the presence of the spirits of the an-

Plate 1. Family tomb dedicated to the ancestral spirits of the *Ie* of the Yagis

Plate 2. *Kamidana*, Shintoist 'divine shelf'

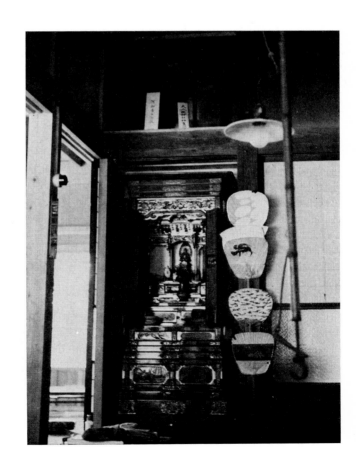

Plate 3. *Butsudan*, Buddhist 'altar'

Plate 4.  *Irori*: in the living-kitchen-dining room

Plate 5.  *Kamado* 'furnace': the roof of the *kamado* at the extreme left serves as the seat of the *Kojin* (Fire Deity) (scale: 1 to 25)

Plate 6.   Wooden *stupas* erected beside the *sekitō* 'stone tower' (scale: 1 to 33)

Plate 7.   *Alternate stupa* for a
fiftieth anniversary (scale: 1 to 20)

Plate 8. *Butsudan* without image of Lord Buddha and with only monumental wooden tablets (scale: 1 to 8)

Plate 9. New Year's ancestral ritual: holy pine tree dedicated to the Rice Spirit (scale: 1 to 15)

cestors, but unlike other objects of ancestor worship it SYMBOLIZES the body of Buddha. However, the use of wood is considered typically Japanese and the indigenous form of ancestor worship is still maintained in this way. On some memorable occasion such as thirty-third or fiftieth anniversary of the death of a person an alternate wooden *stupa* may be erected (Plate 7). This is interpreted as an even clearer manifestation of the form of ancestor worship as it had existed before the introduction of Buddhism into Japan.

## THE *KAMIDANA*, SHINTOIST 'DIVINE SHELF'

Such a divine shelf is found in almost every house in Japan. But it differs according to which deity each family chooses to worship. The most popular one, however, is the guardian god of a village or province.

## THE *BUTSUDAN*, BUDDHIST 'ALTAR'

The fact that there is such a Buddhist altar in the house does not necessarily mean that the family are adherents of the Buddhist faith. Nor is it customary to build a new altar whenever someone of the family is converted to Buddhism. A Buddhist altar is built sometimes when someone of the family dies, but it is not absolutely necessary to do so all the time.

The *butsudan* is essentially an altar dedicated to the ancestors and as such is symbolic of ancestor worship. Therefore it is quite acceptable to build one without a Buddhist image. But the wooden tablet with the name of the dead member of the family written on it is indispensable (Plate 8).

It has been suggested by some scholars that *kamidana* and *butsudan* may be regarded as a miniature shrine and temple respectively. For, although the general practice might have been for several families who were of the same *ie* lineage to hold jointly and as a group the rites for the ancestors — either at a village (clan) shrine or temple — it became no longer possible to do so once the member families were scattered and the clan dissolved. After some time, the custom gradually developed by which each family held the rites for the ancestors separately; and in the meantime a copy was made of the village shrine or temple, which had been the place of worship in old times, in the form of a *kamidana* or *butsudan*. They are both the symbols of ancestral spirits in this sense as well.

## THE *IRORI* 'HEART' AND *KAMADO* 'FURNACE'

According to recent scholarship they were one and the same thing for a long time; that is, before the forms, the positions and functions of the two became differentiated. It is generally assumed that the *kamado* 'stove' which is now mainly used to cook meals grew out of the *irori* 'hearth', which not only has the function of heating the house but also is the place for eating and visiting.

Both *irori* and *kamado* are the symbol of *ie*. For one, the seats around the hearth are specifically as signed to the patriarch, his wife and the rest of the family, and it is imperative that they observe the order. For another, the word *kamado* is used synonymously with *ie* in some areas of Japan. For example, in the Tohoku (northeastern) area, to "split a *kamado*" means to set up a separate family.

The *irori* and *kamado* are not without religious significance. First, at both of these places the Fire Deity (*Kojin*) is enshrined. It is this deity that is supposed to protect the house from fire and other catastrophes. Second, it is customary at New Year to place pine trees, which are considered holy, near these places on top of a straw bag or tub containing newly harvested crops (Plate 9). It has been pointed out that this custom is the remnant of the old ritual of calling into the house the spirits of the ancestors who were identified with the Rice Spirit and various agricultural deities.

From the foregoing discussions it may be concluded that one cannot understand fully the meaning of ancestor worship in Japan, which is the family religion there, without referring to the social and religious significance of the *ie* lineage concept. The *ie* was the social basis of ancestor worship for two reasons: in the first place, it was the basic unit of Japanese society and as such required the existence of the ancestor as a postulate if not as a fact; in the second place, the ancestor of the *ie* was traditionally identified with agricultural deities in general and the Rice Spirit in particular — hence the notion of the ancestor as a spiritual, sacred being.

The influence of foreign religions such as Buddhism is discernible, but in reality these did not alter substantially the unique form of ancestor worship in Japan. It is probable that it underwent some change but, more important still, the foreign religions had to undergo more notable changes when introduced into Japan. Such metamorphosis or transformation was necessary in order for them to be assimilated to Japanese culture. The case of Buddhism will serve as a good example.

The institution of *ie* was so deeply established and ancestor worship was such an integral part of the religious life of the Japanese that when the work of modernizing the country was commenced in the latter half of the nineteenth century, it was deemed wise — and socially more desirable — to keep them intact. Both the *ie* and ancestor worship were recognized as social institutions of long standing, legalized, and various folk customs regarding them were made into law. For example, Article 987 of the Civil Code under the Old Imperial Constitution of 1889 recognized the succession of the patriarchal status and defined the supervision of genealogy, ceremonial tools, and the family tomb as a right attached to such status.

The institution of *ie* is not legalized under the present Civil Code, which was enacted after the Second World War, nor is ancestor worship enforced. But the facts of the *ie* lineage are admitted as shown by the following excerpt from the present Civil Code:

The possession of genealogy, ceremonial tools and the family tomb shall be inherited by the person who, ACCORDING TO THE CUSTOMS OF SOCIETY, will assume the responsibility of SUPERVISING THE RITES FOR THE ANCESTORS. (Article 897; emphasis added.)

## REFERENCES

ARIGA, K.
1943   *Nihon Kazoku Seido to Kosakuseido* [The family system and tenancy system in Japan]. Tokyo: Kawade.
1972   *Nihon no ie* [The family in Japan]. Tokyo: Shibundo.
FUKUSHIMA, M.
1967   *Nihon shihonshugi to "Ie" Seido* [Japanese capitalism and *ie* system]. Tokyo: University of Tokyo Press.
FUKUSHIMA, M., *editor*
1959   *Koseki seido to "Ie" Seido* [Census registration and *ie* system]. Tokyo: University of Tokyo Press.
FUKUSHIMA, M., *compiler*
1959–1967   *"Ie" Seido no Kenkyū* [Study of *ie* system]. Tokyo: University of Tokyo Press.
HORI, I.
1968   *Folk religion in Japan, continuity and change.* Tokyo: University of Tokyo Press.
HOZUMI, N.
1938   *Ancestor-worship and Japanese law.* Tokyo: Hokuseido.
KAWASHIMA, T.
1957   *Ideologi toshitemo Kazoku Seido* [Family system as an ideology]. Tokyo: Iwanami.

KITANO, S., K. OKADA, *editors*
1959   *Ie, so no Kōzō-Bunseki* [*Ie*, an analysis of its structure]. Tokyo: Sobunsha.
OKAWACHI, K., *et al.*
1968   *Ie.* Tokyo: University of Tokyo Press.
TAKEDA, A.
1970   *Ie o meguru Minzoku Kenkyū* [Study of folk customs of *ie*]. Tokyo: Kobundo.
TAKEDA, C.
1957   *Sosen-Suhai, minzoku to rekishi* [Ancestor-worship in Japanese folklore and hisory]. Kyoto: Heirakuji Shoten.
1971   *Minzoku-Bukkyō to Sosen-shinko* [Folk-Buddhism and ancestor-belief in Japan]. Tokyo: University of Tokyo Press.
TAKEDA, C., M. TAKATORI
1957   *Nihonjin no Shinko* [Japanese folk faith]. Osaka: Sogensha.
TAKEUCHI, T.
1969   *Kazoku Seido to Ie Seido* [Family customs and *ie* system]. Tokyo: Koseisha.
TODA, T.
1937   *Kazoku Kōsei* [The structure of the family]. Tokyo: Kobundo.
TSURUMI, S., H. ADACHI
1972   *Ie no Kami* [Deities of *ie*]. Kyoto: Tankosha.
YANAGITA, K.
1946a   *Senzo no Hanashi* [About our ancestors]. Tokyo: Chikuma Shobo.
1946b   *Ie Kandan* [Lectures on *ie*]. Tokyo: Kamakura.

# Recent Trends in Studies of Ancestor Worship in Japan

CHOSHU TAKEDA

## HISTORICAL BACKGROUND

*Ancestor Worship and the Modern Civil Code*

Japan's first modern civil code, based upon a survey of folk practices that had been customary in different regions until then, was enacted in 1898, the thirty-first year of the Meiji era, and was in force until the end of World War II. (Today it is referred to as the old or Meiji civil code.) Various articles in the code explained and firmly decreed that

1.  every family *(kazoku)* must belong to a specific *ie* [a house or house line],
2.  the *ie* is the structural unit of society,
3.  the *ie* itself is the main body for ancestral worship and the main locus for celebrating ancestral rites, and
4.  thus the *ie* (and, therefore, ancestral rites) exists in perpetuity and must never be allowed to lapse.

Because freedom of belief had been guaranteed by the 1889 constitution (now called the old or Meiji constitution, in effect until 1947), the old civil code declared that ancestor worship was not a religion but a matter of national ethics.

The current civil code, enacted after World War II, totally abolished the *ie* system as a legal entity and thus nullified legal controls over ancestor worship. But the institution of the *ie* as a basis for ancestor worship survives widely in social behavior, and the fact that it survives has had to be acknowledged in legal practice.

## Classical Myth and the Imperial Institution

When Japan's classical myths were written down in the Chinese script in the eighth century A.D., political goals, including the idealization and justification for the control of the ancient state by the Imperial House or Imperial Institution loomed large. The main purpose of the myths was to explain the origin of the ruling house. Amaterasu Ōmikami [Sun Goddess] was named as the first ancestor of the Imperial House, and throughout the many years since the mythical age it has been believed that every Emperor, generation after generation, is a direct-line descendant from Amaterasu. Thus the Emperor's political power has been bolstered by religious authority. In the ancient state each of the chief officials surrounding the Imperial House was the head of a powerful clan. The myths designated each of the ancestors of these powerful clans as a *kami* [god], and in the narrative the line of descent begun by each of these *kami* is explained as a form of branching off from the line of the Imperial House.

During the feudal period, in the middle ages, actual political power was held not by the Emperor but by the shogun or military ruler. Nevertheless the shogun had to be appointed by the Emperor to be the supreme military commander and political authority; his position thereby differed from that of a feudal lord in medieval Europe. Emperors were divorced from power but continued to be the wellspring of authority. This is because they were commonly thought to be direct descendants of Amaterasu.

Once Japan had become a modern state under the changes wrought by the Meiji Restoration, the Emperor again held supreme political power, and the Meiji constitution expressly declared his status as the source of all religious authority "sacred and inviolable." The constitution decreed that the Emperor's power to rule was supported and defended by Amaterasu the foundress, by the sanctified Emperors of past generations, and by myriads of other *kami* as well. So the legitimacy of the Emperor's religious authority and of the right to rule based upon it was rooted in the belief that the Emperor was carrying on the line of the ancestral Sun Goddess. Ancestor worship by the Emperor was not his private affair but was a state or official matter. And an ideology, based upon classical myth and regarding the Imperial House and all the people as one great lineage, powerfully controlled politics and education after the Meiji era.

## The Japanese Language and Chinese Script

The early Japanese had a language of their own but had not created a script for it. Chinese graphs were imported into ancient Japan, translated into Japanese, and used for recording the local language. The Chinese graph for ancestor, *tsu* (in modern Japanese, *so*) was translated into ancient Japanese as *oya* [parent]. It seems that in ancient Japanese there was no word that referred only to ancestors; one used the same term for them as for parents. To indicate lineal ascendants other than parents one used the term *tōtsu oya* [parents of older generations]. In general the Japanese vocabulary became markedly enriched by the importation of Chinese words and script. Eventually the Chinese term for ancestors, *hsien-tsu,* which entered the Japanese language as *senzo,* came to be widely used in preference to the native *tōtsu oya.* Honorific prefixes or suffixes commonly are attached to it, e.g. *go-senzo-sama.*

## Kamidana and Butsudan

Except in the apartments of nuclear families composed of only one or two generations that now are located in some housing tracts around large cities, all Japanese homes contain two sacred altars, one to the buddhas *(butsudan)* and one to the native gods *(kamidana).* The *kamidana* enshrines talismans from Amaterasu Ōmikami and from the guardian gods — usually called *ujigami* [clan gods] or *ubusunagami* [birthplace gods] — of the various regions. People go to shrines to receive such talismans, which are also distributed by the local and regional shrine organizations; and in the case of Amaterasu they are distributed by the supreme shrine dedicated to her, the Great Shrine of Ise.

The practice of preserving these talismans arose in the latter half of the feudal period. In terms of the ideology that posits Amaterasu as Imperial Ancestress and the Imperial House as the great head family of the whole nation, the *kamidana* in each home indirectly is a means for that family's ancestral worship. Village and town guardian gods have names of their own, and in the classical myths recorded in the eighth century most of these gods are described as having some sort of connection with the line of descent of the Imperial House.

In the latter half of the feudal era, during the Tokugawa period, the shogunal government *(bakufu)* forced every family to have a *butsudan* and to enroll in a local Buddhist congregation, as a step in the total suppression of Christianity. This meant that families unavoidably were obliged to carry on the worship of their ancestors in Buddhist style. In its external appearance the *butsudan* is an altar to the buddhas and boddhisattvas, but in its essence it is a Buddhist-style altar consecrated to the family's ancestors. The various buddhas and boddhisattvas consecrated in the altar are referred to collectively as *hotoke*, but this word also means "ancestor." Since the latter part of the feudal era, the custom of making grave markers out of stone became widespread in Japan, and these gravestones were called *sekitō* because ancestors were assumed to be synonymous with buddhas. That is, *seki* means "stone"; and *tō* is short for *sotōba*, which is the Japanese version of Sanskrit *stupa*, the sacred grave containing a buddha's remains. The fact that every family gravestone is called a *tō* reflects the idea that what is buried beneath it is a manifestation of the Buddha.

For a home to contain both a *kamidana* and a *butsudan* is an indication that the *ie* is a constituent unit in the structure of society. From the latter part of the feudal age the use of dual altars became conspicuous in association with a developing process of *ie* subdivision and independence. Before that time the stronger tendency was for each family to exist as a subunit within a larger lineage. During that earlier period, it is thought, the *kamidana* and *butsudan* had not yet been separated; but just what form the family altar took then has not yet been made very clear.

## MODERN STUDIES

### Hozumi Nobushige

Ancestor worship is thought to have been widely practiced by the Japanese people long before it was compelled to adopt Buddhist forms under feudal political authority; aboriginally it was a pure folk religion with no relationship to the state or to the Imperial Institution. But with the end of the feudal era and the coming of the modern state, ancestor worship became tied to the Imperial ideology and was written into the constitution and the civil code as a national ethic. In the drastically accelerated modernization of society after the Meiji period, ancestor worship was spread universally among the populace by the power of national law. And so long as the Imperial ideology held sway in government, education, and even in everyday life, is was strictly taboo to make scientific studies of ancestor worship (except for purposes of advocating the ideology) no matter what one's field of scholarship. To question the sacred and inviolable power and authority of the Emperor was absolutely unacceptable.

While the old civil code was still in effect, i.e. until World War II, the most noted study of Japanese ancestor worship was Dr. Hozumi Nobushige's *Ancestor worship and Japanese law* (1917). The original book was based on lectures, which Dr. Hozumi had given in English in 1899 to the International Congress of Orientalists in Rome, and his work already was widely known overseas. In his preface he says he is attempting to clarify, in terms of jurisprudence and sociology, the pervasive influence of ancestor worship on different aspects of modern Japanese law. Dr. Hozumi was Professor of Civil Law at Tokyo Imperial University, and he had played a major role in the drafting of the Meiji civil code.

In his book Dr. Hozumi divides Japanese ancestor worship according to the features shown in Table 1.

Table 1. Features of Japanese ancestor worship (from Hozumi 1917)

| Type of home altar | What is consecrated | Type of ancestral offering |
|---|---|---|
| | talismans of the Imperial Ancestress Amaterasu | (1) offerings by all Japanese to the Imperial Foundress |
| *kamidana* | (a) talismans of the guardians of the area where the family lives: *ujigami* and *ubusunagami* <br> (b) talismans of other gods | (2) offerings by residents of an area to the local guardians |
| | in a Shinto family, *mitamashiro* [tablets to the ancestral spirits of the *1e*] | (3) offerings by every family to its ancestors |
| *butsudan* | in a Buddhist family, *ihai* [mortuary tablets bearing posthumous names of the ancestors of the *1e*] | |

The old civil code decreed that ancestor worship was the national ethic but did not specify whether it should take Shintō or Buddhist form. To decree one form or the other would have run contrary to the freedom of belief guaranteed by the constitution. In actuality, however, ancestor worship was practiced in each home either according to the

Shintō form or according to the Buddhist form. Buddhism has spread far and wide among Oriental peoples, but the mixed form of ancestor worship found in Japan cannot be found among any other national group.

As Dr. Hozumi pointed out, in Japan ancestors may take either the form of *kami* or the form of *hotoke*. This dualism is frequently puzzling to foreign observers. Dr. Hozumi was the first modern scholar in Japan to make the special characteristics of Japanese ancestor worship the major theme of his research and to ground his work in a thorough understanding of Western research and theory on the nature of ancestor worship. He also is thoroughly representative of the scholars of his time in the sense that his understanding of the problem was, after all, under the influence of the Imperial ideology. Furthermore, his studies were not based upon intensive scientific field investigation. This reflects the scholarly standards of the time in Meiji Japan. He was able to some extent to call attention to the surface reality of *kami-hotoke* dualism in Japanese ancestors, but he did not go deep enough to be able to account for the causes or sources of this dualism.

*Yanagita Kunio*

Twentieth-century Japanese folklore science has made remarkable advances toward its goal of reaching a general understanding of the folkways, both mental and material, of Japanese daily life. This is especially true of the work of Yanagita Kunio and his school. They have planned and carried out thoroughly scientific studies and surveys of popular ways of life, based on empirical research on families and villages over long periods of time and covering broad districts and fields of endeavor; and they have been utterly free from the influence of the Imperial ideology and other orthodoxies. As a matter of course Japanese folklore science has considered the practices and ethos of the ancestor worship, which has so fundamentally regulated Japanese ways of life for so many centuries, as one of its central problems. Research by these folklorists has given us the first elements of a scientific explanation of the unique and extremely complex features of ancestor worship, as it is practiced by the ordinary Japanese person. And this is not limited simply to accounting for the sources of the dualism which, as I mentioned, Dr. Hozumi already had pointed out years ago.

Yanagita Kunio's *About our ancestors*, published soon after the end of World War II is the first study of Japanese ancestor worship from the folklorist point of view and may be regarded as representative of it. The book has exerted a guiding influence over the work of many scholars. Examples are Dr. Hori Ichiro's research on folk-beliefs (1951, 1953) and Mogami Kokei's research on the dual grave system (1956). Hori and Mogami have clarified important aspects of ancestor worship, and each is an outstanding disciple of Yanagita.

Japanese ancestor worship was practiced extensively by the populace in many forms independently of the old civil code and long before that code was enacted. Quite a number of records and documents have been preserved in Japan since ancient times, but because ancestor worship as practiced in the ordinary home was such an everyday occurrence, it seldom was described in writing. Thus the topic was long ignored by historiography, which uses written records as its primary source material. Broad scientific inquiry into Japanese ancestor worship and ancestral beliefs did not take place until a folklore science developed that makes unrecorded everyday practices its direct objects of study.

RECENT RESEARCH

The end of World War II brought an end to the taboo, which had been imposed on thought and scholarship since the Meiji era by the Imperial ideology. Japan's government and society were thoroughly democratized, and the *ie* system, which had been the basis for ancestor worship, was legally abolished. Fortunately just at that time Yanagita's book was published. This seems ironic in a sense, but it was in part an expression of the times.

My own study, *Ancestor worship in Japanese folklore and history* (1957), is an attempt to make clear the basis on which Buddhism, which in its doctrines is fundamentally unrelated to ancestor worship, was able to amalgamate with ancestor worship in Japan. In my later *Folk Buddhism and ancestor belief in Japan* (1971), I offered evidence to show that almost all popular Buddhist temples in Japan had been established with the support of the independent ancestral faith, which was latent among the general populace, long before the temples were forced by feudal political authorities to adopt a uniform Buddhist style. In short I demonstrated that these popular temples had originally been established for their funerary functions. My aim was to modify and develop Yanagita's theories by using information from the field studies that I had conducted on village and clan festivals, on funeral customs, on temple functions, and so on. My views on the general nature of ancestral belief have been derived wholesale from Yanagita's work and have been greatly influenced by the studies of Hori and Mogami.

Ancestor worship is a social as well as a religious phenomenon. Sociologist Dr. Maeda Takashi is pursuing a unique investigation, from a sociological point of view, into the patriarchal system, as the societal base from which ancestor worship has emerged in Japan, and into the social influence and background that ancestor worship provides (Maeda 1965).

The late Dr. Moroto Sojun a scholar of religions, investigated classical Chinese ancestor worship from a religious standpoint, drawing mainly on the Chinese Confucian classic *The book of rites* for his source material (see Moroto 1972). But the book contains almost nothing directly related to popular ancestor worship in Japan, and so I omit comment on it here.

## MAIN FEATURES OF JAPANESE ANCESTOR WORSHIP

Seen in terms of recent folklore research, Japanese ancestor worship as an extralegal phenomenon has, in outline, the following chief characteristics:

1. The Japanese popularly believe that ancestors provide an origin for the existence of the *ie*; that through the generations the ancestors have the utmost concern for the family's well-being, and that they provide its greatest protection and security.

2. Thus absolute respect for the ancestors of the *ie* is an ethical imperative binding upon all members of the family. This is utterly different from any specifically religious faith, which is a matter of personal freedom to believe or to disbelieve. In Japan it is held that every religion should conform to this ancestral ethical imperative.

3. Conceptually, ancestors are the wellspring from which the family line derives. In practice, though, they are not seen as being particular deceased persons. Rather, they are thought of as the souls of all family members who have carried on the *ie* generation after generation from its founding to the present, and who have gradually lost their individuality in a common composite image. Spirits of family members retain their uniqueness for a set interval after death, but in time they are sacralized, shed their individuality and the pollution of death, and are assimilated into the collectivity of ancestors of the *ie*. In this sense "ancestor" is a generalizing concept, not a particularizing one.

4. As ultimate guarantors of the family's well-being through the gen-

erations, the ancestors must exist at the root-source of the *ie* line. In this regard "ancestor" is not an existential concept (Being), but a postulate (Having to Be), a conception of an entity that cannot not be. The unique Japanese view of the soul, which I mentioned above, has been nurtured by this sense of ancestors as postulated primal source.

5.    Aside from the Imperial House and some aristocratic families, most Japanese in general do not know the personal name or the origins of the founder of their *ie* line. But in all families the ancestors of the *ie* exist in majesty in people's minds, guarding the lives of their descendants. They are believed to demand reverence from their descendants, and to grow wrathful if not revered.

6.    These postulate ancestors are to be given respect as suprahuman beings, but beyond that there is no absolute requirement that they bear individual names or personalities. The myriad *kami* of Japan, and the buddhas and boddhisattvas of Buddhism, also readily meet these conditions. This is why ancestors easily can change form into *kami* or *hotoke*, and conversely an existing *kami* or *hotoke* easily can come to occupy an ancestral seat. Herein lies the basis of the dualism to which Dr. Hozumi called attention.

7.    Japan's folk culture fundamentally rests on the culture of paddy rice farming, and the well-being of an *ie* is best symbolized by an abundant rice crop. And because it was believed that an abundant crop was a blessing from the gods, the ancestors, the eternal guardians of the security and happiness of the lives of their descendants, frequently were thought of as agricultural gods or as the spirits of cereal crops. Also in Japanese folk belief the mountains have commonly been regarded from very ancient times as sacred abodes for the gods. Because of this, the ancestors in their guises as cereal or agricultural gods were thought to dwell in the mountains from the time the harvest was completed in autumn through the winter, and then to descend into the villages and fields from the beginning of paddy work in the spring through the summer. Thus the sacred ancestral dwelling continued to alternate with the seasons, shifting every half-year from the mountains to the paddies.

Such are the major features of Japanese ancestor worship as they have been brought to light by the recent research of Japanese folklorists.

# REFERENCES

HORI, ICHIRO
1951 *Minkan shinkō* [Folk beliefs]. Tokyo: Iwanami.
1953 *Wagakumi minkan shinkō no Kenkyū* [Studies on the history of Japanese folk beliefs]. Tokyo: Sōgensha.
HOZUMI, NOBUSHIGE
1917 *Sosensaishi to Nippon höritsu.* Tokyo: Yūhikaku. (English edition 1938 *Ancestor worship and Japanese law.* Tokyo: Hokuseidō.)
MAEDA, TAKASHI
1965 *Sosensūhai no Kenkyū* [Studies on ancestor worship]. Tokyo: Aoyama Shōin.
MOGAMI, KOKEI
1956 *Mairibaka* [Homage graves]. Tokyo: Kōkon Shōin.
MOROTO, SOJUN
1972 *Sosensūhai no shūkyōgakuteki Kenkyū* [A religious study of ancestor worship]. Tokyo: Sankibō.
TAKEDA, CHOSHU
1957 *Sosensūhai, mingoku to rekishi* [Ancestor worship in Japanese folklore and history]. Kyoto: Heirakuji Shoten.
1971 *Mingoku-bukkyō to sosenshinkō* [Folk Buddhism and ancestor belief in Japan]. Tokyo: Tokyo University Press.
YANAGITA, KUNIO
1946 *Sengo no hanashi* [About our ancestors]. Tokyo: Chikuma Shobō.

# Ancestor Worship in Japan: Facts and History

TAKASHI MAEDA

## THE RELIGIOUS CONTENT OF ANCESTOR WORSHIP

An "ancestor" is not necessarily a sage or hero, but may be anyone who can be traced genealogically. "Worship" must include the recognition of (the ancestor's) worth and supernatural power. Hence, ancestor worship is different from the "worship" of prophets, magicians, sovereigns, or totems.

Further, the element of love and respect must be greater than that of fear and avoidance, for ancestor worship to arise.

### Funeral Customs

Many customs still in existence partly reveal the attitude of our forefathers to the dead, e.g. *tama-yobai* [calling the soul] is performed among those believing in the indestructibility of the soul, in Japan, China, Southeast Asia, and Africa. For some time after breathing has stopped they try to revive the dead by calling his name, sometimes from the rooftop, or, in some districts in Japan, from the edge of a well. The latter practice may arise from the belief that the next world is underground.

Fear of the dead is still seen in such practices as breaking open a hole in the wall, taking the coffin out through it, then closing it up

This paper is a translation of parts of Maeda's book (1964). It includes an outline of chapters one to three and a detailed translation of chapter four. The work was translated by Christina Naylor, University of Sydney.

again immediately, to prevent the spirit's return. In many places in Japan they make a "temporary gate" of reeds and bamboo, for the coffin to pass under. Even if the spirit returns, it will think its former house has gone, because the gate it passed under has disappeared. Other devices are used in most villages today to confuse the spirit on the way to the graveyard, so that it will not be able to find its way back. In some places they maltreat the corpse, for example, by binding it up very tightly.

However, there are many other customs arising from love and respect for the dead, or from a desire to protect them from evil spirits. *Tsuuya* [passing the night] is very common. People stay by the coffin all night to comfort the spirit. (In former times the spouse or child of the deceased would actually sleep the night on the same mattress as the deceased. Surely this indicates strong love and respect.) Nowadays, *tsuuya* is often finished at 10:00 p.m. But we have seen older people who still practise the old customs.

Some call *tsuuya, hotoke mamori* [guarding the *hotoke*]. This arose from the belief that for some time after death, the corpse may be attacked by evil spirits. Even in the cities, we may also see knives or swords above or near the body, to avert attack. Or on the way to the graveyard, if the coffin suddenly feels heavy, they get the priest to chant sutras with might and main, to ward off the spirits that have made the coffin heavy.

*The World of Ancestral Spirits*

In Japan and many other countries the dead are supposed to be living in the graves, or homes, but at the same time to be going on a long journey. Yanagita Kunio points out that the Buddhist practice of sending off the spirits to some distant place, with the object of attaining buddhahood, is contrary to the long-held Japanese belief that the spirits do not sever relationships with their posterity, but return at stated times during the year to guard them. The "other world" was often thought of as a nearby mountain guarded by the spirits.

Judging by local variations in *bon* (also *Obon*) observance, and the fact that the core of this festival has nothing to do with what is taught in the *Ullambana sutra*,[1] we may assume that the spirit festival predated the advent of Buddhism in Japan.

[1]   This is the sutra offered to the Buddha and priesthood for the benefit of the preta [hungry ghosts]. This sutra was composed in China.

*Urabon* [the festival for greeting and sending off spirits] is a holiday for everybody, to allow people to return to their natal *ie*. Spirits are treated as though still living with the family. The path made for them leads not from the graveyard but from a nearby mountain, their supposed dwelling.

## Ancestral Spirits as Protective Gods, and their Tatari [Curse]

Ancestral spirits, to be worshiped, must be thought to confer positive benefits through their supernatural power. It is not enough to believe they are close at hand.

But should they be neglected, they will in resentment inflict distress and sickness on their posterity. This is called *tatari*. In Takaoka village, Ibaragi Prefecture, if there is a succession of deaths, especially among young people, the villagers will say, "It's because they don't perform the ancestor festivals properly" (Omachi 1951: 85). If disasters continue even after ancestral rites are observed carefully, they are blamed on *muenbotoke* [unrelated spirits, with no descendants to worship them].

## THE SOCIAL BASIS OF ANCESTOR WORSHIP

### Feudal Isolation and Emotionalism

In self-sufficient, isolated communities, people are absorbed into the community, and have a very exclusive attitude to outsiders. Such communities in Japan may call outsiders such names as *nurewaraji* [wet sandals, to be taken off]. Cultural differences are perpetuated, and understanding of others is lacking.

Within the group, there is a much higher degree of intimacy and understanding than is found in ordinary families. So death can hardly turn a friendly relationship into cne of fear and mistrust, nor will enmity be abandoned. As Dr Usui says, "In narrow, isolated societies, . . . objects become known intuitively. . . . Then the memory representation of those objects comes to include all the emotional characteristics of the object actually perceived. So it is very natural that some memory representations of some objects should become endowed with the same intuitive feeling as the actual objects" (n.d.a: 36–44). The same would hold for ancient isolated families. When they remember something, or some ancestor, it is as though it (or he) were actually present. Ancestor worship is very likely to arise in such societies.

But in Japan, distant ancestors are also remembered as *kami*. (This word, used for gods, literally means "above".) This does not happen in primitive societies, but in places like the paddy farms of China and Japan, where families settle for a long time.

## THE SOCIAL INFLUENCE OF ANCESTOR WORSHIP

Ancestor worship greatly reinforced paternal and elder brother authority. The legal position of women was very low, but as soon as a woman gave birth to a male heir, her position changed completely. After death, she could occupy an honored position among the ancestors.

Property inheritance underlined the importance of inheriting the duties of ancestor worship. But how could equal inheritance in China be compatible with the superior position of the eldest son in ancestor worship?

As Shimizu points out (1953: 94) property division was not carried out till after the death of the father. Until then, the sons' families would all have been living together, so they could pass on the ancestral tradition even after the horizontal unity was broken. This is very different from where new families are set up in every generation.

Further, during the T'ang and Ming dynasties it was considered proper not to hasten the division of the property right after the death of the father. During mourning it was forbidden. On the other hand, there was a system under T'ang law, like the Japanese *inkyo* [retirement], whereby the property was divided before the death of the father, who just reserved enough for himself, dividing the rest. Where there was insufficient property for the father, the sons had to support him. After his death, his remaining money was used for ancestral rites.

When the division was finally carried out, they tried to increase the amount of land, so this should have lessened the danger of *ie* collapse.

The Chinese inheritance system was closer to common inheritance than the Japanese system. And despite equal inheritance, the eldest son had greater rights and position. He was often given a small extra portion of the property. This is probably a result of the ancestor worship system.

But in Japan, where the eldest son has the whole burden of maintaining ancestral rites, he receives over half the property.

In our study we asked villagers what they thought of the custom of eldest-son inheritance. Over half were in favor of it, and adding those who thought it was unavoidable, we found 73 percent accepting it (Maeda 1964: Table 9, 190). The justification by 57 percent was "to ensure continuance of the *ie*." Further, younger sons, accepting inheritance by the eldest son, said, "if we divide the property, neither the *honke* nor the *bunke* could continue."

Widows expect only to be looked after by the heir. Those who demand some of the inheritance are ridiculed by the villagers as "strangers" (*mizukusai*).

Most in our study agreed it should be the eldest son who inherits — "just because it's the custom of our village."

The new Civil Code, although it lays down equal inheritance, does not ignore ancestor worship. Clause 899 states that the one who inherits ancestral rite duties also inherits the lineage, the *butsudan* and other things connected with ancestor worship. Some contend that this violates freedom of religion, by indirectly strengthening ancestor worship. (Nakagawa 1949: 6–8). They say that if ancestor worship is not a religion, but based on human nature, then it should be removed from the realm of law.

Those defending the clause say that law is a compromise with reality. Changing it too quickly only causes harm.

## THE DECLINE OF ANCESTOR WORSHIP

### *The Actual State of Ancestor Worship in Japanese Villages*

It was often said by scholars during late Meiji and Taisho (1900–1925) that the first faint signs of the decline of ancestor worship were seen then. But everyone must admit that the decline now is incomparably greater. As it is quite impossible to lay bare all the causes of decline, I shall here inquire into only two or three from the point of view of sociology. First I shall consider what level of belief is held by villagers in Japan, on the basis of material gathered by direct questioning, and arranged according to age and sex.

The materials given below are part of the study conducted under the sponsorship of the Rockefeller Foundation and the Ministry of Education (Japan), by researchers from the Kyoto University Department of Sociology under the direction of Professor Usui. In particular the study of the nine villages is part of the study conducted by Usui during 1958 and 1959, with a research grant from the Ministry of Education. The area for study was divided into agricultural, mountain, and fishing villages among old, "natural" villages, with from 50–60 to 120–130 households. For the first three to four days the villagers were gathered in a hall for group interviews when we enquired into age groups — twenties, thirties, forties, fifties, sixties — then each age group was interviewed for one hour. Below is a general description of each of the nine villages.

HACHIBUSE, ISHIKAWA PREFECTURE, KAWAKITA GUN, UNOKI MACHI, HACHIBUSE BURAKU  Situated in the northern part of the Noto Peninsula, it is about two kilometers east of Unoki railway station. The 75 households are strung out almost in one line between the hills and the low-lying paddy fields. As there is an uphill walk of 1.8 kilometers to the next *buraku*, it is fairly isolated, sometimes in winter it is completely cut off by three or four heavy snowfalls per year.

Ninety-four percent of the households are farming. The others are priests or unemployed. The total arable area is 92 hectares, 72.1 percent of households having over one hectare. Yield averages 7 bales of rice per *tan* (28 bales per acre).

UWADA, TOCHIGI PREFECTURE, KAWAUCHI GUN, KAMIKAWACHI MURA, UWADA BURAKU  Situated 12 kilometers north of Utsunomiya, it has 82 households. In the middle running north is a road 9 feet wide, with 29 *honke*-lineage *ie* on either side. To the north and south of the *buraku*, on the arable land, are scattered clusters of *bunke* and those who have come from outside. There is distance of 1.5 kilometers between the houses on the extreme north and the extreme south, an indication of how extensive is the residential land owned by the *honke*. There are 9 households with over 800 *tsubo* (1.96 acres) of residential land; 19 with over 500 *tsubo* (1.23 acres). About half the farmers own over 2 *cho* (4.9 acres) of arable land; 76 percent own over 2.5 acres. It is said to be the most prosperous *buraku* in old Haguro Mura, which is itself famous in Tochigi Prefecture as a rice-growing area. But 16 percent of the farm households are very poor, having come to the *buraku* after the war. Most of these own less than 5 *tan* (1.23 acres).

SUYE, KUMAMOTO PREFECTURE, KUMA GUN, SUYE MURA  This *buraku* was studied by Embree (1939) before the war, and its general condition is described in detail in *Sengo no Suye mura* [Postwar Suye] edited by Usui (n.d.). Because the number of households in each *buraku* is small, three *buraku* were studied. The village is four kilometers from both Menda and Taragi railway stations. Forty-five of the 75 households (60 percent) are purely agricultural. Over 80 percent are either purely or partly agricultural. Only 12 households manage over five acres of arable land, but people are fairly well off, possibly because over 80 percent of the paddy fields can be harvested twice a year.

YOKOTE, AICHI PREFECTURE, NISHIO SHI, YOKOTE BURAKU    Unlike the previous three *buraku*, this is a "suburban" rural village, along the famous Hekisai railway line, only four kilometers from the center of Nishio City. When one crosses the Yasaku River flowing through the eastern sector of this *buraku*, it becomes Yokosuka Town, with schools, post office, picture theaters, etc. It is only two hours to Nagoya, so there are a lot of commuters. With buses and trains, it is said to be the most progressive *buraku* of the nine we studied. There are 52 households, but no farming household owns many paddy fields. Income is mainly from orchards and cash crops like tomatoes (for the ketchup factory in Yokosuka).

TEBA, TOKUSHIMA PREFECTURE, KAIFU GUN, MUGI MACHI, TEBA ISLAND This island, four kilometers from the mainland of Shikoku, was first settled in 1789, by exiles, and had about ten households at the end of Edo. But through the sharp increase in *bunke* since Meiji, it now has 190 households. But it is very isolated as the only transport is a boat four times per day. Formerly the villagers caught fish by single lines, from one-ton boats, but recently industrial pollution has made fishing nearly impossible. So those of 30–40 years of age leave their families, to fish at other ports. Only the older ones remain to fish (round the island).

HAZAMA, CHIBA PREFECTURE, TATEYAMA SHI, HAZAMA BURAKU    Situated on the southernmost extremity of Boso Peninsula, Hazama has always engaged in fixed-net fishing. There are now 121 households. Before the war the villagers belonged to one or two head fishermen (*amimoto*). After the war they joined a fishermen's cooperative, and are thus relatively prosperous. With abundant fish and a shortage of fishermen, they have 10–20 young men coming in from Iwate each year, between May and October. Each *ie* has 2–3 *tan* (0.5 to 0.74

acres) of dry fields, and a few paddy fields, averaging one *tan* (0.25 acre). But work in the fields is left almost entirely to the women. Paddy field farming has only begun recently. According to the old folk, they used to eat only barley with a little rice, a lot of seaweed and fish, and a few peanuts, etc. These people were once renowned for their longevity, a possible result of this diet.

SHINOHARA, NARA PREFECTURE, YOSHINO GUN, OTO MURA, SHINOHARA BURAKU    Situated nearly in the center of Yoshino Gun, Shinohara is like a lonely island, surrounded on all sides by mountains and still thirteen kilometers from a bus stop. Only a little food can be produced by the 82 households, as the fields are on a slope of 40 degrees. Even the biggest landowner has only nine *tan* (0.9 hectares). No one else has even 5 *tan* (1.23 acres) and 43 percent have just over one *tan* (0.25 acres). At the beginning of Meiji they made a living from making ladles, but since mass production drove them out of business they have eked out a living from timber transportation. Even so, only 4 households have more than 20 hectares of forest land, and only 9 percent have over 5 hectares. The majority are laborers without land.

The *inkyo bunke* [retirement *bunke*] system persists here, and traditionalism is very strong.

OBORA, GIFU PREFECTURE, MASUDA GUN, KOSAKA MACHI, OBORA BURAKU    This mountain *buraku*, now 30 minutes by bus from the Kosaka railway station on the Takayama line, was under early Taisho only accessible from Kosaka by foot, from Kiso Fukushima on the Chuo Line, through Kaneyama and Shimomura, to Obora. At that time their staple diet had to be not rice but millet, deccan grass, and other cereals. It may be for that reason they still use a wooden *hera* [spoon] in place of toilet paper.

Only two households engage in farming only. Nearly half of them own from 0.5 to under one hectare. Thirty percent have less than 0.74 hectares. It was not till 1930–31 that 6 hectares of rice were planted. There is still only one family with over a hectare of paddy field. Half have less than 0.74 hectares. Therefore many are engaged in forestry.

AONE, KANAGAWA PREFECTURE, TSUKUI GUN, TSUKUI MACHI, AONE (FORMERLY AONE MURA)    On the southwest extremity of Tsukui Gun, Aone is adjacent to Doshi Mura in Minami Tsuru Gun, Yamanashi prefecture. To the northwest the Doshi River forms the border. We selected three of the *buraku* in Aone for study. All the 133 households worked in dry field cultivation, forestry, or charcoal burning till the end of Taisho. There were no paddy fields. When buses and trucks for the first time were able to get into Aone in 1947, they brought great changes. Not only younger sons, but nearly all the eldest sons and daughters too, as soon as they had completed middle school, began seeking jobs in Tokyo and Yokohama. Young people's groups came to exist only in name. Further, after the road was widened and private cars could also come and go, it became possible to go and watch night baseball in Tokyo and return the same night, whereas the journey once took two days.

Table 1. Showing numbers in each age group affirming or denying the existence of ancestral spirits in five *buraku* (Hachibuse, Suye, Yokote, Teba, and Aone)[a]

| Age group | Sex | Affirm | Deny | Don't know | Total |
|-----------|-----|--------|------|------------|-------|
| 20's | M | 20 | 18 | 2 | 40 |
| 20's | F | 36 | 12 | 3 | 51 |
| 30's | M | 20 | 18 | 3 | 41 |
| 30's | F | 38 | 8 | 5 | 51 |
| 40's | M | 24 | 12 | 3 | 39 |
| 40's | F | 35 | 6 | 7 | 48 |
| 50's | M | 31 | 5 | 5 | 41 |
| 50's | F | 35 | 1 | 2 | 38 |
| 60's | M | 21 | 4 | 3 | 28 |
| 60's | F | 22 | 5 | 1 | 28 |
| Totals | | 282 | 89 | 34 | 405 |

[a] Table 1 is a summary of Tables 1A–1E in Maeda (1964).

Table 1 indicates to what extent people of these *buraku* still believe in the existence of ancestral spirits, without which there can be no ancestor worship.

In Table 1 are included two purely agricultural villages, and one each of suburban, fishing, and forestry villages. Although there are differences in belief in the existence of ancestral spirits, according to age and sex, in each village the majority did believe in them. In Hachibuse 80 percent did. But in the mountain forest village of Aone hardly any young men in their twenties or thirties did, so it averages out to about half each.

Table 2 gives the average for the nine villages. The most striking feature is the relatively high proportion of those affirming belief, in the three purely rural villages, and the relatively low proportion in the two forestry villages of Obora and Aone.

Table 2. Totals of those affirming and denying the existence of ancestral spirits

| Buraku | Prefecture | Affirm (percent) | Deny (percent) |
|---|---|---|---|
| Hachibuse | Ishikawa | 88.3 | 11.7 |
| Suye | Kumamoto | 85.6 | 14.4 |
| Uwada | Tochigi | 81.1 | 18.9 |
| Shinohara | Nara | 68.6 | 31.4 |
| Teba | Tokushima | 61.9 | 38.1 |
| Hazama | Chiba | 60.6 | 39.4 |
| Obora | Gifu | 59.3 | 40.7 |
| Yokote | Aichi | 56.1 | 43.9 |
| Aone | Kanagawa | 50.1 | 49.9 |
| Average | | 67.9 | 32.1 |

We have observed in a study of over 10 other villages that tradition in weddings, funerals, food and clothing is maintained much more strongly in rural than in mountain villages. Even though Obora and Aone are incomparably more inaccessible than Uwada and Hachibuse, the paddy farmer is much more attached to the soil, and there are more cooperative activities in the village. But in Obora and Aone, subsistence off the land is impossible, and they do not consider 10 to 15 kilometers too far to travel to work. According to our mobility studies there are generally more leaving home to work from mountain villages than from rural ones. It is mostly those who leave home who deny the existence of ancestral spirits. I think this may be why there are fewer believers in mountain villages than in purely agricultural ones. But we cannot generalize too much. For example, Shinohara, although a mountain village, is so cut off, and requires such special skill to cultivate the slopes, that it is very different from other mountain villages developed since the war.

But despite local variations in degree of belief, the concept of immortality of the soul is still generally evident in different annual events and customs in rural villages. Offerings and prayers to ancestral spirits for worldly blessings, and fear of *tatari* are obvious examples.

Table 3 shows the degree to which these beliefs are held. The ques-

Table 3. "Will the *ie* decline if the ancestors are neglected?" (Nishi Ashida)

| Age group | Think so (percent) | | Think not (percent) | | Total |
|---|---|---|---|---|---|
| 20's | 7 | 41.2 | 10 | 58.8 | 17 |
| 30's | 13 | 68.4 | 6 | 31.6 | 19 |
| 40's | 14 | 63.6 | 8 | 36.4 | 22 |
| 50's | 12 | 63.1 | 7 | 36.9 | 19 |
| 60's | 9 | 64.3 | 5 | 35.7 | 14 |
| Total | 55 | 60.4% | 36 | 39.6% | 91 |

tion asked was: "Will the *ie* decline if the ancestors are neglected?" Study locality was Nishi Ashida Buraku in Aogaki Machi, Hikami Gun, Hyogo Prefecture. It is a typical flat-land agricultural village.

As the table shows, most people in their twenties do not believe in *tatari*. From the thirties up, 60 percent or more do believe that the *ie* will decline if offerings are neglected. When sickness continues for some time, the villagers, believing the ancestors have been neglected, will often purify the *butsudan*, be diligent about morning and evening ritual, tidy the graves and call in the priest to chant. But should good health and fortune continue for some time, many will pay deep thanks to the ancestors, as may be seen from Table 4 (analysis of Uwada

Table 4. Beliefs about indebtedness to gods and buddhas (Uwada Buraku)

| Age | Sex | 1ᵃ | percent | 2 | percent | 3 | percent | 4 | percent | Don't know | percent | Total |
|---|---|---|---|---|---|---|---|---|---|---|---|---|
| 20's | M | 1 | 11.1 | 4 | 44.4 | 1 | 11.1 | – | | 3 | 33.4 | 9 |
| 20's | F | 2 | 20.0 | 5 | 50.0 | – | | 1 | 10.0 | 2 | 20.0 | 10 |
| 30's | M | 1 | 16.6 | 2 | 33.4 | 2 | 33.4 | 1 | 16.6 | – | | 6 |
| 30's | F | 1 | 10.0 | 7 | 70.0 | 1 | 10.0 | – | | 1 | 10.0 | 10 |
| 40's | M | – | | 5 | 55.5 | 1 | 11.1 | 3 | 33.4 | – | | 9 |
| 40's | F | 1 | 25.0 | 3 | 75.0 | – | | – | | – | | 4 |
| 50's | M | 1 | 14.3 | 4 | 57.1 | – | | – | | 2 | 28.6 | 7 |
| 50's | F | 1 | 20.0 | 4 | 80.0 | – | | – | | – | | 5 |
| 60's | M | 2 | 33.3 | 4 | 66.7 | – | | – | | – | | 6 |
| 60's | F | 2 | 25.0 | 5 | 62.5 | – | | – | | 1 | 12.5 | 8 |
| Total | | 12 | 16.2 | 43 | 58.3 | 5 | 6.7 | 5 | 6.7 | 9 | 12.1 | 74 |

ᵃ 1 "I believe all is due to the gods and buddhas."
  2 "I am grateful to the gods and buddhas."
  3 "I believe gods and buddhas exist but do not feel especially indebted to them."
  4 "Gods and buddhas do not exist."

Buraku in Tochigi Prefecture). Here, 75 percent "believe that all is due to the kindness of the gods and buddhas."

What is the meaning of the words *hotoke* [buddha] and *kami* [gods]? Takeda Choshu explains why the dead are called *hotoke* (a word derived from imported buddhism) in the following way.

The final goal of buddhism is the repose of the individual soul. It has nothing to do with ancestral spirits or the *ie*, being an individualistic religion. It is really contrary to the *ie* concept (Takeda 1957: 241). But this is a purely superficial difficulty, and Japanese religion has always been influenced by buddhism in various ways. Although Nirvana had originally nothing to do with physical death, ordinary people, finding the doctrine of Nirvana difficult, likened it to physical death. So from the idea that those who have entered Nirvana are *hotoke*, all the dead were called buddhas, regardless of whether the persons had any affiliation with buddhism during their lifetime, and regardless of their character (Takeda 1957: 232).

Suzuki Eitaro states:

"It is no exaggeration to say that by joining itself to ancestor worship, buddhism became thoroughly Japanized and popularized, and was able to dominate people's hearts for a long time. One may say that today's buddhism cannot be anything more than ancestor worship. Shinto also, although it has left the popular customs of ancestor worship to buddhism, was originally mainly an ancestor-worshipping faith" (1941: 264).

Buddhism, which is deficient in concepts about the dead, was unable to change Japan's peculiar belief that deceased ancestors still live as before with their families. Rather, buddhism adapted itself to the native belief, and had its content changed by it, e.g. the Urabon memorial service was originally meant to send the departed spirits on to Nirvana, but in Japan it became one to welcome them back.

Further, yearly memorial services were first instituted in Japan, as were other customs quite beyond explanation in (purely) buddhist theory (Usui n.d.b: 26).

Europeans and Americans find it very strange that Japanese villagers have a quite different attitude to priests and religionists, that some consider buddhism as merely a means of worshiping their ancestors, and that the priests also make their living through visits to the ancestors by the *danka* (Beardsley, et al. 1959: 447).

This can further be said of the *butsudan* [ancestral shelf] in any home, which is a variation on the Indian and Chinese ancestor shelves. Although it is normal in Japanese villages to have a picture or statue of the buddha in the centre, and *ihai* [ancestral tablets] to the left and right of this, many have *ihai* only, with no statues. This is because, to the villagers, the ancestors themselves are the *hotoke*. So it is not the existence of buddhas, but of ancestors that occasions the setting up of a *butsudan*. This is illustrated by the frequent comment "We have no *butsudan* because we have no *ihai* as yet."

There are variations in the size and shape of *butsudan* according to sect, type of village (agricultural, forestry, or fishing), social class, and religious zeal. Some may be content with something one *shaku* [one foot, or 30 centimeters] square. Others may be six feet (1.82

meters) high. There are some big *butsudan* that are seen to occupy the whole Buddha chapel.

Some may specially select the materials and have the *butsudan* made and decorated to order, spending tens of thousands of yen. But in the 20-odd villages we studied, we found the more showy ones were in the agricultural villages. People were often proud to show off *butsudan* much too grand for the household's economic condition. Building splendid *butsudan* and tombs is thought to be one way of taking great care of the ancestors.

Further, we who stayed in Suye and Hachibuse were able to witness religious families gathering before breakfast each morning to burn incense, while the head of the house chanted a simple sutra passage. In Hazama (Chiba Prefecture) and other places it was considered only proper to first offer the freshly cooked rice to the ancestors each morning, and in the evening to also light lamps and burn incense and read a simple passage, then clap hands and close eyes. On the other hand, there were two or three villages where not even one person sat before the Buddha.

Table 5. Degree to which ancestor worship is practised (in the same five *buraku* as Table 1)

| Age group | Sex | Worship daily | Worship sometimes | Worship on special days | Never worship | Total |
|---|---|---|---|---|---|---|
| 20's | M | 9 | 10 | 7 | 14 | 40 |
| 20's | F | 19 | 11 | 12 | 9 | 51 |
| 30's | M | 7 | 14 | 10 | 10 | 41 |
| 30's | F | 32 | 10 | 6 | 3 | 51 |
| 40's | M | 16 | 7 | 13 | 3 | 39 |
| 40's | F | 27 | 13 | 5 | 3 | 48 |
| 50's | M | 20 | 9 | 7 | 5 | 41 |
| 50's | F | 29 | 4 | 1 | 1 | 35 |
| 60's | M | 14 | 6 | 6 | 2 | 28 |
| 60's | F | 21 | 7 | | | 28 |
| Totals | | 194 | 91 | 67 | 50 | 402 |

Table 5 shows whether people worship the *ihai* daily, sometimes, or only on special days and memorials. The most striking feature is the difference according to age. This is also plain in Table 6.

of those in their 20's,   20 percent worshiped daily
of those in their 30's,   30 percent worshiped daily
of those in their 40's,   40 percent worshiped daily

of those in their 50's,    50 percent worshiped daily
of those in their 60's,    60 percent worshiped daily

Table 6.    Percentage in each village worshiping *ihai* daily and always bowing to *ujigami*

|            | 20's | 30's | 40's | 50's | 60's |
|------------|------|------|------|------|------|
| Suye       | 58.0 | 58.3 | 83.4 | 80.2 | 100.0 |
| Hachibuse  | 33.3 | 43.7 | 46.7 | 85.7 | 70.0 |
| Yokote     | 21.7 | 45.0 | 46.1 | 71.2 | 66.6 |
| Teba       | 25.0 | 68.2 | 59.2 | 62.0 | 75.0 |
| Hazama     | 50.0 | 44.4 | 72.6 | 76.8 | 100.0 |
| Mera       | 54.5 | 45.0 | 65.6 | 61.1 | 72.2 |
| Obora      | 25.0 | 24.0 | 46.6 | 57.2 | 75.0 |
| Shinohara  | 5.8  | 23.8 | 37.5 | 33.3 | 66.7 |
| Aone       | 25.0 | 4.5  | 10.1 | 20.0 | 37.4 |
| Okamibuchi | 0.0  | 5.0  | 22.5 | 45.6 | 22.2 |
| Average    | 29.8 | 36.2 | 49.0 | 59.3 | 68.5 |

In some villages, 100 percent of those in their sixties worshiped daily. Will the same correlation prevail in the future? This is very difficult to calculate, but at least one can hardly expect more than twenty-to-thirty percent of the present generation of twenty-to-thirty-year-olds to be worshiping *ihai* each day by the time they reach sixty. There are various reasons for thinking this. For instance, young people, especially young wives, are too busy with children and business to sit quietly. Hence they neglect the *butsudan*. Further, young people often have hale and hearty grandparents, but have never known any of the deceased ancestors. So compared with older people who have lost immediate relatives, they have little inclination to worship the *ihai*. They leave it to the family representative to make the offerings. In Uwada, Tochigi Prefecture, where we asked "Does someone invariably worship the *ihai*?", it was plain that nearly always a grandparent did. But only 4.8 percent of families said they did not always make offerings each morning. It is easy to think, from other materials gathered, that had we asked the same question in the other villages, we would have found that in most homes some person every day made offerings. But had we made this study in the cities, we would probably have found that most do not. But this is only surmise.

Table 7 indicates the great differences in depth of belief. The left side of the table shows in 21 *buraku* the percentage in two broad age groups (20–49 and 50–69) of those worshiping the *ihai* daily. The average is 33 percent for the younger, but 56.6 percent for the older group.

Table 7.   Differences in depth of belief

| | Percentage worshiping ancestral *ihai* daily | | Percentage never worshiping | | |
|---|---|---|---|---|---|
| | Age 20–49 years | Age 50–69 years | Age 20–49 years | Age 50–69 years | Number of interviewees |
| Suye | 65.2 | 100 | 6.1 | 0.0 | 69 |
| Hachibuse | 41.2 | 75.0 | 11.7 | 0.0 | 77 |
| Teba | 52.8 | 65.6 | 10.9 | 9.4 | 89 |
| Aone | 20.0 | 28.1 | 34.6 | 15.6 | 88 |
| Hyaro | 1.8 | 24.0 | 27.7 | 4.0 | 91 |
| Hashigami | 11.9 | 44.2 | 31.3 | 5.9 | 105 |
| Hotta | 33.3 | 63.6 | 54.4 | 22.7 | 85 |
| Hinoemata | 18.6 | 50.0 | 25.6 | 11.1 | 49 |
| Mera | 22.8 | 51.2 | 21.4 | 10.8 | 56 |
| Ozakai | 13.9 | 25.8 | 11.1 | 16.1 | 58 |
| Obora | 29.4 | 63.6 | 7.3 | 0.0 | 90 |
| Kajika | 43.1 | 50.0 | 18.9 | 27.2 | 80 |
| Shinohara | 25.6 | 42.9 | 15.4 | 4.7 | 60 |
| Nishi Ashida | 32.8 | 67.5 | 15.7 | 2.5 | 110 |
| Natsudomari | 17.3 | 50.0 | 28.8 | 3.5 | 78 |
| Mitabe | 26.4 | 43.6 | 20.6 | 6.2 | 50 |
| Okamibuchi | 21.7 | 51.9 | 25.0 | 5.2 | 79 |
| Momoki | 49.8 | 87.0 | 32.7 | 4.3 | 77 |
| Hetsuka | 47.9 | 64.6 | 18.7 | 9.7 | 100 |
| Ibarajima | 30.0 | 62.0 | 36.6 | 3.4 | 90 |
| Mukasa | 67.2 | 90.0 | 0.0 | 0.0 | 97 |
| Average | 32.0 | 57.5 | 21.6 | 7.7 | 80 |

Table 8.   Differences in those bowing to *ujigami*

| | Percentage always bowing before *ujigami* | | Percentage never bowing before *ujigami* | | |
|---|---|---|---|---|---|
| | Age 20–49 years | Age 50–69 years | Age 20–49 years | Age 50–69 years | Number of interviewees |
| Suye | 67.4 | 85.0 | 2.0 | 5.0 | 69 |
| Hachibuse | 40.4 | 80.0 | 9.6 | 0.0 | 77 |
| Teba | 40.4 | 80.0 | 9.6 | 0.0 | 89 |
| Aone | 8.7 | 29.0 | 31.7 | 9.7 | 88 |
| Hyoro | 12.5 | 52.0 | 19.6 | 8.0 | 91 |
| Hashigami | 21.7 | 27.8 | 29.0 | 0.0 | 105 |
| Hotta | 41.2 | 59.0 | 9.5 | 4.6 | 85 |
| Hinoemata | 39.4 | 68.8 | 9.1 | 0.0 | 49 |
| Mera | 50.0 | 52.8 | 16.6 | 10.0 | 56 |
| Ozakai | 15.6 | 30.8 | 12.5 | 19.2 | 58 |
| Obora | 29.4 | 63.5 | 7.3 | 0.0 | 90 |
| Kajika | 43.1 | 50.0 | 18.9 | 27.3 | 80 |
| Shinohara | 25.6 | 42.9 | 15.3 | 4.7 | 60 |

Table 8.  (Continued)

| Nishi Ashida | 32.8 | 67.5 | 15.7 | 2.5 | 110 |
|---|---|---|---|---|---|
| Natsudomari | 14.0 | 50.0 | 30.0 | 3.5 | 78 |
| Mitabe | 26.5 | 43.7 | 20.6 | 6.2 | 50 |
| Okamibuchi | 11.6 | 26.3 | 16.6 | 5.2 | 79 |
| Momoki | 32.7 | 40.9 | 14.5 | 0.0 | 77 |
| Hetsuka | 59.4 | 90.4 | 8.7 | 3.2 | 100 |
| Ibarajima | 13.5 | 58.1 | 15.3 | 6.4 | 90 |
| Mukasa | 67.1 | 90.0 | 1.5 | 0.0 | 97 |
| Average | 33.0 | 56.6 | 14.9 | 5.5 | 80 |

Table 9.  List of prefectures and *gun* of *buraku* not previously listed

| Buraku | Prefecture | Gun (or shi) |
|---|---|---|
| Hyoro | Aomori | Higashi Tsugan |
| Hashigami | Iwate | Kokonohe |
| Hotta | Akita | Senboku |
| Hinoemata | Fukushima | Minami Aizu |
| Ozakai | Tomiyama | Nagami (*shi*) |
| Kajika | Mie | Owase (*shi*) |
| Natsudomari | Tottori | Ketaka |
| Mitabe | Shimane | Chiburu |
| Momoki | Kumamoto | Yatsuhiro |
| Hetsuka | Kagoshima | Kimotsuki |
| Ibarajima | Niigata | Higashi Kambara |
| Mukasa | Fukui | Mikata |

The left side of Table 8 shows for the same two groups how many always bow when they pass the *ujigami*. Again the average for the younger group was about 30 percent, and 57.5 percent for the older.

I cannot think that mere business or remoteness from ancestors can adequately explain this difference. Surely it must be difference in belief. It is noteworthy that there are some religious groups which attract more young believers than old. But as ancestor worship is tied to the conservative *ie* system, the older ones are more likely to adhere to it, even though the proportions vary according to locality and social class.

We can gain some idea of this difference in attitude to tradition by the following "spontaneous study." (This is a study of responses made without reflection. Such responses are seen most typically among primitive peoples, to whom all things have been as they are now long before they were themselves born. In such completely traditional societies there is hardly any criticism of tradition, as they unconsciously maintain it.)

Before we conducted our research, we studied the folk traditions of each village, then during the interviewing sessions, asked questions of a random sample of interviewees.

In Mazaki (Mie Prefecture, whose residents are mainly engaged in pearl culture, there is a saying: "It is bad to go out into the soybean fields after *hangeshō* [11th day after summer solstice]." Why? "If you do, a priest will appear, people will be drawn after him and finally die."

Table 10 divides people into those who know this and those who do not, then further into those who believe it and those who do not. If we include those who "do not believe, but still worry about it," 90 percent of those in their fifties and sixties believe, but only 22 percent in their twenties and thirties do. This correlates with the proportions of those not believing in the existence of ancestral spirits (Maeda 1964: Table 2, 169). Thirty-two percent denied their existence (27.2 percent in the 20 villages not tabulated), but only 10 percent did not worship them. If we compare Tables 1 and 2 we find that in Teba Island, whereas 44.1 percent in their twenties and thirties denied the existence of ancestral spirits, only 14.7 percent said they did not worship them.

Table 10. Those believing the saying that it is bad to go out into soybean fields on *hangeshō* (11th day after summer solstice)

| Age | Sex | Indifferent | Believe so | Not believe, but worry | Not believe | Not know saying | Total |
|-----|-----|-------------|-----------|------------------------|-------------|-----------------|-------|
| 20's | M | 2 | 2 | 3 | 2 | 4 | 13 |
|      | F | 1 | 2 | 4 | 6 | – | 13 |
| 30's | M | – | 2 | 3 | 6 | 1 | 12 |
|      | F | – | 5 | 3 | 2 | 1 | 11 |
| 40's | M | – | 2 | 1 | 2 | 1 | 6 |
|      | F | – | 6 | 2 | 2 | – | 10 |
| 50's | M | – | 2 | – | 1 | – | 3 |
|      | F | – | 6 | – | 0 | – | 6 |
| 60's | M | – | 1 | 2 | 1 | – | 4 |
|      | F | – | 6 | 2 | – | – | 8 |
| Total |  | 3 | 34 | 20 | 22 | 7 | 86 |
| Percent |  | (3.5%) | (39.5%) | (23.3%) | (25.67%) | (8.1%) |  |

One young man gave this reason for the discrepancy: not to participate in morning worship or village rites meant becoming a social outcast, and inviting scorn and criticism.

However, few even among the young men were able to give such a clear answer. Those that did had usually experienced city life during their childhood, then been forced to return to the village by evacuation and defeat in war. Most of the others, even though they tried to give a rational answer to our questions about the existence of ancestral spirits, were, on the emotional level, incapable of standing before the ancestral tablets without joining hands, or of passing the graves without bowing. So the results of the interviews, which demanded clear-cut answers, cannot be expected to correlate too closely with actual conduct.

A similar discrepancy is seen in attitudes to inheritance (see Table 11). While only 19.5 percent of the youths we questioned opposed equal inheritance as required under the new constitution, only one to two percent had actually divided it equally.

Table 11.   Opinion on inheritance by eldest son only (in percent)

|  | Good | Cannot be helped | Not good | Don't know |
|---|---|---|---|---|
| Hachibuse | 76.1 | 15.9 | 1.3 | 6.7 |
| Suye | 62.7 | 17.4 | 11.4 | 8.5 |
| Teba | 70.0 | 10.3 | 14.9 | 4.8 |
| Mera | 55.3 | 20.3 | 18.6 | 5.8 |
| Hazama | 61.5 | 20.0 | 7.7 | 10.8 |
| Yokote | 68.9 | 13.0 | 10.4 | 7.7 |
| Okamibuchi | 54.2 | 22.7 | 16.8 | 6.3 |
| Obora | 49.0 | 24.4 | 22.2 | 4.4 |
| Aone | 44.3 | 26.1 | 19.4 | 10.2 |
| Shinohara | 16.9 | 3.0 | 72.5 | 7.6 |
| Average | 55.9 | 17.3 | 19.5 | 7.3 |

Similarly, many youth groups call on the villagers to cut down on wedding expenses. Yet the leaders of these groups often do what they condemned, when they themselves marry.

The reason for such discrepancies is probably that the new ways of thinking have not grown spontaneously from their way of life, but have been imported from outside cultures. Hence, although they show quite a degree of intellectual understanding, their personalities, nurtured in a conservative environment, still direct them towards village tradition. Yet the steady decline in ancestor worship among younger people, and the very discrepancy between thought and action, could not have taken place without some liberation of the *buraku* itself.

So in the following section I wish to look at the decline of ancestor worship again.

## VARIOUS CONDITIONS AFFECTING DECLINE

In ancient Rome, the position of women was raised during the Punic Wars, as the absence of men brought women into public office. Contrary to expectations, they remained in office after the men returned. Cato's saying, "We have been dominated by women since the war," recalls the postwar Japanese quip, "Since the war, women and socks have become stronger."

This has contributed to the decline in patriarchal authority, which is part of the basis of ancestor worship.

Despotism by elders has also been undermined in China and Japan by the development of modern capitalism. However, in China the old family and religious life were not affected much as long as agriculture remained the mainstay of the economy.

But the revolution of 1911–1913 brought great change, from a static to a mobile society. Politically, Western-type law overturned the family system from the roots, and dealt a heavy blow to paternal authority. The law completely ignored ancestor worship, the mainstay of the clan system. New government schools with vernacular textbooks and scientific subjects despised the Confucian system. Villages were gradually freed and lost their self-sufficiency. In people's houses, new lamps and factory-made cloth and bicycles mingled with things handed down from the ancestors (Lang 1946: 71–74). As in Japan, this not only destroyed the self-sufficiency of the village, but drove villagers as laborers to factories in the towns. When they returned home, they brought with them some of the life-style of the towns, which gradually spread among the villagers.

Use of machinery made it possible for women also to work in

Table 12. Family size (in Uwada)

|  | Number of households | Number of people | Number of family members (average) |
|---|---|---|---|
| 1873 | 35 | 278 | 7.9 |
| 1907 | 47 | 377 | 8.2 |
| 1910 | 50 | 409 | 8.0 |
| 1925 | 61 | 439 | 7.1 |
| 1930 | 57 | 440 | 7.7 |
| 1953 | 82 | 568 | 6.9 |
| 1956 | 81 | 553 | 6.8 |

factories, raising the question of their liberation, and entry into politics. As in Japan, the pattern and size of families were also affected.

Fewer maintained the patriarchal extended family of over three generations, and numbers in the family declined (see Table 12).

Decline in the formerly absolute authority of elders most directly contributed to the decline of ancestor worship. Lang says: "This is because in a mobile society the experience of elders has gradually become useless and harmful, not only in industry but even in agriculture."

In Japan, it was the Meiji Restoration, bringing the destruction of feudalism, that is said to have started the decline of ancestor worship. Capitalism, and defeat in war, accelerated the decline. But why?

Under feudalism, life was very restricted. Travel was restricted. Peasants were absolutely tied to the land, especially by the *danka* system. Division of land and long-term buying and selling of land were forbidden or restricted, making expansion impossible.

Further restrictions were placed on peasants from time to time; e.g. in 1649, they were forbidden to buy sake or tea, or to eat rice. Only plain cotton or linen clothes could be worn. *Tokonoma* [ornamental alcoves] and other ornaments were not allowed in their houses. (Ono n.d.: 132.)

The Restoration abolished the class system, and allowed freedom of occupation, travel, and buying and selling of land. Movement throughout the country was made easy by a uniform currency. Conscription brought the collapse of paternal authority, and also brought the young boys out of their feudal enclave for a while.

Table 13.   Form of *Kazoku* (in Uwada)

| | Number of households | |
|---|---|---|
| | 1873 | 1956 |
| *Dōzoku* | 8 (23%) | 2 (2%) |
| Direct lineage *kazoku* | 22 (63%) | 50 (62%) |
| Modern small *kazoku* | 4 (11%) | 28 (35%) |
| One person | 1 (3%) | 1 (1%) |
| Total | 35 | 81 |

Then the need to withstand Western capitalism spurred on great economic development. Rail, road, and telegraph brought remote villages within reach of the cities, for trade and pleasure. Mass-produced articles were sold cheaply to villagers, who made up 80 percent of the population, thus destroying their economic self-sufficiency and causing them to sell their labor to buy the goods.

For instance, in Uwada, Tochigi Prefecture, farmers who had previously kept rice for their own consumption would load two bales of rice on a horse each day during autumn and winter, and set out at 7 A.M. to sell it in Utsunomiya, four kilometers away. They would return with fertilizer, or perhaps farm implements, looms, thread, sugar, soy sauce, salt, or sake, etc. But to buy these things they often had to borrow at ruinous interest. So if they heard that rice was getting a better price in Nikko, they would not grudge the double distance to take it there.

The same sort of thing happened in forestry villages, such as Shinohara, Nara Prefecture. The money economy invaded this village from the beginning. When they had made about 300 ladles, they would travel three days each way, two or three times each month, to Shimoichi, to sell them. But to use their expression, they "exchanged a mountain for a bale of rice" (because of poor selling prices).

The resultant drift to the cities to find work meant that people in their twenties and thirties are hardly seen in villages now, although the census shows these people are far more numerous than those in their forties and fifties.

Japan was ten years ahead of China in the liberation of women. Coming into a larger world, and coming to understand the broad principles underlying it, women began to develop a more rational attitude. Then the Second World War destroyed, for a time, the traditional discrimination between the sexes, as did the Punic Wars in ancient Rome. Although many men returned to their jobs after the war and women retreated once more to their homes, the old attitude of submission was less prevalent.

The new constitution also gave equal legal rights to women. In particular, a woman who married into another *ie* can now inherit an equal share of her natal *ie* property. If this becomes widespread in practice, the *ie* spirit and property will become impoverished, losing its supraindividual character. This will accentuate the decline of ancestor worship.

The authority of elders has been further undermined by education. Under recent educational reform, several administrative villages have joined to manage middle schools, and pupils must now travel greater distances to school. For instance, the school at Teba has closed, and pupils go by ferry each day to the Shikoku mainland. The great widening of the sphere of acquaintances undoubtedly is having a liberating effect. Furthermore, the school and society at large are now having a much greater part in education than the elders have.

According to Lang, open confrontation between father and son, never seen in old China, is now gradually appearing. Still, the authority of the father in the countryside is still strong, despite the decline in his economic importance. But this is not so in modernized parts. For example, among Shanghai laborers, there is not one family where an old man is recognized as family head, if he is not working. Further, even if the father still holds all the authority in the home, it is not as easy for him as before to exert his authority over his grown-up sons.

The law also restricted the rights of the father, both in China and Japan. In China he lost the right to kill his children without punishment, or to choose their marriage partners. In Japan, under Meiji law, children were in theory no longer regarded as the property of their parents. The *nenki* [period of service] of apprentices was limited, and it was forbidden to let them be maltreated at the whim of their masters.

Further, Meiji law laid down equal inheritance of property not belonging to the household head. Marriage was held to be a contract between the partners themselves, requiring only the agreement of the father, and that only when the man was under 30 and the woman under 25. This was a great leap forward, in comparison with the previous rule disallowing marriage without the consent of the parents.

Patriarchal rights were still recognized under Meiji law as household head rights and parental rights, but discrepancies arose with the increase in nuclear families. With the new constitution in 1948, patriarchal rights disappeared completely, along with the *ie*, household head rights and inheritance of *ie* supervision. Further, marriage by adults is permitted without any consent or agreement by the father.

Decline in ancestor worship was inevitable with the decline in authority of the patriarch. This authority, which was based on great affection and superiority, lessened with the decline in mutual love and understanding of the family members.

Lang reports that in China, of 305 persons interviewed in Peking, Shanghai and Wu Shih, 35 reported that they did not conduct ancestor worship in their homes. This would indicate a much greater decline in ancestor worship than in Japan, for they did not even have *ihai* in their homes. But she does not assert that all those who have abandoned worship claim it is irrational. There were not only buddhists but worshipers of other gods in her survey. Further she says that of 52 upper-class families interviewed in Peking and Shanghai, 10 had no ancestral rites. But of these, the heads of six were university professors and the other four were Christian. Further, in villages like those in our survey, it was also the twenty to forty year-olds whose ancestral faith was weakest.

The complete disappearance of ancestor worship in Japan was doubtless delayed by the prewar state and the emperor system. But state authority alone cannot explain its continuance, which lies more in the spontaneous attitude of villagers, more than half of whom still actively engage in it.

## REFERENCES

BEARDSLEY, R. K., J. W. HALL, R. E. WARD
  1959   *Village Japan.* Chicago: University of Chicago Press.
EMBREE, J. F.
  1939   *Suye mura: a Japanese village.* Chicago: University of Chicago Press.
LANG, O.
  1946   *Chinese family and society.* (Reprinted 1968 by Shoe String Press, Hamden, Conn.)
MAEDA, TAKASHI
  1964   *Nihon no senzasuhai Jijitsu to rekishi.* Aoyama Shoinkan.
NAKAGAWA, ZENNOSUKE
  1949   *Sōzoku hō* [Inheritance law].
OMACHI, TOKUZO
  1951   Jonku Takaoka Mura. *Minzoku shi.*
ONO, TAKEO
  n.d.   *Nōgyō shi* [Agricultural history].
SHIMIZU, MORIMITSU
  1953   *Shina kazoku kōzō* [Structure of the Chinese family].
SUZUKI, EITARO
  1941   *Nihon nōson shakaigaku genri* [Principles of the sociology of Japanese rural villages].
TAKEDA, CHOSHU
  1957   *Sosen suhai: minzoku to rekishi* [Ancestor worship in folklore and history]. Heirakuji Shoten.
USUI, NISHIO
  n.d.a   *Mikai shakai ko* [Thoughts on primitive societies]. *Tetsugaku kōkyo* 400.
  n.d.b   *Kokka kokumin no shōchō to site no Tennō* [The Emperor as symbol of state and people].
USUI, NISHIO, *editor*
  n.d.   *Sengo no Suye mura* [Postwar Suye].

# Ancestors and Nobility in Ancient Japan

RICHARD J. MILLER

Ancestral cults and beliefs have played significant roles throughout
the approximate 1,250 years of Japanese recorded history. Even today
an observer can hardly avoid being impressed by the conscientious
observance by the vast majority of Japanese families of ceremonies
relating to both distant and immediate ancestors. The ritualistic details
involved in the funeral ceremonies for the deceased, the preparation
of appropriate grave sites, and the subsequent periodic ceremonial
observance of death anniversaries require most careful thought and
planning by modern Japanese. Means of remembrance and of expressing respect for the departed family members have been in evidence
in virtually every Japanese home this writer has visited. The home
generally has either a family shrine (*kamidana*) or a family Buddhist
altar (*butsudan*), in the latter of which are placed memorial tablets
(*ihai*) for the deceased. A variety of complex beliefs, feelings, and
traditions result in such ceremonies and observances, and undoubtedly
they involve, at least in part, the desire of the living to both amelio-
rate the lot and to placate the spirits of the departed.

"Ancestor worship" is a convenient though very loose term used to
describe this modern situation which traces its history back for many
centuries. I believe that one of the reasons modern Japanese render
respect to their ancestors derives from the fact that the social and
political status of social groups depended in ancient times on the status and types of ancestors that they possessed or believed they possessed. In ancient Japan, ancestry constituted one of the numerous
symbolic means utilized to differentiate the relative ranking and status
of clans that comprised the noble stratum of society. A noble clan in

ancient Japan was called an *uji;* and while clan is a satisfactory rendition for the term, it would be more accurately rendered if translated as descent or lineage group. The important and intimate relationship that existed in ancient Japan between ancestral types and clan status will be discussed here.

From at least as early as the seventh century A.D. clan status and ancestry were officially and systematically coordinated. This fact is clearly reflected in the extant historical sources of the period. It should be stated at the outset, however, that the nature of the primary sources for the period restricts our consideration to noble clans. As interesting and desirable as it might be to consider the relationship between ancestry and clans of low social status, the available data permit us no such freedom of choice. Members of the imperial family and the various noble clans were the ones responsible for the compilation of our sources, and their interest in the gathering of facts and writing of history seldom strayed beyond the limited values of their own class. Their primary concern was their own status, or, more accurately, their own RELATIVE status within the complex clan grouping which constituted the sociopolitical hierarchy of their own time. While records are replete with genealogical references concerning the founders or progenitors of noble clans, genealogical references relating to individuals or social groups of lower than noble status are extremely rare.

Two of our primary sources of genealogical information on Japan's ancient noble society derive from her earliest extant historical records compiled under official auspices in the early eighth century. The first work, entitled *Kojiki* [Record of Ancient Matters] referred to below as KJK, was completed in A.D. 712 (Philippi 1968). It contains mythological accounts concerning the origins of the Japanese archipelago, the imperial house, and important clans. Genealogical references abound, as do stories and myths, as well as what purport to be historical narratives from mythological times down to the reign of Empress Suiko in A.D. 628.

The second work, entitled *Nihon Shoki* [Chronicles of Japan] (NSK) was completed in A.D. 720. It covers much the same ground as the KJK but carries the historical account down to A.D. 697, the last year of the reign of Empress Jitō. While both of these works are of value in the study of genealogical matters, it is only the NSK that provides us with relatively reliable historical data for the analysis of aristocratic sociopolitical structure in the seventh century (Aston 1956; see also Robinson 1961).

A few remarks are required here concerning the historicity of the two works. Japan's foremost historians generally agree that the materials contained in the KJK and the NSK for the period prior to the sixth century A.D. are not reliable historically. Myth and fancy are intertwined in that early period with what purport to be facts of history. In the absence of corroborating documentation, the accounts of these two texts for the period prior to the sixth century must be regarded as echoes of a dimly remembered past or as backward projections of the early eighth-century beliefs and thinking of court-appointed compilers. The KJK account of the sixth and early seventh centuries is exceedingly brief and consists primarily of genealogical matters dealing with the imperial family itself. By contrast, the NSK account of the sixth and seventh centuries is quite detailed and is generally accepted as being far more reliable (Sakamoto 1970 : 31).

The sixth and seventh centuries were periods of marked change, characterized by clan factionalism and struggles to gain political and social hegemony. The power and prestige of the imperial house greatly increased, and the available evidence indicates that many clans tended to manufacture genealogies in an effort to establish fictive collateral relationship with the imperial line as a means of enhancing their own prestige. During the period of its growing ascendancy, it is entirely possible that the imperial house was aware of this tendency and gave tacit approval to it as a means of extending imperial control over more clans (Abe 1966 : 34, 67). However, the attitude of the court in this regard had changed markedly by the early eighth century when the KJK and NSK were compiled. By that time the controlling elements of the Yamato state regarded false genealogies as a threat to the very stability of the state. Numerous references in both of these works support this fact. One of the best examples appears in the preface to the KJK where we find Emperor Tenmu (A.D. 673-686) saying,

I hear that the *Teiki* [Imperial chronicles] and *Honji* [Fundamental dicta] handed down by the various houses [clans] have come to differ from the truth and that many falsehoods have been added to them. If these errors are not remedied at this time, their meaning will be lost before many years have passed. This is the framework of the state, the very foundation of the imperial influence. Therefore, recording the *Teiki* and examining the *Kuji* [Ancient Dicta], discarding the mistaken and establishing the true, I desire to hand them on to later generations (Philippi 1968: 41; brackets mine).

It is apparent that this fundamental policy statement guided the compilers of the KJK, and it appears also that it influenced the compilation of the NSK. For example, in an NSK notation of the fourth year of the reign of Emperor Ingyō (traditional date, A.D. 415) we find the emperor lamenting the fact that irregularities existed in regard to clan names and titles and affirming that he must rectify the situation. In a decree we find him saying,

The ministers, functionaries, and the Miyakko of the various provinces each and all describe themselves, some as descendants of Emperors, others attributing to their race a miraculous origin, and saying that their ancestors came down from Heaven (Aston 1956: I, 316–317).

He then commanded the people of the various clans bearing titles to submit themselves to the ordeal of boiling water in order to determine the authenticity of their clan names and titles.[1]

In A.D. 815, a century after the completion of the KJK and NSK, a genealogical work was compiled under official auspices; it is entitled the *Shinsen Shōjiroku* [New Compilation of the Register of Families] referred to below as SSJR. It is of fundamental importance for the study of genealogical matters and lineage classification prior to the ninth century. It lists the original progenitors of 1,182 clans arranged by lineage type and grouped under seven geographical categories. Data from the KJK and NSK and other documentation, such as clan records and local gazeteers, were used in its compilation.[2]

Despite the policies that governed the compilation of the KJK and NSK, the record is clear that genealogical confusion continued to exist throughout the eighth century. Toward the end of that century, the record indicates that on several occasions the court ordered the compilation of corrected clan genealogies. While those works are not extant, it is believed that some of them were utilized in the compilation of the SSJR at the beginning of the next century. The preface of this work takes note of the same type of genealogical confusion that had existed in much earlier times, and refers to the event in the reign of Emperor Ingyō that was mentioned above. In addition, it states that another source of confusion was the many immigrant or foreign clans that bore Japanese-style clan names, making it difficult to distinguish which were of immigrant origin and which were not. It further informs us that some immigrant clans even claimed Japanese deities as their

---

[1]   This notation is of value in illustrating the policy of the compilers of the NSK, but if the event occurred at all, it more than likely refers to a happening of a considerably later period in history. See also Kitamura Bunji (1964: 98).

[2]   No translation nor comprehensive study of this work is available in English, except for a valuable translation of its preface to be found in Ryūsaku Tsunoda, et al. (1958: 89–90). For the latest critical edition in Japanese, see Saeki Arikiyo (1966).

progenitors, constituting another problem leading to the compilation of the SSJR.

In view of this background it is not surprising to note that in the compilation of the SSJR a clear distinction was maintained between native and foreign clans. Actually, the work is divided into three books, the first of which lists those clans that claimed descent from former emperors. The second book lists those clans that claimed descent from Japanese deities or *kami,* and the third book lists clans that claimed descent from Chinese and Korean progenitors. For the sake of convenience these three types of clans will be termed here "imperial clans" for the Japanese *kōbetsu,* "deity clans" for *shinbetsu,* and "foreign clans" for *shoban.* It should be noted that these are the classifying terms of the SSJR and while they do not appear in the NSK, such distinctions were certainly made in the early eighth century when those works were compiled. It is therefore acceptable to apply this classification of the early ninth century to the data relating to the late seventh century found in the NSK.[3]

It is clear that in dealing with the genealogical matters of ancient Japan prior to the ninth century one is dealing as much with belief as with historical fact. However, it is important to remember that what WAS believed in regard to genealogy in the eighth and ninth centuries is in itself a fact of history that influenced what the powers of the Yamato state considered to be the proper stratification of noble clans. The principal means we have for studying the stratification or relative ranking of noble clans is through analysis of clan titles or what were called *kabane.* All noble clans bore a clan title in addition to a clan name, and all members of a given clan bore in common the same clan title. Prior to the last quarter of the seventh century as many as twenty-five different clan titles were employed. The origin and evolution of the system is obscured in antiquity, but the use of such titles probably began as early as the fourth century. Considerable uncertainty exists as to the relative ranking of most of those early titles, except that it is known that a few of them were borne by the more important and prestigious clans. It is certain that by the end of the seventh century relative ranking of the most important clan titles was determined largely by the type of ancestors possessed by the clans bearing them.

The following is intended to illustrate this situation. According to

---

[3]  A word of caution is required in this context regarding such terms as "imperial clans" and "clans of imperial lineage." These terms refer solely to noble clans whose original progenitor was an emperor; the terms neither refer to nor include the imperial family itself. One will find the imperial family also referred to in works in English as the imperial clan, the imperial house, the Sun Line, etc.

the NSK, Emperor Tenmu established a new system of clan titles in
A.D. 684 to be integrated with the earlier traditional system.[4] The new
system was called the *Yakusa no kabane* or the "Eight-Rank *Kabane*
[System]," and in a two-year period Tenmu granted the top four ranks
to four groups of clans, comprising 126 in all. These four ranks, beginning with the highest, were *mahito, asomi, sukune* and *imiki*. An analysis of the 126 recipient clans in terms of their ancestral types and the
particular new titles they were granted demonstrates that the relative
ranking by ancestral types was in the order of imperial clans, deity
clans and foreign clans. The first rank of *mahito* was reserved exclusively for certain imperial clans; the second rank of *asomi* was
reserved primarily for certain other imperial clans; the third rank of
*sukune* was reserved primarily for certain deity clans; and the fourth
rank of *imiki* for both deity and foreign clans.

Table 1 shows the percentile distribution of these ancestral types by
clan titles.

Table 1.   Analysis of clan titles granted during reign of Emperor Tenmu A.D. 684,
in percentages

| Number of clans | *Kabane* rank | Imperial clans | Deity clans | Foreign clans | Information lacking |
|---|---|---|---|---|---|
| 13 | First rank (*mahito*) | 100 | 0 | 0 | 0 |
| 52 | Second rank (*asomi*) | 85 | 14 | 0 | 0 |
| 50 | Third rank (*sukune*) | 14 | 74 | 2 | 10 |
| 11 | Fourth rank (*imiki*) | 0 | 45 | 45 | 10 |

It will be seen here that 100 percent of the clans awarded the top
*kabane* rank of *mahito* were of imperial lineage; that 85 percent awarded the second rank of *asomi* were also of imperial lineage; that 74
percent awarded the third rank of *sukune* were of deity lineage; and
that the clans awarded the fourth rank of *imiki* were evenly divided
between deity and foreign lineages at 45 percent each. Although not
shown in the table, the overall percentages based on ancestral types
without reference to the particular rank of title granted demonstrate
that clans of imperial lineage were in the majority as follows: 51 percent were of imperial lineage; 39 percent were of deity lineage; 4.5
percent were of foreign lineage; and 5.5 percent were of unknown
lineage.

Throughout the eighth century, following the implementation of

---

[4]  For many details concerning clan titles see my monograph (1974), "Ancient
Japanese nobility."

Tenmu's eight-rank system of clan titles, the top four ranks of the new system were granted to numerous clans. The SSJR of the early ninth century lists the genealogies of 292 clans bearing one of these four titles. Table 2 is an analysis of those clans in terms of their ancestral types and titles.

Table 2. Analysis of clan titles listed in SSJR of the early ninth century, in percentages

| Number of clans | *Kabane* rank | Imperial clans | Deity clans | Foreign clans |
|---|---|---|---|---|
| 44 | First rank (*mahito*) | 100 | 0 | 0 |
| 108 | Second rank (*asomi*) | 73 | 18 | 9 |
| 92 | Third rank (*sukune*) | 13 | 60 | 27 |
| 48 | Fourth rank (*imiki*) | 2 | 13 | 85 |

A comparison of Tables 1 and 2 shows that a close parallel exists between their respective percentile distribution profiles of ancestral types as related to clan titles. Although not shown in Table 2 the over-all percentages based on ancestral types without reference to the particular rank of the clan titles demonstrate that clans of imperial lineage enjoyed a plurality over the other two ancestral types, as follows: 47 percent were of imperial lineage; 27 percent of deity lineage; and 26 percent were of foreign lineage.

The schematic listing of clans in the SSJR also reflects the fact that relative ranking was dependent on the clans' ancestral types. For example, of the three books that comprise the work, clans of imperial lineage are listed in Book One, undoubtedly to symbolize that their social ranking was superior to that of deity or foreign lineage. Clans of deity lineage were listed in Book Two to symbolize that their social ranking was inferior to that of clans of imperial lineage, but superior to that of foreign clans listed in Book Three. There seems to be little question but that those clans accepted as being descendants of former emperors enjoyed superior social ranking, because the imperial house was the social and political apex of the state by the last quarter of the seventh century. And through most of the balance of Japanese history the emperor was considered to be the fountainhead of legitimacy. Collateral blood relationship with the monarch, even though very distant, constituted a distinct advantage for many noble clans. This idea remained active through subsequent centuries, despite the fact that emperors most often reigned more than they ruled. The *de facto* powers of government were exercised for them, first by the Fujiwara family from the ninth until the mid-twelfth centuries, and then by military leaders (*shōgun*) during the Kamakura, Ashikaga and Tokugawa periods until the middle of the nineteenth century.

The degree of collateral relationship with the imperial house was often reflected in the particular clan titles borne by the more important clans. For example, clans descending from emperors who had reigned in the fifth century enjoyed a higher social ranking than those that descended from emperors of earlier centuries. This generalization is supported by analysis of the clans of imperial lineage that were granted either the highest clan-title rank of *mahito* or the second highest one of *asomi* during the reign of Emperor Tenmu in the last quarter of the seventh century. At that time, sixty-five clans were granted these two top clan titles, thirteen being granted the former and fifty-two the latter. The available sources provide us with specific genealogical information on only eleven of the clans awarded the highest rank and on thirty-six clans granted the second highest, yielding a total of fifty-five clans for consideration. Now each of these clans, before being granted one of the two top ranks of the new clan-title system, had borne one of three clan titles of the earlier traditional system. For convenience's sake let us just term these three possible clan titles as traditional clan titles one, two, and three. Table 3 schematizes the ranking of these fifty-five clans in terms of their respective imperial ancestors, their traditional clan titles, and the new clan titles granted them in the reign of Emperor Tenmu.

Table 3. Ranking of clans in relation to imperial ancestors, traditional clan titles, and new clan titles granted

| Reign | Emperor | | Traditional clan titles | | | New clan titles | |
|---|---|---|---|---|---|---|---|
| | | | Three | Two | One | Rank two | Rank one |
| 1 | Jinmu | | 1 | | | *asomi* | |
| 5 | Kōshō | | 6 | | | *asomi* | |
| 7 | Kōrei | | 2 | | | *asomi* | |
| 8 | Kōgen | Dates | 26 | | | *asomi* | |
| 9 | Kaika | uncertain | 1 | | | *asomi* | |
| 10 | Sujin | | | 6 | | *asomi* | |
| 12 | Keikō | | | 2 | | *asomi* | |
| 15 | Ōjin | | | | 3 | | *mahito* |
| 26 | Keitai (507–531) | | | | 3 | | *mahito* |
| 28 | Senka (535–539) | | | | 2 | | *mahito* |
| 30 | Bidatsu (572–585) | | | | 2 | | *mahito* |
| 31 | Yōmei (585–587) | | | | 1 | | *mahito* |
| Total number of clans | | | 36 | 8 | 11 | | |

It will be seen from this analysis that eight of the clans that were granted the highest ranking clan title of *mahito* in the new system were ones that traced their clan progenitors to emperors who reigned during the sixth century and had previously borne traditional clan title one. As such they were the closest collateral relatives of Emperor Tenmu outside of the imperial family itself in the last quarter of the seventh century. The additional three clans that were granted *mahito* traced their clan progenitor to Emperor Ōjin, whose reign dates are uncertain but who may have reigned in the latter part of the fourth century. In their case, however, their ancestry is traced back through a cadet line of Ōjin's descendants from whom Keitai was selected. In other words, none of the recipients of the clan title of *mahito* traced their ancestry through other cadet male lines descending from Ōjin, nor through the main line of descendants of Ōjin that included ten emperors between his reign and Keitai's. It is quite clear that the prestige of these three clans was based as much or more on their descent from Keitai as from Ōjin, and for this reason they also had previously borne traditional clan title one.

Next, it will be seen that forty-four clans were granted *asomi*, the second highest of the new clan titles. Under the earlier system eight of them had borne the traditional clan title two, and thirty-six of them had borne the traditional clan title three. Their being granted the second highest rank of the new clan-title system was based on their more distant blood relationship with Tenmu than the clans that were granted the highest rank of *mahito*. The eight that had borne the traditional title two traced their clan progenitors to Emperors Sujin and Keikō, (emperors 10 and 12), whose reign dates are moot points. The thirty-six clans that had borne traditional title three traced their clan progenitors to even more remote imperial ancestors (emperors 1, 5, 7, 8, 9), for whom we possess no corroborative documentary evidence of their existence outside of the eighth-century accounts contained in the KJK and NSK. In summary, these correlations between clan title and clan progenitors demonstrate that stratification of the highest-ranking clans of imperial lineage at the end of the seventh century was based on varying degrees of blood relationship with the then reigning monarch.

It has been demonstrated thus far that the relative ranking of clans of imperial lineage at the end of the seventh century involved a sort of triangulation, the elements of which comprised the reigning monarch, the degree of blood relationship to him a given clan possessed, and the clan's title. But there were other dimensions involving rank and prestige, one of which was of a spatial nature. This dimension is reflected in the fact that the SSJR groups 1,065 clans with authenticated lineages not only under the three ancestral categories of imperial, deity and foreign clans described above, but also under seven geographic categories within each of the ancestral categories. The seven categories are as follows: clans resident in the left sector of the capital, in the right sector of the capital and in each of the five Home Provinces, namely, in the provinces of Yamashiro, Yamato, Settsu, Kawachi and Izumi. It is apparent that the court compilers of the SSJR wished to restrict consideration to the genealogies of clans resident in areas that were relatively close geographically to the emperor and the court.

The SSJR contains authenticated genealogical references to a total of 739 clans of imperial and deity lineage resident in the two sectors of the capital and in the five Home Provinces. Those of imperial lineage amount to 46 percent of the total, while those of deity lineage amount to 54 percent. Overall more deity than imperial clans are listed in the SSJR, but within the capital itself imperial clans are in the majority. Again expressed in percentages, imperial clans in the capital amount to 55 percent and deity clans to 45 percent. If we consider the relative percentages of imperial and deity clans in both the capital and the Home Provinces, we find that the former were more concentrated in the capital and the latter more concentrated in the provinces, as in Table 4.

Table 4.

|  | Imperial clans | Deity clans |
|---|---|---|
| Capital | 25 percent | 19 percent |
| Provinces | 21 percent | 35 percent |
|  | 46 percent    + | 54 percent = 100 percent |

This same pattern is reflected in the relative percentages of imperial clans in the capital and the Home Provinces, and the relative percentages of deity clans in the capital and provinces. In addition, there is a closer balance in the distribution of imperial clans as between the capital and the provinces than in the case of deity clans, as will be seen in Table 5.

Table 5.

|  | Imperial clans | Deity clans |
|---|---|---|
| Capital | 54 percent | 36 percent |
| Provinces | 46 percent | 64 percent |
|  | 100 percent | 100 percent |

It is possible that this relative distribution pattern of imperial and deity clans in the capital and provinces represents a status factor based on the distance of residence from the monarch and court. At least the pattern clearly demonstrates that clans of imperial lineage were primarily centered in the capital and those of deity lineage, in the provinces.

The social patterns that emerge from the various analyses presented above possess important implications for gaining an understanding of the stratification of noble clans in Japan in the seventh and eighth centuries. They show that ancestry traced back to an exalted clan progenitor was of less status value than collateral relationship with another important clan or individual that claimed the same ancestry. A collateral blood relationship with a ruling monarch, no matter how distant or how lacking in historical validity the relationship, provided a clan with higher social status than other noble clans of deity or foreign lineage. Even within the stratum of noble clans of imperial lineage, a clan that claimed as its progenitor an emperor of relatively recent centuries enjoyed a higher social status than one that claimed a more remote imperial progenitor.

There can be no doubt but that this scheme grew out of the trend of the previous century or two in which the emperor and the imperial family, the direct descendants of the Sun Goddess, attained social and political paramountcy. Our sources for the early sixth century portray the emperor as being but one among a number of clan chieftains who were politically and militarily powerful and who jointly ruled the state. By the end of that century one of the clans, the Soga, had eliminated other competing clan chieftains and had formed a dyarchy with the emperor. By the early seventh century, Chinese political theory was exerting strong influence on the thinking of some elements of the imperial family. In A.D. 604 one of its members, Prince Regent Shōtoku, issued a moral code in seventeen articles for governance. That code provided the ideological basis for the growing claim that the emperor constituted the social and political apex of the state. In the following forty years this claim drew increasing support from clan chieftains who were opposed to the Soga clan, and in A.D. 645 they forcibly eliminated Soga leadership and undertook fundamental reforms. In the next half-century they gradually formulated new legal and governmental structures, the broad outlines of which were directly borrowed from the politically centralizing theories of the Sui and T'ang dynasties of China. These developments are known in history as the *Taika Kaishin* [Reforms of (the Period of) Great Change]. It is only within the context of these historical events that the patterns of social stratification of noble clans of ancient Japan can be understood.

The strong impression I gain from the study of available sources is that the whole genealogical fabric of the late seventh and eighth centuries was consciously manufactured. It is my belief that political considerations, more than truth, were of pivotal importance in the evolution of that fabric. The most important political consideration was the preservation and protection of the position of the emperor and the imperial family. Emperor Tenmu was quoted above, in relation to the correction of errors and falsehoods in older chronicles, as saying, "This is the framework of the state, the very foundation of the imperial influence." But it is apparent from the sources that "correcting" those errors really involved arranging the sociopolitical hierarchy to protect the imperial influence, even if it did involve genealogical falsifications.

The restructuring of the state in the second half of the seventh century required the cooperation and support of many clans. The clans that had supported the throne in its struggles with the Soga clan, as well as with other opposing groups, naturally were rewarded with rank and position. It is this element of reward that strongly colors the history and social stratification portrayed for us in the KJK and NSK. It was the victors in the political struggles of the seventh century, or their heirs, who compiled those works in the early eighth century. In describing the mythological origins of Japan, they used the opportunity to note that certain deities and emperors were the progenitors of clans that were important during the seventh century. This process resulted in stratifying deities and monarchs of a mythological past on the basis of the relative ranking of their supposed descendants at the end of the seventh century, and not the other way around.

The compilers of the KJK and NSK could not have been in possession of the extensive and reliable historical documentation that would have been required to support such claims of ancestry. We know that Japan until at least the fifth century was in a preliterate stage. While some documentation of the sixth century was available to the compilers, the events and personages mentioned in these two sources for periods before the sixth century are lacking in reliability. It is for these reasons that the genealogical references of the KJK and NSK are almost exclusively devoted to the mere designation of the names of clan founders or progenitors. None of these sources provides a single genealogical tree for a noble clan, which traces through either the paternal or maternal line all of its direct ancestors back to a clan founder. The genealogical notations of these sources are confined largely to interlinear glosses that inform us that this or that deity or personage was progenitor of a given clan.

Drawing upon these sources and later documentation, the SSJR likewise goes little further than the briefest notations of clan progenitors; they usually consist of little more than the name of a given clan, its clan title, and the name of its progenitor. In some cases the progenitor is noted as being the descendant of a given emperor or deity in such and such a generation. In many other cases the genealogical references consist of nothing more than a clan name and title, followed by such notations as "same ancestor as [clan listed] above" and "same ancestor as [such and such a] clan." The transparent manufacture of genealogies to fit a certain political and social scheme of things, combined with the shallow history of Japanese literacy, inevitably resulted in the enormous lacunae that exist in the available sources.

In conclusion, it can be said with certainty that ancestry in ancient Japan of the seventh and eighth centuries was an important factor in defining the social hierarchy of noble clans. Unfortunately, the available sources tell little about the "worship" of ancestors. We must content ourselves with the political and social roles ancestors played.

## REFERENCES

ABE, TAKEHIKO
1966   *Shisei.* Tokyo: Shibundo.
ASTON, W. G., *translator*
1956   *Nihongi: chronicles of Japan from the earliest times to* A.D. *697.* London: George Allen and Unwin. (Translation of *Nihon Shoki* [Chronicles of Japan]. Aston's translation first appeared in 1896.)
KITAMURA, BUNJI
1964   Kabane no seido ni kansuru shinkenkyū josetsu. *Jinbun kagaku ronshū* 3:98. Sapporo: Hokkaido University.
MILLER, RICHARD J.
1974   *Ancient Japanese nobility: the kabane ranking system.* Berkeley: University of California Press.
PHILIPPI, DONALD, *translator*
1968   *Kojiki* [Record of ancient matters]. Tokyo: University of Tokyo Press.
ROBINSON, G. W.
1961   "Early Japanese chronicles: the six national histories," in *Historians of China and Japan.* Edited by W. G. Beasley and E. G. Pulleyblank. London: Oxford University Press.

RYŪSAKU, TSUNODA, WILLIAM T. DE BARY, DONALD KEENE, *compilers*
1958   *Sources of the Japanese tradition.* New York: Columbia University Press.

SAEKI, ARIKIYO
1966   *Shinsen Shōjiroku no Kenkyū* [New compilation of the register of families], two volumes. Tokyo.

SAKAMOTO, TARŌ
1970   *Rikkokushi* [The six national histories]. Tokyo: Yoshikawa Kobunkan.

# Dōzoku *and Ancestor Worship in Japan*

SHOJI YONEMURA

## THE HOUSEHOLD AND THE CULT OF THE ANCESTORS

It has been said that the patrilineal descent system and patriarchal family structure of many African peoples is closely bound up with an ancestral cult (Fortes 1970: 183). This also holds true for Japan. Ancestor worship in Japan is the key foundation of the household (*ie*) and the *dōzoku* form of lineage. Ancestor worship follows the pattern of household and *dōzoku* ancestor worship. The congregation of worshipers in the cult of ancestors comprises either only a household group or, exclusively, a corporate *dōzoku* group. This involves two kinds of ancestors. The one, according to Yanagita, is a founding ancestor of the household who became such either by creating his own household or by creating branch households for nonsucceeding sons. But an ancestor also is any departed forebear who has been acquired ancestorhood by a series of household rituals performed by his legitimate successor for thirty-three years after his death. Both have the household as the unit in which the ancestral cult is performed as a common feature (Yanagita 1946: 1, 3–4, 154–155). We will discuss the position of the first or *dōzoku* ancestor in the next section.

In Japanese tradition, in order to become an ancestor, one needs to have a specific living descendant or legitimate successor to whom the household headship is transferred. A man becomes an ancestor when he dies not only because he is dead, but because he leaves a legitimate successor. Death alone is not a sufficient condition for becoming an ancestor entitled to receive worship. A living specific descendant has the right and duty to offer ritual service to his departed predecessor. This responsible person is usually either the deceased's eldest son or successor. He carries the tablet (*ihai*) of his dead father in the funeral procession to the graveyard and undergoes obligatory mourning interdictions such as social isolation, or inability to enter the village shrine, etc. for fifty days. This mourning period is the longest one among various categories of kin. This is why the eldest son is termed the tablet holder (*ihaigo*) in some parts of Japan. In the Family Code of A.D. 718 the most important right and duty for the succeeding son was to officiate in the cult of ancestors by moving into the status of the dead father. Nonheir members who created new household lines in their own households could not worship their fathers, although they could carry with them a duplicate tablet of their parents. In Wada village of Fukui Prefecture, the head of the original household forbade his branch to duplicate the ancestral tablet of his dead father for the reason that the dead father would be puzzled as to which tablet to choose (Kamishima 1961: 267).

Even when parents established their own branch households, moving out to live with their unmarried sons and daughters at their time of retirement, their own mourning rites could be held only by the successor of their original households. Their tablets were to be kept on the altars of their original households. In some places in Japan, a head of the branch household created by parental retirement could carry out mourning rites for his dead father, but the eldest son held the father's tablet in the funeral procession to the graveyard. In a recently created branch household, when the most senior member died, his descendant should worship him there, yet still go to the original household to take part in the worship of more distant ascending generations. One who had no descendants could not become an ancestor. He was termed *gaki* (*preta*, or hungry ghost) and became a wandering and ill-disposed ghost. Accordingly, at set times in each month and at the *bon* (also *Obon*) festival of August, men made special provision for the wandering hungry ghosts. At Takaya village of Okayama-shi, Okayama Prefecture, a memorial tablet with no Buddhist names, in which wandering spirits installed themselves, was put on the ancestral altar of the household, lest they should disturb the cult of ancestors. Nor could children who died become ancestral spirits, though they were specifically identified with a particular household, for they did not achieve parenthood. They were termed *muenbotoke* or *hotoke* without *en*, without obligation. *Hotoke*, the term generally applied to an ancestor, means deified Buddha. Many *muenbotoke* have no tablets to be worshiped. To avoid this calamity, at Sama village of Tottori Prefecture, if a beloved child or a grandchild dies, his parents or grandparents make their own ancestral tablet in their lifetime and write the Buddhist death name of their child or grandchild between their own posthumous Buddhist names on the tablet.

When a father dies, a tablet (*ihai*) is made for him and a posthumous Buddhist name is written on it. He is termed the new *hotoke* or *senzo* [ancestor]. The tablet is placed either on the altar or on a temporary special altar on the floor in the main room. A Buddhist memorial service is held on the 3rd, 7th, 21st, 33rd, 49th and sometimes 100th day after death for the purpose of preventing his wandering about and causing misfortune or trouble in this immediate period. This also establishes him as an ancestor in the context of mourning rites as a whole. During this period, the household members of the departed make it a rule to pay visits to his grave and offer a cup of water and rice to him on the altar or at the grave. After the Buddhist memorial service on the 49th day after death, the tablet of the new *hotoke*, hitherto covered with white cloth, is exposed on the altar, or else it is transferred from the temporary special altar to the original altar in the main room. This ritual means that the new *hotoke* is purged of death pollution and is accepted among the ancestors of the household.

However, persons who died abnormal deaths need much longer periods of mourning than forty-nine days. They are principally those who have died in the prime of life before completing a normal life cycle. Such deaths are those caused by violence, sudden disease or epidemic, drowning, and unsuccessful childbirth. Their spirits are said to hover on earth and do harm because of their unfulfilled interest in, and attachment to, life in this world. Accordingly, they need more frequent and more devout ritual services for them to become *hotoke*. In several villages of Japan, men set up the wooden tablets or spread bleached cotton cloth inscribed with a holy text by the river for persons who have died abnormal deaths. Men and passers by use a scoop to splash water on the tablets or cloths until the characters written on them are defaced (Minzokugaku Kenkyūsho 1956: I, 1099, 1331).

After the first intense period, an anniversary memorial service is held on the 3rd, 23rd, 33rd and later years after death. This may continue for upwards of fifty years. It is generally believed that after thirty-five years, the *hotoke* becomes an ancestor. The *hotoke* loses its individuality and is assimilated into the collectivity of ancestors from the first founding ancestor of the household. Thereafter, the annual memorial service is abolished. The tablet of the new *hotoke* is either buried in the grave of the person for whom it stands, deposited in the temple or, in the northern part of Okayama Prefecture, cast into the river. At Ino-cho of Miyazaki Prefecture, the tablet of the new *hotoke* is removed from the altar to a small shrine in the yard called *uchi gami* [household tutelary deity] after thirty-three years (Naoe 1972: 101). It is believed that the spirits of the departed ancestors become *jino kami* or *jigami* [earth deity] and function as *yashiki gami* [the deity for the household and its grounds] after thirty-three or fifty years. This belief is spread over Saitama, southwestern Fukui, southwestern Hyogo and Shizuoka Prefectures (Naoe 1972: 75–101). The *yashiki gami* is originally the household tutelary deity and is introduced into a small shrine at the corner of the yard or in a distant field or forest owned by the household.

On the 33rd deathday, a branch with green leaves is fixed at the grave-yard in place of the wooden symbol of the fivefold tomb. A branch with green leaves becomes the sacred symbol signifying the presence of the ancestor. This custom is widely practiced throughout certain remote is-lands and is based on the idea that the departed is gradually purged of death pollution until he loses his own individuality and is merged into the collective body of ancestors thirty-three years after his death. In various parts of Japan, the old grave, in which the corpse is buried, is abandoned, and a new grave for worship is set up near one's home or on a hillside as the token of assimilation of the departed into the col-lectivity of ancestors (Mogami 1956).

In the ancestral collectivity, the deceased is worshiped at annual major festivals such as New Year, the *bon* festival and the Equinoxes of spring and autumn, together with the collective body of ancestors as-cending to the founding ancestor of the household. Many founding an-cestors, however, still have their own individuality in spite of their re-moteness in the past and are enshrined at small shrines at the graveyard or hillside owned by their descendants. Some of them are termed *jigami* or *yashiki gami*. For example, seventeen out of eighteen earth deities in the northeastern part of Hyogo Prefecture are the founding ancestors of a household (Hinonishi 1972: 3). The founding ancestor represents ancestral authority and the honor of the household. He functions as the organizing principle of the succeeding ancestors as well as his *dōzoku* members. The founding ancestor functions as the focus of the *dōzoku*, and his small shrine is the symbol of *dōzoku* solidarity.

Thus a man-become-ancestor resides somewhere on the mountains above his birthplace, watching over his descendants and demanding their attention, wishing them to be happy and prosperous. He visits his de-scendants either if he is invoked or on his own initiative as the protector of his household and crops. He descends upon his descendants at the beginning of the rice-farming and harvesting season of the year and as-cends to the mountains of his homeland in winter. It is believed that the hope of the departed at his last moment is achieved in his afterlife without fail and that he is able to be reborn three times. His last hope is, as stated above, the happiness and prosperity of his offspring. The tradition has been handed down from generation to generation that, in case of fire, the ancestral tablets have to be removed for safety first of all, and if one succeeds in doing so, he will reinstate his household without fail through the blessings of his ancestors. Until recently, in rural Japan a grandson was given the name of his grandfather, and a granddaughter that of her grandmother. At Miura Peninsula of Kanagawa Prefecture, the successor is thought to be reborn as one of his ancestors. People say that an ancestor is born when the eldest son is born, at Yoshitsuson of Mie Prefecture (Takeda 1970: 33). In short, an ancestor is constantly urged to return in a new incarnation among his descendants. This belief in and desire for reincarnation refers to the dependence of the household for its continuity on the renewal of personnel and to the emphasis upon the direct descent line.

As is well known, a household in Japan is a corporation and a durable unit. A household is conceived as persisting through time by the succession of its members. To this end, a head of household has undivided authority and inherits the estate intact for the continuity and welfare of the corporation. This authority is acquired only by the succession to the headship and comes by transmission from his ancestors. An ancestor is the fountainhead of the household and has mystical power over his descendants. The household head holds his authority in the names of the ancestors. He stands before other household members with an array of ancestors behind him. He admonishes his children for bad conduct, reproaching them in front of the ancestral altar with, "Do you think you can give any excuse to the ancestors for behaving thus?" He reiterates, "Don't bring shame upon your forefather's memory." Thus standing before the ancestors, a sluggard is shamed.

The household head is the sole figure to make a final decision. He is the one father-of-the-household in the sense of the person with supreme authority in the household. He can even decide upon his successor. He can appoint as his successor an adopted son, superseding a real son. Thus he can demand obedience and reverence from his children as his inalienable right. Children have to respect and honor their father without regard to his character and treatment of them. They have to put his wishes before their own and support him in his old age. The father may be neglectful of his son, but his son should be dutiful. The loyalty of children to the interests and wishes of their father is thought to outweigh all other duties and is venerated as the supreme virtue in the relationship of sons to their parents in Japan.

The authority of the household head extends over his younger siblings who establish new household lines. The household head is able to order his younger siblings to undertake service on important ceremonies such as at New Year's or at a wedding. For example, in Koresato of Oka-yama Prefecture, the Written Oath (*Tegata-no-koto*) of 1712 tells us that the eldest son of the original household ordered his two younger siblings to attend and offer service to his household at New Year's and a wed-ding ceremony (Yonemura 1962: 9). In a Receipt for Grant of Arable Land signed by a younger sibling of the Norioka household in Tennoji, Osaka, he promised his elder brother of the original household in a writ-ten form in 1856 that he would ask his elder brother's advice on every-thing without fail and, handing over the whole estate intact to his de-scendants, would never mortgage or confer ownership of the arable land given him in usufruct (Otake 1962: 201).

The eldest son is addressed as *oyakata* [father] by his younger brothers and is treated piously as a father in various parts of Japan. In the south-ern part of Kagoshima Prefecture, newly established branch households are unable to build a small shrine for their immediate seniors. Only af-ter the fifth generation beyond establishment are they permitted to do so and to carry out independent worship in their own households (Hori 1961: 154). As stated above, in Wada village of Fukui Prefecture, the head of the original household forbade his branch to duplicate the an-cestral tablet of his dead father. Even at sixteen villages of the midwest-ern and western parts of Japan, where parents established their own branch households with their unmarried children upon retirement, the eldest son kept the ancestral tablet of his dead father on the altar of his household, while his younger sibling was permitted to hold only the tab-let of either his departed mother or one of his remote kin not in the direct ascending line (Naoe 1972: 446). This tells us clearly that the right to officiate in ancestral cult confers on the household head the authority to control his younger brothers in place of the dead father, although he is unable to call his dead father to harm his brother or sister for bad be-havior, as in West Africa.

On the other hand, the household head is also subject to the ancestor's authority and is obliged to invoke it as the sanction for his headship. According to the *Minka Yojitsu* [Folk- and technic ways of common people] in feudal days the successor was to his founding ancestor and ancestor-father as a house-clerk was to his master. He was only a kind of caretaker of the household property deposited by his ancestors;

then he had to honor his ancestors and hold annual memorial services for them, supporting his wife and children through the use of the household property, and handing over the whole estate intact to his descendants (Otake 1962: 292). In short, the household head holds his authority to control property and descendants and to monopolize the right to officiate in the cult of ancestors through the continual submission to the higher authority that was vested in his father before his death.

Authority, however, implies responsibilities. Therefore, it imposes heavy responsibilities upon the household head. He has to carry not only material responsibilities for dependents but also ritual responsibilities to his ancestors. These ritual responsibilities are especially heavy and onerous. The household head can never be sure whether he is fulfilling his ritual responsibilities satisfactorily or not. Only when he can compile various deeds for piety's sake, following the dictates of faithful worship, will he have faith in the justice of his ancestors who were morally constrained by his pious worship (Fortes 1970: 194). If misfortunes or ills befall him and his household, they are interpreted as due to his negligence — the manifestation of dissatisfaction on the part of the ancestors. He has no other way but to accept what comes from the ancestors and to offer them what they demand in sacrifice and service.

What they require from him is to submit to their discipline and to revitalize faithful worship. A household head is a servant of higher authority, and the ancestor is the last tribunal. A household head is to his ancestor what a son is to his father. In this sense, as Professor Fortes pointed out, "ancestor worship is in essence the ritualization of filial piety" (Fortes 1959: 29). Thus an ancestor becomes disciplinary and applies a negative sanction to his descendants. Yanagita (1946) has asserted that a Japanese ancestor is benign and protective. The ancestor in Japan represents protectiveness and benevolence indeed. And yet he has the right to be worshiped in the household cults for ancestors through observance such as memorial services on deathdays and annual festivals. As long as he receives the ritual services due to him, he will be content to preside as the benign protector for his living descendants. If his rights are denied, they lead him to cause misfortune or sickness to his descendants. He will punish them if he is offended by any form of behavior or neglect that affects him.

For example, in Tokunoshima on the Amami Islands, where children are as reverent to their parents as to God, if they suffer from unknown diseases it is interpreted as a fault of negligence to their ancestors. People say that they are being punished by their ancestor parents. It is said, too, in Bichu-cho, Okayama Prefecture, that if misfortune or ill befalls the household head and his household members, his *hotoke* is punishing him. There is a story handed down from generation to generation and widely known in various parts of Japan of a young couple who, though diligent, did not provide ritual objects for their ancestors at the *bon* festival of August. Thereupon an angry ancestor thrust their child into the hearth to get burnt while they were out working in their fields (Yanagita 1946: 187). Yoshida (1972: 114–115) tells us of a fourth son in U village of Kochi Prefecture who became sick. A medium said the illness was a mystical retribution sent by his grandfather, who was angry over neglect by the boy's father. It was known that the grandfather had been on bad terms with his son for a long time before his death. In the end he had committed suicide. The fourth son went to the hospital and died. Twenty years ago, a woman in her thirties, also of U village, injured her health and consulted her priest. While he prayed for her, she suddenly hit at the sacred branch with ceremonial, cut paper and ran out to the graveyard, saying "I want to eat ricecakes at the Equinoxes of spring and autumn." She ran round one of her household graves three times and sank down on the ground on her back. When she recovered, she realized that she had never offered ricecakes to her ancestors and therefore had been possessed by an angry ancestor (Yoshida 1972: 120). A ricecake is an indispensable offering for the ancestral cult of the household at the Equinoxes of spring and autumn.

According to Yoshida's study in U village, where hierarchical organization of the *dōzoku* is weak and Shintoism is dominant, fifteen out of eighty-three cases of sickness were diagnosed as caused by retribution and spirit possession by ancestors or kin (Yoshida 1972: 114–116). Six of them were attributed by mediums to mystical retribution by ancestors for failure in religious submission and service on the part of afflicted descendants. Although they then prayed and worshiped them through mediums at their graves or before their altars, four of them died. Japanese ancestors in this way are punitive and intervening. Thereby they recover their rights and authority and restore order and discipline. To this time it has been asserted that Japanese ancestors are beneficent and protective within the cult group but may be harmful outside the cult group (Naoe 1972: 428). However, the two are just different faces of the same coin. Japanese ancestors are benign and kind as long as they receive ritual service due to them. However, it must be recognized that they are punitive to their descendants if their right to be worshiped in the ancestral cult of the household is denied.

Along with this fact, it must be noted that eight persons who did harm to others and nine who were afflicted in U village were women and that women played significant roles in retribution and spirit possession. This is partly due to the fact that married women in households may bring into play hostile activity, which is attributed to ancestors; thereby they become harmful ancestors as well as victims by retribution and spirit possession. On the other hand, although the head of the household takes formal charge of the ancestral cult of the household, the routine of ritual tending is carried out by women. It has been pointed out already by Professor Hagiwara that women played a significant role in the household cult routine for ancestors in the Meiji period (1869–1912) and that the more women became the prime agents in the cult of ancestors, the more they were apt to become victims of unfavorable reactions from the ancestors (Hagiwara 1954: 365–367). It still holds true of Japan today. Women occupy a crucial place in the ritual routine of tending to their ancestors (Koyama 1967: 283–284; Hori 1963: 318–319).

Four of the eight harmful females afflicted five living kinsmen within their households. One stepmother was ill treated by her unrelated son because of her weak status as the second wife of his father; after committing suicide she afflicted him with a high fever. One blind mother-in-law was maltreated by her daughter-in-law and possessed her two children so that they became blind. One husband's father's maid (concubine) who died from tuberculosis was not buried with due ceremony but was burnt to ashes by setting fire to her isolation hut; thereafter, in 1955, she possessed the wife of her dead husband's son. Another patrilateral aunt was divorced and, being forgotten, brought harm to her niece, who had married an adopted son in her household. None of these harmful women had been able to establish a firm position as mistress or housewife in their households. They were placated only when they made themselves felt in a malevolent manner. In this way they not only compelled ritual service due to them, but also the unity of their households.

Two patrilateral aunts out of four other harmful females committed suicide, and one junior sister died from unsuccessful childbirth. One sister married out but died without children. She had no one to worship her. Accordingly, she harmed her brother's son. As stated above, the persons who die unnatural deaths and have no one to worship them linger on earth wanting homes. Especially the young man who dies a victim of abnormal death and the pregnant woman who dies in childbirth are malevolent and uncontrollable because of their lingering interest in, and unnatural escape from, this world. Accordingly, they need more frequent and more pious ritual attention to become *hotoke*. Their spirits search for and attack their living close kinsmen because of their previous attachment to kin, property and house. Such spirits possessed two nieces, one nephew and one elder sister, although they had belonged to another household after marriage. These cases tell us that the ritual responsibilities still remained with their brothers and that there is attention to bilateralism. This may be partly explained by the fact that the patrilineal descent system is weak in U village (Yoshida 1972: 119).

However, these phenomena are by no means restricted to U village alone; they are, for example, observed in various parts of Okayama Prefecture (Wakamori 1963: 236–238; Miura 1958: 23–42). This kind of afflicting spirit is detached from the strict patriline. In Daisen-cho of Tottori Prefecture, they are termed *kyakubotoke* [guest *hotoke*] and if their tablets are made and put on the altars of the afflicted one's household, they are separated by a thin board from the original ancestral tablets of the worshiper's household. The patriline still dominates the scene. Thus we establish the very real and close sense of ancestral concern in traditional households of Japan.

## *DŌZOKU* AND ANCESTOR WORSHIP

A *dōzoku* form of lineage is a set of households composed of the original household *(honke)* and its branch households *(bunke)*. They are connected with one another through a genealogical relationship based upon the household. In other words, *dōzoku* is a group of households which recognize mutually their genealogical relationship in terms of their origin and the branches derived from it. It performs unitary functions as a corporation on the basis of their relationship; and local terms for it such as "stock" *(make* or *kabu)*, "one descent" *(itto)*, or "one household" *(ikke)* signify its corporate nature. The genealogical relationship becomes explicit only when the original and the branches recognize their respective statuses and roles. The head of the original household has to give a portion of its household property to its branch at the time of fission and to help it spontaneously; and the branch household has to submit to the legitimate authority of the stem because of its status as the fountainhead of the genealogical relationship. The branch offers various services to the original household whenever needed.

Accordingly, if the original household does not assume its duty to the branch — for example, if it does not grant the branch a portion of the household property or some other kind of help — a genealogical relationship is not formed between them. That is, if a new household is established by a son even in the stem's village but without any help from his parental household, it does not form a genealogical relationship with the parental household. This new household is termed an independent household, or an independent hearth (*hitori-kamado*) and is distinguished from the branch household, called a hearth division (*kamado-wake*) in the true sense of the term. Indeed, there is a generic relationship between stem and branch in terms of father and son, but no personal genealogical tie is automatically sufficient to establish a household relationship. In short, in order to form a *dōzoku*, all constituent households have to recognize mutually the genealogical relationship among them. Then they have to perform roles assigned to their respective status as the original or the branch in a genealogical relationship. Therefore, economic help has to be accompanied by a genealogical relationship.

*Dōzoku* ancestor worship has close relations with the unity and identity of *dōzoku*. As was stated above, a *dōzoku* is a set of households, consisting of the original and its branch households. This household persists and continues throughout generations irrespective of the birth and death of its constituent members. This leads in turn to thanks to the ancestors as the source of its being and ultimately to the worship of the founding ancestor of the original household as the fountainhead of the genealogical relationship. This corresponds to the fact that the notion of the ancestor in Japan stands for the founding ancestor as well as for succeeding ancestors, or the collectivity of ancestors. The founding ancestor symbolizes the continuity of the *dōzoku* and represents its honorable tradition. *Dōzoku* ancestors stand at the center of the attention of *dōzoku* members. The collectivity of ancestors from the founding ancestors of a *dōzoku* is the common spiritual property of that corporate *dōzoku*. Hence it is said that the *dōzoku* ancestor is the justifying authority for the cooperation of the living members. It is a rallying point for the *dōzoku* which at the rituals for the cult of its ancestors brings together all its members into ritual unity.

The continuation of the cult of *dōzoku* ancestors lies in the rite of solidarity. Because of this, *dōzoku* households have to continue their ancestor worship as their right and duty. This is why *dōzoku* ancestor worship excludes non-*dōzoku* members. Even those kin members who have married other *dōzoku* members and have been adopted into non-*dōzoku* households, are not permitted to join in the cult of *dōzoku* ancestors. In this respect, it differs sharply from the anniversary Buddhist memorial services for forebears which have their personal kindred as members of the cult group. The *dōzoku* worshiping their founding ancestor in the six hamlets of Koresato, Okayama Prefecture (Yonemura 1962: 1–19) are described here to show how the solidarity and cooperation of *dōzoku* are linked with the cult of the ancestors.

Table 1.   The composition of *dōzoku* in the western part of Koresato

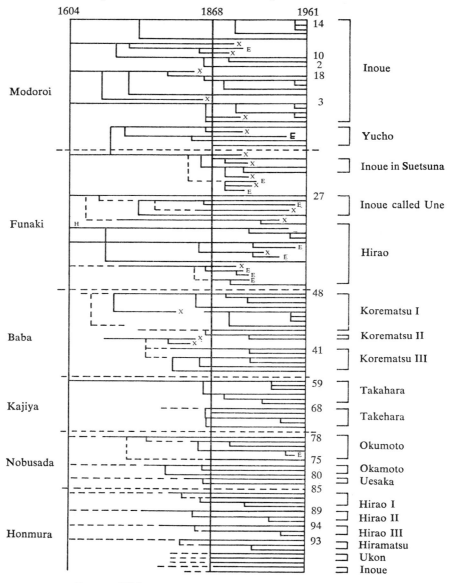

------- Presumed link
x  Abolition
E  Emigration

The Inoue stock in Modoroi is composed of eighteen households and is the largest one in Koresato (see Table 1). It is said that the main original household came of *samurai* class, retiring to Modoroi after a defeat in 1577. By 1604 it had established three branch households, one of which was founded for a servant of the main original household. The original Inoue household head was recorded as the official ward headman in documents of both 1669 and 1763, though it yielded to a branch in 1702. By 1868 it had established yet another branch household. This main original household's fortunes declined after that period; notably, its taxable land holding had dropped to only 0.15 acres by the time of the 1938 cadastral survey; yet, even so, it had established three more branch households, with land totaling 3.78 acres in house lots and arable fields. By this effort, it has fulfilled its responsibilities to its branch satisfactorily. The three latest branch households readily accept the authority of the main original household, and unanimously declare it to be a very dependable household.

The second and third branch households died out sometime between 1868 and 1912. Then Number 10 and Number 18 assumed leadership and formed subgroups. Number 18 especially forms an active subgroup with its three branch households, partly because it is one of the most wealthy and influential in Koresato. This *dōzoku*, or sub-*dōzoku*, jointly owns a threshing machine and shares in the work. In contrast to this case, the subgroup under Number 10 has ceased cooperative work, disputing who should have the right of seniority. Household Number 10 and Household Number 2 are at odds on a genealogical point as to which is senior to the other. Another subgroup consists of the original household, Number 3 (established by a servant of the main original household), its three direct branches and one branch-of-a-branch (i.e. indirect branch). Today, Household Number 3's third branch is the most wealthy and influential and initiates most action, while two of the remaining four households in the group depend considerably on it for support. Interestingly, this Inoue substock has acquired its own name "Tawa," and carries on an independent ancestral cult.

In summary, the Inoue stock today has no hierarchical organization with a main original household at its apex but is now gradually differentiating into four equally remote subgroups. Above all, Tawa stock shows a high degree of independence. However, all *dōzoku* household heads except for Household Number 2 have a clearly known genealogical connection and conduct funeral ceremonies as a unit. They eagerly wish to keep their *dōzoku* connection forever and still maintain a strong group solidarity.

What is more, the Inoue stock holds *dōzoku* ancestor worship ceremonies. All household heads gather in front of a small shrine inside the house lot of the main original household for the worship of the founding ancestor to commemorate February 28, when the founder settled in Modoroi after his defeat. They offer him a cup of wine and rice and worship him. The written Shintō prayer on the 360th anniversary for the founding ancestor in 1936 states:

We have carried your precepts into practice faithfully and devoted ourselves to our jobs so that our *dōzoku* has developed and prospered; all these we owe to the benefits and blessings of you and your successors. There is no one but us to worship you. Every one cherishes your memory. Today we gather in front of you and offer cups of rice and wine with all sorts of fruits and vegetables to you on your 360th anniversary. We will follow your precepts without fail and pursue our business with diligence and worship you forever. Replenish our descendants on the earth like an arrowroot and make us prosper like branches of a strong mulberry tree.

After worship, they eat rice with red beans. This is prepared by the person on duty on a shift system and expenses are allotted equally to the eighteen households. The main original household does not play any special role in this ancestral cult, and this reflects equal ranking of the Inoue stock. It is, however, not too much to say that this ancestral cult strengthens the Inoue *dōzoku's* solidarity, which is apt to loosen in daily secular life. It is in this sense that it is said, "the *dōzoku* is ancestor-centered."

An interesting sidelight within the Inoue stock is the fact that the Tawa stock, in addition to participating in the Inoue ancestral cult, carries out its own subgroup ceremony on February 24. The five Tawa households celebrate at the foot of a pine tree the festival of the long-nosed goblin (*tengu*). It is said that this tree has some historical connections with the founding ancestor of this stock and that it is the sacred vehicle of the presence of ancestors. After the ceremony, rice with red beans and sweet fermented rice gruel (*amazake*) are consumed in front of the pine. Possibly the separate ceremony reflects some old segregation of the Tawa stock, which, after all, was founded by a servant of the main original household, although it is not supposed to matter whether a branch was formed by kin or by nonkin.

In the Baba hamlet we find three *dōzoku*: Korematsu I, II, and III. It is said that the founding ancestor of the Korematsu I stock came from the *samurai* class, retiring to Baba hamlet from Kawai manor. This stock did not grow without setbacks. Though two branches had been established by 1703, they both died out rather quickly. Now the original household forms a *dōzoku* with four direct branches and four that are branches of branch households. Their genealogical connection is unquestioned and they exchange labor frequently. Household heads still visit each other to pay respects in New Year rounds, and join together both for the mid-summer *bon* festival for collective forebears and for the ceremony of veneration of the Korematsu I *dōzoku* ancestor. They conduct the funeral ceremony with the Korematsu II group because there are only three component households in the latter. Note, however, that in the various joint ceremonies among the Korematsu I group, the original household plays no special role. Even for the ancestral cult, each household in turn takes over the responsibility of the performance, rather than having this responsibility reserved as a privilege of the original household, as is usual. Each household in this stock intends to keep up the *dōzoku* relationship in the future.

On the contrary, the Korematsu II stock, consisting of three households, has a somewhat vague genealogical relationship, and the three do not attempt to help each other economically. And, as already noted above, the three households of this stock need the aid of the Korematsu I group to cope with a funeral.

The Korematsu III stock consists of six households. The original household of *samurai* descent settled in Baba in 1613 but died out at some time between 1830 and 1840. Consequently, the genealogical relationship between Number 41 and Number 44 is vague, though each recognizes that they both come from the same stock. There is a fair amount of cooperation among the six households. Number 41 lends machines to, and frequently exchanges work with, its newly established branch. The other four households, including Number 44, exchange work during the rice-planting season. This stock holds not only *dōzoku* ancestor worship, but also the funeral ceremony as a corporation. They also follow the custom of visiting each other at New Year's to pay respects. The households of Korematsu III clearly intend to maintain the solidarity of the *dōzoku* in the future.

The Korematsu I and III stocks hold *dōzoku* ancestor worship. The Korematsu I stock worships the founding ancestor with lighting a lamp in Shintō rites and offers a soldier's helmet to his grave every 11th day of the third lunar month. This soldier's helmet is kept by the original household. The Korematsu III stock, too, offer their genealogy (*keifu*) and the armor case to the founding ancestor in front of the ancestor's grave on the 24th day of the third month. After the ritual, all the household heads of both stocks eat the sour fish and rice at the homes of the persons on duty on the shift system. It is interesting that they offer their traditional soldier's helmet and armor case to the founding ancestors and are proud of their noble birth. It is also to be noted that by offering their genealogy to the founding ancestor, they reaffirm their genealogical relationship every year. In some places, *dōzoku* ancestor worship is termed the festival of the genealogy (*keizu-matsuri*). Thus they keep their genealogical relationship and solidify their *dōzoku* solidarity. In this respect, they are in sharp contrast with Korematsu II stock where the genealogical connection is nebulous and no ancestral cult is held.

There are two *dōzoku* in Kajiya hamlet: the Takahara stock and the Takehara stock. The Takahara stock consists of six households. The original household of this stock was itself a branch from the main household in a neighboring hamlet; its head was named a village headman in 1682. Since 1868, it has established and formed three direct branch households, and two indirect branches with a somewhat attenuated relation to the original household and its stock in a neighboring hamlet. The head of the original household retired, keeping with him his unmarried sons. Then the eldest son acquires the ancestral tablets along with 0.12 acres of arable land that provide rice for ancestor worship rituals. The eldest son builds himself a new house. From that point on the eldest son regards his household as the original or main household. The other *dōzoku* members, however, continue to recognize the retired father's household as the original. This disagreement does not appear to have disturbed the *dōzoku* members' understanding of their mutual genealogical relationships, and they intend to maintain their *dōzoku* relationships in the future. Above all, this stock conducts the funeral as well as wedding ceremony together with the Takahara stock in a neighboring hamlet. This tells us clearly that the *dōzoku* bond is far stronger than the *kumi* [ward] bond, which is based upon neighborliness.

Although the origin of the Takehara stock is unknown, all five households of this stock recognize their genealogical relationship. They work together in rice planting and in the harvest season. They join each other for many of the traditional ceremonies: funerals, the anniversaries of recently deceased family members, Buddhist services for the dead, and worship of the ancestral *dōzoku* deity. They insist that *dōzoku* exists only for its ancestors so that *dōzoku* members should keep the genealogical relationship forever and enjoy the intimate human contacts it affords.

Both Takahara and Takehara stocks celebrate Wakamiya-sama [harmful deity] as their anecstor. The Takahara stock worships it at a small shrine on the 17th day of the tenth lunar month and the Takehara stock, on the 13th day of the ninth lunar month. In this respect they differ sharply from other *dōzoku*. Formerly, the Takahara stock worshiped Gongen-sama as its founding ancestor on the autumnal Equinox. The worship of Wakamiya-sama stems from a time when, as legend has it, the head of the original household, who was at that time also the official village head, killed a burglar. Thereupon the departed burglar's spirit haunted and brought a curse upon the *dōzoku* members. The *dōzoku* then dedicated a small shrine to Wakamiya-sama to rid themselves of the curse. Now, Gongen-sama is assimilated into Wakamiya and is worshiped with Wakamiya by the *dōzoku* members on the 17th day of the tenth lunar month.

The Takehara group also venerates Wakamiya-sama as its ancestor, but since they address this deity as Takehara-sama, everyone accepts that in this case, too, the deity is conglomerate. The ceremony is conducted on the 13th day of the ninth lunar month.

In Funaki hamlet there are three *dōzoku*; the Hirao stock, and Inoue stock in Suetsuna (a locality in Funaki), and an Inoue stock in Une (another locality). The five households of the Hirao stock are differentiated at present into a single household and a group of four, all of the latter being branches of the original household H. This original household, owning 4.42 acres of paddy fields and a house lot of 0.6 acres in 1604, was then one of the largest landowners. In 1693 its head became the official *kumi* [ward] headman, and from 1803 to 1817 he served as official village head. He monopolized the right to officiate in the cult of *dōzoku* ancestors as well as the Shintō ceremony of the Konomine shrine. As for the Konomine shrine, the founding ancestor brought along the shrine god as the guardian deity of his *dōzoku* when he settled in Funaki and since then has served it as a secular priest as well as the key holder of the shrine. In addition, one of the household heads of the original stem provided the paddy fields of 0.61 acres for the shrine repair in 1664. Such prerogatives of headship brought great prestige to the original household. To reinforce the everlasting dominance of the original household, its heir in 1712 obtained from his two younger brothers the following written oath (*tegata-no-koto*):

### Written Oath

To the original household head                          March 18, 1712
    Zenshiro Esq.

In both New Year Ceremonies and the Wedding Ceremonies the two of us pledge to attend and offer our services willingly to the original household without fail. Moreover, we will hand down this oath to posterity.

the Branch Households
Seigoro          (stamp)          Chozaemon          (stamp)

In this way, the original household enjoyed the highest prestige as the originator of the genealogical relationship and exercised its authority upon its branch households.

Permanent institutions do crumble over time, however, and recently the original household moved away. No one else has assumed the full role of *dōzoku* leadership and, consequently, the New Year visits have been abolished. Nevertheless, the Hirao stock still holds the cult of *dōzoku* ancestors on the early morning of the 22nd day of the seventh lunar month. All five household heads go to the small shrine for the founding ancestor and to the Konomine shrine at Konomine with dumplings and bottles of *sake* [wine] for worship. After the ceremony, all eat together, exchanging cups of wine and talking until evening, at the home of the person on duty. They appear anxious to maintain cooperation and solidarity with the *dōzoku* relationship.

The original household of Inoue stock in Une owned the house lot of 0.9 acres and was attended by a servant household in 1604. Its head became a ward headman in 1862 and established five branch households before 1868. Since that time, however, two branch households have died out, and one branch has drifted away. The original household at present forms a *dōzoku* with three branch households and holds *dōzoku* ancestor worship on the deathday of the founding ancestor, though there is no economic cooperation among them.

Three branch households of the original Inoue stock in Suetsuna have become extinct, while two other branches have drifted away. Only three *dōzoku* households now remain; of those, only two that are connected by a close personal kin tie cooperate on a genealogical basis. Nevertheless, all three households worship the founding ancestor at his grave on the 14th day of the 11th lunar month with three households of the Yucho stock in Modoroi, whose original household was established by this Inoue stock in the 1600's. After the ceremony, they gather and eat rice with beans at the home of the person whose turn it is.

This holds true for *dōzoku* in both Nobusada and Honmura. There are three *dōzoku* in Nobusada hamlet: the Okumoto stock, the Okamoto stock and the Kamisaka stock. The original household of the Okumoto stock was so powerful that it established a community shrine in 1767. After that time, however, because of numerous fissions in the branch households, the genealogical relationship of the original stem to its first and second branch households has been forgotten. Thus, this stock is now subdivided into three subunits. In essence it is far from being a *dōzoku* type of structure. According to one of the branch household heads, the *dōzoku* relationship was very important when the branch was first established, but, as a long time has elapsed there is no help for it. Most *dōzoku* members do not want to continue the genealogical relationship. Both the Okumoto stock and the Kamisaka stock are composed of three households. But a genealogical relationship of the original to the first branch for both groups is not recognized so that they are subdivided into two households and one household. Thus the *raison d'être* of the *dōzoku* has been lost. Formerly, all *dōzoku* in Nobusada hamlet worshiped Wakamiya as their ancestor on the 15th day of the ninth lunar month. This Wakamiya worship, however, has been abolished since 1920. The old ancestral shrines are found now only in upland fields and lower reaches of mountains. They remain unrepaired.

In Honmura there are six *dōzoku*: Hirao, I, II, and III, Hiramatsu, Ukon, and Inoue. In each case the main household disagrees with its assumed first branch as to their genealogical relationship. The three households in the Ukon group and the two households in the Inoue group say that they cooperate by reason of sharing the same surname, but all households claim to be genealogically independent. Nevertheless, there is an inexplicit, residual consciousness in these as well as the other sets of households in Honmura hamlet that each set once belonged to a common stock. The household members of the Hirao II, Hirao III, Hiramatsu, and Inoue stock used to gather on April 8 for a ceremonial repast at the home of the person on duty. Recently, however, the date has been shifted to the first Sunday of April for the convenience of schoolchildren and their mothers. The gathering is seen as an entertaining social event and the original meaning of the ancestral ceremony has been lost. Thus the holy day has become a holiday. Occasionally the Ukon stock celebrates Wakamiya as its ancestor on September 7, but inasmuch as this ceremony includes non-*dōzoku* members it is no longer properly the veneration of a founding ancestor. The Hirao I stock conducts no ancestral ceremony at all.

To sum up, the *dōzoku* depends in its rise and fall upon the *dōzoku* ancestor worship. It can be safely said that *dōzoku* ancestor worship is an indication of an effective *dōzoku*. In Nobusada and Honmura, where *dōzoku* ancestor worship has become purely nominal or abolished, the *dōzoku* has become weak and inactive. In Modoroi, Baba, and Kajiya, where *dōzoku* ancestor worship is still held, the *dōzoku* is strong and performs a function as a corporation. Such worship functions as the focus of a *dōzoku* and solidifies the unity of *dōzoku*. One of the most severe punishments upon a *dōzoku* member is to disqualify him from membership in *dōzoku* ancestor worship. So far, *dōzoku* ancestor worship is the ritual expression of *dōzoku* solidarity. The attachment of living members to the *dōzoku* is reinforced in the course of ritual acts. Thus *dōzoku* ancestor worship in Koresato can be defined in terms of rites of *dōzoku* solidarity.

Above all, *dōzoku* ancestor worship in Koresato is a world of men or household heads. All ancestral cults in Koresato are conducted by and in the presence of men at the grave or at small shrines of founding ancestors. This is in sharp contrast with the ancestral cult in the household, where women are becoming the prime agents. There are, indeed, some exceptions to this. For example, to glorify the ritual all *dōzoku* household members, including their wives and children, join in the cult of *dōzoku* ancestors in both Oka and Imai stock at Hisatsune village of Katsuta-cho, Okayama Prefecture on the 28th day of the twelfth lunar month (Okayama Minzokugakkai 1957: 48–50). The head of the original household of the Konan stock in Hara village of Katsuyama-cho, Okayama Prefecture presides over the ancestral cult of his *dōzoku* once every four years on the 19th day of the eleventh lunar month and invites all members of the eighteen branch households (Wakamori 1963: 151).

Along with this, *dōzoku* members generally offer their ancestors rice and cups of wines which are produced and brewed by the worshipers themselves. After the ritual, they eat rice with red beans and exchange cups of wine with one another at the home of the person on duty or in front of the graves or small shrines of founding ancestors. This dinner is termed *naorai*. It means that *dōzoku* members eat at the same meal with their ancestors, with whom they hold communion. By merging into one, the living *dōzoku* members encourage their ancestors to continue their concern in them, while they consolidate and solidify the unity of the *dōzoku*.

A circular system, too, is widely used in Koresato in the cults of *dōzoku* ancestors. But it does not necessarily apply to all *dōzoku* ancestor worship in the village commmunities within Okayama Prefecture. As Professor Pelzel points out, "lineage in Japanese usage is an organization of certain households into an expanded or compound *ie*" (Pelzel 1970: 235). A branch household is to its original what an household member is to his household head. The head of the original household extends his authority over his younger brothers, who create new household lines. In the southern part of Kagoshima Prefecture, newly formed branch households cannot build their small shrines for their immediate seniors until the fifth generation after establishment. They have to go to the original household to take part in ancestor worship of the more distant generations.

We can cite many cases of the same kind even in Okayama Prefecture. In Yamamura village of Tsuyama-shi, where branch households have to pay a New Year's visit to their original household first of all and then go round to visit one another; the original household of the Yoko-yama stock invites the two branch households to his household and celebrates Marishiten as his ancestor through a Shintō priest (Wakamori 1963: 1337). The original household head of the Shomatsu stock in Om-achi village of Katsuta-cho collects all the ancestral tablets of his nine branch households on the altar of his household and worships them through a Shintō priest when the harvest is over. After the ritual, they go and pay respect to the graves of their ancestors. All rites are presided over by the original household as a right and duty. This holds true of another five *dōzoku* in the northern part of Okayama Prefecture. Even in *dōzoku* where ancestral cults are held on a shift system, the original household takes the seat of honor and other branches sit at the table according to their status on the genealogical table as is seen in the Tamagi stock at Naka village of Chuo-cho (Wakamori 1963: 152–153). The branch household that is bound to hold an ancestral service in a given year borrows the ancestral tablet of the founding ancestor from the original household and conducts the cult of *dōzoku* ancestors of the Asano stock at Hara village of Katsuta-cho (Wakamori 1963: 151–152).

Thus in some well-ordered *dōzoku* the original household monopolizes the right to officiate in the cult of *dōzoku* ancestors and holds the legitimate authority over its branches in the names of its *dōzoku* ancestors. *Dōzoku* ancestor worship is a ritual expression of both *dōzoku* solidarity and the status structure of the *dōzoku* group.

In concluding this report, *dōzoku* ancestors themselves have to be discussed. As is seen in the cult of *dōzoku* ancestors of Koresato, *dōzoku* members worship mainly their founding ancestors. Many of the founding ancestors have their own names and individuality. A typical example of this is the founding ancestor of the Inoue stock in Modoroi. According to the written Shintō prayer of 1936, the founding ancestor of this stock is Mitsuzaburo Inoue, sixteenth child from the fifty-sixth Imperial generation. Being defeated at the battle of Tenjinyama Castle in 1577, he retired to Modoroi with the youngest son of his lord and the son's nurse. The descendants of the Inoue stock regard him as the founding ancestor, though he is a descendant of the Emperor. Thus they glorify his noble birth, through which they distinguish the stock from other *dōzoku* of like order. To take another example, the genealogy of the Daicho stock tells us that the founding ancestor, whose father was the lord of Saka-maki Castle, being defeated, retired with his family in 1575 to O village of Tomi-son. He changed his household name from Kondo to Dai-cho (Yonemura 1966: 75). It is said, according to the brief sketch of the Tomomori stock (Seishi Ryakkuki), that the founding ancestor was Kihe Tomomori who returned to agriculture in Tomomori. His father, who was defeated as a citadel steward under the lord of Tenjinyama Castle, became a priest and assumed the name of Genshobo in Kento-ku temple in Terabe of Takebe-cho. Kihe Tomomori ordered his eldest son, Mangoro, to worship him as the founding ancestor in his brief sketch of the Tomomori stock in 1600 (Yonemura 1971: 100).

Insofar as my knowledge is concerned, the founding ancestors of the thirteen *dōzoku* in the northern part of Okayama Prefecture came from the *samurai* class and returned to agriculture. They not only represent symbolically the long history of their stocks as the fountainheads of their *dōzoku* but also glorify the honorable tradition of their stocks through their noble birth. As stated above, they function not only as the focus of their *dōzoku* but also as the representatives of their subsequent ancestors or as the symbols of the collectivity of ancestors. In other words, they function as the organizing principle of these ancestors as well as their *dōzoku* members. In this respect, the founding ancestors themselves have to be worshiped as the source of their being in the structural context of *dōzoku*.

What is more, the merits accumulated in their lifetimes provide protection and prosperity for their descendants. So men offer their founding ancestors sacrifices and beg them to descend and enjoy them. Men pray for their protection and benevolence. In return for the blessings of their ancestors, men have to glorify them and bring more honor to them by accumulating deeds for piety's sake. They hold the cult of the founding ancestor at the anniversaries of the memorial day in addition to the yearly observance of the commemorative day. As was noted above, the Inoue stock in Modoroi held the 360th anniversary in 1936 (Yonemura 1962: 1–19). The Kuroda stock at Komori of Kamogawa-cho held their 350th anniversary in 1953 (Yonemura 1973: 612) and the Yamamoto stock at Koen village of Nagi-cho held their 600th anniversary around 1950 (Okayama Minzokugakkai 1957: 50). Furthermore, if circumstances permit, men erect splendid stone tombs for their founding ancestors including their succeeding ancestors. For example, the Kuroda stock at Komori erected a monumental stone for the founding ancestor at the 350th anniversary in 1953.

Around the 1870's the Tomomori stock, too, erected a small shrine and a monumental tomb for their founding ancestor, including his succeeding ancestors, as a cooperative project of the original stem and its first branch household. Since that time this stock has held the cult of *dōzoku* ancestors in cooperation with the branch segment of the Tomomori B stock in commemoration of the occasion. In this way, they glorify their ancestors. It is in this sense of the terms that the Terasaka and Uehara stock offer their founding ancestor's original armor at the ancestral cult of the *dōzoku* in front of the grave or altars, just as do the Korematsu I and II stocks in Modoroi. In addition, a line of successful and famous ancestors not only raises the status of their founding ancestors, but glorifies their descendants too. They are worshiped with their founding ancestors by their *dōzoku* members. The Takatori stock in Yono village of Katsuta-cho worships and glorifies the ancestor who was raised to the senior grade of the fifth Court rank, on the 10th day of the fourth month. Thus they glorify their ancestors as the source of their being and *dōzoku* ancestors cast honor upon the solidarity and unity of their *dōzoku*.

On the one hand, Wakamiya is worshiped by two *dōzoku* in Kajiya. As for Wakamiya of the Takahara stock, the spirit of the departed burglar, who was killed by one of the heads of the original household, is enshrined in Wakamiya because a medium divined that his spirit brought curses upon the *dōzoku* members. This holds true of Ashida at Hina village of Ochiai-cho, and the Honmyo stock at Tane village of Yubaracho (Wakamori 1963: 237). Wakamiya is dedicated to all departed spirits who die unnatural deaths. They have some connections with the ancestors of worshipers, their graves, or house lots. Through this connection, they afflict some of the worshipers and urge them to worship Wakamiya through the divination of mediums.

On the other hand, the Takehara stock worships its ancestor, or Takehara-sama as Wakamiya. The Toguni stock in Kanahara village of Katsuta-cho, the Nagao stock and the Miki stock at Sora village of Bizenshi worship their ancestors as Wakamiya. The predecessor of the Nagao household dedicated Wakamiya to his ancestor who afflicted his household members. It is said that this departed ancestor harmed his descendants whenever they consulted doctors. A typical example of this is the Tomisaka stock at Tomisaka village of Katsuta-cho. According to the Contribution Record of Erecting Ancestral Wakamiya Shrine (*Sosen Wakamiya Jinsha konryu ni tsuki kifucho*) in 1886, the founding ancestor, Tomisaka, Magoroku held Hoshiyama Castle against Ukita but, being defeated, took his own life. Then his people made off with his bones to Kajinami and buried them at the foot of Shirono mountain and dedicated Wakamiya to him. Since that time they worshiped him yearly on the 20th day of the tenth lunar month. However, with the lapse of time, the shrine fell into disrepair. Around 1886, many of the *dōzoku* members had nightmares so that they could not sleep. Accordingly, they consulted a medium and, through his divination, realized that the founding ancestor deplored the descendants' neglect. Then they erected a small shrine to console him as part of their duty. They prayed for his benevolence and protection so that they could be happy and prosper. This tells us clearly that Wakamiya is nothing but a founding ancestor. Take one more example from Shikoku. The Imashiro stock in Taka-gushi-honmura of Uwajima-shi, worships a founding ancestor called Hyogonokami Imashiro as Imashiro-sama who died in battle. This ancestor is capricious and harmful. Whenever one cuts grass and trees in the grove around the shrine, some of the *dōzoku* members, without fail, fall ill or are badly hurt. So *dōzoku* members worship him with utmost care. They hold this rite on the 15th day of both the fourth and eight lunar months. Fifty years ago, in addition, they held cult celebrations on the Equinoxes of spring and autumn. Besides, before the ritual, all *dōzoku* members swept the grave clean and made all sorts of preparations for the festival. Even now, when some of the *dōzoku* members fall ill or suffer an unlucky year, they expel evil spirits in front of the shrine through the purification of a medium first of all and then exorcise the founder in front of the ancestral altar of their household (Sakurai 1972: 62–65).

Thus it is believed that Wakamiya is a *dōzoku* ancestor who died an unnatural death. Whenever his right to receive ritual service is denied, he afflicts his *dōzoku* members. Mediums such as mountain monks and shamans are instrumental in spreading Wakamiya belief. Nevertheless, it may be said that punishing is inherent in the behavior of ancestral spirits notwithstanding their benevolence. Through this harmful character of the *dōzoku* ancestor, the *dōzoku* cult and Wakamiya belief readily assimilate. In this respect, a *dōzoku* ancestor may be harmful not only outside the cult group, but even within it. It may be admitted that the *dōzoku* ancestor is benign and protective as long as he receives ritual service due to him, but he is punitive and harmful to his descendants if his right to be worshiped by his *dōzoku* members is denied. *Dōzoku* ancestor worship functions effectively as the focus of a *dōzoku* and strengthens the solidarity and unity of the *dōzoku*.

## REFERENCES

ARUGA, KIZAEMON
1959  "Nihon ni okeru senzo no kannen [The notion of ancestors in Japan]," in *Ie — sono kozobunsheki* [*Ie* — its structural analysis].

Edited by Kitano Seiichi and K. Okada, 1–33. Tokyo: Sobun-sha.

FORTES, MEYER
1959   *Oedipus and Job in West Africa.* Cambridge: University of Cambridge Press.
1965   "Some reflections on ancestor worship," in *African systems of thought.* Edited by M. Fortes and G. Dieterlen, 122–142. London: Oxford University Press.
1970   "Pietas in ancestor worship," in *Time and social structure and other essays,* 164–200. London: Athlone Press.

FREEDMAN, MAURICE
1958   *Lineage organization in southeastern China.* London School of Economics Monograph on Social Anthropology 18. London: Athlone Press.
1966   *Chinese lineage and society: Fukien and Kwantung.* London School of Economics Monograph on Social Anthropology 33. London: Athlone Press.
1970   "Ancestor worship: two facets of the Chinese case," in *Social organization.* Edited by M. Freedman, 163–187. Stanford: Stanford University Press.

HAGIWARA, TATSUO
1954   "Fujin no seikatsu" [Life of women], in *Meiji bunkashi* [The cultural history of the Meiji period]. Edited by K. Yanagita, 365–367. Tokyo: Yoyo-sha.

HINONISHI, SHINTEI
1972   Tajima ni okeru jigami no kenkyū [The study of earth deities in Tajima]. *Nihon Minzokugaku* [Bulletin of the Folklore Society of Japan] 82:3.

HORI, ICHIRO
1961   *Minkan shinko* [Folk belief]. Tokyo: Iwanami-shoten.
1963   *Shukyō-shuzoku no seikatsukisei* [Religion and custom as norms of life]. Tokyo: Mirai-sha.

KAMISHIMA, JIRO
1961   *Kindai nihon no seishinkōzō* [The ideology and thought of modern Japan]. Tokyo: Iwanami-shoten.

KOYAMA, TAKASHI, *editor*
1967   *Gendai kazoku no yakuwari kōzō* [The role analysis of modern families]. Tokyo: Baifukan.

MINZOKUGAKU KENKYŪSHO
1956   *Sōgō nihon minzoku goi* [Japanese folklore glossaries]. Tokyo: Heibon-sha.

MIURA, SHUYU
1958   Okayama-ken no misaki [Misaki in Okayama Prefecture]. *Seto Naikai Kenkyū* 11:23–24.

MOGAMI, TAKAYOSHI
1956   *Mairibaka* [Visiting graves for worship]. Tokyo: Kokin-shoin.

NAKANE, CHIE
1967   *Kinship and economic organization in rural Japan.* London: Athlone Press.

NAOE, HIROJI
1972    *Yashikigami no kenkyū* [The study of yashiki gami] (third edition). Tokyo: Yoshikawa-kobunkan.

OKAYAMA MINZOKUGAKKAI
1957    *Nagi sanroku no minzoku* [Folklore at the foot of Mt. Nagi]. Okayama.
1958    *Hattoji shuhen no minzoku* [Folklore around Hattoji]. Okayama.

OTAKE, HIDEO
1962    *Hokenshakai no nomin kazoku* [Peasant families in feudal society]. Tokyo: Sobun-sha.

PELZEL, JOHN C.
1970    "Japanese kinship: a comparison," in *Family and kinship in Chinese society*. Edited by M. Freedman. Stanford: Stanford University Press.

SAKURAI, TOKUTARO
1972    *Minkan shinko* [Folk belief]. Tokyo: Hanawa-shobo.

TAKEDA, AKIRA
1964    *Minzokukanko to shiteno inkyo no kenkyū* [The folkloristic study of retirement practices]. Tokyo: Mirai-sha.
1970    *Ie o meguru minzoku kenkyū* [Folkloristic study on household]. Tokyo: Kobun-do.

TAKEDA, CHOSHU
1961    *Sosen suhai* [Ancestor worship]. Kyoto: Heirakuji-shoten.

TAKEDA, CHOSHU, M. TAKATORI
1957    *Nihonjin no shinkō* [Religious belief of Japanese people]. Tokyo: Sogen-sha.

WAKAMORI, TARO, *editor*
1963    *Mimasaka no minzoku* [Foklore in the northern part of Okayama Prefecture]. Tokyo: Yoshikawa-kobunkan.

YANAGITA, KUNIO
1946    *Senzo no hanashi* [About our ancestors]. Tokyo: Chikuma-shobo.

YONEMURA, SHOJI
1962    Saishisoshikito sonrakukōzō [The organization for Shinto rituals and the village structure — Koresato of Yoshii-cho]. *Shakai to denshō* [Society and Folklore] 62:1–19.
1966    Ichi sanson ni okeru dōzoku to shinzoku [*Dōzoku* and kindred on a mountain village — O village of Tomi-son]. *Okayama-Daigaku Kyōikugakubu Kenkyūshuroku* [The Bulletin of the School of Education, Okayama University] 22:67–119.
1970    Saishisoshiki to sonrakukōzō — Okayama-ken, Katsuta-cho, Kozo buraku [The organization for Shintō rituals and village structure — Kozo of Katsuta-cho, Okayama Prefecture]. *Sonraku Shakai Kenkyū* 6:73–119.
1971    Sasihisoshiki to sonrakukōzō [Shintō ceremonies and social structure in a suburban village near Okayama-shi]. *Okayama Daigaku Kyōikugakubu Kenkyūshuroku* 31:91–117.
1973    "Ichi sanson ni okeru dōzoku to shinzoku" [*Dōzoku* and kindred in a remote mountain village — Komori of Kamogawa-cho, Okayama-ken], in *Village structure and kinship system*. Edited by

the Editing Committee of articles presented to Professor Kitano, 579–646. Tokyo: Mirai-sha.

YOSHIDA, TEIGO
1972 *Nihon no tsukimono* [Retribution and spirit possession in Japan]. Tokyo: Chuokoron-sha.

YOSHIDA, TEIGO, T. AYABE
1967 "Seinan Nippon sonraku ni okeru chitsujo to henbō" [Social order and change in a village community in southwestern Japan]. *Hikaku kyōiku bunka kenkyūshisetsu kiyo* 18.

# The Malevolent Ancestor: Ancestral Influence in a Japanese Religious Sect

KAREN KERNER

Like millenarian cults throughout the world, the *shinkō shūkyō* [newly arisen religions] of Japan have as their goal the transformation of society. While some of the new religions postulate the presence of the millenium, and others seek to prepare for it, all are concerned with changing the very substance of social ties. Most of these new religions, like the traditional religions of Japan, are theologically syncretic and tolerant in outlook.

Two of the new religions, however, Sōka Gakkai and Tensho-Kotai-Jingu-Kyō, are exclusivist in orientation. They specifically prohibit members from worshiping in any fashion other than that dictated by sectarian religious affiliation. My concern here is with a single aspect of religious belief and practice in the exclusivist sect Tensho-Kotai-Jingu-Kyō, namely the relationship of its members (called *dōshi*, literally "comrade") to their ancestors.

## ANCESTOR WORSHIP: STRUCTURE AND SENTIMENT

If attendance at shrines and temples during holidays is the public form of religious observance for non-*dōshi* Japanese, then the veneration of ancestors within the household is the primary private form. In strict

The research on which this paper is based was supported by NIMH Research Grant 1-RO4-MH13636 and NIMH Research Fellowship 5-F1-MH25,332, and a supplementary grant awarded by the East Asian Institute, Columbia University. The author would like to express her gratitude to the Associates of the Institute for the Study of Human Issues, Inc. for their encouragement and assistance. Particular thanks go to David Feingold for his stimulating comments.

structural terms, in the Japanese system only the household founder and his wife and those in succeeding generations who replace them as household heads, the "progenitors" (Smith, conference discussion, 1973), can be defined as true ancestors. However, the popular use of the term *senzo* to refer to both these true ancestors and to other dead household members blurs distinctions between categories of household dead honored at the domestic shrine. In consequence, many authorities have used the English term "ancestors" to refer to occupants of both the category of progenitors and that of those other persons who were regular members of the household at the time of their deaths.

While there is no invariable one-to-one correspondence between social structure and patterns of ancestor worship throughout the world, the ways in which people structure relationships within the boundaries of significant social groups, such as the family, illuminate the ways in which they regard deceased occupants of social roles within those groups. Thus, in regions in which lineage organization is stressed, patterns of ancestor worship reflect that unilineal emphasis, and in regions in which bilateral kinship or other horizontal social ties are strong those nonunilineal emphases are reflected in the identification and choice of ancestors to be worshiped. Conversely, the ways in which people structure relationships between the living and the dead are clues to the nature of ongoing social organization.

It appears, for example, that in the northeastern areas of Japan where *dōzoku*[1] organization is important, veneration of ancestors occurs only within the patriline. In southwestern Japan, where the *kokumi*[2] type of organization (Befu 1963) predominates, age-grade organizations persist, and the bilateral kindred is strong, worship of both paternal and maternal ancestors is common. These patterns of veneration thus reflect the constitution of social relationships existing on the ground.

Ancestors, linked to their descendants by a chain of ritual and remembrance, represent both those-who-have-gone-before and those-who-shall-come-after: all properly constituted household or family members know that they will one day assume ancestral status and merge

---

[1]    Befu (1971: 57) provides a succinct definition of the *dōzoku*: "Structurally, the *dōzoku* is composed of several stem families organized into a hierarchical group, with one family at the top, known as the main family (*honke*) and the others called branches (*bunke, bekke*), occupying subordinate positions in the system. The hierarchy ... implies political, economic, and ritual disparity among families ...."
[2]    The *kokumi* type of community organization found in southwestern Japan is characterized by an association of households on an egalitarian basis, in which kinship plays only an incidental part, in contrast to the *dōzoku* type of community. In *kokumi* communities, households are organized into formal organizations known often as *ko* or *kumi*: hence the name "kokumi type."

with the previous generations of ancestors. In some sense, reverence for the ancestors is also reverence for the position that the venerator shall himself someday occupy. Ritually expressed regard for the ancestors thus affirms the continuity of social relations through time.

One important concern of scholars dealing with ancestor worship has been to ascertain the disposition of ancestors toward their living descendants. Ancestors are presumed to exercise in some degree jural authority over their descendants, much as the living occupants of power-holding roles exercise authority over their juniors (Fortes 1961). Indeed, Kopytoff (1971) suggests that in certain African societies, those who have been called ancestors are more appropriately regarded as "dead elders." He notes that in Suku society, "a single set of principles regulates the relationship between senior and junior; a person deals with a single set of *bambuta* [elders living and dead] and the line dividing the living from the dead does not affect the structure of the relationship" (Kopytoff 1971:133). However, the line dividing living and dead occupants of the elder role is ritually demarcated if affectively blurred, as various scholars, including Fiawoo, Newell and Uchendu, have noted.

Ancestral volition and authority are demonstrated by the legitimate intercession of ancestors in the lives of their descendants. A reciprocal concern, the disposition of the living toward their dead ancestors, is similarly important: role alters are presumed to participate equally in the definition of relationships obtaining between the living and the dead. Thus, Chinese ancestral spirits may dwindle into the piteous if dangerous "Hungry Ghosts" without proper mediation and provision by the living (Jordan 1972). Moreover, as Freedman (1967: 86–88) suggests, relations with the ancestors may be redefined according to the contexts in which they occur: Chinese ancestors in their shrines are reverenced and tended; Chinese ancestors in their tombs are used in *feng-shui* [geomancy] as media through which their descendants seek to attain material desires.

Ancestors may be conceived of as actively benevolent: for example, among the devotees of Melanesian cargo cults (Worsley 1957) and among adherents of the American Indian Ghost Dance of 1890 (Mooney 1896), venerated ancestors were believed to be the source of all good fortune and were expected to return to offer the benefit of direct guidance to their troubled descendants. In the golden millenia portrayed by cult leaders, the eagerly awaited ancestral dead would arrive with goods and techniques to enrich the lives of their descendants. It is significant that these beliefs developed in areas characterized by traditional beliefs in the legitimate and usually beneficent involvement of the dead in the affairs of their living descendants (Lawrence and Meggitt 1965).

Ancestors may be viewed as passively benevolent: Hsu (1949) and Freedman (1966) have suggested that, in the main, Chinese ancestors are well disposed toward their descendants so long as a modicum of respectful attention is paid them, and Yanagita (1946) and Hozumi (1912) have maintained that Japanese ancestors are similarly invariably beneficent. Jordan (1972) suggests that, at least in part, Chinese ancestors are benevolent because they are relatively ineffective: they are not moralistic arbiters of their descendants' behavior.

On the other hand, ancestors may be actively malevolent, as is the case among the Ifaluk (Spiro 1952) and the Nayars (Gough 1958), and descendants appropriately regard their ancestors with awe and fear. Recent work by Wolf (cited by Freedman 1966) in Taiwan, and Yoshida (1967) in southwestern Japan suggests that ancestors in these societies may, under certain circumstances, harm the living. Since such harm is not the invariable consequence of interaction between ancestors and descendants, its cause may be diagnosed only by a medium.

Ancestors may punish their descendants by exacting retribution for the failure of descendants to observe ceremonial obligations toward the dead, as Fortes (1961) reports for the Tallensi. Under such circumstances, punishment is acknowledged to be the just, if deplorable, exercise of ancestral right, and can ideally be avoided if the ritual obligations toward the dead are faithfully carried out.

But ancestors may also harm their descendants in a manner that is neither wilful nor punitive: misfortune may occur to the living because of the links binding together a suffering ancestor and his descendant. Under these circumstances, the descendant must alleviate his ancestor's suffering in order to eliminate his own suffering. Among the Akha, for example, the spirits of those ancestors who have died "bad deaths" are redeemed by descendants to forestall personal misfortune (Feingold, personal communication, 1969). The similar case of the hungry ghosts in Taiwan (Jordan 1972) has already been mentioned.

This study presents the case of a religious sect in which ancestors are believed capable of harming their descendants either wilfully or as a consequence of personal suffering. Avoidance of such harm is accomplished not through the propitiation or commemoration of the affecting ancestors, but through the symbolic and ritual severing of the ties binding the ancestors to their descendants. Among members of Tensho-Kotai-Jingū-Kyō, the ritual remembrance of the household *senzo* is abruptly terminated when one assumes regular membership in the religion. This symbolic disjunction is paralleled by the performance of disjunctive rituals in other aspects of sectarian social life.

The case under discussion is that of Tensho-Kotai-Jingū-Kyō (hereafter referred to as Tensho), a Japanese messianic sect discussed more fully in a previous publication (Kerner 1970). Extensive information about sect branches in Hawaii may be found in the fine published work of Lebra (1970a, 1970b, 1972).

Tensho was founded by Kitamura Sayo, a farmer's wife, in 1945, after three years of itinerant preaching. Mrs. Kitamura reported herself to be the repository and spokeswoman of a *kami* known as Tensho Kotai Jin [Absolute Almighty God of the Universe], who represented, according to sectarian theology, a tripartite merging of the female *kami* Amaterasu Omikami, the male *kami* Kotaijin, and Mrs. Kitamura. The headquarters of the religious group remains at the site of the Kitamura family home in the town of Tabuse, Yamaguchi Prefecture, Japan.[3]

Mrs. Kitamura's followers believe her to have been divine: they call her, therefore, Ogamisama [the Great Venerable Goddess]. Her granddaughter, Kitamura Kiyokazu, who is Ogamisama's spiritual successor, is known as Himegamisama [Princess-Goddess]. Mrs. Kitamura's son Yoshito, the present director of the religious organization, is called Wakagamisama [Young God].

The division of powers between Himegamisama, the successor to the foundress' charismatic office, and Wakagamisama, the director of the religious organization who is also the head of the Kitamura *ie* [household line], parallels in some respects the organizational split reported for Tenri kyō (Newell and Dobashi 1968) between the Nakayama *ie* line and the charismatic line of succession. In Tensho at the present time the distinctions between the two lines are only potentially significant, as Miss Kitamura has not yet married. With her marriage and the birth of children, and her eldest brother's marriage and parenthood and eventual assumption of the Kitamura *ie* headship, a possible basis for

---

[3]   The religion has excited some attention in the Japanese popular press. In the Occupation years, the outspoken criticism leveled by Mrs. Kitamura against the government, and the ecstatic public behavior of her followers (including speaking in tongues, loudly praying, and dancing in public places) was frequently reported in a negative fashion by the newspapers of the time. In 1966, the religion assumed further prominence when its massive new headquarters complex in Tabuse, designed by Otani under the direction of Tange, one of Japan's foremost architects, was awarded a prize for outstanding architectural excellence. More recently, the religion again achieved national prominence when, at the death of the Foundress, her seventeen-year-old granddaughter Kiyokazu (Himegamisama) assumed the mantle of *Kyōso* [religious leader] for the faith.

future factional splits would be established. If, however, Miss Kita-mura's husband were to be adopted into the Kitamura *ie,* the potentially fissiparous situation could be avoided.

Although syncretic in nature, the religion carefully redefines and re-structures concepts found also in Buddhist, Shintō, Confucianist, and even Christian sources. It claims a total worldwide membership in excess of 360,000, of which approximately 300,000 members are Japanese. The overseas branches were established as a consequence of the foundress' repeated missionary trips abroad. At the time of field-work between June 1967 and May 1969,[4] there were 207 Japanese branches of the religion. With construction of a Tokyo headquarters complex now under way, the total number of Japanese branches has grown to more than 300.

In Japan, Tensho is often referred to as Odoru Shukyō [the Dancing Religion], a name distasteful to adherents. It acquired that name in reference to the *muga-no-mai* [nonego dance] which is performed pub-licly by members to symbolize selfless union with the *kami.* The *miga-kino-kai* [mutual disciplinary session], a form of *hoza* discussion group, is the core of the members' religious practice.

## RELATIONSHIPS BETWEEN ANCESTORS AND DESCENDANTS

Members of Tensho frequently state that they were attracted to the faith because it promised alleviation of suffering, particularly that occa-sioned by illness, family trouble, or economic misfortune. The sect de-fines suffering as the consequence of negative supernatural interference. Sick persons may be possessed by a variety of causative agents: spirits emitted from living persons; spirits of the dead (both ancestral and un-related); and spirits of animals. Each of these types of spiritual beings may manifest itself in various forms of disease ranging from mild respiratory ailments to seemingly incurable cases of cancer.

---

[4] I resided for nine months during 1967 and 1968 at the headquarters of the religion in Tabuse. Additional visits were made also to sect branches and homes of followers throughout Japan in 1968–69 and in 1969 for a period of three weeks in Hawaii. Between 1969 and 1972 I exchanged visits with Himegamisama and her brother, who were then students at American colleges. Information about ancestral spirits was acquired as a by-product of an investigation into notions of privacy and vulnerability among sect members. Interviews were conducted with the resi-dents of the headquarters community, including the Foundress and her successor, and with sect branch leaders and members. Additional information was acquired through semiparticipant observation, both as a resident of the headquarters com-munity and as a visitor to sect branches and members' homes.

In Tensho-Kotai-Jingū-Kyō belief, ancestral spirits are more frequently defined as malignant than among nonmember Japanese. Some
of these ancestral spirits are seen as wilfully and actively malevolent.
Others, because they have not yet been redeemed according to Tensho
belief, are themselves innocent of evil intent, but contrive to make their
descendants suffer through their own misery. Ogamisama, the foundress
of Tensho, described the condition of such unhappy souls as follows:

If a person remains engrossed in this world and becomes an unsaved soul,
he will become an obstacle for this world. Even after death he becomes an
obstacle to the world in the state of an unredeemed spirit. Unredeemed
ancestors are in this way bringing you misfortune.

The category of ancestral spirits *(senzō no rei)* in Tensho belief includes
both remote ancestors and newly departed kin or household members.
Tensho members do not distinguish terminologically between true ancestors (the progenitors of the household line and their successors) and
other household dead, nor is any apparent distinction made between
lineal, collateral, or cognatic kin as the locus of supernatural influence.
The spirits of deceased individuals below Ego's generation, including
the spirits of aborted fetuses, are capable of affecting kinsmen —
particularly, but not only, parents and siblings. The spirits of all non-
*dōshi* dead, including those ancestors who have not previously been
redeemed through Tensho practice, are called *akurei* [unredeemed
spirits, earthbound souls]. These unredeemed souls are believed to
suffer intense agony.

Most of these unredeemed souls occasion misfortune for their living
kin as a consequence of their own suffering. Others, however, are believed to be actively malevolent. Wilfully malevolent spirits frequently
affect their in-laws: for example, a mother-in-law may become the object of spiritual attack by her deceased daughter-in-law, and vice versa.
However, other actively malevolent ancestral spirits may affect both
lineal and collateral kin. The malevolent spirits of first wives frequently
affect their husbands' living spouses.

In contrast to traditional practices in Japan, Tensho members utilize
neither the double grave system, nor the complex system of burial
names and rituals. The typical funeral is an extremely simple affair,
accompanied by neither feasting nor long eulogy. The deceased individual is laid out without undergoing embalming (yet believers maintain that the bodies of departed members are unusually pliable and
healthful-looking even after death). Members of the family and the
local sect branch visit the funeral parlor or the home in which the body

reposes, and congratulate the members of the deceased individual's family on the departed person's accession to a higher spiritual plane. A local sect leader will say a few words over the body, reminding listeners of the gratitude they owe to Ogamisama, and the security all enjoy who follow Tensho precepts.

Prior to her death, Ogamisama herself officiated at the funerals of individuals resident at the sect headquarters in Tabuse. At the present time, her son, Wakagamisama, the director of the religious organization, performs the same function. The bodies of the departed *dōshi* are cremated, and the ashes scattered. Ogamisama herself was buried on the grounds of the sect headquarters across from the main sanctuary, and the tumulus erected over her coffin is regarded as a shrine by her followers.

Despite common fears held by nonmember Japanese about the dangers resident in the soul of the newly deceased individual, members of Tensho express few overt fears about the newly deceased. It is believed that faithful practice of the teachings of Tensho, or the intercession of one who is a devout practitioner, nullifies any contaminating capacity of the earthbound spirit. After all, it is said, "our headquarters is built on the grounds of a traditional cemetery, and Ogamisama redeemed all those souls so that they would not bother us." The nonbeliever dead, particularly if they have died as a result of suicide or murder, are considered to be dangerous — but no more dangerous than long-dead, unredeemed spirits.

It should be noted that Tensho members distinguish neither terminologically nor behaviorally between the spirits of the newly dead and those of remote ancestors. Among non-*dōshi* Japanese, as Kirby (1910), Plath (1964), and Smith (1966) have noted previously, these categories of the dead are labeled with the single term *senzo;* they are, however, distinguished in terms of the behavior of descendants toward them.

Tensho members, on the other hand, distinguish between two significant categories of spirits of the dead only in terms of the moral status of those spirits: those that are redeemed and those that are not. Redeemed spirits, identified with *tenshi* [angels], reside in heaven, returning only infrequently to earth to give a bit of assistance to particularly devout *dōshi*. Unredeemed spirits, the *akurei*, are forced to linger near the earth, causing illness and misfortune through their attachment to living people.

Sickness caused by spirit possession is sometimes diagnosed by the sufferer, but more frequently a fellow sect member or leader must diagnose the spiritual cause of the ailment. In one case discussed with me, a young man was afflicted with palsy. He was described as "shaking and quivering like an old man." He was diagnosed by the leader of his branch congregation as being possessed by the spirit of the older brother of his father's father, who had suffered from palsy in his old age. When the young man recovered, he had lost all trace of the palsy, and no longer resembled "a shaky old man."

In another case, a woman dreamt repeatedly that a frightening apparition with uncombed long hair kept appearing by her bedside, making threatening motions toward the dreamer's throat. The woman would awake gasping for breath. When she took her problem to the Foundress, she was informed that the ghost was the jealous spirit of her husband's first wife, who had to be released from bondage by the second wife's intercession. Ogamisama told the woman that, without such intercession, "many second wives die of the same sickness as the first wives because they are not aware of the spirit world. The earthbound spirits of the first wives usually attach themselves to the second wives and take their lives."

Central to Tensho belief is the concept of *innen* or karma. *Innen* is conceived of as the sum of credits and debits from past incarnations, both ancestral and personal. It is believed that persons in this life are linked by karma both with their ancestors and other household members and with other compatriots from their own past lives. Tensho members believe that nothing happens by chance in this life: present activity is the product of "the old debts in our book of karma."

The curing of illness caused by spirit possession is accomplished by breaking the ties between suffering individuals and the afflicting spirits. Because spirits are believed to be attracted to an individual as a consequence of karmic linkage, malevolent ancestral spirits — indeed, all malevolent spirits — are controlled through "cutting the karma" of the affected person. Ogamisama was believed to possess a remarkable capacity to release individuals from their karmic bonds: through her intercession, an individual could be divorced completely from his past affective connections and their causal implications for his future. Devout *dōshi* possess this capacity to a lesser degree, and may intercede for suffering individuals.

Moreover, the redemption of afflicting spirits — and thus the severing of karmic links — may even be accomplished by the afflicted individual himself, through faithful recitation of the Tensho prayer and through the performance of the *muga-no-mai* [nonego dance]. However, he must pray unselfishly for world peace and the redemption of all evil spirits. He must NOT pray to be relieved of a specific afflicting spirit, or this selfish desire will nullify the effects of the prayer. Followers believe that the involuntary upward movements of the hands and arms during prayer or in the dance indicate the redemption and departure of afflicting spirits, with a consequent lessening of the weight of the believer's limbs.

Central to Tensho belief is the destruction and abandonment of ancestral soul tablets, and the household "god shelf" (the Shintō *kamidana* or the Buddhist *butsudan*) on which they are normally placed. No offerings are made to the ancestors, nor are they informed of important household events. They are not commemorated on holidays, nor are they considered to participate in the ongoing life of the family. Once redeemed — and one is obliged to redeem ancestors in order to avoid personal suffering — the ancestors are considered no longer to be symbolically or ritually linked to their descendants. Although the ancestors of Tensho members continue to occupy significant positions in the family genealogy, they cease to occupy significant positions within the social and religious life of the household.

In the homes of Tensho members, the *tokonoma* [shelved alcove: a semisacred space] is also stripped of all other non-Tensho religious articles. Instead, followers frequently, though not invariably, place photographs of Ogamisama and of the sect headquarters, copies of the sectarian motto for the year (e.g. *"Mikuni daiji,"* glossed as "God's country above all," was the motto for 1969), a clock, and Tensho literature on the shelves formerly used for the household shrine. Performance of the required twice-daily (or more frequent) household devotions, involving ten to fifteen minutes of prayer and the singing of sectarian hymns, routinely takes place before these displayed paraphernalia of the Tensho faith.

The symbolic severing of ties with the ancestors is paralleled in the social life of the sect by the segregation of sect members from their nonmember families, by rituals performed in the adoption of children whose natural parents are still living, and by sectarian insistence on a period of service for young people, away from their families, at the headquarters of the faith.

On the social level, the sect seeks to redefine and restructure the believer's personal universe; by loosening or eradicating ties to any groups or persons dwelling outside the boundaries of Tensho, it serves symbolically and socially as the primary  and often only reference group for followers. Sect members are thus often separated from their families and warned not to interact with them until such time as all family members convert. Such segregation is explained as necessary for the ultimate health and well-being of the follower. Similarly, both brides and *mukoyōshi* [adopted husbands] are told to forget their natal homes and families as if they had never existed. Moreover, sect marriages are frequently arranged between Japanese and Nisei *dōshi*, involving the permanent departure of one of the spouses from his or her own familiar society.

*Dōshi* children are not infrequently given in adoption to totally un-related members: it is quite common for Nisei members of the sect to request and receive Japanese children. The children selected for adop-tion are most often those of impoverished or widowed parents, and they are adopted by other childless couples. The transfer of the children is effected after a few words said by a leader and a short period of prayer in which the leader, the adoptive parents, and the child or children participate. The newly adopted children are expected to leave their natural parents free of sentimental attachment to them. Instead, I was told, "they turn to their new parents as if they had been born to them."

In terms of community participation, particularly significant in rural areas, sect members are prohibited from participating in rituals performed at community shrines. Particularly in the early days of the religion, the prohibition on such participation frequently occasioned community ostracism for the nonparticipating Tensho followers. Simi-larly, sectarian prohibitions on the giving of gifts, the ritual economic exchange that defines and delineates Japanese social relationships, in-sure that the friendships of Tensho members tend largely to be with other Tensho members.

Even in the business world, the ideal economic institution is defined by Tensho as one that is operated entirely by Tensho members, with no union employees. The simultaneous affiliation of Tensho members, even for economic reasons, with any groups outside the boundaries of the religion is viewed with antagonism.

In sum, all ties of sentiment linking Tensho members to groups out-side sectarian boundaries, including even the family, are expected to weaken or cease. Tensho therefore redefines the nature of social ties. All of a sect member's living role alters, whether family members, co-workers, or coreligionists, are defined as *gyō no aite* [mutual disci-plinary partners]. The individual is expected to rise spiritually through interaction with his *gyō no aite*; he "polishes his soul" through contact with his disciplinary partners, who thus become defined as primary participants in sect social life. In consequence, the Tensho member learns to think of himself not as a member of several different social groups with occasionally conflicting requirements, but primarily as a *dōshi,* who participates in a social world conceptually unified by the precepts of his faith.

## REFERENCES

BEFU, HARUMI
  1963   Patrilineal descent and personal kindred in Japan. *American Anthropologist* 65:1328–1341.
  1971   *Japan: an anthropological introduction.* San Francisco: Chandler.
FORTES, MEYER
  1961   Pietas in ancestor worship. *Man: Journal of the Royal Anthropological Institute* 91(2):166–191.
FREEDMAN, MAURICE
  1966   *Chinese lineage and society: Fukien and Kwangtung.* London: Athlone; New York: Humanities Press.
  1967   "Ancestor worship: two facets of the Chinese case," in *Social organization: essays presented to Raymond Firth.* Edited by Maurice Freedman. Chicago: Aldine.
GOUGH, E. K.
  1958   Cults of the dead among the Nayars. *Journal of American Folklore* 71:446–478.
HOZUMI, NOBUSHIGE
  1912   *Ancestor worship and Japanese law* (second edition). Tokyo: Maruzen.
HSU, FRANCIS L. K.
  1949   *Under the ancestors' shadow: Chinese culture and personality.* New York: Columbia University Press..
JORDAN, DAVID K.
  1972   *Gods, ghosts and ancestors: the folk religion of a Taiwanese village.* Berkeley: University of California Press.
KERNER, KAREN
  1970   Japan's new religions. *The Japan Interpreter* 6 (2):135–150.
KIRBY, R. J.
  1910   Ancestral worship in Japan. *Transactions of the Asiatic Society of Japan* 38:233–267.
KOPYTOFF, IGOR
  1971   Ancestors as elders in Africa. *Africa* 41:129–142.
LAWRENCE, P., M. MEGGITT
  1965   *Gods, ghosts and man in Melanesia: some religions of Australian New Guinea and the New Hebrides.* Melbourne: Oxford University Press.
LEBRA, TAKIE S.
  1970a  Logic of salvation: the case of a Japanese sect in Hawaii. *International Journal of Social Psychiatry* 16:45–53.
  1970b  Religious conversion as a breakthrough in transculturation: a Japanese sect in Hawaii. *Journal for the Scientific Study of Religion* 9:181–196.

1972 "Religious conversion and elimination of the sick role," in *Transcultural research in mental health.* Edited by W. P. Lebra. Honolulu: East-West Center Press.

MOONEY, JAMES
1896 *The ghost dance and the Sioux outbreak of 1890.* Reports of the Bureau of American Ethnology 14 (1892–1893) II. Washington, D.C.

NEWELL, W. H., F. DOBASHI
1968 "Some problems of classification in religious sociology as shown in the history of Tenri kyokai," in *The sociology of Japanese religion.* Edited by K. Morioka and W. H. Newell. Leiden: E. J. Brill.

PLATH, DAVID
1964 Where the family of God is the family: the role of the dead in Japanese households. *American Anthropologist* 66(2):300–317.

SMITH, R. J.
1966 Ihai: mortuary tablets, the household and kin in Japanese ancestor worship. *Transactions of the Asiatic Society of Japan,* third series, 9:83–102.

SPIRO, MELFORD E.
1952 Ghosts, Ifaluk and teleological functionalism. *American Anthropologist* 54:497–503.

WORSLEY, PETER
1957 *The trumpet shall sound: a study of cargo cults in Melanesia.* London: MacGibbon and Kee.

YANAGITA, KUNIO
1946 *Senzo no hanashi.* Tokyo: Chikuma Shobo. (English translation 1970: *About our ancestors.* Translated by F. H. Mayer and Ishiwara Yasuyo. Tokyo: Japanese National Commission for UNESCO.)

YOSHIDA, TEIGO
1967 Mystical retribution, spirit possession and social structure in a Japanese village. *Ethnology* 6:237–262.

# Ancestral Influence on the Suffering of Descendants in a Japanese Cult

TAKIE SUGIYAMA LEBRA

## OBJECTIVE AND DATA

One of the anthropological preoccupations regarding ancestor worship has been to identify ancestral volition or disposition toward the living. Attempts have been made to ascertain whether ancestors in a tribe or in a society under study are benevolent, malevolent, ambivalent, indulgent, or punitive toward their descendants. A judgment on this matter appears significant or necessary primarily because it assumes the following kinds of relationship between the two generations.

First, ancestral will is responsible for an experience undergone by a descendant. If well disposed, forebears will benefit descendants and may "never cause disasters to befall the coming generations," as postulated by Hsu (1948: 241) regarding Chinese ancestors. If an ancestor is malignant, revengeful, envious, or punitive as is a Nayar ancestor (Gough 1958), then misfortune will be the inevitable outcome for the living. This logic can be reversed: if the living experience a misfortune, ancestral malignancy or wrath must be suspected.

Second, this causal relationship between ancestral volition and the experience by the living presupposes the power or authority held by ancestors over descendants. This has been extrapolated from the structural imbalance within this world between the power-holding generation (father, mother's brother) and the deprived succeeding generation (son,

This research was funded by an NIMH grant (MH-09243) and assistance received from the Social Science Research Institute, University of Hawaii; this aid is gratefully acknowledged. Thanks are also due to Ms. Freda Hellinger for her editorial suggestions.

sister's son). The inevitable dilemma involved in intergenerational transmission of power may find its solution in ancestor worship as among
Tallensi who believe ancestors "retain final authority, chiefly by virtue
of the pain and misfortune they inflict on their descendants from time
to time" (Fortes 1960: 176).

Conversely, the same dilemma may result in repressed hostility, rather
than "worship," toward ancestors; and this hostility may underlie a frequent attribution of illness to ancestral influence as among Okinawans
(W. P. Lebra 1969). In either case, ancestral power or authority as the
basis for efficacy of sanction seems unquestioned. Freedman (1966:
151) echoes this position when he sees Chinese ancestors in light of
both their "relative ineffectiveness" and "general air of benevolence."
The implication is that Chinese ancestors are not punitive because
their will is not bolstered by their power under the Chinese system of
inheritance.

Third, ancestral influence is justified as a legitimate or at least natural
response to the way the living are conducting themselves. A misfortune
must be accepted as punishment for neglecting the welfare and wishes of
an ancestor; whereas the proper attention to the needs of the ancestors
will be rewarded by good fortune. Implied herein is the acknowledgment
of guilt on the part of the suffering descendant. This projection of justice
makes ancestral influence doubly contingent: upon the offspring's behavior as well as upon ancestral predisposition.

The main objective of this paper is to present another case of ancestor
worship where the above rationale for experiences by the living generation does not apply in any significant degree. A misfortune or suffering
endured by a descendant, when attributed to ancestral influence, does not
necessarily stem from an ancestor's malevolence or wrath, or demonstrate an ancestor's power over the sufferer, or verify the latter's guilt. A
benign, powerless ancestor may well cause trouble to an innocent descendant. What is the rationale behind this, then? I will attempt to answer
this question.

The case introduced here is a Japanese cult which has been identified
as the Salvation Cult in my previous papers (Lebra 1971, 1974, ip.).
Founded in 1929, the Salvation Cult with its "headquarters" in Tokyo
commanded roughly 500 local branches scattered all over Japan, and
claimed a membership of more than 170,000 as of 1970 (Shūkyonenkan
1971). The doctrine of the cult is highly eclectic, accepts Buddhism,
Shintō, Taoism, Confucianism, and even Christianity, and grants a legitimate supernatural status to every conceivable deity or spirit, be it a
Buddha, nature deity, animal spirit, village tutelary god (ujigami), or

deceased human. (For more detailed descriptions of the cult see my previous papers.)

Fieldwork was conducted during the summers of 1970 and 1971 with a primary focus upon two branches in what I will call Eastern City, central Japan, whose combined membership was estimated at around 200. This paper is based upon information obtained through interviews with the two branch leaders and fourteen members. All but two members were female — this sex distribution roughly corresponds with that of those attending branch meetings regularly — their ages ranged from thirty-eight to seventy-eight, and their occupations (active or retired) varied widely and included storekeepers, cabaret operators, schoolteachers, a maid, and a fisherwoman. Further information was added through semiparticipant observation of rituals as well as casual conversation with attendants at branch meetings. "Lecturers" invited from other branches or the headquarters were another source of information.

## RELATIONSHIPS BETWEEN ANCESTORS AND SUFFERING DESCENDANTS

In the course of fieldwork, it became apparent that the cult members almost without exception have undergone a variety of suffering, particularly illness and family disharmony. Like many other "new" cults, the Salvation Cult finds a ready explanation for suffering in supernatural influence or in a certain relationship between the sufferer and a spirit. The responsible spirit is identified either by the sufferer himself, by a leader or a fellow member, or cooperatively by both. While an informal talk often leads one to "discover" the spirit, the cult offers its own ritual for spirit possession which induces the sufferer to be possessed by a specific spirit causing the trouble.

Among the spirits thus identified are ancestral spirits (*senzo no rei*). A *senzo* may be a remote ancestor, "ten generations old," or a recently departed parent or other kin. A remote ancestor is traced patrilineally in conformity with the Japanese ideal of succession pattern, while no such rule is applied to the recently deceased, a cognatic or collateral kin claiming a *senzo* status. A married woman finds a trouble-causing *senzo* among the dead members of either her natal house or her husband's house, more often among the former.

A consanguineally linked *senzo* makes no sex discrimination in selecting a descendant as a target of his influence, but in-laws do: a woman would find herself caught up by her departed mother-in-law, but not by her father-in-law. A *senzo* can be recruited from Ego's own generation (sister) and even from a succeeding generation (child).

The cult thus includes a variety of classes of dead people under the one term *senzo*, and this indiscriminatory attitude towards ancestors is by no means unique to this cult but widely shared by Japanese, as shown in past studies (Plath 1964; Smith 1966; Newell 1969; Kirby 1910). It may be partly due to this structural ambiguity of the ancestor category that the assumptions sketched above regarding ancestor worship, which are likely to have been derived from more rigidly structured systems of ancestor beliefs, turn out to be irrelevant.

Suffering by the living, if identified as related to ancestral influence, is attributed to the ancestor's own suffering. A suffering ancestor floats around this world because he is blocked from attaining a *hotoke* [Bud dha] status and is thus unable to join the ancestral group (*senzo no nakamairi*). Such a lonely, homeless spirit is described as *muen* [affinity-less]. Ancestral suffering accounts for a descendant's suffering under the assumption of one or more of the following relationships recognized between preceding generations and succeeding generations.

*Inheritance*

What stands out as the most basic premise is the belief that a descendant, by necessity rather than by choice, has inherited his identity from his ancestors to the extent that his experience or whole person is a near or exact replica of those of his ancestors. The same holds true with suffering.

Three levels of inheritance appear mixed together in the minds of the cult members: genetic-constitutional ("The blood running in my body IS my *senzo*, therefore I must keep it clean"); jural (inheritance and succession of assets and liabilities attached to the *ie* [house] handed down over generations); and metaphysical (destiny, karma, reincarnation, or metempsychosis). All these ideas are put together under the folk-meta-physical term *innen*.

A retired schoolteacher looks back on her hardship-ridden career and says, "All this is because many of my *senzo* have had hardships. I must cut this *innen* bond within my generation so that my *shison* [offspring] will not inherit it." An informant's daughter almost died from excessive bleeding. It was found out later that her paternal great-grandfather had bled to death in the Russo-Japanese War. Another informant's daughter suddenly disappeared from home under the pressure of the *innen* inherited from her great-grandmother who had led a wandering life. A former cabaret owner had to suffer because of her promiscuous husband since she had inherited this *innen* from her mother-in-law who also had suffered from the same problem. The *innen* inheritance by the daughter-in-law from the mother-in-law in this case, of course, is anchored in the consanguineal *innen* bondage between father and son in sharing the same promiscuous disposition. A male informant specified the number of generations for completion of an *innen* cycle: "You can judge someone's personality if you know his three-generation-old ancestor. You will reappear in your offspring three generations ahead." The weight of *innen* varies according to the status, wealth, and power of ancestors: "The wealthier the *senzo*, the heavier the *innen*."

*Reflection*

The idea of *innen* inheritance is further extended into the esoteric belief that one's behavior or suffering is a mirror-reflection of an ancestor who is, at present, behaving or suffering in a similar way. Many instances of *innen* inheritance involve this reflection. The girl's bleeding is an indication that her great-grandfather still suffers from the same affliction. If one cries, it is because one's ancestor is crying. An informant came to realize why her adopted daughter (niece), being mistreated by the adoptive father (the informant's husband), cried so often: "It was her real grandfather who was crying behind her; it was he who allowed her to be adopted." A husband who is selfish and uncooperative is understood to be a reflection of his father acting through him.

This judgment does not result, as might well be suspected it would, in accusation of or hostility toward the ancestor behind the actor, not even in admitting that ancestors cause trouble for descendants. Instead, the idea of reflection, in the view of informants, can reverse the causal connection between an ancestor and a descendant. If a descendant's state reflects that of an ancestor, it is reflected back onto the ancestor's mirror. That is, Ego's suffering is equal to the suffering of his ancestor and vice versa. Furthermore, Ego's happiness will be reflected into happiness for the ancestor, and this feeling of joy will, in turn, come back to Ego. Thus Ego's suffering results in self-accusation for permitting an ancestor to remain unhappy.

Such bilateral reflection takes place not only between Ego and an ancestor but also between Ego and a descendant. A delinquent child is a reflection of an undisciplined parent, and in turn, such delinquency reflects back to cause the parent to suffer. A suffering mother then must apologize to both her ancestors and to her children. Masochism demonstrated here involves acknowledgment of guilt; and yet, bound by the "logic" of mutual reflection, is far from recognition of a moral dichotomy between a guilty party and a punitive party.

Mutual reflection ends with a total fusion or identity between generations: "My ancestors, I, and my descendants — we are one and the same." "Ancestors are myself, ancestors are descendants. *Innen* from ancestors is me." "Ancestor worship means self-worship."

*Vicarious Retribution*

One major reason why an ancestor is deprived of *hotoke* status and continues to suffer is because he committed *tsumi* [sin] while in a fleshly form. The *tsumi* most frequently mentioned is *shikijō no tsumi* [sexual sin] which takes different forms. Extramarital indulgence and a number of remarriages are examples of such *tsumi* committed by male ancestors; whereas female ancestors are associated more with the *tsumi* of love suicide.

Among other *tsumi* are: homicide by *samurai* ancestors; abortion which left the fetus neglected in the state of *muen*; ruthless power manipulation and exploitation of the poor by ruling-class ancestors. Not all *tsumi* involve violation of a moral standard. A state or action of an ancestor which has anything to do with bloodletting is regarded as *tsumi*-ridden for the simple reason that blood is polluting and thus invites punishment from the god controlling the place, the natural element, or object that has been polluted. Menstruation, miscarriage, and being stabbed as well as stabbing someone all constitute *tsumi* commitment in this sense.

One more important ancestral *tsumi* must be mentioned. It is believed that most distinguished families — and most informants presented themselves as descendants of such families — used to have their respective guardian gods enshrined on their estates, well tended and worshiped. During the age of civil warfare, *samurai* ancestors, busy fighting and moving from one battlefield to another, either completely neglected the guardian gods or even destroyed their shrines. This constituted a serious *tsumi*.

It is one or more such *tsumi* committed by his ancestors that makes a descendant suffer. According to this interpretation, suffering is understood and accepted as a vicarious retribution by the sufferer on behalf of the sinful ancestor. A male informant, who claims direct descent from Taira, the first warrior ruling family in Japanese history, attributes his suffering as a husband and businessman to the unforgivable *tsumi* committed by his *senzo*. His first wife left him and his present marriage is

also a frustrating one; meanwhile every business venture he has undertaken has been successful up to a point but has always ended in failure.
All this was because his godless ancestors had committed *tsumi* of sex
and money — by taking advantage of female retainers and robbing the
poor of money.

A divorcee attributes her own marriage predicament and that of her
relatives to the curse of an ancestor's maidservant who committed suicide after being impregnated and who was subsequently discharged by
her master. "She died, cursing all descendants of the Yoshii family." A
conclusive statement was given by another informant: "Every time I
face a difficulty, I convince myself that my ancestors have done wrong
things."

An instance of ancestral *tsumi* against the family guardian god, the
fox spirit, resulted in the god's punishment of a descendant, an informant's husband, by making him mentally ill. The idea of vicarious retribution was put across by a leader of the cult when he said, "If you loan
money to somebody and worry about its return, both the loaner and the
debtor will become unhappy. You ought to think that your ancestors did
something that necessitated your loaning — that they were in debt."

Vicarious retribution applies to Ego's descendants as well as to Ego's
sin. One of the branch leaders revealed that she committed *tsumi* by dis-
obeying her parents' wish to allow herself to be adopted by her childless
brother as a daughter and successor to the *ie*. Realizing that her *tsumi* of
*oyafukō* [unfaithfulness to parents] was punished through her daughter's
illness, she knelt by her daughter's bed, bowing to the floor and tearfully
begging her forgiveness.

Vicarious retribution ceases to be "vicarious" once the boundary between ancestors and descendants is obliterated as stated in the preceding
section.

*Communication*

Suffering is further interpreted as a means of communication between an
ancestor and a descendant. Illness then should be taken as a message
transmitted through the patient's body. Without receiving such a signal,
one would remain uninformed, fail to rectify one's misconduct, and make
more serious errors.

A mother once lingered on the verge of death from asthma, and this
corresponded with the time of her son's death in the war. He "notified
his death," it was understood later, through the pain undergone by his

mother. This message signified that religious services and sacrifice should be rendered for the dead son to become a *hotoke*.

Communication sometimes involves a degree of elaboration of codes. Injury, for example, is a signal from someone who died an unnatural death or committed suicide; gynecological disorder is a message either from an ancestor who committed a sexual sin or from the spirit of a neglected infant; the problem of bed-wetting should be coded in relation to someone who drowned.

Gratitude is the proper response to receiving a message. The mother of two unfilial children became awakened to how rebellious she had been against her ancestors and how much displeasure she had caused them. "I would have been blind to this if my children had not turned away from me." In this case, ancestors used the children as a means of communication. She thanked the children for letting her know of her own rebelliousness. The more suffering, the more enlightenment.

As in the last case, the receiver of the message may happen to be too insensitive unless he "sees" it through somebody else. An intelligent high school boy suddenly developed a school phobia, ran away from home, and ended up as a "hippie" in a mountain hideaway. This incident was explained as his dead grandmother trying to inform her son and daughter-in-law of her homelessness. The latter would have been unreceptive to this message unless their intelligent, sensitive son were selected to act as a medium.

Ancestral communication is not always "instructional" but occasionally "instigative." An ancestor who used to disappear from home instigated a descendant and father of the house to run away from home with stolen money. Even this kind of communication is accepted as beneficial by informants who interpret the family, not the victim, to be the true message receiver.

*Reliance*

All the above relationships are channelled into this final one, reliance of a suffering ancestor on a descendant for his salvation. A descendant's suffering is taken as a result of such reliance. The behavior of the ancestor is described as helpless, solicitous for help, hanging or mounting on, clinging, hugging, or attached to the person to be relied upon. Reliance may be localized as when a spirit hangs on the neck, leg, eye, breast, head, etc., which is realized through neck pains, leg injury, eye disease, breast cancer, mental illness. An infant tends to cling to a woman's breast or womb.

Being an activation of the *innen* bond, reliance tends to be upon a con-sanguineal kin or a member of the *ie* where the spirit once belonged. There appear to be varying degrees of legitimacy in the choice of the object-person for reliance. Reliance upon the eldest son and succeeding or incumbent head of the *ie* in the direct line is regarded as most legiti-mate but rarely practiced.

An informant took a neighbor to the branch church for a possession ritual to find out why her neighbor was forced to lead such a miserable life of illness and with an unfaithful husband. The informant's neighbor was possessed by her husband's grandmother who had drowned during a flood. The spirit held on to her and refused to let go because she loved the granddaughter-in-law more than any of her blood children or grand-children. This meant that the woman looked "like insane" and did not come back to consciousness for a long time. The informant, feeling re-sponsible, tried to persuade the possessing spirit to release the neighbor. "I told the spirit that relying upon your granddaughter-in-law makes no sense. 'Rely on the direct main line, on the first son,' I said." The neigh-bor's house turned out to be a branch house established by a younger son.

Such structural constraint, as shown by the above example, is, how-ever, often superseded by the spirit's preference for a certain personality type regardless of kinship and succession rule. In some cases it is the weakest, most vulnerable person, and in some other cases the person who resembles the spirit the most, that the spirit comes to rely upon. However, in an overwhelming number of instances it is the most reliable and helpful person who is selected by the spirit.

The ultimate objective of ancestral reliance is attainment of *hotoke* status which requires the spirit's contentment through sacrifice and at-tendance by the living. The *tsumi*-ridden spirit — and most suffering spirits are sinful — must make an apology to the angry god before it can enjoy the nurturant care given by the living. For that apology, too, the helpless spirit must rely upon the living. A descendant, thus relied upon, must visit a shrine to make a vicarious apology for the *tsumi* committed by an ancestor.

## CONCLUSION

The above analysis of relationships between ancestors and suffering descendants, as observed in a Japanese cult, suggests the following. First, all the five relationships — inheritance, reflection, vicarious retribution, communication, and reliance — obscure the boundary between an ances-tor and a descendant. What emerges here is a fusion or interlocking, instead of differentiation and confrontation, between two generations, between subject and object in ancestor worship. Anthropological assumptions, as delineated at the outset, such as ancestral volition, ancestral causation of misfortune, ancestral power and justice, seem derived from a clear demarcation line between ancestors and descendants. I am tempted to conclude that these assumptions do not apply meaningfully where one does not know or is indifferent to where an ancestor ends and a descendant begins. This may further relate to the difference between a culture which invests in social relationships and solidarity and a culture which cherishes individual autonomy.

Second, the consistent theme, appearing and reappearing in the Salvation Cult, is masochism and nurturance on the part of the sufferer. This may reflect a woman's role as a link between ancestors and descendants in a society where patrilineal ideology predominates and yet the woman looks after not only the children but the dead members of the household as well. The Salvation Cult, its members being predominantly women, may represent such a sexual bias more than other Japanese cults which are more male oriented.

Third, locked with the above two points is the structural ambiguity of the ancestor category as previously described. If *senzo* can include one's child as well as ascending generations, the mother's attitude toward a dead child may well be duplicated toward forebears. Indeed, it is the mother, selfless and reliable, who seems to offer a role model in the whole tenet of the cult. This may underlie both the lack of differentiation between ancestors and descendants, and the stress on masochism and nurturance.

## REFERENCES

CROOKE, WILLIAM
1926   "Ancestor worship and cult of the dead," in *Encyclopaedia of religion and ethics,* volume one. Edited by James Hastings, 425–432. New York: Scribner's.
DORE, R. P.
1958   *City life in Japan: a study of a Tokyo ward.* Berkeley and Los Angeles: University of California Press.
FORTES, MEYER
1960   Pietas in ancestor worship. *Man: Journal of the Royal Anthropological Institute* 91(2):166–191.
FREEDMAN, MAURICE
1966   *Chinese lineage and society; Fukien and Kwangtung.* London: Athlone; New York: Humanities Press.

GOODY, JACK
1962    *Death, property and the ancestors.* Stanford: Stanford University Press.
GOUGH, E. K.
1958    Cults of the dead among the Nayars. *Journal of American Folklore* 71:446–478.
HOZUMI, NOBUSHIGE
1912    *Ancestor worship and Japanese law* (second edition). Tokyo: Maruzen.
HSU, FRANCIS L. K.
1948    *Under the ancestors' shadow; Chinese culture and personality.* New York: Columbia University Press.
KIRBY, R. J.
1910    Ancestral worship in Japan. *Transactions of the Asiatic Society of Japan* 38:233–267.
LEBRA, TAKIE SUGIYAMA
1971    "Social ecology of a healing cult." Paper presented at the 30th annual meeting of the Society for Applied Anthropology, April 1971, Miami, Florida.
1974    The interactional perspective of suffering and curing in a Japanese cult. *The International Journal of Social Psychiatry* 20:281–286.
i.p.    "Taking the role of supernatural 'other': spirit possession in a Japanese healing cult," in *Culture-bound syndromes, ethnopsychiatry and alternate therapies.* Edited by W. P. Lebra. Honolulu: University of Hawaii Press.
LEBRA, WILLIAM P.
1969    *Ancestral beliefs and illness in Okinawa.* Reprinted from *Proceedings of the VIIIth International Congress of Anthropological and Ethnological Sciences 1968,* volume three: *Ethnology and archaeology.* Tokyo and Kyoto.
NEWELL, W. H.
1969    "Some comparative features of Chinese and Japanese ancestor worship," in *Proceedings of the VIIIth International Congress of Anthropological and Ethnological Sciences 1968,* volume three: *Ethnology and archaeology,* 300–301. Tokyo and Kyoto.
PLATH, DAVID W.
1964    Where the family of God is the family: the role of the dead in Japanese households. *American Anthropologist* 66(2):300–317.
*Shūkyonenkan*
1971    *Shūkyonenkan* [Yearbook of religion], compiled by Bunkachō, Japan.
SMITH, R. J.
1966    Ihai: mortuary tablets, the household and kin in Japanese ancestor worship. *Transactions of the Asiatic Society of Japan,* third series, 9:83–102.
YANG, C. K.
1961    *Religion in Chinese society.* Berkeley and Los Angeles: University of California Press.

230 TAKIE SUGIYAMA LEBRA

WIMBERLEY, HOWARD
1969  Self-realization and the ancestors: an analysis of two Japanese ritual procedures for achieving domestic harmony. *Anthropological Quarterly* 42:37–51.

# A Note on the Enshrinement of Ancestral Tablets at Zamami Island, Okinawa

MAKIO MATSUZONO

I.   Zamami is an island of the Kerama group roughly forty kilometers west of the Okinawan main island.

The ideal form of enshrining ancestral tablets among the Zamami villagers today is as follows: the family altar accommodates only the tablets of family heads and their wives in successive generations, and those successive family heads should be agnates in relation to the apical ancestor, preferably lineal ones. There are two constituent elements of the ideal form: family altar, the one-generation one-couple principle, and the agnatic principle.

The variations of real life, however, never allow conditions perfect enough for this ideal form to exist for any length of time. When a man dies, a tablet must be made which has to be worshiped by someone else. The most likely worshiper is the firstborn son of the deceased. The second son can take the place of the first son if the latter dies young or has been on a long trip away from the island. If the deceased had no real son, but adopted beforehand a boy from his own *munchū* [agnatic descent group] the latter succeeds him as family head and worships his tablet.

Thus far, there exist no real problems that can trouble villagers, because the deceased already secured his successor before his death and the one-generation one-couple principle ought not to be violated. But what if a man without sons, real or adopted, were to be killed in war or drowned in a storm at sea? His tablet may be safe in his family altar while his wife is alive. A daughter is not permitted to bring a father's tablet into her husband's house. Therefore, unless the widow adopts someone into her family, the worship of her late husband's tablet will finally be imposed on one of his male agnates, i.e. members of his *munchū*. The most probable and, in actuality, most frequent worshiper of the deceased's tablet is one of his brothers. If they have all died, then one of their sons or the father of the deceased, if he is still alive, will be expected to act as caretaker of the tablet. When one dies before marriage, his father or one of his married brothers is again the most probable worshiper of the tablet.

There have been numerous reports from wider areas of both the main island and offshore islands to the effect that people are strongly opposed to enshrining two or more siblings' tablets on one altar. Zamami is not an exception. This tabooed action, usually labeled *chōde kasabai* [repetition of sibling's tablet], leads to a breach of the one-generation one-couple principle. This situation calls for a compromise practice which meets both the principle and the demands of real life. Many family altars in Zamami enshrine two kinds of tablets, here called the main tablet and the side tablet for convenience. The main tablets represent successive family heads and their wives. They are inserted in one tablet case, which is always placed in the center of the topmost platform inside the altar. A side tablet represents a sibling or any other collateral agnates of the present family head. It is usually placed on the left side of the main tablets on the same platform or one step below. Sometimes two or more side tablets are placed separately on the right and left of the main tablets; in this case, those on the left represent closer agnates to the family heads than those on the right. The side tablet is smaller in size than the main tablet, and an incense pot put in front of the former is again smaller than the one in front of the latter.

The side tablet, distinctly separated from the main tablet in this way, is in the eyes of villagers nothing but a compromise. They never give up the idea of correcting this inconsistency to actualize the one-generation one-couple principle. They would say they were forced to enshrine the side tablet only temporarily, to be removed in the near future to a proper place. Some would even go to extremes to insist that the side tablet should not be placed on the family altar but had better be removed to a tiny shrine-hut to be specially built on the ground inside the compound, although a real instance of this was not observed by the writer. The most popular strategy was to hand over the side tablet to the second or third son when he established a new branch family. Put in another way, the main family tries to adhere to the principle by assigning one of its branch families to enshrine those side tablets that cannot comfortably reside inside its family altar. Undoubtedly, this course of action on the part of the main family gives the same kind of burden to the branch family.

A newly founded branch family normally does not have an ancestral tablet to be worshiped inside the house. Thus it follows that a second or third son who reluctantly inherited a side tablet is placed at a disadvantage from the very moment of establishing his own family. When there are several side tablets, it is sometimes decided, far ahead of the time of the sons' marriage, which side tablet the second son should take over and which one the third son should, etc. A new branch family that inherited the side tablet would, in the next generation, probably try to get rid of it by handing it over to one of its own branch families. Thus the problem is never settled.

The above description may sound logical enough. But in point of fact, the demand of a main family is not always met. A son may strongly resist enshrining the side tablet, and the father's expectation may only be fulfilled in the next generation when one of his grandsons establishes a branch family. The transference of a side tablet back and forth between the main family and a branch family or between branch families is not rare. A man wishing to get rid of the side tablet is generally the one who initiates the action. His arguments are most often based on the oracle of a *yuta,* or shaman, to the effect, for instance, that a recent misfortune of his family, such as sickness, death, or bankruptcy has come about because of an unjustifiable enshrinement of a collateral or nonagnatic side tablet. As a matter of fact, the *yuta* seems to be the most obstinate advocate of the two principles already mentioned in connection with the tablet enshrinement.

There seem to exist two paradoxical factors to be considered by villagers in determining who should enshrine the side tablet. The prevalent ethical creed compels the son to listen to a father's request on his inheriting the side tablet. Although from a third person's viewpoint, it is generally considered better for the side tablet to remain as close as possible to the main family which first enshrined it, if the transfer of the tablet from the main family to the branch family is repeated through several generations then the lines of worshipper and worshipped become more remote. The personalities and religious attitudes of those concerned, and the *yuta's* oracle, are among the most influential elements to determine which of these two factors is to be stressed over the other.

II.  Now let us turn to some historical considerations relevant to the two principles.

It may be wise to start by elaborating somewhat on the local term *shiji-tadashi* (correction of *shiji*). *Shiji* can be defined as an agnatic relationship in a biological sense as it is understood by villagers. To understand fully the actual operation of *shiji-tadashi,* it is important to know what kind of changes have taken place in the practice of adoption and how they have affected the make-up of the *munchū* in Zamami village.

The *munchū* in Zamami today is composed of those who are linked to each other by *shiji*; that is, they are agnatic descendants of the founding ancestor. But this is not true of the past. In the past, a man was not infrequently adopted from other unrelated *munchū*, and the lack of *shiji* did not prevent him from acquiring legitimate membership in his adoptive father's *munchū*. Today, however, adoption always occurs within the same *munchū,* and those without *shiji* are considered unqualified to be a *munchū* member. An investigation of the census register of the village reveals that cases of adoption from outside one's own *munchū* were not infrequent during Meiji, Taishō, and early Shōwa Periods, and the last incident of such adoption is the one which took place in Shōwa 14 (1939). Thereafter not a single case of this has been recorded. The current ideology (borne out by the villagers), which emphasizes the agnatic tie as the essential prerequisite to membership in the *munchū*, contradicts the previous type of *munchū*, which included members lacking *shiji* to the founding ancestor. This ambivalent situation has caused villagers to take corrective actions in regard to tablet enshrinement and membership of the *munchū*. *Shiji-tadashi* means correcting irregular kinship relations in the past in such a way as to make them conform to today's strict agnatic ideology.

The family line in the previous type of *munchū* was frequently continued by a family head with a different *shiji,* and villagers today describe this kind of hybrid family line by an apt local term *tachii-majikui* [mixture of different lines]. Today's strictly agnatic *munchū* is taking shape as a result of the correction of *tachii-majikui* that was common in the more loosely agnatic *munchū* of the past. For convenience we designate the former type of *munchū* as Type Y and the latter as Type X.

The following fact should not be missed in the discussion on changes taking place in the *munchū* structure in Zamami: Type Y *munchū* does not enjoy the same religious function and the same depth of scale as the Type X *munchū*. Uncompromising agnatic ideology today tends to be resorted to as a means of breaking down Type X *munchū* into a certain number of disjointed families or family groups by ostracizing those anomalous families whose successive line was proved in one way or another to have been interrupted in the past by one or more non-agnatic family heads. It may sound paradoxical, but we maintain that agnatic ideology, in its strictest form, has been emphasized among villagers concurrently with the regressive process of kinship ideology in general, as an integrating force in their social and religious life, that is, in accordance with the rising tide of voluntary social relationships.

The ideal form of enshrining ancestral tablets discussed above is connected with the now dominating Type Y *munchū*, but only partially relevant to the previous Type X *munchū*. Of the two principles comprising the ideal form, i.e. the one-generation one-couple principle, and the agnatic principle, the former seems to have been maintained consistently from mid-Meiji (the 1890's). This is the earliest point of time to be traced back with any certainty in the history of the village, whereas the agnatic principle seems to have been gradually put into force during and after the Taishō Period (1912–1925) in accordance with the changing attitudes of those villagers receptive to a rigid agnatic ideology and the concomitant rule of avoidance of adoption from outside the *munchū*.

Should a family be known to have adopted a nonagnatic male as a would-be family head in the past, the living members of the family often worship only those tablets representing agnatic family heads downward from the adopted, thereby excluding those representing nonagnatic family heads in the preceding generations, including the adoptive father. The actual procedures taken in this case are not uniform, but the following three methods seem most common: (1) to bring down a main tablet to the status of side tablet; (2) to send away a tablet to the custody of the family believed to have the same *shiji*, not always in the same island; and (3) for the family to move to another house together with their agnatic tablets, leaving nonagnatic ones in the present house which would eventually be deserted.

III.   The correction of *shiji* observed in tablet enshrinement ultimately leads to reorganization of a Type X *munchū* into a Type Y *munchū*. A change of *munchū* membership is frequently demonstrated by a change of house name. Every indigenous family in the village, as long as it has an independent house to shelter its members, has, apart from a family name, a name for the house. The house name of a branch family is generally formed by adding a certain descriptive word to the house name of the main or most senior family of the *munchū*. This additional word in most cases means "small" or otherwise states the location of the house in relation to that of the main family such as east, west, front, back, up, or down. Therefore, families belonging to a particular *munchū* are easily identified by their house names.

In case adoption from a different *munchū* took place only one or two generations previously, and the incident is clearly remembered by both families, agnatic descendants of the adopted may find it relatively easy to shift their membership from the present *munchū* to that of the head's natal family, and to take a new appropriate house name. When the memory has been lost, a *yuta's* oracle is sometimes asked to discover the *munchū* from which the adopted came. Again in this case, unless the main family of the agnatic *munchū* thus identified raises objections, the adopted may be entitled to membership in the *munchū* and a suitable house name. However, this kind of smooth renewal of *munchū* membership is not common. In far more numerous cases, families severed from their former *munchū* become isolated, and do not obtain membership in any other *munchū*. Not infrequently, the natal family of the adopted in question, no matter whether it is believed to exist inside or outside the village, cannot be detected in such a way as to satisfy both the parties concerned. Even if a *yuta*, in his client's interest, suggests a particular *munchū* as a possible natal place of the adopted, the judgment may be denied by the oracle of another *yuta* approached by members of the implicated *munchū* unwilling to approve their membership. Such isolated families have to abandon the house names indicative of their membership in the previous *munchū* and instead will eventually be referred to by other villagers by their family names only.

Suspension of membership disqualifies them from participating in any form in the pilgrimage to the main island whence the founding ancestor of the *munchū* is believed to have come to the village. This pilgrimage is made once a year or once every three, five, or seven years, depending on the decision of the *munchū,* for the purpose of paying homage to the original family of the founding ancestor and attending the memorial service dedicated to his ascending ancestors at the main island. In recent years, only a few representatives go on this pilgrimage, but all the member families of the *munchū* must share the cost. Eliminated families stop paying their share, either willingly or reluctantly.

As may be understood from the above discussion, the correction of *shiji* has exerted a greater influence in disorganizing Type X *munchū* by alienating nonagnatic families than it has in rebuilding Type Y *munchū* proportional to the former in scale and integrity. This is well demonstrated by the fact that the more forcefully agnatic ideology is put into actual operation, the fewer the number of tablets to be worshiped in the family or in the *munchū*. People are forced to dispose of the nonagnatic tablets, and on the other hand it is rare that these discarded tablets find the right place to be enshrined in the capacity of main tablets forever. The correction of *shiji*, as villagers view it, is significantly associated with the correction of tablet enshrinement.

IV.    The structural change from Type X to Type Y *munchū* does not seem to be limited to Zamami Island. There have been reports to the same effect from other offshore islands west or northwest of the main island, such as Tonaki and Aguni, and also from northern parts of the main island. These reports are mainly concerned with recent changes in the structure of cult groups and the practice of adoption. Although they do not provide us with necessary information on the local practices of tablet enshrinement, the same sort of change as is observed in Zamami is inferred as taking place or having taken place there.

In the southern parts of the main island, including Shuri and Naha, the change from Type X to Type Y *munchū* apparently ran its course to the final phase many years ago; the reason may be that the area was the stronghold of the unified Ryukyuan Dynasty and it was probably the warrior class residing there who was most active in adopting strict agnatic ideology from China as the core of their value system. Not surprisingly, cases of tablet removal reported from the southern and central parts of the main island are predominantly those taking place inside the *munchū*, as compared with the more frequent cases in Zamami where nonagnatic tablets are thrown out of the *munchū*. In those areas in the main island where the Type Y *munchū* has prevailed for many years, the correction of *shiji* has been long forgotten. When there is confusion of memory regarding the family of the senior line in the *munchū*, the judgment of a *yuta* or other kinds of local diviners is frequently asked for, which may tell them to remove the tablet of their founding ancestor to another particular family now considered to be senior descendants. To take another example, in case the first-born son of the senior family is known to have been adopted into a junior family a few generations ago, the present head of the junior family, prompted by the belief that he is justifiably the senior member of the *munchū*, may lay claim to the earliest ancestral tablet from the senior family.

In any event, all the motivations on the part of those initiating the removal of tablets seem well in line with the ideal form of tablet enshrinement, consisting of two principles. And the removal of tablets takes place inside the *munchū* or between different *munchū*, or in both ways, depending on the extent to which the *munchū* of a given area is "agnatized" in the strictest sense of the word; in other words, whether it is Type X *munchū* or Type Y *munchū*.

V.   It is very probable that the introduction of strict agnatic ideology from the southern parts of the main island, beginning several decades ago, was instrumental in bringing about Type Y *munchū* in offshore peasant societies such as Aguni, Tonaki, and Zamami. In this connection, it is interesting that Type X *munchū* still appears predominant in those parts of insular Sakishima areas southernmost and farthest from the main island. But as is evident from the case of the Yaeyama Islands, an adopted son is not always recruited from one's own *munchū*, and therefore the *munchū* does not exclude nonagnatic members.

On Zamami Island there are seven mountains, four of which are considered sacred by villagers. Every indigenous villager belongs to one of these four mountains. On a certain "lucky" day of every autumn, they climb the mountain to which they belong and on hallowed ground on the summit they perform the ceremony of praying toward the direction of Shuri, which is believed to be the birthplace of their original ancestors, and at the same time they pray for blessings from beyond the sea. It is worthy of note that acquisition of membership in the mountain group still remains consistent with the structure of the previous Type X *munchū*. The correction of *shiji* does not seem to have invaded this domain. A man adopted from outside the *munchū* and his offspring do not cease to belong to the mountain to which his adoptive father belonged. Even if they have shifted their membership to their agnatic *munchū* by discarding nonagnatic ancestral tablets and taking up a new house name, it does not affect their membership in the mountain group. Contradiction is obvious between the way members are recruited into the *munchū* and the way they belong to the mountain group. The former is in line with Type Y *munchū* structure and the latter is in line with Type X *munchū* structure. But today, at least, the question never seems to arise in villagers' minds as to how to dispose of this contradiction. They simply do not care about it.

This annual religious ceremony has become obsolete since the end of World War II. Most of the female religious functionaries in charge of service on the mountain summit have died without being succeeded by members of the next generation. Those who survive are in their seventies and eighties and find it extremely difficult to perform their duties properly. In addition, religious old men now find it hard to climb the mountain under the burning sun, and youngsters are generally indifferent to the traditional way of life. At present, not many people dare to climb the mountain, and this annual ceremony has become something like an excursion of school children, taking place on a Sunday and not necessarily on a lucky day. This may be the reason they do not venture to take action to correct the membership of the mountain.

After World War II, kinship relations in general, as an integrative force in village society, have lost their strength to a considerable degree in Zamami Island. Several factors are responsible for this tendency. In Okinawa, the technology and necessary implements for bonito fishing were first introduced to Zamami Island around the turn of this century. The fishing industry is organized round the catching of bonito. Most people stayed in the village throughout their life and engaged in fishing at sea or in processing dried bonito on the land. The traditional life-style was maintained intact, or rather strengthened by cooperative work needed for the village economy, based on a single industry. However, the once prosperous fishing economy drastically slackened after the war, as a result of the dwindling fishing grounds and the scarcity of bait fish. Also, fishermen from other islands or coastal villages of the main island eventually challenged Zamami's monopoly in this field.

Currently, there is only one fishing boat in the village, and only one out of every six or seven families lives by fishing and processing. Many adults are forced to leave the island in search of jobs in places such as Naha, Koma, and the big cities in Japan proper. Because there is not a high school in the island, children eventually go to the Okinawa main island and some of them find jobs there. A considerable number of persons have emigrated from the indigenous village population in this way since the war. Some *munchū* were deserted by about half or more member families including the senior one. On the other hand, thirty out of a total of 151 families of the village are those who came to live there after the war, most of them being unrelated to indigenous families in terms of kinship. Thus, the proportion of heterogeneous elements in the total population is ever-widening.

About two hundred villagers are recorded as having died (mostly by suicide) at the time the United States troops landed on the island in March 1945. The death toll mounted with the addition of those who perished in air raids. A great many houses were burned to ashes, and many ancestral tablets were lost in the fire. As a result, many families in the village were extinguished without successors. The Japanese government grants a yearly allowance to surviving families of those killed in the war — veteran-returnees and disabled persons. It is very difficult to find in the village a family which does not receive any kind of allowance. It is, in fact, no exaggeration to say that most of the indigenous families live on allowances. Agriculture and pig rearing are negligible and little staple food is produced.

Traditionally, in Okinawa, the *munchū* functions primarily in the sphere of ancestor worship rather than in economic and other worldly spheres. Outlined above are the social and economic backgrounds which have made dysfunctional any kind of descent groups in Zamami, no matter whether it is a disintegrating Type X *munchū* or an emerging Type Y *munchū*. And now that the value of the traditional religion is being impaired, bilateral kinship and individually motivated voluntary relations in daily activities are becoming the most important human ties or contacts in the village.

Under these circumstances, it may be only a matter of course before the Type Y *munchū* loses its reason for existence just as the Type X *munchū* of the past lost its reason. As a matter of fact, I am a little hesitant to speak of the Type Y *munchū*, at least as it is found in Zamami, in terms of descent group in any sociological sense. Membership in the *munchū* is described by villagers not as something like eligibility to participate in any corporate actions — as in economic cooperative systems or the rites of ancestor worship — but rather as belongingness *per se*, as demonstrated symbolically in the enshrinement of incontestable agnatic tablets and their bearing proper house names. Accordingly, Type Y *munchū* may well be thought of as falling between an agnatic and a descent relationship.

In any event, villagers attribute the most significant value to the Type Y *munchū* as an entity. This is a true agnatic system with offspring descending from a common apical ancestor, even though the active functioning as a corporate descent group seems dormant at the moment.

The support of the Type Y *munchū* seems to have been occasioned by a sweeping tide of changing attitudes; the villagers are swift to absorb the value system of the higher culture prevailing in the southern parts of the main island. The dogma of strict agnation was considered by them to be the most important code for this behavior, as it was in marked contrast with the loose, compromised ideology once prevalent in the village.

# Ancestor Memorialism: A Comparison of Jews and Japanese

HOWARD WIMBERLEY and JOEL SAVISHINSKY

Any discussion of Jewish and Japanese life between individuals who are familiar with only one of the two patterns is likely to give rise to the exclamation, "You don't mean to say they're like that too!" Plath (1964) in his inquiry into how the Japanese treatment of the dead reflects the institutional molding of affect, noted that these particular effects might be comparable to those of other peoples, such as Americans. Zenner (1965) briefly elaborated on this point by noting a number of interesting similarities between Japanese and Jewish memorial practices. However, since Zenner's initial comparisons, little systematic ethnological work along these lines seems to have been undertaken. Finding Zenner's observations rather remarkable, in the winter of 1972–1973 we undertook a preliminary study of middle-class, Jewish New Yorkers of Ashkenazic descent in which we attempted to integrate library research materials with field observations in order to develop a balanced account of this American subculture for further comparisons. In this report of our findings we have analytically divided our data into historical, structural, and psychological categories for comparison with the well-documented Japanese case.

## JEWISH MEMORIALISM [1]

### The Historical Dimension

The Jewish religion is suffused with metaphors of kinship and it derives its charters of authority from genealogy. The dominant figures

[1] Maurice Freedman (1958) distinguishes between ancestor worship and memo-

of the Old Testament are patriarchs in a literal and corporate sense: the Jewish people are "the seed of Abraham," they are his "household" and the "house of Aaron"; their God is the "God of our Fathers," i.e. of Abraham, Jacob, Isaac and their descendants. And the people are, by virtue of their heritage and the covenants made by their "Fathers" with Yahweh, the "Children of God." In the Old Testament, and subsequent commentaries on it, religious, priestly, and political authority are usually validated on a genealogical basis, and there is, throughout, a strong consciousness of patrimony, family ties, and kinship obligations. In more recent centuries, the inhabitants of the rural communities (*shtetls*) of Eastern Europe maintained this kinship imagery at both the communal and the "national" levels: they saw themselves as members of *Klal Isroel*, "the entire Jewish people the world over" and, as Landes and Zborowski indicate, "The *shtetl* Jews consider all members of the Jewish community to be related to each other through kinship ties, a belief expressed formally in the collective term *B'nai Israel*, Children of Israel, and in the acceptance of the three Biblical patriarchs as the ancestors of all Jews" (1950: 462). Despite the pervasiveness of kinship in early Jewish history and its writings, there is no Biblical sanction or authority for actual ancestor worship or memorialism, nor do these appear as a formal part of early orthodox Jewish ceremonialism. Some Biblical scholars suggest that early Hebraic religion actually contained many remnants of ancestor worship from pre- and non-Israelite sources in the Middle East, but that the early patriarchs and prophets attempted to suppress these practices from the faith. In the case of the two liturgical prayers most directly related to memorialism and commemorating the dead, *Kaddish* and *Yizkor*, the former, an ancient Aramaic text, is literally a "sanctification" of God which only later became associated with ceremonies of mourning. The prayer itself lacks any mention of the dead, although after its incorporation into the liturgy, its recitation was believed to help "redeem the dead parent from the sufferings of Hell (*Gehinnom*)" (Zenner 1965: 481).

---

rialism, using the latter term to refer specifically to domestic household rites. In this essay we are dealing with both household and communal modes of memorializing deceased persons and have not followed a strict dychotomy in our use of these terms. We suggest in the text that neither Jewish nor Japanese people literally "worship" their ancestors, and hence we employ the term memorialism in a broad sense to cover activities and observances that have elsewhere been designated as "worship."

It is probable that the Kaddish was formulated after the destruction of the first Temple and was recited primarily after a lecture or discourse on a Torah theme. It then slipped easily into the worship service into which its themes and responses fitted admirably (Lamm 1969: 52).

The memorial service of *Yizkor* [Recalling the Dead] was introduced into Jewish services during the period of medieval pogroms, and it was "instituted so that the Jew may pay homage to his forbears and recall the good life and traditional goals" (Lamm 1969: 196). In both cases, then, memorial prayers have become part of the liturgy either through the reinterpretation of a prayer from another context or through the introduction of a service during a specific historical period.

In contrast to the relative silence of early Biblical and liturgical sources on the theme of ancestors, and as the history of the above prayers illustrates, there has developed an unmistakable complex of beliefs and services directed towards helping, placating, memorializing, and maintaining ties with the deceased. The specific content of the *Yizkor* and *Kaddish* prayers also reflects the fact that orthodox Judaism rejects the notion of direct WORSHIP of ancestors, and instead conceives of memorial prayers and observances, in the words of one of our rabbinic informants, as "REVERENCE and RESPECT for the dead," a reverence which this rabbi derived from the Biblical injunction to "honor thy father and mother."

While some Jewish memorial observances incorporate Biblical and liturgical elements, others exist outside of the formal framework of Judaism, and they have evolved as an adjunct set of participations, some of which are clearly folkloristic in nature. Rabbinic authorities, for example, repeatedly emphasize the Biblical, Talmudic, and orthodox rejection of ancestor worship as a "monstrous blasphemy" (see, for example, Lamm 1969: 211). Yet cultural and historical studies of European Jewry consistently reveal a belief in the efficacy of prayers directed to ancestral spirits as a mode for obtaining help and guidance. Trachtenberg provides extensive documentation of these and similar practices among Ashkenazic Jewry in the medieval period, noting their similarity to non-Jewish beliefs of this era and their persistence among Ashkenazic Jews into more recent times (1970; Pollack 1971). The practice of paying annual visits to the grave of the deceased, the pattern of naming their children after ancestors, the making of charitable donations on behalf of the deceased, and the belief that the dead and the living can intercede on one another's behalf are widespread Ashkenazic patterns which have no specific Biblical sanction.

244 HOWARD WIMBERLEY, JOEL SAVISHINSKY

On a number of these memorial practices, Ashkenazic and Sephardic beliefs show some basic divergences. Sephardic Jews, for example, name their children after living rather than deceased ascendants. These differences are indicative of the fact that observances and beliefs pertaining to the dead show a great deal of regional and historical variation among the many Jewish groups that have developed during the last 2,000 years.

*Structural Features*

To understand the structure of Jewish memorialism, it is necessary to look at the structure of both the Jewish family and the Jewish "people" as a religious and historical community. Ancestral practices among East European Jews are bilateral in breadth but shallow in genealogical depth. Observances, memories, and involvements concerning the deceased usually include a person's own and his parents', children's, and grandparents' generations, but rarely extend deeper into genealogical time. That is, they center on people of whom there is still a living memory among family members. There is no specific kinship principle which designates which persons, beyond parents, spouses, siblings, and children, should be memorialized. In the case of parental siblings, for example, our initial research indicates that decisions in the matter of memorialization may be made in an *ad hoc* and personal manner. That is, the decisions on kinsmen such as aunts and uncles may more often be situational rather than strictly ideological in nature: those kinsmen with whom an individual had close, warm ties are most likely to be memorialized, regardless of their specific degree or line of relatedness. In some cases this may result in mostly patrikin being memorialized, in other cases matrikin, and in still other instances there is a combination of deceased persons from both lines.

From a personal point of view, then, significant kinsmen among Jews constitute a bilateral, consanguineal kindred rather than a unilineal, corporate descent group. This noncorporate tendency is reinforced by the lack of any consistent unilocal, postmarital residence pattern among Jews. It is from among this bilateral network of people that memorialized kin — those for whom *Kaddish, Yizkor,* and *Yahrzeit* are observed — are most likely to be found. Also, unlike systems which emphasize unilineal descent, men and women do not become responsible for the memorialization of members of their spouses' families of orientation or identified with them. It should be noted, however, that the literature on *shtetl* cultures of Eastern Europe indicates that people were often likely to have warmer and more extensive ties with matrikin than patrikin, due to the fact that mothers provided the expressive focus of family relationships and often turned to their own kin for assistance in raising their children. This fact could conceivably lead to a matrilineal emphasis in memorial practices, a possibility worth further statistical investigation (Landes and Zborowski 1950: 452–453, 459). [2] *Shtetl* Jews also occasionally practiced an initial uxorilocal residence pattern called *kest*, in which a young couple lived with, and were supported by, the bride's parents for a period stipulated in the marriage contract; this pattern, too, could have conceivably contributed to a matrilineal emphasis. If confirmed, such a matrilineal trend in memorial practice would contradict the patrilineal ideology of Jewish family life.

Another important structural feature of Jewish life is the pervasive sense of community that Jews have fostered among themselves both before and since the Diaspora. Jews have lived their complementary lives, as family and as community members, with equal intensity, and there are several ways in which the individual involvement at both these social levels is revealed in memorial practices. For example, death notices are displayed in public places in many New York Jewish communities, and funeral services, especially for particularly righteous persons, become as much communal as family affairs. In the culture of the *shtetl*, all the members of a community would memorialize a well-loved scholar or rabbi, for the deceased's spirit was believed to watch over and guard the village as it had in life. Such a communal orientation in mourning observances, in which death is seen as affecting "the entire group and not only the surviving relatives . . ." has applied, generally speaking, from Biblical times to the present day, in relatively self-contained Jewish communities. To the members of a *shtetl* community, the *shtetl* itself was an extended family; and in death, as in all life crises, both the family and the community took an active part.

These communal overtones are further emphasized by the fact that the recitation of major memorial prayers, such as *Kaddish* and *Yizkor*, can only occur in the presence of a *minyan*, a group of ten adult Jewish males; and hence these are most often said in a communal

[2]   The authors comment (1950: 452): "It often happens that the mother's relatives are the ones best known to her children, even, in cases, to the entire ignorance of the father's kin. Informants born and reared in the *shtetl* area have told us of never having met paternal grandparents, especially the paternal grandfather, until the age of thirteen or fourteen."

context at a synagogue. One rabbinical commentator on Jewish mourning has observed that: "The Jewish experience has taught that such values as peace and life, and the struggle to bring heaven down to earth, of which the *Kaddish* speaks, can be achieved only in concert with society, and proclaimed amidst friends and neighbors of the same faith" (Lamm 1969: 163–164).

There are other ways in which the community has become both a participant in and repository for the memorialization of the dead. Prominent public places have often been used by a dead person's survivors to commemorate his or her memory. Since at least Roman times, a prime means of doing this has been by making contributions to synagogues in the name of the deceased: traditionally, such acts are publicly advertised by the display of permanent plaques or mosaics in the temple bearing the names of the donors and the person being commemorated. This practice is still followed extensively among Ashkenazim in the United States. In a similar vein, it is customary for a person reciting *Yizkor* in a synagogue to make a donation to the temple on behalf of the deceased. Zenner notes:

In both Israel and the United States, Jewish religious and secular institutions are full of plaques which are in honor of a contributor and in memory of that person's deceased relations. In one synagogue, even the fluorescent lights contained the name of a contributor. Synagogue ornaments, Israeli forests, and institutional buildings commonly are named in memory of deceased relations of the contributors. The relations remembered are generally parents, spouses, siblings, and children of the donors (1965:482–483).

Four things are accomplished simultaneously by means of these charitable acts. First of all, the deceased is memorialized, and he is honored by means of an act of generosity and charity — actions which are among the most righteous and praiseworthy that a Jew can perform. Furthermore, as one Yiddish saying goes, "Charity saves from death" (from Proverbs 10: 2), and so the generous individual is both honoring a kinsman and thereby assuring his own good fate in the afterlife. "Thus, he who performs a good deed is taking out 'afterlife insurance in *Olam Habo*,' the world to come." [3] Third, and most visible in the case of memorial plaques, the deceased's memory is enshrined and displayed in such a way and in such a place that the

---

[3]   Zborowski and Herzog (1962: 195). Cf. the latter's comments (1962: 191–213) for an extended discussion of the place which charity occupies in traditional Jewish culture and psychology. Trachtenberg (1970: 157) provides some specific examples from the medieval period of Ashkenazic Jewry.

whole community of worshippers has its attention drawn to him and his name; and the memory is thus guaranteed of perpetuation, honor, and homage as long as the synagogue or institution itself shall survive. Fourth, and perhaps less consciously, the deceased's surviving kin have drawn attention and honor to themselves as well, for each thought of the dead that the plaque invokes carries with it a reminder of the concern, love, and respect which the dead person's family bore him both before and after his demise. As was customary in the *shtetl* concerning all such benevolent acts, people thus publicly display their generosity and their care for family, and thereby demonstrate the increase in their personal *zkhus* [merit] (Zborowski and Herzog 1962: 196–197). Memorials at the communal level thus become a commemoration for the dead and self-advertisements for the living.

Memorial plaques and *Yahrzeit* candles provide a physical clue to the structure and function of memorial practices, and there are a number of other visible symbols which also reflect (in part) the content of Jewish ancestral behavior. These other symbols include annual grave visits, the recitation of *Yizkor* and *Kaddish* by the deceased's survivors, the display of memorabilia in family homes, and the very names borne by a person's descendants. Particular given names, for example, may be passed on indefinitely within family lines; and since the bearer of a name is believed to honor and incorporate the nobler qualities of his or her namesake, there is created a conscious sense of continuity and identity which, at a given point in a family's history, may often include the living memory of individuals whose lifetimes cover a span of four or five generations. Furthermore, the structure of the naming pattern offers a good reflection of the bilaterality of the Jewish family kindred: individuals may be named in memory of either male or female ancestors on both their father's and their mother's side.

*Psychodynamics*

Psychodynamically, Jews experience a strong sense of obligation towards parents and ancestors, including the obligation to honor their wishes and ideals and prove oneself worthy of their heritage. This behavioral pattern is reinforced and given poignancy by parental adherence to an ethic of suffering and sacrifice for one's progeny. *Alles for die kindere* [everything for the children] is a saying which embodies the parental ideal that life is lived for the sake of one's offspring, and that all necessary sacrifices are to be made on their behalf. While the content of the maxim carries with it an air of altruism, Jewish family life also possesses a strong undercurrent of obligation and indebtedness. The children are repeatedly — sometimes directly, sometimes indirectly — reminded of the parental sacrifices which have been made for them, and so they grow up with a strong consciousness of their parents' expectations and hopes. In the United States, as Zborowski and Herzog note for the *shtetl*: "Children are reminded constantly of all their parents have done and suffered in their behalf" (1962: 294).

Balancing this sense of obligation is an awareness of the advantages which a person acquires as part of his ancestral heritage. That is, a person benefits reciprocally from the reputation and accomplishments of his forbears through *yikhus ovos,* which is high status based upon a person's ancestry and genealogy. In the *shtetl* the number of learned and wealthy individuals that a person could count among his family ancestors was a prime determinant of his social position. This form of ancestral status and self-consciousness still persists among Jews of Ashkenazic descent in the United States. People are quick to point out that their ancestors in Eastern Europe were *sheyneh layt* (literally "beautiful people," i.e. high class, learned, and/or wealthy) rather than *prosteh vidn* [low class, working, or common Jews].

An individual is thus proud and fortunate to have a learned person or rich individuals in his genealogy, for such people can thus invoke *zkhus ovos* [the merits of their ancestors], when appealing to God for help. The ancestral merit of this kin can benefit not only individuals, however, but families and communities as well. The influence of a righteous man is indeed great, as Zenner notes, for he "may protect or atone for his ancestors, his contemporaries and his posterity, through his righteous deeds" (1965: 482). People who enjoy high status and spiritual help based on *yikhus ovos* and *zkhus ovos* thus live their lives against a backdrop of family and community history; and they are consequently likely to feel a strong sense of indebtedness to their ancestors, coupled with the obligation to honor and to prove themselves worthy of this ancestral inheritance and merit.

Within this psychological context of sacrifice, expectation, and honor, homage to significant ancestors may be shown in a number of ways: these include not only such aspects of formal worship as *Yahrzeit* lights and the recitation of *Kaddish* and *Yizkor*, but also the fulfillment by those living of the deceased's wishes. Parents and elderly Jews give frequent expression to their concern for what they want their descendants to achieve in life. The Jewish concept of *naches*, denoting the joy and gratification enjoyed by a person because the worthy actions of someone else both please and favorably reflect upon him, is most salient within the realm of kinsmen. Parents and grandparents look to their descendants, rather than to their own accomplishments, as the prime source of their *naches*: for a person to give a parent or grandparent *naches* is to perform a great secular *mitzvah* [good deed]. The establishment of a family, the pursuit of righteousness, the love of learning, and the rewards of a profession — these and other goals may be urged upon a child or adult either directly by an elderly grandparent or, indirectly, through the invocation of a deceased parent's or grandparent's memory by a concerned (and psychologically subtle) parent. Childhood and later life are thus experienced against a backdrop of ancestry and with a sense of continuity which links the hopes of one generation with the accomplishments of another.

The psychological efficacy of these family patterns rests upon a mutual dependency between elders and youngsters, and between the living and the dead. The young depend upon their elders not only for physical necessities and emotional support, but for approval and validation as well. A parent honored in life may be further honored in death, and the neglect of a parent's wishes during his lifetime may be compensated for after his demise.

Conversely, the living look upon their eventual death with a comparable sense of dependency directed toward their survivors and descendants. The living are very concerned about how their survivors will remember and honor them after their death. Religious Jews are especially anxious for an heir — particularly a male heir — so that there will be someone to say *Kaddish* for them upon their demise: their happiness and security in the afterlife and their chance to avoid the dismalness of *Gehinnom* [Hell] are believed to rest upon the efficacy of this prayer and the regularity and sincerity of its recitation.

The problem of family psychodynamics warrants some special consideration of the role of women and mothers within the theoretically patriarchal Jewish households. Mothers often have a predominant position of power and moral authority, and their sway over husbands and children is notable as their induction of feelings of guilt and obligation in their children is pervasive and characteristic. In seeking to understand some of the structural and psychological dynamics of these situations, it is relevant to consider the jural and legal position of women in Jewish culture. First, Jewish women are in possession of fewer rights and privileges than men; and if women are to express themselves and realize their capacities, they will have to do it outside of the economic, political, scholastic, and religious spheres permitted to men. The household and its family members, on the other hand, provide an arena where women are not nearly as restricted as they are outside the home, and the concentration of their expressive and instrumental activities into these channels thus becomes comprehensible. If husbands and children are one of the main creative and expressive outlets available to women in Jewish culture, then the emotional investment by women in their spouses and offspring is an understandable consequence; and the development of certain psychodynamic bonds between them, such as guilt, resentment, and obligation, is an expected outcome.

Given these family and ancestral pressures upon Jews, there are a number of ways in which resentment and guilt may arise within families. The dynamics of guilt within the family may have several sources: persons may be oppressed by the sense that they mistreated the deceased during his or her life, perhaps through stinginess, a lack of care, or a failure of understanding. In the case of the death of an elderly parent, if the later years were characterized by declining health and were spent in a nursing home, hospital, or similar setting where people other than his children cared for him, then the children may be particularly susceptible to guilt feelings over their lack of commitment and personal attention to the stricken parent. Grown children who have lived their adult lives with an intense awareness of what their parents wanted them to become and to accomplish, but who feel that their lives have been an inadequate realization of their parents' dreams, may experience self-recrimination and shame along with the guilt occasioned by a parent's death. A married person who has lost a spouse may suffer a comparable sense of personal failure and inadequacy if the spouse's death engenders feelings that one never provided for or treated the deceased with the care, consideration, and consistency that was deserved and which one had promised. Guilt may also arise from the unresolved resentments, quarrels, and jealousies of the relationship, the psychological residue of which becomes especially oppressive when death seems to prevent any possible reconciliation. And the death itself may be a cause of anger and resentment, stemming from the sense of loss, abandonment, and rejection experienced by the survivors.

In each of these circumstances, Jewish memorial practices provide a number of ways for dealing with the emotions involved. People may try to achieve forgiveness from the dead through certain customary procedures. In one such observance, when a dead person lies on his deathbed, it is customary for relatives, neighbors, friends, and acquaintances to "ask pardon" of the deceased "for all possible insults or offenses they may have inflicted on him during his life." One Israeli custom "has the mourners place a stone on the covered grave and ask forgiveness for any injustice they may have committed against the deceased" (Lamm 1969: 67).

Of deeper psychological import are those memorial observances whose purpose is to display respect and reverence for the deceased. *Kaddish, Yizkor,* and *Yahrzeit* are prayers said at periodic intervals over a long span of time, and they thus serve to maintain a tie with the deceased and exhibit the sincerity of the mourner's love. The necessary recitation of the first two prayers in a congregational setting, among a group of fellow-mourners, provides the bereaved with a continual reintegration into the community and its supporting sentiments and is thus productive of a sense of comfort and consolation. The mourner may derive satisfaction not only through directing his prayers and thoughts to the deceased, but may also reinforce his own conviction regarding the sincerity of his feelings and sense of bereavement. Guilt and grief may thus be simultaneously assuaged.

Naming one's child after a deceased parent or grandparent also provides a highly visible embodiment of respect and continuity. Traditional Jews are especially concerned about having their spirit and memory perpetuated by means of their name. As one Hebrew text says, "a man's name is his person" and "his name is his soul" (cf. Trachtenberg 1970: 78). It is considered to be both a personal and family tragedy if an individual lacks descendants who could honor and perpetuate his memory in this way, "for a namesake is another link with the continuing community" (Zborowski and Herzog 1962: 321). In traditional families where such a naming pattern is followed, a young child will be reminded of the ancestor after whom he or she has been named, and special emphasis is often put on the personal qualities of the deceased which the child is expected to emulate. Here again, then, a memorial observance weaves the threads of history and morality into the fabric of a young person's life and takes a life from the past — a memory, an ancestor, and a name — as a model for the present.

While not an orthodox practice, many Jews do direct certain memorial prayers to the deceased themselves, often asking for forgiveness, aid, or advice, or inviting the departed to share in some *naches* which the family or community is enjoying. It is customary to visit gravesites during times of individual or family crises; and the anxiety-ridden person may seek to communicate, by prayer, with a deceased parent, grandparent, or spouse, asking them for guidance or for help in his dilemma. Trachtenberg notes that in the medieval and subsequent periods, there has always been a belief that the deceased could help the living, especially the righteous and the related among the departed. Thus, "the ancient practice of visiting the cemetery to entreat the good offices of deceased relatives or scholars persisted . . . In addition to such individual visits, there grew up the custom of the entire congregation repairing to the cemetery annually on several occasions . . . 'that the dead may beseech mercy on our behalf' " (Trachtenberg 1970: 64). Another type of communication between the living and the departed is reflected in the dream folklore of the *shtetl*, which "abounds in ancecdotes of fathers, mothers, grandparents, rabbis, who appeared in dreams to save someone [or a community] from disaster or point the way to success. . . . [In sum, then], the deceased continues to live within the community" (Zborowski and Herzog 1962: 310–311, 380).

Charity, as we have seen, may also provide an avenue for memorializing the deceased and maintaining ancestral ties. As an illustration of this, we cite the case of one female informant in New York who keeps a *pishke* [charity box] in her desk drawer — a *pishke* to which her recently deceased mother had regularly made contributions. Whenever this woman's own children face a crisis, such as an important job interview or a school exam, she places some coins in the *pishke* and calls on her mother to intercede on the children's behalf. This woman also keeps her deceased mother informed of family *naches*, such as good school report cards, weddings, and births, and places money in the *pishke* on each of these occasions as a charitable thank-offering.

This case is neither unique nor isolated, because Jewish folk practice, both in New York and Eastern Europe, seems to have consistently held to such beliefs, even in the face of orthodox disclaimers. Relationships between the living and the dead were thus viewed in terms of a reciprocity of interest and influence. For the believing, but somewhat less-than-orthodox Jew, one can thus reestablish, through memorialism, the kind of dependencies that one had with the dead during their lifetime. From this mutual interdependence between the living and the dead, one thereby achieves the kind of comfort that can be derived from continuing intergenerational ties beyond the individual's lifetime. Dependency, comfort, and continuity, so intrinsic to the ethics and psychodynamics of the Jewish family and community, acquire a degree of permanence and pervasiveness through their embodiment in the mechanics of memorialism.

Death can also be an intensely moral experience among Jews. It is in regard to this ethical dimension that memorial observances may involve the individual and the family in a wider sense of communal and ethnic responsibility. Through the experience of guilt, remorse, and bereavement, a sense of moral obligation can be reawakened (or created) in the individual to better fulfill his parents' hopes and dreams — a moral sense often involving the consequent need to reform his or her life. The dual intimations of mortality and responsibility, which are reinforced by repetitive memorial practices over time, may thus impel family members to treat kin and community members more humanely and adhere more closely to the moral tenets of the religion and the community. Since such a consciousness is usually phrased and experienced in terms of one's proper behavior "as a Jew," there is also a reaffirmation of one's collective responsibility and conscience in the community of *Klal Isroel,* the Jewish people.

The intensified sense of mortality may not only lead to a personal reformation, but it may also alter an individual's perception of specific family ties. A surviving spouse or child may turn to his or her own child now as a means for fulfilling the dreams and wishes of the deceased spouse or parent, just as the mourner may now see that same child as his or her own vehicle for personal immortality. The obligatory period of joint family mourning, *shiva,* and the somewhat less intense period of *shloshim,* fully bringing together by force the spouse, children, and siblings of the deceased into a therapeutic community of brief duration, provides a setting in which a range of contradictory emotions may be resolved, just as it simultaneously allows the family to draw lessons from the life of the deceased by remembering and recreating his or her personality and life history. The reunion of the mourning group at the time of the unveiling of the deceased's gravemarker again illustrates the repetitive nature of memorialism, a feature which enhances its moral and psychological efficacy. While Jewish memorial beliefs do not attribute to the dead the kind of jural authority which anthropologists have identified in some other cultural systems of ancestor worship, Jewish patterns do enable the deceased to exercise a degree of moral authority and to convey a sense of comfort and dependency which may even exceed that which they exercised in life.

The moral experience of death, like other aspects of Jewish memorialism, also has a dimension of reciprocity to it. That is, as a complement to the notion of ancestor *zkhus*, it is possible for the living to have a moral impact upon the dead, a feature which finds its embodiment in the concept of "the merit of the children." Adults whose lives were marked by faults and vices may be redeemed after their death through the exemplary behavior of their progeny. Both their memory in the community and their fate in *Olam Habo* may be blessed and preserved by virtue of their children's merit. While a parent cannot redeem an erring child by virtue of his own good deeds: "The reverse is possible! The deeds of the child CAN redeem the life of the parent, even after the parent's death. It is a neat reversal, a 'merit of the children' " (Lamm 1969: 159–160).

Finally, the moral experience of death can occur not only at the individual and family levels, and engender, in these persons, a communal consciousness; but, structurally and psychodynamically, the moral impact of death can be seen to operate at the actual level of the community itself. The community not only participates in the funeral, but it traditionally takes over the responsibility for funeral and burial arrangements for the bereaved family, just as the community bears a corporate responsibility to support scholars, widows, orphans, and the indigent. The death of a great scholar, rabbi, or leader may prompt a community, by means of various memorial practices, to restate and reaffirm his ideals; renew a sense of moral commitment and purpose; and often institutionalize the continuity of the deceased's work and memory through a memorial fund, the creation of scholarships, or the formation of an association, school, or other institution dedicated to his ideals. While certain medieval Ashkenazic beliefs emphasized the punitive, retributive, and threatening nature of deceased spirits and couched the language of death and mourning with many euphemisms, more recently contemporary Jews appear to have played down these aspects of belief in comparison to the supportive and moral role of the deceased.

The members of a community may observe *Kaddish*, *Yizkor*, and *Yahrzeit* for an honored person, just as they would for a member of their own family: they thereby reflect the familial nature of the Jewish community, and the congregational nature of the Jewish family. One can suggest that perhaps compensating for the relatively shallow genealogical depth of Jewish familial memorialism is the great breadth of its communal dimension. While these community practices may fall short of the actual worship of the deceased or the bureaucratization of his charisma, they may in fact constitute the communalization of his memory and morality.

At this larger structural level, the community thus does for itself what the congregation does for the individual mourner. The mourner, through necessarily communal participation in the more formalized aspects of memorial observance, renews his sense of affiliation with Jewish history and custom and the Jewish people; and he benefits from the comfort of tradition and a sense of dependency on the community, God, and his ancestors. Just as the individual recites *Kaddish* in a community of mourners and thereby calls to the attention of others his grief, his loss, and his piety, now the community itself calls the individual's attention to this greater loss and involves him in a community which is itself bereaved.

These multilevel psychodynamic effects illustrate the relationship of ancestral practices to social solidarity and continuity. In the Jewish case, the dimensions of solidarity and the depth of continuity are broader and deeper than those of some other cultural systems: solidarity and continuity are simultaneously familial, communal, and "national"; but since jural authority rests more with Talmudic tradition and rabbinical precedent than with the ancestors, the focus is more on moral authority, which finds its sources in the existential, historical, and ancestral forces which animate the individual's life.


DISCUSSION

Historically, we note that ancestor memorialism has been an important component of both Jewish and Japanese folk religion since the earliest of recorded times. However, its significance in the prevalent religious orthodoxies of the two peoples is quite different. In Japan, ancestor memorialism plays an important role in both Buddhist and Shintō rites. In orthodox Judaism, on the other hand, ancestor worship as well as many of the aspects of ancestor memorialism described here are specifically condemned by Jewish religious authorities. A number of functional models can be erected which could conceivably account for this difference, but a historical inquiry into its origins is well beyond the scope of this study.

At the structural level of analysis we find that while both cultures employ kinship terminologies which reflect bilaterality, the lineal parent-child relationship is expanded into a descent ideology which employs ancestor reverence as a major theme. Among Japanese the focus of this ideology is the household, although it may be extended to the national level via the concept of the family state. In the Jewish case, the focus has been the local community with historical extensions to the broader concept of the "People of Israel." The rural *shtetls* of Eastern Europe provided a prime social context within which deceased persons were memorialized, and this has been continued, to some extent, among Ashkenazic Jews in the United States. Our pilot study (in New York City and its suburbs) of the saying of *Kaddish*, the lighting of *Yahrzeit* candles, and the naming of children after ancestors shows that spouses separately memorialize the dead of their natal families — there is no Jewish equivalent for the Japanese *ie*.

At the psychological level of analysis, we note many similarities in the emotional content of the memorial practices of the two peoples which we feel arise from similar child rearing experiences. Japanese and Jewish children are highly prone to feelings of guilt when they fail to meet expectations as communicated to them by their parents. And parents in both societies, especially the mother, are able to produce this response by their expressions of pain and self-sacrifice when the child fails to achieve objectively stated goals. Furthermore, rejection of family and community dependence is both difficult and laden with anxiety, such that memorial practices find suitable psychological support.

If our supposition that similarities in child-rearing experiences together with their consequences with regard to personality formation and family dynamics account for the observed similarities in Jewish and Japanese memorial customs, then this conclusion may be of help in the resolution of certain questions regarding Japanese memorial practices alone. Smith (1966), Plath (1964), and Ooms (this volume) have presented data which answer the questions "Who are the ancestors?" "What emotions do they engender?" and "How are they symbolized?" They show how the identification of the ancestors is related to household structure, how their assumed emotional attributes are related to the institutional molding of affect, and how the symbolic conceptualization of the ancestors is structurally similar to the life cycle of the living. However, when we consider the question of why there are ancestral practices in Japanese society, we are not quite satisfied with the answers provided. Smith alludes to the force of tradition, though it was not his objective to answer why, but rather, who. Ooms points out that most Japanese no longer believe in the reality of ancestral spirits or in their ability to affect the living — an observation which we suspect is equally true of American Jews. At

one point, he attributes the continuation of Japanese memorial practices to the emotions they induce without indicating why these emotions should provide sufficient motivation. Later, he suggests that
contemporary Japanese memorial rites have been weakened by semantic depletion and that they now exist as survivals perpetuated by
a kind of historical momentum. To illustrate their terminal state, he
reports the view of an informant who felt that "ancestor worship was
meaningless and rather a burden," though this informant also reported
that she would eventually undertake these activities at the proper
time. Plath suggested that Japanese ancestor worship provides its
adherents with comfort and emotional security due to the importance
of maintaining family ties — ties which include those between the
living and the dead. With regard to the emotional content of these
ties, he noted that hostility directed toward the ancestors is suppressed
and that they are thought to be benevolent and concerned with the
welfare of their descendants.

In our view, Japanese ancestor memorialism is not perpetuated by
tradition, nor by the feeling of security it provides in Plath's sense. In
light of our comparison with Jewish data, we conclude that ancestor
memorialism among Jews and Japanese exists as an expressive model
of idealized social relations through which participants overcome
feelings of hostility and personal deprivation. [4] Human institutions,
such as the family, are often less than perfect and seldom wholly
satisfying to individual members. Cooperation within any cultural
enterprise is likely to involve certain psychic costs — costs which
somehow must be accounted for and justified. Within the memorial
practices of Jews and Japanese, the attitudes of gratitude and dependence are stressed which would, when sincerely felt, promote cooperation. But the rites also stress an identification of oneself with one's
ancestors who are the forbears of one's living group such that any
sacrifice for it is equally a sacrifice for oneself. Lebra (in this volume)
notes that members of one Japanese religious sect specifically equate
ancestor worship with self-worship. Wimberley, elsewhere, also noted
that members of the Japanese religion Seichō-no-Ie hold a similar
view (1969, 1972).

We do not suggest that ancestor memorialism among Jews and
Japanese exists solely to contain hostility, to expiate guilt, and to
promote selfless devotion to one's group. Other ends may equally be

---

[4] For a bibliography and discussion of expressive models as cultural units related
to the resolution of psychological conflict, see Roberts and Ridgeway (1969: 223–
245).

served. However, in the Japanese case, it is notable that in those cases where ancestors are held responsible for the suffering of their descendants, the social affairs of the descendants are seldom in order. Lebra notes that this disorder need not arise from the simultaneous application of different principles of social organization, in which case a structural explanation would be called for, but rather that it typically arises from various individual circumstances. What is particularly impressive about her findings is that again and again the reason given for an ancestor having harmed a descendant is not because he was acting in the capacity of a moral arbiter, but rather because he desired assistance. In short, he needed a descendant on whom he could depend, as do the living with regard to each other. In the Seichō-no-Ie case, the prevailing view is that, if we get right with our ancestors, we'll get right with one another.

In this paper, we presented a synoptic view of memorialism among American Jews and discussed its form and significance as they relate to a further understanding of Japanese memorial practices. At this juncture we suggest that detailed case studies of instances of Jewish memorial activities be undertaken either to establish or to disprove our expectation that the intensity with which they are undertaken is related to the degree of self-deprivation and hostility engendered within the individual by the group with which he is identified. Furthermore, we suspect that as a result of memorial practices, the participant becomes less individuated and comes to see self-sacrifice for the group as an objective good.

## REFERENCES

FREEDMAN, MAURICE
  1958  *Lineage organization in southeastern China.* London School of Economics Monographs in Social Anthropology 18. London: Athlone.
LAMM, MAURICE
  1969  *The Jewish way in death and mourning.* New York: Jonathan David.
LANDES, RUTH, MARK ZBOROWSKI
  1950  Hypotheses concerning the eastern Jewish family. *Psychiatry* 13: 462.
PLATH, DAVID W.
  1964  Where the family of God is the family. *American Anthropologist* 66:300–317.

POLLACK, HERMAN
1971 *Jewish folkways in Germanic lands (1648–1806).* Cambridge, Mass.: M.I.T. Press.
ROBERTS, JOHN M., CECILIA RIDGEWAY
1969 Musical involvement and talking. *Anthropological Linguistics* 11: 223–245.
SMITH, ROBERT J.
1966 *Ihai:* mortuary tablets, the household and kin in Japan. *Transactions of the Asiatic Society in Japan,* third series (9):1–20.
TRACHTENBERG, JOSHUA
1970 *Jewish magic and superstition — a study in folk religion.* New York: Atheneum.
WIMBERLEY, HOWARD
1969 Self-realization and the ancestors: an analysis of two Japanese ritual procedures for achieving domestic harmony. *Anthropological Quarterly* 42:37–51.
1972 The knights of the golden lotus. *Ethnology* 11:173–186.
ZBOROWSKI, MARK, ELIZABETH HERZOG
1962 *Life is with people.* New York: Schocken.
ZENNER, WALTER P.
1965 Memorialism — some Jewish examples. *American Anthropologist* 67:481–483.

SECTION TWO

# Characteristic Features of Ewe Ancestor Worship

D. K. FIAWOO

With minor exceptions, the ancestral cult is the focal point of the social organization in West African societies, including the Ewe of Ghana. As the basis of the entire religious system, ancestor worship is at the root of the African's philosophy of life and the orderly social relations upon which the well-being of society depends. On all ceremonial occasions the ancestors must be invoked through customary libations.

On the occasion of a libation among the Ewe, the ritual celebrant raises his calabash of maize flour soaked in water three times to the east and says, *amevɔwo tɔe nye esi*, meaning "May the wicked design of evil men be frustrated and nipped in the bud." Then turning to the west, he says, *fievia fie wodena*, meaning "The child destined for the evening must see evening, i.e. the good man must see fulfilment; he must live to a ripe old age even as the sun runs its full course when it sets in the west." This entreaty sums up the role of the ancestors among the Ewe: to eliminate evil from society and to reward goodness. This is also the basis of the Ewe juridical system. The ancestor cult is the embodiment of the values of the lineage/clan and the ritual expression of the Ewe social order. The following material is based on long-term field research conducted among the Aŋlɔ and Tongu Ewe of Ghana.

## The Ewe-speaking People

The Ewe-speaking people, who now number about one and a half million, occupy the southeastern triangle of Ghana and the southern half of the Togo Republic. They are a patrilineal society with virilocal residence, but substantially acknowledge cognatic kinship ties. Titles and property rights, though transmitted in the agnatic line, do not rigidly exclude maternal kinsmen.

A married woman does not sever ties with her own patrilineage. She is always a member of this corporate group to which she will turn in times of crises. At death, she is instantly claimed and buried by her own patrilineage.

The Ewes have never had a unified political system. On the contrary, they have been fragmented into a number of small independent chiefdoms. Their unity lies mostly in their claims to migration from a common source in western Nigeria and a common language. This common language is made up of four mutually intelligible dialects, each representing a distinct subtribal group. In Ghana, these groups are identified as the Aŋlɔ of the littoral, the Tongu along the lower reaches of the Volta River, west of Aŋlɔ, and the northern Ewe who occupy a position north of Aŋlɔ. The Togo Ewe refer to themselves as Genyi[1] which also identifies the dialect spoken by them. Collectively, they are conscious of their common cultural heritage, although Ewe scholars have also emphasized certain structural differences inherent in their social organization.

## The Cosmological Background

Ewe traditions are almost completely silent about the origins of the world, except that it was created by an immanent supreme being, *Mawu*, who later removed himself from the reach of man. But the Ewe have very definite ideas about life and death and the sources of certain fundamental beliefs and values which regulate their lives.

The Ewe believe that human life is compounded of two souls or two components of the same element; the one comes from *Mawu*, the supreme being, and the other from *Tsiefe*, the spirit world. At death, the union is permanently dissolved. The part of the soul from *Mawu* returns to the creator while the one from *Tsiefe* goes back to the spirit world, after the appropriate mortuary rites. *Tsiefe*, a place from which one does not return,[2] is not an exact spot that one can locate in space. It is loosely

---

[1]   Glidyi appears to characterize this group in Westermann's study (1935).

[2]   Note the contradiction. *Tsiefe* is from *tsife* [place of confinement]. At least by etymology, *Tsiefe* conveys the idea of a region of no return. In Ewe thought, however, the souls in *Tsiefe* are not abandoned to the spirit world. The continuity between life and death is made possible only by the rebirth of the souls in *Tsiefe*.

identified with man's original home or the portions of the earth inaccessible to the average Ewe. Five or more decades ago, when Nigeria seemed physically remote from Eweland, adventurous traders to Nigeria had interesting tales of their encounters with dead kinsmen in the Yoruba markets of that country. The dead disappeared into thin air when their identity became known. To the average illiterate Ewe, Nigeria remains *Nolime* [ghost land, the place of departed souls].[3]

Prior to the union of the soul elements and entry into *Kodzogbe* [the world of the living] the newborn has already led a full life in *Tsiefe*. There he is believed to have parents, siblings, spouse(s), and children. In short, he belongs to an ethereal family which duplicates that of the living world. To succeed in earthly life, he must adopt a pattern of life which corresponds to that of *Tsiefe*. As far as it is possible, occupation, hobbies, and personal interests must reflect those left behind. To do otherwise is to court disaster.

To make his way into the world, a soul must find an earthly mother. He is then led by an elder of *Tsiefe* towards two large oak trees (*adidowo* or *ametiwo*), whose branches serve as the gates of *Tsiefe*, demarcating it from *Kodzogbe*. As the branches interlock, the gates are said to be shut. It is an ill omen to arrive when the portals of *Tsiefe* are barred. Still-birth and infant mortality are attributed to this event. That is, a soul has left the spirit world, but has been denied entry into *Kodzogbe*.[4] On the other hand, a successful exit from the portals of *Tsiefe* signifies a new birth. Eventually, death will intervene when man resumes his place in *Tsiefe*. Thus a perpetual link, more or less cyclical, is forged between *Tsiefe* and *Kodzogbe*, between life and death.

In this brief narrative of the sources of life and death, the underlying belief in prenatal destiny is manifest. The soul's life on earth, short or long, filled with ease and wealth or pain and poverty, is predetermined. But fate is not altogether immutable. At least in theory, there are extenuating circumstances in which fate may be frustrated by the evil designs of men, probably assisted by sorcery or some supernatural power. Thus at the separation rites following burial, the spirit of the deceased is admonished to confront its assailant, if death was not the outcome of *gbe si miefo* [a bargain with one's soul in the spirit world].[5]

---

[3] Studies in Aŋlɔ clanship reveal that according to popular myths, some of the founders descended from the sky. However, the sky is seldom equated with *Tsiefe*.

[4] This suggests the existence of a "no man's land" separating *Tsiefe* from *Kodzogbe*. This limbo is also equated with the region to which the souls are confined, pending the appropriate mortuary rites which usher them into *Tsiefe*.

[5] Death at the hands of an assailant does not always suggest a negation of destiny. Such death may well have been predestined.

In rational thinking, prenatal destiny seems unethical because it fails to hold man accountable for his behavior in life.[6] A failure in society can always exclaim, *xɔvexɔvee* or *mele ŋunye o* [it is not with me], implying that he is not favorably endowed by his destiny. Nevertheless, as Fortes has shown with reference to the Tallensi, this alibi in itself has a functional role. The social misfit can escape the perpetual condemnation of society. Furthermore, prenatal destiny provides an index of man's total dependence upon supernatural will which is reflected in the absolute obedience demanded of children in the near-patriarchal Ewe system. In the context of socialization, *amebubu* [obedience] is said to be the kernel of education. Nowhere is this supernatural will more evident and meaningful than in ancestor worship — the relationship between former living members of the community and their descendants.

## BASIC STRUCTURAL PRINCIPLES OF WORSHIP

Ewe spiritual beings fall broadly into two categories, ancestral and nonancestral spirits. The latter comprise a large number and variety of community and personal spirits who exert a pervasive influence on individuals and the community at large. The former are specifically concerned with the regulation of the conduct of the lineage and its wider dimensions. The values set on kinship find expression in the ancestor cult.

The basis of Ewe ancestor worship, as in other parts of West Africa, is that there is life after death and that the dead members of the lineage and clan continue to show active interest in the mundane affairs of their living descendants. Life is compounded of two soul elements, one from *Mawu* and the other from *Tsiefe*, the spirit world. During ancestral rites, it is that part of the soul from *Tsiefe* which returns to feed through the medium of a stool as its shrine. Various categories of stools are recognized. The spirit of a chiefly lineage returns to inhabit a chiefly stool, while the spirit of a wealthy man in life returns to inhabit a stool of wealth. Ordinary lineages have humbler stools.[7]

The stool serves as the material symbol of the link between the living and their deceased antecedents. The occasion for feeding and/or cleansing

[6]   In spite of a seemingly tight philosophy of prenatal destiny, the Ewe claim that the soul returning to *Tsiefe* is held accountable for its deeds. It is not clear whether the souls are held responsible for their prenatal destiny or their actions in life (cf. Gaba 1965).

[7]   The Ewe also acknowledge stools of valor, established in memory of brave men whose deeds are nationally recognized (see fuller discussion of stools below).

the stool is also an occasion for acknowledging the role of the ancestors in society. This is the ritual basis of collective ancestor worship. In less collective expressions, the simple act of pouring out a drop of water or gin on the ground before satisfying oneself, or dropping the first morsel of a meal to the ground, testifies to the watchful presence of the ancestors in everyday life. At night especially, the souls of the departed are up and about, and the lineage enjoins taboos and certain prescribed forms of behavior which will ensure amity between themselves and their guests. Thus, unlike the Ewe belief in the supreme being, *Mawu*, belief in the ancestors and the departed members of the lineage is cultic and finds meaningful ritual expression.

*Tɔgbeawo* or *tɔgbeŋoliawo* is the Ewe term for the lineal ancestral spirits, while all the departed members of the lineage are collectively identified as *awlimeawo*, *tsieawo*, or *ŋoliawo*. Two points immediately arise from these terminological categories. First, the distinction between the departed members of the lineage and the objects of ancestor worship suggests that death and incorporation into the spirit world do not automatically entitle a deceased person to the status of ancestor. The calendrical offerings which are characteristic of ancestor worship are directed primarily to the *tɔgbeawo* who receive them on behalf of themselves and their junior kinsmen. This is borne out by the ritual language at offerings. Secondly, *tɔgbe* is derived from *tɔgbui* [grandfather] and gives a masculine bias to the objects of ancestor worship. This is in conformity with the near-patriarchal authority of the father of the family and the masculine leadership of the lineage and clan.

Ewe ancestor worship is not firmly linked to the political system – at least, not to the same extent as the Ashanti cult. There is no concept of royal or chiefly ancestral spirits who must exercise authority or exert influence over a people corresponding to the political community over which they once held sway. At the national level, the paramount ruler may appeal to his ancestors on behalf of the nation or the relevant political community, but he has no ritual or juridical obligation to do this; nor is there obligation on the part of the public to participate in festivals or rites to commemorate royal ancestors as the Ashantis do on the occasion of the *adae*. Among the Ewe, it is the nonancestral cults which unite nonkin groups around the paramount ruler as an ex-officio priest. Similarly, subjects owe no special allegiance to the ancestors of their divisional chiefs or local village chiefs. Thus the fundamental character of the ancestor cult as the embodiment of the values of the descent group is quite strong. Nevertheless, the crowd at an ancestral ritual is not necessarily limited to the descent group. The crowd will include affines, maternal kin, nonkin sympathizers, and, if a chiefly lineage, subjects who owe political allegiance to the stool — the latter only from a sense of respect for the chief.

### Ritual Character of Worship

A striking feature of Aŋlɔ ancestor worship is the marked irregularity of ritual offerings. Collective lineage worship is far from being a regular calendrical event. Obviously, a congregation which convenes once in five, ten, or twenty-five years is not likely to create a sound religious impression on its members, let alone develop a sense of identity with the relevant deity. To fill in the gap and forestall an attitude of indifference, what started as emergency consultations have become regular weekly features. The cult permits individual and family consultations. Although these personal contacts began only as emergencies they have since become accepted institutionalized modes of acknowledging the role of the ancestors in everyday life.

Implicit in Ewe ancestor cult is the conceptual distinction between cult of the dead or mortuary rites and ancestor worship. In the ritual events of the postburial rites when the dead members of the lineage are helped in their final journey to *Tsiefe* [the spirit world] the ancestors are invoked, but only as witnesses to the occasion. Similarly, when the ancestors are fed, it is customary to remember all the dead members of the lineage. Thus there is some overlap between the two events, but in the mind of the Ewe actor, there can be no mistaking the one for the other. Nonparticipant observers may fail to make the distinction, but not the actors themselves.

For purposes of analysis, and in view of the scant literature on Ewe ritual life, it is necessary to isolate the main procedures by which the Ewe establish contact with the dead and with the ancestors. The first postburial rite is *yɔfofo* [levelling the grave] which represents the first stage of the long journey to ancestral spirithood. Between four and seven days after burial, the exact date determined by the clan membership of the deceased, members of the lineage reassemble at the grave to perform the final rites. The main feature of the ritual is *nudedeyɔme*, consisting of presenting the parting meal to the deceased and closing the grave. The dead man is addressed as follows: "Some couple of days ago, you left us unceremoniously. As mortals, we are at a loss to understand the meaning of this hasty departure. But if this is the act of man, then I exhort you to vengeance. Share your assailant's water and drink with him. On the other hand, if this has been preordained, then rest in peace when you reach the portals of *Tsiefe*. May your children and the family enjoy good health."

The grave is then covered and levelled. The ritual takes its name from this act of levelling the grave.

*Yɔfofo* is reminiscent of the days when burial was conducted at home in the backyard. The corpse was only lightly covered with earth pending the *yɔfofo* ritual, when the grave was fully covered and levelled. Today burial takes place away from home, but the ritual persists in a slighty different form. The *nudedeyɔme* [ritual feeding] is done in the public cemetery, where a tiny hole is dug alongside the grave at a position analogous to the head of the corpse; but the ritual of final closure or levelling is performed elsewhere — in the bath hut where the corpse was washed for burial, and on a simulated grave, as public sanitation does not permit half-covered graves in a public cemetery.

*Yɔfofo* has a direct bearing on the ancestor cult as it provides the primary bridge to the ancestral world and ultimately to ancestral spirithood. The physical separation between the dead and the living is final: thereafter, the spirit of the deceased may revisit home and kinsmen, but mainly upon a specific invitation.

It is believed that the dead wander in limbo after *yɔfofo* and the crossing of the proverbial Styx. Permission to enter *Tsiefe* must come from the lineage in *Kodzogbe*. Hence the importance of the second major ritual, *yɔfewɔwɔ* in the chain of mortuary rites.

*Yɔfewɔwɔ* represents the final mortuary ritual which incorporates the dead members of the lineage into the ancestral family in *Tsiefe*. On this occasion, there is a considerable reenactment of the first burial rites: a funeral bed is made and a "corpse," simulated by a decorated stool, is laid in state and surrounded by mourners. There is a complete rehearsal, except for the physical interment. Among the Tongu, the relics which have been preserved are buried on this occasion.

The ritual begins with a procession of members of the lineage from the *afedome* [ancestral compound] to the homes of deceased members of the lineage. The procession is marked by drumming and dancing which is typical of all funerary rites. As the procession calls at each home, a libation is poured and the spirits of those who have died since the last *yɔfe* ritual are invited to join the procession to the ancestral home in order to partake of the ritual there.[8] The typical expression is *va afedoa*

---

[8] In theory, all deceased members of the lineage are invited; in practice, *ϑumekukulawo* [members who have died unnatural deaths] — by accidents involving the shedding of blood, contagious diseases, snake bites, or drowning — are excluded. By customary

*me nanɔ dzotia nu* [come to the ancestral home and sit by the bonfire]. This formal invitation to the spirits concludes the first part of the ceremony.

When members reconvene in the evening, the first major event is *dzotikpekpe* [lighting the logs], symbolizing the union between the living and the dead. The *adefola* or *gbedodatɔ* [ritual celebrant] picks up an *atra* [log] and says: "Grandpa, I call upon you and all your children. Tonight we invite you to join us as we kindle the logs." He puts down the log, picks up a second, and then a third, repeating the same phrases as before. The three logs are set down in a formation resembling the letter Y turned upside down:

He then lights the logs from the point of contact and the vigil officially begins amidst wailing, drumming, singing, and dancing. By the early hours of the morning, the funeral beds have been made and the important ceremony of *zibabla* [tying up the stools] has been concluded. These stools provide the media by which the lineage communicates with the spirits.

It is not essential that every spirit should have its own stool symbol, but status in life receives due recognition. Former elders and distinguished personalities of the lineage are singled out and accorded special veneration befitting their status in life. The stools are wrapped in silk and velvet and the most beautiful cloths the lineage can afford; they are then placed on a common funeral bed which is also tastefully decorated. Under the canopy of large chiefly umbrellas, the stools are fanned by girls and women adorned especially for the occasion. There is wailing on all sides, reminiscent of burial rites.

Various rituals are performed, including special offerings to the lineage stool. It is to this stool that the major ancestral spirits of the lineage are invited to be a witness to the events of the day.

Funerals properly concern the lineage of the deceased but sympathy on the part of the wider community is always a welcome gesture. Such

---

practice, *ɔumekukulawo* are regarded as social lepers and must be buried at the *tagba* [outskirts of the town] because they have "died bad deaths"; however, they resent these discriminatory practices. For fear of malice on their part, they may be placated by brief ritual attention outside the house. On no account must they be fed with the ancestors. The rationale is that indifference to the welfare of these souls eliminates or reduces the incidence of unnatural deaths in the lineage.

sympathy may take the form of contributions and/or reverent attendance at the rites. Nonkin sympathisers may step forward and throw a few cowries into the funeral bed and mutter a familiar ritual expression, *metsri nu na mi loo!*

Then follows the final ceremony of *tsadidi* [taking a stroll with the spirits], amid drumming, singing, and dancing. On return to the ancestral compound, a few rounds of musketry are fired to finish the ceremony. At night, the stools are dismantled. If personal effects of the deceased were featured in the ceremony they are buried the same night. Articles contributed by lineage members are restored to their owners.

*Zibabla* or the ritual wrapping of stools in *yɔfe* may take other forms. At Tefle (Tongu) where the author has witnessed the *yɔfe* ritual on various occasions, no stools are wrapped up, but silk and velvet cloths are arranged to simulate the corpse. The ritual itself is a clan-centered affair as members of the constituent lineages cooperate with the clan head in the ancestral compound. When the ritual involves several spirits, two or more representations of the deceased are made according to their social status in life. At the climax of the events, clansmen send gifts to their dead kinsmen through the ritual of *nudede vu* [loading the canoe].

*Yɔfewɔwɔ* may be simple or elaborate, according to the resources of the lineage or clan. When it is elaborate expenditures run high, as mortuary rites often do in contemporary Ghana.

Among the Aŋlɔ, *yɔfewɔwɔ* has long ceased to be a regular calendrical event. The high cost of ritual is a restraining factor. Thus the interval from one *yɔfe* to another may vary widely, from five to twenty-five years. At Tefle where the *yɔfe* ritual has been grafted onto the local annual festival, determined efforts are made to observe the ritual annually. Among the Aŋlɔ where annual festivals have not yet found firm footing, elaborate *yɔfe* rites are often linked to some major stool festival, say the installation of a chief. Thus the *yɔfe* ritual is performed more frequently in chiefly lineages than in ordinary lineages.

The Aŋlɔ parallel to the clan-centered ritual at Tefle is found only at the level of the paramount ruler and divisional chiefs. These offices are vested in specific clans and the occasion for a stool festival is also an occasion for acknowledging the role of the clan ancestors.

On this occasion, the core group of ritual participants is the clan supported by the relevant political community. During the reign of the late paramount chief, *Tɔgbui* Sri II of Anlo, a *yɔfe* ritual was organized for his predecessor in 1947. It featured the *Adzɔvia* clan as the active ritual participant, but in its festive character, the event was an Aŋlɔ national affair.

The contributions of women to the success of the *yɔfe* ritual are readily acknowledged by the men, but these roles are not different from their feminine duties in the domestic group. At the *yɔfe* ritual, women are seated by the funeral bed as principal mourners, fanning the stools with their handkerchiefs — symbolic of fanning the corpse laid in state — and singing familiar dirges. They are also responsible for the elaborate cooking which the occasion demands. Women who have only conjugal ties with the lineage are easily absorbed and perform similar chores as those who are members by birth even though they properly belong to their own ancestor cult to which they have definable obligations. Only menstruating women are excluded from participation. Should these deliberately infringe the rule, they are said to be afflicted with perpetual menstruation. Widows are also excluded, but on different grounds. Their presence at the ceremony is not a defilement, but society expects them to withdraw from active participation in the normal social rounds while they are mourning.

In spite of the useful roles of women at mortuary rites, the spirits of deceased women receive differential treatment at the *yɔfe* ritual. In some parts of West Africa women serve as queen mothers, are elected as chiefs and paramount rulers in their own right, and have stools as their symbol of office.[9] The Aŋlɔ have not developed this kind of so-phistication.[10] The dead women of the lineage are remembered faith-fully in the *yɔfe* rites, but instead of a stool an *abaxe* [straw bag] which is identified with their sex is used.

The main ancestral ritual is directed to the ancestors themselves. In *yɔfe*, the ancestors are invited, more or less in the capacity of wit-nesses, but the principals are the spirits of the departed who are yet to be incorporated into the ancestral kingdom.

When the ancestral ritual is performed in a chiefly lineage, it is iden-tified as the *zikpuinuwɔwɔ* or *zinuwɔwɔ* [stool ritual]; otherwise it is an *afedomenuwɔwɔ* [ritual of the ancestral compound]. However, the generic expression for all ancestor rituals is *zinuwɔwɔ* [doing things related to the stool] since the stool — whether chiefly or not — is the ritual symbol of all the ancestors. In their differential character the ritual content of *zikpui-nuwɔwɔ* may vary little from an *afedomenuwɔwɔ*, but the former is likely to be more elaborate, expensive and possibly will attract a wider

[9]    The Akans of Ghana and the Mende of Sierra Leone are examples. Among the latter, women paramount rulers are nominated to serve alongside the men in the country's highest legislature.
[10]    There are rare exceptions. A woman who demonstrates high qualities of leadership or shows exceptional bravery in time of war is honored as a *hanua* [community leader] of women.

range of observers and sympathizers than the latter. The stool of a chiefly lineage may very well attract the subjects of the stool to the ancestral ritual, but there is no obligation on either side.

Like *yɔfe*, ancestral rites are not regular calendrical events. It is circumstances which dictate the rites. A run of misfortunes in the lineage may be interpreted by the *bokɔ* [diviner] as a sign of ancestral displeasure. Probably the ancestral spirits have been neglected for too long or the lineage has been remiss in the performance of traditional duties. After ascertaining the wishes of the spirits, the head summons a meeting of the lineage and conveys the message of the forebears. Funds are collected and a day is set aside for offerings.

There is meticulous compliance with the wishes of the spirits lest deviation should occasion further displeasure. Only the animals demanded by the spirits are sacrificed. The rites are performed by the lineage head or chief and in the *afedome* [ancestral compound]. The animals are slaughtered and drinks are offered with supplications to the ancestors to pardon offenses committed against them, winding up with prayers for the life and prosperity of the members of the lineage. It is important that all the ancestors are mentioned by name, or at least references are made to them in order to avoid the displeasure of a forgotten spirit. To play safe the ritual celebrant calls the most senior ancestor by name and says: *Na tɔgbeawo, nyanyeawo kple manyemanyeawo keŋ* [To all the ancestors, the known and the unknown].

The occasion for a stool ritual is the most memorable event of the lineage and full lineage participation is enjoined. Demographic and economic factors may disperse the lineage but on the occasion of an ancestral offering, members will try to be reunited with their kinsmen in the *afedome*. This is an important unifying function which is shared by all Ewe lineages.

*Zikpuinuwɔwɔ* has two formal aspects: *zitsilele* [stool cleansing] and *dzawuwu* [stool feeding]. The latter is simpler and less expensive and provides a shortcut to the placation of the ancestors. The former is more elaborate and always includes the latter. The stool is not cleansed without also being fed. There are no fixed periods in the year for the ceremony, but they generally take place between July and December when there is an abundance of food.

Indeed, the availability of food and the means to acquire it are probably the most decisive factors in the celebration of a stool ritual. In the distant past, stool festivals were celebrated annually; but with the rise in the cost of living and the attendant economic hardships, the ritual has become less regular. Thus the irregularity of the ritual has become a characteristic feature. Some stools have not been washed for several years. The lineages concerned wait until there is some threat to life or a specific disaster which the diviners have interpreted as the direct expression of the displeasure of the ancestors. In chiefly lineages, the installation of a new chief is also a suitable occasion for a stool ritual, as stool washing and feeding usually form an integral part of an installation ceremony. As discussed above, the cult also permits individual and personal contacts.

On particular days of the week, usually Thursdays and Saturdays,[11] the stool hut is open to members of the lineage or clan who are privileged to make offerings and to solicit blessings from the ancestors. The cult priest-in-charge knocks at the door of the hut and pauses a few moments before opening it. In characteristic obeisance, he greets the stool and in the custom of *adefofo na zikpuia* [singing the praises of the stool] reveals his mission: so-and-so wishes to remember the ancestors and has brought such-and-such a gift.

The Ashanti stool house generally has as many stools as there have been chiefs in the lineage or clan. Among the Ewe, especially the Aŋlɔ, this duplication is thought unnecessary. But there are important exceptions. A chief who may have distinguished himself in battle, and particularly one who has succeeded in capturing an important stool from an adversary, brings home his prize as an extra symbol of his chiefly authority and as a memento of his deeds of valor. At death, such a stool is deposited with the original one and forms a part of the clan's heritage.[12] Nevertheless, during ancestral rites, all the spirits are invited to the original stool. In the preliminary invocation, the youngest and latest stool, in its role as *tsiami* [spokesman], is addressed by name and requested to carry the message to his seniors in office. In the pouring of libations, however, the original stool, as father of the stools, is invited to "come and have some drink for yourself, your children, and grandchildren." The other stools may be given supplementary libations in their own right.

The respect for seniority which marks this ritual is a direct expression of social conduct in the lineage. The Ewe do not recognize the rights of primogeniture, but age and seniority are widely respected. In the political system a chief is not addressed directly, but through a spokesman.[13]

[11]   The days vary among the lineages, but it is generally agreed that Fridays are not propitious for such consultations.
[12]   The duplication of chiefly offices in some lineages or clans is sometimes traced to this event. In the midst of dissent, a faction may break away to install a rival chief, supporting its action by the historical accident of an extra stool in the lineage or clan.
[13]   Compare the Ashanti political system (Busia 1954; Rattray 1923).

In chiefly lineages, the chief, as the spokesman of the lineage, is also its spokesman before the ancestors. In practice, he delegates most of his functions to a member of the lineage whose roles he supervises. In his ritual role, the appointee bears several names: *gbedodatɔ* [initiator of prayer], *adefola* [one who sings the praises of the stool]. Other titles are *tsino, ziiɔ,* and *fiantɔ.* His duties include the weekly opening of the stool hut for personal offerings by members of the lineage; he pours libations on behalf of the lineage and washes the stool at the appropriate ceremonial function. During stool festivals, the chief must stand by his *gbedodatɔ,* as the latter offers libations and prayers. The slaughter of sacrificial animals may be assigned to a specialist, the *lakawula,* but bathing the stool in blood or offering it meat is the privilege of the chief himself. He rarely delegates this role.

The office of *gbedodatɔ* is not a remunerative one, for it is an honor to be appointed. In some lineages he may be offered ten or twenty percent of the ritual gifts given by members of the lineage. The office is not hereditary and is not regarded as full time; cult priests are often farmers, fishermen, or craftsmen.

In a metaphorical sense, each member of the lineage is his own ritual specialist, communing directly and spontaneously with his ancestors in the privacy of his home and farm. Thus a man who has met with a piece of good fortune exclaims: *"Tɔgbega gadi nam!"* [Here is good luck from great-grandpa], and pours a libation of maize flour and water at the threshold of his house. As far as is known, the ancestors are not any less pleased with these humbler, personal, and spontaneous offerings. Quite apart from providing extra machinery for acknowledging the presence of the ancestors in everyday life, they add flexibility to the worship of the ancestors. Without stools and characteristic symbols, the individual can address his ancestors, and feel that he has been heard.

## Lineage Stools

Four categories of ritual stools are recognized:

1.  The *fiazi* [stool of the chief], the best known ancestral ritual symbol, is also the symbol of the office of a king, a paramount ruler, or subordinate chief. During ancestral rites, the forebears are invited to this stool. Thus the *fiazi* symbolizes the political and ritual roles of the occupant (see Plate 1).

2.  *Afedomezi* [stool of the lineage's ancestral home] is peculiar to nonchiefly lineages and performs only a ritual role in relation to the

ancestors. In all cases of *afedomenuwↄwↄ* [lineage ancestral rites] the *afedomezi* is the central symbol.

3. *Kalezi* [the stool of valor] is less well known in Aŋlↄ because they are so few. Originally, the man who distinguished himself in war was presented with a sword as an accolade of bravery. It was the nation's highest honor reserved for men of exceptional valor. Men whose leadership inspired others to notable feats were similarly honored. In the days of internecine warfare, it was fashionable to find successors to chiefly offices among the valiant on the battlefield. In this event, the two statuses became merged in an incumbent who was highly respected as a chief and as a man of valor.

On the other hand, not every man of valor acceded to the office of a chief. However, to perpetuate the memory of such a proud son of the lineage when he died, a stool was carved as a *memento mori*. This is the act of *zikpuidodo* [immortalizing by stool]. It is such men of distinction whose memories are treasured in ancestor worship. The stool so carved is deposited in the stool hut as part of the lineage heirloom. On the occasion of the ancestral rites, such a stool receives ritual attention. The *kalezi* has no political significance, but in a maximal lineage it may provide the point of fissure along which future lineage segmentation will develop.

4. *Hozi* [the stool of wealth] is relatively new and does not appear to have originated from *Hogbe*, the Ewe ancestral home.

In spite of a doctrine of prenatal destiny, the Ewe have wide respect for personal achievement. In the past, the relatively wealthy man, typically one with a retinue of slaves, was literally a chief in his own right and carried a stool as a symbol of his achieved status. When he died, the stool was enshrined and treasured by the lineage. On the anniversary of his death, his children and grandchildren made offerings to the stool. As part of the lineage stools, it also received ritual attention on the occasion of the communal worship of the ancestors.

Important distinguishing features of the *hozi* are: (a) it is decked in cowries, the traditional West African currency; (b) unlike other stools, it is never smeared with, or bathed in, blood at ritual offering; (c)ritual offerings are made by the son or grandson of the man in whose honor the stool is established.

On the occasion of an offering the ritual celebrant prays thus: "In connection with the ritual in hand, we ask for life and health so that we can work and achieve fulfilment and prosperity, and thereby recapture the former wealth of this house, and more abundantly."

The emphasis of the prayer is on life and health to work and accumulate

Plate 1.   An ancestral stool from a chiefly lineage in Aŋlɔ. Note the paraphernelia: two state swords and a headgear on the stool, and two interpreter staffs in front

wealth which can perpetuate a wealthy house. In the days of cowry currency, a wealthy man was said to have *kpɔhotsui* [found cowries]. Thus all stools are decked in cowries, symbolic of their function.

The *hozi* is venerated by the lineal descendants of the man in whose honor it is established. Its primary function is to honor a wealthy man for his achieved status and to inspire descendants to industry and possibly wealth. The lineal ancestors are there to help achieve these objectives of the lineage.

Since the colonial days, slave ownership has ceased to be a status symbol, but men have learned to achieve socio-economic distinction in other areas: as successful farmers, fishermen, craftsmen, entrepreneurs, and traders. It is not known how many of these modern successful men are immortalized by *hozi*, but informants maintain that the tradition has survived. It is claimed that at least one or two new *hoziwo* (plural of *hozi*) are established each decade and that there are scores of *hoziwo* scattered throughout Aŋlɔ land.

By encouraging achievement, the *hozi* principle emphasizes the eternal reward for hard work. Industry and success are much admired. The stool is also an expression of desirable filio-parental relationship. It is the son who perpetuates the memory of the father in the *hozi*.

## The Functional Role of Worship

The Aŋlɔ clan is not a localized group, but is corporate in character. On the occasion of the clan ancestral offerings, members are enjoined to return to the clan ancestral compound at Anloga, where they renew their kinship ties and loyalty to the head of the clan. Both belief and ritual symbolize important values and sentiments held in the kinship, juridical, and political systems. A case study will be illuminating.

In 1965, after a period of ritual inactivity, the ancestral spirits of the *Agave* clan, symbolized by their stool, *Kaklaku*, suddenly decided to arouse their wards to action. A chain of unfavorable events had been interpreted as an expression of the displeasure of the ancestors, who had not been ceremonially fed for a few years.

The head of the clan and its spokesman before the ancestors was also the *Awadada* [field-marshal], the second highest political office in the Aŋlɔ land next to the office of the paramount ruler. Thus *Kaklaku* [his stool] had considerable ritual and political significance. Besides its duties to the clan, the stool had important military functions in time of war. In peace, it served national juridical functions, providing a powerful means of trial by ordeal. According to belief, it could also neutralize the effects of disease and epidemics threatening the whole Aŋlɔ nation. At the lineage and clan level it offered individual and collective security to its members.

The stool itself was six inches long, four inches wide, and five inches high. For most of the year, it was heavily greased with the fat of a ram and placed on a much bigger stool. There were other ritual objects, including swords, daggers, machete, and leg-cuffs. Some of the swords were three-pronged and were said to represent the three military divisions of Aŋlɔ. The leg-cuffs were said to be magically useful especially in arresting the mobility of an aggresive enemy. Fleeing enemies were also arrested by the same magical power. Theoretically, the stool festival was said to be an annual affair; in practice, it depended on the availability of funds.

The traditional method of collecting funds was to estimate total expenditure and assess all able-bodied men and women through their segmentary clan units. Donations were also accepted from well-to-do individuals. Any deficit was shared and paid in the same manner as *xɔmefi* [funeral debt].[14] Surplus funds were deposited in the stool house as savings for the next ritual. The ritual specialists were drawn from one *kpɔnu* [division of the clan] and included the *tsilelawo* [stool-washers], the *lakawulawo* [animal slaughterers], and *gbedodatɔwo* [prayer-makers].[15] The second division of the clan consisted of cult servants, while the third group, the chiefly wing, provided the candidates for the stool.

For the stool washing, several varieties of herbs were gathered and classified as warm herbs or cool herbs. The stool was first cleansed in sea water using the warm herbs, and then in a well using the cool herbs. Several rams were slaughtered and the blood made to drip on the stool and the other ritual objects. Parts of the raw meat were offered to the stool. The rest was cooked ritually, and after presenting portions to the stool and clan members, the general public was invited to partake of it.

While the meat was cooking, several members of the clan came forward to *wudza* [make offerings]. These took the form of the redemption of pledges or the expression of gratitude for favors shown. A middle-aged woman offered an amount of money and a chicken and testified as fol-

---

[14] When expenditures exceed lineage resources at a given time the difference is customarily met at a meeting of the elders. Even though a funeral is the responsibility of the lineage, the local community often comes to the aid of the lineage in a system of mutual aid.
[15] In a relatively small descent group these offices may be filled by only one ritual specialist.

lows: "I came to you last year to complain of childlessness. I shed tears and implored you to help me. As you know, I often had miscarriages. Last year, I made a promise that if my prayers should be answered I would show my appreciation. I now have a baby and I wish to redeem my pledge." This woman's testimony is typical of the traditional favors requested.

Others who came forward with gifts included farmers, fishermen, teachers, mechanics, truck drivers, and traders. A migrant fisherman based at Abidjan offered a ram and explained that he had suffered a reverse in his fortunes at his station. Through the help of a diviner, he realized that he was being punished by the stool for his long indifference to rituals at home. Thus he had been deserted by the stool. After making the offering, he prayed to the stool to restore all the fishermen who had deserted him and gone to join other fishing companies. According to the belief, clan and lineage "deserters" may be brought back into the fold through the mechanism of suffering and misfortune that is traced to the displeasure of the ancestors (cf. Gaba 1965).

After the meat was cooked, part of it was placed in a container on the stool. What followed might be described as a "trial by ordeal" in which the conduct of clan members was tested. Invitations were extended to all members of the *Agave* clan with a "free conscience" to step forward and share the meal with the stool. Any man who steps forward must assure himself that he harbors no evil thoughts against a fellow-man, that at least since the last ritual he has committed no murder, theft, or adultery, and that he has not practiced evil sorcery or witchcraft.

Persons under strong suspicion of causing some scandal might be persuaded by their own family to go to the stool and vindicate themselves. A man who wanted to assure his friend that he had not committed adultery with his wife might invite his friend to the stool and prove his innocence. He would speak as follows: "I have been suspected of an offense of which I am entirely innocent. If I speak falsely, I submit myself to the vengeance of *Kaklaku*." Then he would take a piece of the meat from the stool and drink the water by the stool. If he spoke falsely or was guilty of the offense, he would collapse immediately, according to the belief.

This communion with the stool performed the essential function of an ordeal, identifying the malevolent characters of society, especially those who had transgressed the laws of the clan. The object was peace with fellow-clansmen and peace with the ancestors, the only conditions necessary for the abundance and prosperity which all clansmen desire.

Beyond immediate obligations to the clan, *Kaklaku* is a stool of considerable national importance. After the clansmen had their fill, the secrets of the stool were locked up, but the trial by ordeal was resumed outside the stool hut. The ordeal was opened to the general public and offerings and testimonies were made, similar to those already described. The festival illustrates the combined political, juridical, and social functions of the ancestral ritual.

The example of *Kaklaku* is not an isolated case in Aŋlɔ. In related stool festivals, the same degree of group participation might be lacking, but the function of the festival as a means of uniting the members of a social group and regulating interpersonal relations is never in doubt.

The role of the ancestors in Eweland is quite similar to their role in other West African societies. Among the Mende of Sierra Leone, "misfortune suffered personally or by the family as a group is a sign of supernatural displeasure and is interpreted as a warning that the persons concerned should look closely into their conduct towards relatives as well as towards the spirits themselves" (Little 1954). Among the Ashanti the ancestors are known to punish those who violate the traditionally sanctioned code (Busia 1954).

## CONCLUSION

Parrinder (1949), who has made interesting studies of some West African religions, observes that where there is a strong pantheon of gods ancestral worship is less developed. It might be asked: how strong is Ewe ancestor worship *vis-à-vis* the *trɔwo* [nature spirits]. The number and diversity of the ubiquitous *trɔwo* and their articulate priesthood clearly suggest that the nature gods occupy a very important place in the religious life of the Ewe. But as we have shown, the Ewe-speaking people care for their dead, and their entire philosophy of life is geared to the concept of the ancestors and the hereafter. Belief in the ancestors is necessary to find an answer to the meaning of life and the orderly interpersonal relations characterizing the lineage and the clan.

In this study, we have shown that Ewe ancestor worship sheds light on the social, political, juridical and religious systems. Procedures vary from very simple personal libations without characteristic ritual symbols to a complex form of worship embracing the whole lineage or clan; but the emphasis is mostly on the lineage-centered ritual with stools as the symbols of the ancestors. While the Ewe share with most West African societies the main features of belief and practice, the Ewe ancestor worship should be characterized as lineage centered in contradistinction to the household type so ably described by Fortes among the Tallensi of northern Ghana (Fortes 1945, 1949).

## REFERENCES

BUSIA, K. A.
1954 "The Ashanti of the Gold Coast," in *African worlds.* Edited by Daryll Forde, 190–209. London: Oxford University Press.
FIAWOO, D. K.
1959 "The influence of contemporary social changes on the magico-religious concepts and organization of the southern Ewe-speaking people of Ghana." Unpublished doctoral thesis, Edinburgh University.
FORTES, M.
1945 *The dynamics of clanship among the Tallensi.* Oxford: Oxford University Press.
1949 *The web of kinship among the Tallensi.* Oxford: Oxford University Press.
1959 *Oedipus and Job in West African religion.* Cambridge: Cambridge University Press.
FORTES, M., G. DIETERLEN, *editors*
1965 *African systems of thought.* London: Oxford University Press.
GABA, C. R.
1965 "Aŋlɔ traditional religion." Unpublished doctoral thesis, London University.
LITTLE, K. L.
1954 "The Mende of Sierra Leone," in *African worlds.* Edited by Daryll Forde, 111–137. London: Oxford University Press.
PARRINDER, G.
1949 *West African religion.* London: Epworth Press.
RATTRAY, R. S.
1923 *Ashanti.* Oxford: Clarendon Press.
WESTERMANN, D.
1935 *Die Glidyi-Ewe in Togo.* Berlin: W. de Gruyter.

# Ancestorcide!
# Are African Ancestors Dead?

VICTOR C. UCHENDU

Ancestors remain one of the most powerful spiritual forces in Africa where belief in ancestors, particularly in their active role in the social structure, is widespread. African ancestors play an interventionist role in the affairs of the lineage and exercise a countervailing force in balancing the delicate relations between the world of man and the world of the spirits in which they are active participants. Given this active role, and the African world view that articulates and supports the ancestral roles, it is not surprising to me that evolutionary theory of religious development tended to equate African religion with ancestor worship. (Mbiti 1970: 8).

Ancestor worship has a number of attributes. The structural configuration of these atributes is so remarkably uniform in societies where ancestors are recognized and embodied in religious practices, that it has become a great temptation to confuse "ancestral structure" with "ancestral culture." The central fact about ancestors derives from the proposition that "ancestors are made by society." Whatever ancestors are or are not in folk theory and ideology, they are the creatures of society. It is society that accords or denies ancestors "social" or "cultural" status. The problem of interpreting ancestors in religious

The ideas presented in this paper were reported orally at the special symposium on Ancestor Worship held at the University of Illinois, Urbana during the IXth International Congress of Anthropological and Ethnological Sciences. The author expresses his thanks to the participants for the intellectual stimulation received.

The paper represents a small part of a bigger project on *The Igbo religious system: its historical role and contemporary relevance.* I am grateful to The Wenner-Gren Foundation for Anthropological Research for its support of the project.

terms arises from this proposition that ancestors are the creatures of society.

In handling the question of how much of society is embedded or reflected in ancestor culture, theories of ancestorship seem to have come full cycle. With fieldwork data successfully challenging the theory of prelogical mentality as the basis of ancestors worship, ancestors have been restored to the social system, where their sociological and jural roles have been emphasized. But the problem of dealing with ancestors as "part society" and "part spirit world" remains a bone of theoretical contention. Conflicting theories, based on the African material, disturb this writer enough to entitle him to raise the question: Are African ancestors dead?

My aim is to reexamine the theories of ancestor worship which either view ancestorship as a mere projection of the social structure into the world of the spirits or that deny ancestors some attributes of the religious culture which ancestor-worshiping societies accord them. We will do this through the examination of the ancestral traditions of one African people.

## THE NATURE OF THE CONTROVERSY

Despite the persistence of some terminological confusions in the literature, the theoretical achievements in the study of ancestorhood in Africa have tended to build up a high measure of agreement on what the ancestor cult consists of. It is generally accepted that ancestors form an important part of the social structure and are vested with both mythical powers and jural authority. The important distinction between ancestor cults and the cult of the dead made by Gluckman (1937) has helped to focus attention on two interrelated issues: the moral status of ancestors and their countervailing powers; and the relationship between genealogical distance and the effectiveness of the ancestral sanctions. Since ancestorhood is a status in a descent system, a "parenthood made immortal" by the descent structure, ancestors tend to have effective mystical powers only with respect to their descendants (Fortes 1961: 180). In this context only certain dead, occupying particular structural positions in a given social environment, can qualify as ancestors.

## ANCESTORS AS ELDERS

Since ancestors were "restored" to the social system in theoretical terms, the view that they are part of the social system has been widely held. Following the Durkheimian revolution, the precise relationship between ancestors and the enduring social groups with which they are associated has not been easy to define. Durkheim and Durkheimists have tended to explain this relationship on one basis only: the assumption that ancestor worship is essentially STRUCTURAL SYMBOLISM — a projection of the social world to the world of the SELECT dead.

There is also an emergent neo-Durkheimian theory of ancestorhood which regards the application of the term ancestor cult to African materials as nothing more than Western ethnocentrism. This proposition asserts that the "eldership complex" is being paraded as ancestor worship. In my view this theory replaces "structural symbolism" with "structural realism" and, by equating the world of the descent group with the world of the ancestors, it asserts a "structural fusion" that represents the highest form of reductionism.

The logic of the above theory is simple. It is an extension of the widely held African belief that the "lineages are communities of the living and the dead." In a recent restatement of the theory of eldership, Kopytoff (1971: 138–139) makes the following observations:

That African "ancestors" are above all elders (who must) be understood in terms of the same category as living elders . . . . Elders, after they die, maintain their role in the jural relations of successive generations. The ancestor cult is an integral part of the system of relationship with elders. The relationship with dead elders (that is, "ancestors") is seen as being on the same symbolic plane as that with living elders and not as secondary to it or derivative from it.

Kopytoff's propositions are based on the analysis of the materials on the Suku, a corporate matrilineal group in southwestern Zaire. The data supporting Kopytoff's theory of elderhood may be briefly summarized. The Suku are shown to have most of the structural and religious traits that are associated with ancestor worship in some African societies. However, they have no term that can be translated as "ancestor"; make no distinction within the lineage between those who are alive and those who are dead. While authority and power among the Suku vary with age, a single set of principles regulates the relationship between the senior person and the junior person. A person deals with a single category of eldership since the line dividing the living from the dead does not affect the structure of the relationship.

In this society, "the powers with which ancestors are endowed become a 'projection' of the palpable powers of living elders" (Kopytoff 1971: 137). And given the logic of the theory and the facts selected to back it up, Kopytoff's conclusion is not surprising: "The selection by anthropologists of the phrases 'ancestor cult' and 'ancestor worship', in dealing with African cultures, is semantically inappropriate, analytically misleading, and theoretically unproductive" (1971: 140).

While I have no intention of presenting a critique of this theory in this paper, I must respectfully register my disagreement. If this theory supports the Suku folk theory on their attitude to their dead elders, in religious terms, it has also done more violence to many other African folk theories of man-ancestor relationship than to Western ethnocentric views of this aspect of African religion. The culture of ancestors cannot be divorced from the polytheistic system of which it is a part. Any theory of the ancestral cult that fails to look into the various ways in which gods and spirits are manipulated as tools for the achievement of the "good life" — health, wealth, and children — as well as antisocial aspirations has not asked the right questions. Ancestors are not used for all the goals which people want to achieve through their religious system. To assume that they do or must is merely to encourage a great theoretical confusion.

## ANCESTORS AS THE LIVING DEAD

The characterization of African religions simply in terms of "worshiping the ancestors" has been questioned by Mbiti who argues that " 'worship' is the wrong word to describe the religious interaction between the living and their departed relatives." Mbiti contends that to view African religions in terms of "ancestor worship" is to "isolate a single element, which in some societies is of little significance, and to be blind to many other aspects of religion" (Mbiti 1970: 8–9).

Mbiti's approach to African religions and philosophy is through a religious ontology, with the concept of time as the key variable. He postulates that African conception of time is two-dimensional; that it consists of a long PAST, a present, and virtually NO future, (Mbiti 1970: 17), a hypothesis which can be easily falsified by ethnographic evidence.

In Mbiti's paradigm two dimensions of time continuum — the PRESENT (*Sasa*) and the PAST (*Zamani*) — are used to explain the African's destiny. The life cycle — birth, adulthood, old age, and

death and their associated rites of passage — are seen as the process
by which individuals pass from the *Sasa* to the *Zamani* period. In
Mbiti's words (1970: 25):

After the physical death, the individual continues to exist in the *Sasa* period
and does not immediately disappear from it. He is REMEMBERED by relatives
and friends who knew him in this life and who have survived him. But
while the departed person is remembered by name, he is not really dead; he
is alive, and such a person I would call the living-dead. The living-dead is
a person who is physically dead but alive in the memory of those who knew
him in his life as well as being alive in the world of spirits. When, however,
the last person who knew the departed also dies, then, the former passes
out of the horizon of the *Sasa* period; and in effect he now becomes completely DEAD as far as family ties are concerned. He has sunk into the
*Zamani* period.

The logic of Mbiti's paradigm is not to deny the existence of ancestors
but rather to show that they are not, and cannot be, the object of
worship. In this view, objects of reverence, around whom are built
symbols of communion, fellowship and remembrance should not be
called "ancestors" or "ancestral spirits" but the living-dead. On the
first point, there is a wide measure of agreement. However, we hope
to show that the living-dead, long after they have passed from the
status of PERSONAL IMMORTALITY (when there is no memory of them
in the *Sasa*), do not cease to exercise moral authority and impose
spiritual sanctions on the living. In effect, ancestorhood is not destroyed by lack of personal memory by the living since, in my view,
the persistence of the descent structure and a belief system built around
the functional roles of the departed constitute the necessary and the
sufficient conditions for the maintenance and articulation of the cult
of the ancestors.

## ANCESTORS IN IGBO RELIGION

The material on Igbo religion dealing with the subject of ancestors
throws additional light on the subject of ancestorship for which both
Kopytoff and Mbiti have tried to provide alternative theoretical explanations. Although each started from a different premise and used
different methods, their "solution" is similar: a trick of definition in
which ancestors vanish under the label of either elders or the living-
dead. The problem of ancestorship in African religion is not resolved
by an imposition of a new competing terminology. Definitional "solu-

tions" become no solution when it can be demonstrated that ancestral status is an achieved status and that not every living-dead or elder-dead becomes an ancestor, even though each retains the status of parenthood in the spirit world.

A broad outline of Igbo society and culture has been provided by Meek (1937), Forde and Jones (1950), Thomas (1913), and Uchendu (1964). The variations in Igbo regional cultures and traditional institutions have been the subjects of analyses by Green (1964), Ottenberg (1968), Smock (1971) and Shelton (1971).

The Igbo occupy the southeastern part of Nigeria and constitute one of the largest ethnic units in the country. They conform to a segmentary system of social and political organization and live in one of the most densely populated areas in the tropical world. The fact that they subsist on a root crop economy makes the density of their population particularly important. Igbo political culture emphasizes competitiveness and most positions of power and influence are achieved and must be continually validated to be retained. The Igbo world view, and the religious practices that sustain it, share this characteristic of status striving, individual role bargaining, and constant manipulation of social and spiritual forces to achieve desired goals.

Religion, like other subsystems, is viewed by the Igbo as an instrument for attaining important goals. The spirits and divinities are viewed as both objects of worship and instruments for manipulation; they are important tools for the achievement of health, wealth, and children. So in effect, the Igbo would accept the thesis that "religious relationships between a god and an individual are essential instruments of the latter's competitive and even antisocial aspirations" (Horton 1961: 219). A parasitic religious relationship, as the one between a victim and a "bad spirit," provokes protest and drastic ritual activities that are designed to put the spirit to flight.

A schematic paradigm of the Igbo religious system is attached to summarize the role of ancestors in this religion (see Table 1). The important variables in this paradigm are the world of religion, the objects of worship, and the manipulation system.

1. *The world of religion*: This consists of the world of man and the world of the spirits, both of which are linked directly by the ancestors — the only nonhuman beings that belong to both worlds — and the activities of men and spirits as they interact through the instrumentalities and actors in the manipulative subsystem.

Table 1.  A paradigm of Igbo religion

| Objects of worship | | Character and power of objects of worship | | | | | | Manipulative system |
|---|---|---|---|---|---|---|---|---|
| | | **Continuum of** | | | | | | |
| | | Character/morality | | | Power | | | |
| | | Absolute Goodness | Good | Bad/Amoral | Unlimited Power | Limited Less | Limited More | |
| | High God | • • • • • • | | | • • • • • • • | | | |
| Spirits | Good | | • • • • | | | | • • • • • | Good Spirits |
| | Indifferent | | | • • • • • | | • • • • | | |
| | Bad | | | • • • • • | | • • • • | | Bad |
| | Divinities | | • • • • • | | | • • • • • | | |
| Ancestors | Ancestors | | • • • | | | | • • • • • | Deities |
| | Living-dead | | • • • • | | | | • • • • • | Ancestors |
| | Recent dead | | • • • • | | | | • • • • • | Cult of dead |
| | | | | | | | | Ancestors |
| Death | | | | | | | | |
| Man | Humans | | • • • • • • • | | | | • • • • • | Divination Magic Sorcery Shrines Medicine |

2. *The objects of worship:* There are three objects of worship: *Chukwu* [the High God], *Mmuo* [spirits] and *Ndichie* [ancestors]. These occupy radically different epistemological statuses but have one quality in common: they are spirits. As spirits they can only be identified by their effects. The individual cannot see them, hear them, nor have any direct experience of them unless through the medium of experts, and then only in special environments or settings after undergoing the appropriate ritual conditioning.

The objects of worship in Igbo religion are further distinguished on a two-fold continuum — a dimension of morality and a dimension of power. The morality continuum varies from ABSOLUTE GOODNESS, which is attributed to the High God only, and GOOD to BAD or AMORAL qualities. The bad Dead, the ghost of those who, during life, conducted themselves with ruthless disregard of social and moral obligations, occupy the BAD/AMORAL part of the continuum, as do *Agwu* [head spirit] and *Ekwensu* [devil]. Ancestors are by definition moral and cannot expect to attain their status unless they led a transparent and moral life on earth. But some of the living-dead occupy part of the amoral-moral continuum.

On the power dimension, only the High God is accorded UNLIMITED POWER. Other spirits share a continuum of LIMITED POWER and the amount of power and influence exercised by any spirit over the living depends on the configuration of countervailing power which the latter can muster during any given crisis.

Central to the question of countervailing power is the assumption that a man or spirit can develop powers for restricting other people's freedom; that, except for the High God, all other spirits and humans are coercible; and that an individual can augment his power resources through alliances, power quests, and acquisition of medicine and magic.

3. *The instrumental/manipulative system:* In a very provocative article, Horton (1961: 218–219) calls attention to what he describes as "one of the strongest of anthropology's Durkheimian prejudices about religion: the traditional association of religion with collective action and the attainment of socially approved goals, and of secular non-empirical techniques with individualistic action and anti-social goals." In many West African religious practices such a dichotomy between the holy and the profane is artificial. This holds true for the Igbo as well, particularly in that religious relationships between a god and an individual are an essential instrument for achieving the latter's religious and nonreligious goals. We are therefore dealing with a religious system

in which certain categories of objects of worship or reverence are also tools for achieving competitive goals. In the world of man, diviners, magic, sorcery, oracles, shrines, and herbal medicines are among the instruments which are wielded; and in the world of the spirits, both good and bad spirits — the living-dead, the bad dead, deities and ancestors are used. The techniques of manipulation include the "concentration of forces," the matching of one force against the other, and also plain deceit.

## THE PLACE OF ANCESTORS IN THE RELIGIOUS STRUCTURE

Since our focus is on ancestor worship, the role of ancestors in this paradigm deserves more attention. As the diagram shows, ancestors occupy the ontological position between the spirits and men, and they are only one of the important agents or instruments used by man to reach the High God. In Mbiti's words, ancestors "speak a bilingual language of human beings whom they 'left' through physical death, and of the spirits to whom they are now nearer than when they were in their physical life" (Mbiti 1970: 69). Given this position in the religious structure, ancestors are compelled to handle a large portion of the constant and heavy ritual traffic between the world of man and the world of spirits.

The relationship between Igbo and their ancestors is not always a harmonious one. A lot of excitement is generated in anthropological literature over the fact that Africans have an ambivalent attitude towards their ancestors. The equally valid observation that such ambivalence characterizes African relations with other spirits often escapes notice. It is the Igbo practice to keep all spirits at arm's length. To have a recent dead "return and appear" uninvited to his relatives either in dreams or in apparitions is an experience that provides no comfort or enthusiasm; and if the appearance becomes too frequent, people resent it and fight back with ritual remedies. This kind of religious attitude would not support the elder theory of ancestorship which equates the world of the living lineage with the world of the dead lineage.

Ancestors provide more than a countervailing power in the Igbo social structure. They are in fact necessary for other important reasons. They provide the Igbo with an opportunity for the expression of sentiments and help them to relate to people they love. It is to ancestors that the sacrifices of "Thanksgiving" are directed. Many of the concrete achievements which the Igbo can lay claim to have a basis in the parenthood of which the ancestors are the pioneers.

Ancestors help the Igbo to articulate a logical folk theory of their ontology and to explain the MEANING of life. Ancestors possess powers which can CAUSE or PREVENT misfortune. Moral and material failures in Igbo society may be caused by the ancestors directly through the imposition of sanctions on the living or indirectly through their lack of preventive action as intermediaries for the living.

The pillar of Igbo morality is justice. The guardians of this morality are the ancestors and the Earth Spirit. The greatest crimes are those against the Earth Spirit, not those against the ancestors. But the *Ofo*, a symbol of moral and political authority in the lineage, is bequeathed by the ancestors to their present holders who can only retain *Ofo* as long as they uphold morality and show that they do so by living a transparent life.

## THE MORAL STATUS OF ANCESTORS

One of the problems in the comparative study of African ancestor cults is the lack of emphasis on ancestors as moral spiritual beings. One result of this is the tendency to treat lineage elders as ancestors.

Ancestors are NOTHING if they are not MORAL SPIRITUAL BEINGS. Although the moral attributes of the ideal living elders are often applied to ancestors, the analogy is not good enough.

The Igbo require high moral standards for their religious functionaries. Since every family head is a priest, we are not talking about moral standards for a closed professional group. It is from the *patresfamilias*, who hold the lineage *Ofo*, that the ranks of ancestors are eventually recruited. To be able to minister at the shrines of the lineage ancestors, the *Ofo* holders must be seen to be morally fit; and they meet this condition through daily rites of *iju ogu* [the affirmation of innocence] which involve a touch of public confession of the minor transgressions of the day and prayer that the ancestors protect all from the evil machinations of the enemy. Concern for the vindication that the dead led a moral life is so important that no ground burial can be approved until the diviner is able to certify that death is not the result of any known antisocial or immoral transgression. While minor transgressions have ritual remedies, those offenses that fall under the classification of *nso* [abomination] automatically deny the dead "ground burial," the dead being thrown away in the "bad forest." Such a public humiliation creates a status disability that makes it virtually impossible for the dead to qualify for ancestral honor. It is Igbo belief that on the rare occasions where the diviner could detect a major transgression not even a lavish funeral ceremony would ensure the dead a passport to the ancestral land. We are therefore dealing with a highly moral order in which appropriate funeral rites do not constitute automatic canonization for ancestral status. This raises an important theoretical question: What are the qualifications and the selection process for ancestors?

## WHO BECOMES AN ANCESTOR?

The answer to the question of "who becomes an ancestor" will clear up some of the confusion that characterizes the recent ocntroversy in the study of ancestral cults in Africa. We have already called attention to three criteria for ancestorship: parenthood, death, and transparent morality.

Parenthood is a structural imperative for ancestorship. Fortes tends to make the fact of parenthood a sufficient condition for ancestorship. He asserts that:

Among all ancestor worshipping peoples a man becomes an ancestor when he dies not because he is dead but because he leaves a son, or more accurately, a legitimate filial successor, and he remains an ancestor only so long as his legitimate lineal successors survive. Bad parents are just as much entitled to filial piety as good parents. It is an absolute moral rule. A parent may not reject a child, no matter how he misconducts himself. (Fortes 1961: 174, 180).

The Igbo data does not fit this observation. Although ancestorhood is parenthood made immortal, it is not all immortalized parents who become ancestors. In Igbo view, the recent dead, no matter how distinguished they are before death, do not achieve ancestral rank until much later. Following the analogy of Igbo reincarnation theory, they occupy the status of newborn in the spirit world. Igbo linguistic behavior makes this clear. Although the Igbo would say that his father is in *ala mmuo* [the spirit world], he would not refer to a named father in any of the terms used for ancestors. As long as a father's or grandparent's name can be remembered, he occupies the status of the living-dead, not that of ancestors.

All Igbo terms which translate as ancestors are always in PLURAL form. I cannot think of any exception to this rule, and the inventory is small indeed (see Table 2).

Table 2.  Igbo terms for ancestors

| Onitsha dialect | Umuahia/Ngwa dialect | Free translation |
|---|---|---|
| *ndichie* | *ndichie* | Those of old |
| *nna anyi fa* | *nna any ha* | Our forefathers |
| *ndi mbu na ndi abu* | *ndi mbu na ndi abu* | The first and second peoples |
| | *ndi mbu na mbu* | The first and the first (pioneers) |
| *ndi gboo* | *ndi okpu* | The ancient ones |
| | *ndi ikaa* | |

In Igbo world view, the selection process for ancestral honor is a long one. Only the good people can qualify; and the recent dead, who join the ranks of the living-dead, must wait a long time in the spirit world to be incorporated into the ranks of the COLLECTIVE IMMORTALITY called ancestors.

Death is paradoxically both a bridge and a barrier between the living and the dead. As we have seen, not all the dead can achieve ancestral honor, and not all individuals die a "good" or moral death. As Archbishop Arinze observes "not every ancestor is worshipped, not the wicked ones, not the wandering restless ghost, but only the good ancestors, who have reached the spirit land" (Arinze 1970: 18–19). The use of the term "ancestor" in the above context is inaccurate; and the term "recent-dead" or "living-dead" would be more accurate. The point is worth emphasis that the individual whose father is denied ground burial, thus showing *prima facie* evidence that he has lost a good place in the spirit land, does not feel that he has no *ndichie* or ancestors, even though his father has joined the ranks of bad spirits.

Death and birth are great converters of social status. In the reincarnation theory, death is to the spirit world what birth is to the world of the lineage. Death introduces the dead to a myriad of spirits with distinctive statuses, and which status is gained depends on one's activities in the world of man. The cult of the dead occupies a morally inferior status to the cult of ancestors. Whereas the cult of the dead can be manipulated to achieve antisocial and immoral goals, the ancestors can only be used as countervailing forces, for protection and direct aid.

Living a transparent life is an important condition for achieving

ancestral honor. A religious system that operates in a society characterized by an extreme emphasis on manipulating the spirits and other
agents for the achievement of goals can demand no less. It is the
transparent life demonstrated on earth by the dead that lends legitimacy and credibility to their moral authority.

Although parenthood, death, and transparent morality are critical
factors in the selection process of ancestors, an element of time is
involved before an immortalized parenthood is transformed into
ancestorhood.

## CONCLUSION

A number of questions raised by regional ethnographic evidence on
ancestor worship in Africa have long been settled. We know that the
ancestor cult is not the cult of the dead, and that despite the structural simplicity of the institution, its cultural expression is variable.
This variability in African ancestor culture has focussed argumenta-
tion on whether ancestors are to be regarded as elders or as the living-
dead, or perhaps as no more than spirits that have, by a process of
canonization as represented by funeral rites, acquired divine features.
The precise relationship between ancestors and society and social structure has not been satisfactorily settled.

The argument of this paper is that some of the recent interpretations
of ancestor worship in Africa are based on a false premise and that
the "definitional solutions" offered have not resolved any problem.
The thesis that every father or parent automatically becomes an
ancestor is questioned in the light of the multiple criteria for the
selection of potential ancestors that Igbo data provide. By carefully
distinguishing the various status differentials which mark life after
death, the structural position of ancestors in the world of the spirit is
clarified. Furthermore, ancestors are shown to be both objects of
honor and tools or agents which can be manipulated to achieve competitive goals. The appraisal of importance of ancestors in the social
structure, therefore, cannot ignore their role in a manipulative system.

## REFERENCES

ARINZE, F. A.
1970   *Sacrifice in Ibo religion.* Ibadan: Ibadan University Press.

FORDE, D., G. I. JONES
1950   *The Ibo and Ibibio-speaking peoples of southeastern Nigeria.*
London: International African Institute.

FORTES, M.
1961   Pietas in ancestor worship. *Man: Journal of the Royal Anthropological Institute* 91(2):166–191.

GLUCKMAN, M.
1937   Mortuary customs and the belief in survival after death among the southeastern Bantu. *Bantu Studies 9.*

GREEN, M. M.
1964   *Igbo village affairs.* London: Frank Cass.

HORTON, R.
1961   A definition of religion and its uses. *Man: Journal of the Royal Anthropological Institute* 91:201–225.

KOPYTOFF, I.
1971   Ancestors as elders in Africa. *Africa* 41(2):129–141.

MBITI, J. S.
1970   *African religions and philosophy,* London: Heinemann.

MEEK, C. K.
1937   *Law and authority in a Nigerian tribe.* London: Oxford University Press.

OTTENBERG, S.
1968   *A different way of life: double descent in an African society.*
Seattle: University of Washington Press.

SHELTON, A. J.
1971   *Igbo-Igala borderland: religion and social control in indigenous African colonialism.* Albany: State University of New York Press.

SMOCK, A. C.
1971   *Ibo politics: the role of ethnic unions in East Nigeria.* Cambridge, Massachusetts: Harvard University Press.

THOMAS, N.
1913   *Anthropological report on the Ibo-speaking peoples of Nigeria,* six volumes. London. (Reprinted by Negro Universities Press, Westport, Connecticut.)

UCHENDU, V. C.
1964   The status implications of Igbo religious beliefs. *The Nigerian Field* 29(1):27–37.
1965   *The Igbo of southeast Nigeria.* Edited by James Gibbs. New York: Holt, Rinehart and Winston.

# Youth as Elders and Infants as Ancestors: The Complementarity of Alternate Generations, Both Living and Dead, in Tiriki, Kenya, and Irigwe, Nigeria

WALTER H. SANGREE

A recent paper by Igor Kopytoff (Kopytoff 1971) argues that Africanists have been led by their Western conceptual ethnocentrism into creating a false dichotomy between "elders" and "ancestors" in their descriptions and analyses of African societies. He asserts that this has obscured the fact that "elders" and "ancestors" are conceptually as well as terminologically united in many African cultural and social traditions. There are flaws in his assertion, perhaps the most serious of which has been ably countered by James Brain in a recent article (Brain 1973) where he demonstrates that many, if not most, African societies make explicit and clear-cut distinctions both linguistically and conceptually between "elders" (both living and dead) and "ancestral spirits." Nevertheless Kopytoff's article effectively argues that Western scholars have had a tendency to overlook indigenous conceptual continuities between living and dead elders, and this prompted me to reexamine my data on the Tiriki of Kenya and the Irigwe of Nigeria which deal with the traditional relations of the living and the dead (including the not yet born). I found that these relationships, though strikingly different in the two societies, are in each case patterned in ways that are congruent with relationships between both ad-

This article is a revision and expansion of a paper read at the American Anthropological Association Annual Meeting at Toronto, November 1972. The fieldwork on which it was based was carried out in Tiriki, Kenya, between December 1954 and June 1956, and in Irigwe, Nigeria, between September 1963 and June 1965. The fieldwork in Kenya was supported by the Fullbright Program, and the research in Irigwe was funded by the National Science Foundation.

This article is reprinted with the permission of the International African Institute, London, from *Africa* (April) 1974.

jacent and alternate generations.

I shall start by examining the case of the Tiriki, who number roughly 40,000 people, where published material is already available on both intergenerational and elder-ancestor relationships (Sangree 1965: 64–65; 1966: 30–35, 45–46). Tiriki is one of the score or so of "Abaluyia" Bantu speaking peoples with predominantly grain-based economies located between Mount Elgon and Lake Victoria in western Kenya. Traditionally Tiriki political affairs were regulated principally by a system of semigenerational graded age-groups which they borrowed from the neighboring "Nilo-Hamitic" Terik and Nandi. Clan and subclan affiliations of a characteristically Abaluyia type, however, served as the basis for a set of crucial authority relationships in the religious and economic realms.

Traditional Tiriki religious beliefs are quite in harmony with the prevailing Abaluyia and general Bantu idea that the spirits of the deceased have a pervasive influence on the fortunes of the living. A crucial aspect of the relationship the Tiriki feel exists between the living and the dead is articulated by the distinction they make between the fairly recently deceased paternal and mother's agnatic ancestors (*baguga*) and the generalized ancestral spirits (*misambwa*). It is this latter collectivity rather than the recently deceased forebears who are perceived by the Tiriki to be the font of life and well-being. A ritual elder does not expect the ancestral spirits (*misambwa*) to hear his supplications directly; he believes he can effectively reach them only through the intercession of the recently deceased elders who in turn are led to do this by the pleas of the living elders. The relationship between the ancestral spirits, recently deceased forebears, and the living elders is a direct extension of the strongly patterned and formalized set of relationships between three alternate terminologically equated generations, namely the grandchildren, the grandparents, and the deceased great-great-grandparents, all of whom are called *baguga*. I have labelled this the "*baguga* triad" (Sangree 1966: 45).

The complement of this *baguga* triad of three alternating generations is a second triad consisting of three adjacent generations, the grandparental, parental, and filial. Here the relations are essentially economic and authoritarian in nature. A child must respect and obey his father; and the father in turn is expected to discipline his children, provide for their economic needs, and arrange for the bridewealth of his sons.

Competition between siblings over cattle and other property is checked and arbitrated by the parental generation, while competition

between father and son over cattle is controlled primarily by intervention and arbitration by members of the son's grandparental generation. To be sure, members of this senior-most living generation are
often entering their dotage and growing more and more dependent
economically on their middle-aged sons. The middle-aged men, however, are dependent upon their ageing fathers for leadership in the
ritual sphere. Thus the senior elders retain a potent weapon with
which to guard both their own and their grandchildren's rights. The
tense, ambiguous grandfather-father-son relationship is represented,
the Tiriki say, by the three ancestral stones found at every ancestral
shrine. One Tiriki elder told me it was just like Christianity. "One
stone stands for the homestead father, one for his senior son, and one
for the Holy Ghost," he said. It seems likely to me that these three
"stones of the ancestors" (*majina gi misambwa*), as the Tiriki call
them, derive their principal emotional appeal and effectiveness as
religious symbols by covertly representing the harmonious *baguga*
triad.

Grandparents rejoice in the birth of their grandchildren who they
say will be the ones to assure that they are remembered when they die.
No Tiriki ever receives the family name of a living relative; instead
grandparents have the responsibility of finding the name of a deceased
family forebear which suits the newborn and does not appear to cause
a shower of tears when bestowed on the infant a few days after birth.
The grandparents take satisfaction in knowing that the infant they have
named may eventually become an elder who will pray to them by
name at the ancestral shrines, and in turn bestow their names on
newborn children. The traditionalist Tiriki does not believe either in
personal reincarnation or immortality of the spirit or body; but active
remembrance and prayer by one's grandchildren, and the rebestowal
of one's name upon a living person again and again down through the
ages, are sought for imitations of immortality. In addition, every
Tiriki male, upon the birth of his first son, views himself as the founder
of a lineage, and hopes that his name will eventually be exalted as the
founder of a clan.

Thus a Tiriki, knowing he himself cannot bridge the chasm of death,
sees his grandchildren as his personal link with the eternal and vice
versa. His grandchildren (*baguga*) will remember him after he dies
and pass his name on to their grandchildren (*baguga*); and he in
return, as one of their deceased grandparents (*baguga*), will serve as
their link with the ancestral spirits (*misambwa*), thereby furthering
their mortal well-being.

I shall now turn to the Irigwe in Nigeria, a people of around 20,000, situated near Jos, roughly 2,000 air miles from the Tiriki. Both speak highly divergent and in no way mutually intelligible languages of the Benue-Congo subfamily (Greenberg 1966: 7–9) and both practise variant forms of hoe agriculture mainly of grain crops. Neither these, however, nor other cultural similarities provide sufficient basis for a "controlled" comparison anchored either on "common origins" or the impingement of common external political or ecological forces. Thus the underlying commonality which makes this comparison between two such minimally related groups valid is, I believe, a structural one. I am examining the manner in which a structural universal is socially articulated, and ritually and symbolically reified in the two societies. I am using "structural universal" in a sense suggested to me by Radcliffe-Brown (Radcliffe-Brown 1952: 195–196; 1957: 130–131) and by subsequent writings of Fortes and others (Fortes 1969: 45–50). The structural universal I am examining in this instance is the conflict inherent between adjacent generations.

In Irigwe we find, just as we did in Tiriki, a terminological equating of grandchildren, grandparents, and deceased elders, with the tern *üo* being used in Irigwe both referentially and vocatively in all these contexts. But the nature and tone of the interrelationships between the alternate generations does not contrast so much with those between adjacent generations as in Tiriki, and it is noteworthy that the term for "father" (*bɛ*) rather than that for "grandfather" is regularly used in Irigwe to address and refer to ritual elders. Irigwe parents have the principal responsibility for finding their newborn a name within a few days of its birth, although they may extend this privilege to grandparents, other relatives, or friends. The infant may be named for any kinsman or friend, living or dead; those who receive a living person's name, however, have the obligation to "buy" (*sɛ*) the name for themselves at the person's funeral.

Irigwe grandparents characteristically have a lot to do with their grandchildren from infancy on. It is common practice for a grandparent to "beg" for his or her offspring's second son or second daughter. Usually the "begged for" grandchild is "given" to the grandparent at the age of three or so, takes up residence there, and becomes the grandparent's recognized ward. In such cases the grandparent-grandchild relationship becomes virtually indistinguishable from the usual parent-child relationships. Towards their nonadopted grandchildren, however, grandparents are characteristically more demonstrative than parents, and more apt to express open annoyance; also grandfathers in particular are inclined to play the bogeyman, and to make threatening remarks and overtures of an explicitly sexual nature against their preadolescent grandchildren of both sexes.

The Irigwe believe that every living person has a soul (*ōwú*) as well as a corporeal body (*rɛ*). When a person dies, rites are performed to assure that the soul has departed from the corpse which is then put to rest in a lineage crypt. The soul is believed normaly to rise to the firmament and eventually become reincarnated in a newborn baby after returning to earth as a shooting star and then entering the womb of a pregnant woman.

The mortuary rites of men and women who have reached middle age are normally concluded by four successive evenings of circle dancing and chanting, to the accompaniment of two or three male drummers, performed by girls and women related to the deceased. The chants have cryptic lyrics which characteristically include such phrases as, "Where have you gone?", "Why have you left us?", "When shall we see you again?". And the accompanying dance steps, although simple and repetitive, are done at a lively tempo. On the fourth and final evening the chanting and dancing start before sunset. All the girls of marriageable age join in, their bodies washed and oiled, and soon the older women and small girls drop out to join the throng of men and youths from near and far who have gathered around the edges of the dance ground to watch. As darkness begins to fall the mortuary chanting and dancing finally stop once and for all, but after a wait of only a minute or two, the drumming starts again at a more lively and urgent tempo, and the assembled youths rush through the disbanding circle of girls and begin a series of intricate and very energetic impromptu dances which the girls then stand back to watch. Usually this goes on until it gets too dark to see, and then quite suddenly the drumming and dancing stop, youths join their current girl friends waiting among the spectators, and the couples scurry down the paths from the dance ground and quickly disappear into the darkness.

It is not only the youths and girls who enjoy these dances. Comments I overheard elderly participants and spectators make such as, "Won't the deceased be pleased by this," and "How pleasant to know that our deaths will also be the occasions for young people to get together in this manner," and also simply, "How beautiful such times are," all attest to the involvement in and identification with the amours of the rising generation by the senior generation, and to the appropriateness in their minds that death among one of their generation should be linked to such activity. These mortuary rites are firmly established in Irigwe as prime occasions for trysting between youthful lovers who look forward to them very much. A favourite aphorism among young Irigwe is, "It's a tough world when none of the old people die."

The complementary aspect of this association of old people's deaths with courtship is the linking of births with their reincarnation. The appropriate Irigwe aphorism with which to greet the news that a baby has been born is to exclaim, "The grave is now two!" In other words, every birth is both a bifurcation and a reincarnation of a deceased forebear. In this apparent paradox we have expressed the Irigwe belief that every human being is the reincarnation of the soul of someone who lived before, and at the same time a new and unique person. There is something tenuous about the relationship of a living person to his soul. This soul, since it also has a continuing prior existence, so to speak, has to be encouraged and induced by certain periodic and occasional rituals to stay around or return to the body of its current incarnation; for the person whose soul leaves him (or her) for long looses strength and becomes particularly subject to death brought by disease, witchcraft, or some other agent.

The Irigwe world view is profoundly dyadic; everything of importance has its obverse aspect. Male and female, parents and children, mortal and immortal, body and soul, disease and health, and so forth, are, in Irigwe eyes, both proof and objectifications of this underlying principle; but an Irigwe correlate of this principle is that everything contains within itself aspects of its obverse number (Sangree 1971: 68–70). For example, it seems reasonable to be expected by to, and the Irigwe that the ritual, symbolic, and social separation of the sexes at every turn should also contain clear-cut and explicit exceptions to these separations; also every disease, and every poison, is perceived to contain its own cure or antidote within itself. We have already noted that souls do not long remain unincarnate, nor living beings long separated from their souls. Similarly the opposition of parents and children, that is of adjacent generations, is ameliorated by the adoption of junior grandchildren by grandparents, and also by the association of fatherhood rather than grandfatherhood with positions of ritual authority, even though these are, in fact, nearly always held by members of the senior most grandparental generation. There is no need for the opposition of adjacent generations to be counterbalanced in Irigwe, as it is in Tiriki, by grandparents serving as special guardians of the rights of their grandchildren.

We have shown that generational subdivisions are of comparatively little significance in structuring of authority relationships in Irigwe. Instead formal authority is characteristically ascribed in any group simply on the basis of the known or putative agnatic seniority of the men involved; and this leader is then referred to and adressed by the group as "father" (*bɛ*), or "father of the compound" (*bɛ ri*). The Irigwe make no terminological or conceptual distinction between more recently deceased forebears and ancestral spirits comparable to the Tiriki *guga-misambwa* distinction; indeed there are no ancestral shrines, and no ancestor cult, as such. Instead there is a "soul" cult which inexorably links the living and the dead through the "souls" they share in common. It is in Irigwe beliefs about the "soul" that we find the key to understanding the patterned relationships both between the generations of the living, and also between the living and the dead. Elders regard their juniors as possible incarnations of souls of people who have already died who were important to them; and juniors regard their elders as those whose souls may some day be incarnate in beloved ones junior to them. Souls influence other souls, both incarnate and unincarnate, just as living mortals do. To be indifferent about or angry towards a living person is also to be angry or indifferent towards his soul; and an annoyed or angry soul may call another soul away from its incarnation, spelling trouble or death for that incarnation. Those people you are most dependent on in everyday life are also those who through mystical means may most strongly affect your health. It is believed that anger "in the heart" of a parent or a formally bestowed guardian may bring ill-health to a person, and sometimes also to a person's offspring, through the mystical interaction of their souls. Also souls no longer incarnate or just recently incarnated are seen as potential threats to one's health. Thus Irigwe have a compelling reason for treating social relationships with parents and others on whom they feel dependent, and also for treating elderly people and infants, as though their own health, indeed their life, and the welfare of those they love, were at stake.

The Tiriki world is triadic rather than dyadic; for them dualities are innately troublesome and must be subordinated to or at least counter-balanced by some third force or element. [1] Intergenerational conflict or opposition is resolved in Tiriki, as we have seen, by the *baguga* triad. The grandparental *baguga* are the balance point of the triad; they serve as the ritual elders and mediators between their grand-

---

[1] In this context it is noteworthy that in Tiriki the grandparental ritual elders as well as the prepubescent or preinitiation grandchildren are regarded as sexually neuter.

children (*baguga*) whom they perceive as those who will be sure to remember them when they die, and their own grandparents (*baguga*) now dead, but still remembered and regularly beseeched by them at the homestead ancestral shrines (*lusambwa*). The Irigwe world in contrast to Tiriki is profoundly dyadic. Conflict between adjacent generations is structured in terms of the dependency of the child on the parent. A complementary dichotomy, that between the mortal body and the immortal soul, binds together not only senior and junior generations, but also links the still unborn and the deceased with the living.

Kopytoff does us a service by stressing the structural and cultural continuities between elders and ancestors which are so important in many African societies; but it would do violence to the ethnography of Tiriki, Irigwe, and probably every other African society, to lose sight of the indigenous distinctions between the living and the dead which for the Tiriki and Irigwe, at least, clearly both reflect and reinforce their respective structurings and resolutions of inter-generational conflict.

## REFERENCES

BRAIN, JAMES
1973   Ancestors as elders in Africa: further thoughts. *Africa* 43(2):122–133.
FORTES, MEYER
1969   *Kinship and the social order*. Chicago: Aldine-Atherton.
GREENBERG, JOSEPH
1966   *Languages of Africa*. Bloomington, Indiana: Indiana University Press.
KOPYTOFF, IGOR
1971   Ancestors as elders in Africa. *Africa* 41(2):128–142.
RADCLIFFE-BROWN, A. R.
1952   *Structure and function in primitive society*. London: Cohen and West.
1957   *A natural science of society*. Glencoe, Illinois: Free Press.
SANGREE, WALTER H.
1965   "The Bantu Tiriki of Western Kenya," in *Peoples of Africa*. Edited by James Gibbs. New York: Holt, Rinehart and Winston.
1966   *Age, prayer and politics in Tiriki, Kenya*. London: Oxford University Press.
1971   La gémellité et le principe d'ambiguité: Commandement, sorcellerie et maladie chez les Irigwe (Nigeria). *L'Homme* 11(3):64–70.

SECTION THREE

*Note.* Japanese and Chinese names appear in traditional order (i.e. surname first) within the text of each article; in all other cases the names are in Western order.

# Ancestors, Geomancy, and Mediums in Taiwan

G. SEAMAN

The following paragraph presents a synopsis of the documentary film on the behavior of the ancestral dead in Taiwan which was shown at the Congress symposium. Plates 1, 2, 3, and 4 are pictures from this film. [1]

The film follows the case of a family in Taiwan, China, whose daughter-in-law is childless. In a spirit seance, a god tells them that her barrenness is the result of a curse of an uncle who died with no offspring of his own. To remove this curse, one of the sons of the family must be adopted out to the ghost of the uncle, thus providing him with descendants. As proof of their sincerity, the family must dig up the uncle's grave and rebury his bones in a new grave with improved geomancy. A shaman in trance directs the choice of a new grave site and mediates between the ghost and the family in coming to an agreement about the adoption. The film follows the exhuming of the grave, the reconstruction of the skeleton, and the reburial of the uncle in a new grave site.

---

[1] Enquiries about hiring or buying the film may be submitted to Far Eastern Audio Visuals, 1010 w. 23rd St., Austin, Texas 78705.

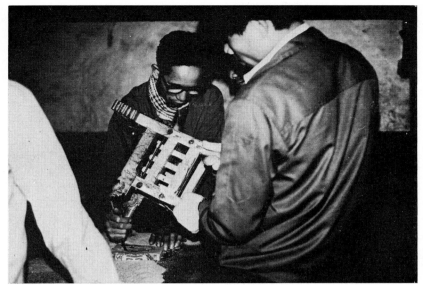

Plate 1. Holding chair. Spirit seances in China often make use of a "divining chair," which, when possessed by a spirit, communicates by writing on a table top. Here the chair writes out a charm to be used in choosing the orientation of the uncle's new grave. Two men hold the chair, while a third clamps a pen to the chair's arm

Plate 2. God on table. The man in the foreground explains the ritual steps prescribed by the "divining chair" to the mother-in-law of the family. The image of the cult god called the "Emperor of the Dark Heavens" rests on the table

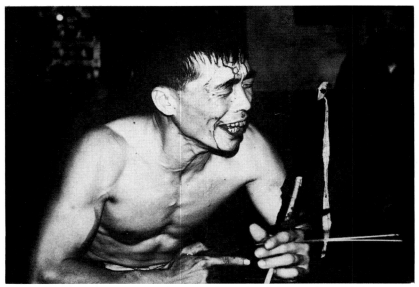

Plate 3. Shaman. After a preliminary diagnosis of the case by "divining chair," the cult god possesses a shaman. The blood on his face is the result of flagellation with ritual weapons used in the cult. The shaman directs the actual performance of further rites

Plate 4. Rice on ground. The location of the uncle's grave is an extremely important consideration. Here, a bowl of rice symbolizes the uncle's bones. He will be required in the exact spot marked by the rise, oriented by the line above

# Prophylactic Medicine and Kin Units Among Yao Ancestor Worshipers

DOUGLAS MILES

The dichotomy Westerners perceive between medical and religious protection against disease is neither ethnographically universal nor unique to contemporary industrialized societies. This paper analyzes the operation of a similar conceptual distinction in the theory and practice of Yao prophylaxis. The subject is especially relevant to an understanding of kinship and matrimonial arrangements in Pulangka community.

My investigation emanates from Freedman's advocacy (1967) of a cross-cultural inquiry into the personality that Sinitic ancestor worshipers attribute to the dead. I suggest that such a pursuit may help to explain the development of effective medical technologies among Far Eastern peoples.

The Yao are Sinitic in origin and cultural orientations. Three quarters of a million live in the southern provinces of China (Moseley 1966: 162). Others inhabit mountains in the northern parts of Vietnam (Nguyen 1968: 221), and Laos (LeBar, et al. 1964: 84). Pulangka, where I studied them, is one of the villages identified with the 16,000 Yao of northern Thailand. (United Nations 1967: 6). It had a population of about 245 in 1966–1968, the period of my fieldwork. The doctrines of an ancestral cult dominate the religious lives of the inhabitants and are fundamental to the ideology of residence and descent.

Nineteen houses stand in the settlement, which straddles a jungle clearing 1,000 meters above sea level. Each accommodates a different *peo* [kin unit], which I call a dwelling group (Figure 1). It extends membership to all relatives living under one roof. Such persons express their corporate identity *vis-à-vis* outsiders by their collective and exclusive allegiance to a distinctive set *(zung)* of deceased humans.

The latter constitute the ancestors of the dwelling group's *tso* (see Figure 1), which resembles a lineage in two respects: it is exogamous and recruits the children of male descendants who marry virilocally; but the offspring of such a man's daughter may also belong if she and her husband live uxorilocally. Individuals who derive from the same *tso* and reside together postmaritally form the core of each *peo* and worship their own ancestors. Not so their siblings whom other dwelling groups recruit as virilocal brides or uxorilocal grooms. They cannot transmit descent to their coresident children and they worship their spouse's ancestors in place of their own.

I stress the Yao belief that the deceased have power to bestow health or inflict illness upon all personnel of the *peo* which serves them in-cluding devotees-by-marriage — but that they lack such influence over any former worshiper who has left that unit and joined another.

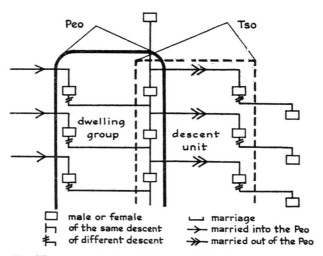

Figure 1.   Dwelling group (*peo*) and descent unit (*tso*)

Figure 1 indicates the range of genealogical links by which members become attached to a dwelling group. The *tso* of the unit may be that of the person's father, mother, wife's father, wife's mother, husband's fath-er or husband's mother. I shall show that Yao invoke ancestral-cult doctrine to justify each alternative. My interest is in the implications of this fact for the use that the people make of medicine which offers pro-tection against disease.

Many techniques for avoiding illness operate in Pulangka society. They belong to one or the other of two types named *tsiang* and *dia*. I express the distinction by translating these terms as CEREMONIAL and MEDICAL prophylaxis, respectively.

Every variant of ceremonial prophylaxis is an ancestral-cult ritual. A performance temporarily counteracts the power of the dead to deliberately render a worshiper vulnerable to sickness. The example I shall give is typical. Members of the patient's *peo* build a wooden replica of a bridge in the jungle on the outskirts of the village. This object becomes the focus for an event where a priest communicates with the deceased by liturgy and animal sacrifice. There is no treatment of the body.

On the other hand, prophylactic medicine *(dia)* subjects the patient to procedures such as skin scarification, flesh cauterization, massage, and a kind of acupuncture, as well as to homemade herbal potions, inhalations, ointments, oil, and other liquid concoctions. The repertoire expands as Pulangka villagers acquire patented drugs and pharmaceutical goods via commercial and other contacts with northern Thai and Laotian towns. None of these techniques, according to the Yao, has any influence over ancestors or other supernatural beings; none entails any of the behavior which characterizes ancestral-cult rituals.

THE PROBLEM AND THE HYPOTHESIS

Why is medicine the more popular of the two prophylactic procedures? As Table 1 indicates, 88 percent of Pulangka's inhabitants use *dia,* while only 39 percent resort to *tsiang.*

Table 1.  How Pulangka inhabitants protect themselves against illness

|  | Number | Percent | Percentages combined | |
|---|---|---|---|---|
| (a)  Medicine exclusively | 130 | 53 | Medicine (a + b) | = 88 |
| (b)  Medicine and ceremony | 88 | 35 | Ceremony (b + c) | = 39 |
| (c)  Ceremony exclusively | 10 | 4 | Any Procedure (a + b + c) | = 92 |
| (d)  Neither procedure | 12 | 5 | Exclusive Use of either Procedure (a + c) | = 57 |
| (e)  No information | 7 | 3 | | |
| Total | 247 | 100 | | |

I initially supposed that the majority had rejected belief in the power of the dead to inflict sickness, that through contact with northern Thai urban centers they had accepted the disease etiologies current in Western-style hospitals and polyclinics. But such appearances were misleading. For example, Uantong's mother (Figure 3:d/9) whom I discuss later, depended entirely on medical methods to counteract her own susceptibility to sickness but willingly underwent economic hardship to sponsor a series of prophylactic rituals on behalf of her son. Further, I found that no member of the community would express scepticism about the powers of the dead even in private or under inducement. On the other hand, every adult with whom I raised the subject volunteered the information that ancestors may be kindly disposed towards some worshipers but regard others with malice.

The sociological implications of this dogma constitute the focus of my inquiry. They become explicit during discussions about matrimonial transfers of personnel from one *peo* to another. The basic principles of negotiation are (1) that no one should worship malevolent ancestors unless adequate protection against the potential consequences is available; (2) that Yao who suffer from the malice of their own ancestors should not marry each other; (3) that a person may escape the hazards of ancestral hatred by taking a spouse who enjoys ancestral grace and joining the latter's dwelling group. Here a more felicitous relationship with the dead may be possible and the individual will be beyond the harmful influence of the deceased humans who formerly demanded his or her devotion.

Comparison of Pulangka with the paradigm of harmonic society places the above observations in the perspective of anthropological theory about descent systems. As in Lévi-Strauss' model, one party to every Yao marriage must join the residential group of the other's exogamous descent unit. In both cases the stationary spouse transmits descent to the couple's children. But in contrast, Pulangka's inhabitants lack any sexual prescription that grooms rather than brides should stay, or vice versa.

On the contrary, Yao ancestors allegedly discriminate between *tso* members who should remain and those who should depart, by their benignity towards the former and their malice against the latter. But how does the choice of the dead gain social recognition? My analysis of prophylaxis in Pulangka is an attempt to answer this question.

I postulate that Yao society classifies an individual as ancestrally blessed or cursed according to the course of protection he or she takes against illness. This argument is the basis of my hypothesis that the difference in popularity between medical and ceremonial prophylaxis depends on the proportion of individuals whose *peo* membership is permanent rather than terminable.

## THE YAO THEORY OF PROPHYLAXIS

The first of these propositions concerns the Yao theory of prophylaxis and requires discussion about several sets of conceptual oppositions: (1) the distinction between the body (*be*), and two other refractions of a human, the double (*uan*) and the anima (*bo*); (2) the differences between forebears and ancestors (*ungthai* and *djaafin*), physiological pedigree and ancestry, progeny and descendants, and (3) the contrast between inherited and ancestrally induced susceptibility to sickness.

### Human Refractions

THE BODY (*be*)  Yao divide the bodies of both sexes into twelve major components: eyes, ears, mouth-and-nose, neck, arms, chest-and-upper-back, abdomen-and-lower-back, legs, left-side-of-the-head, right-side-of-the-head, feet, and hands.

Each component develops liquid embryonic equivalents to itself in the semen or uterine fluid of the maturing adolescent. During conception, counterparts to eleven anatomical divisions of both parties to intercourse synthesize. The exception is the abdomen-and-lower-back, which a male derives exclusively from the genitor and a female from the genetrix. Otherwise, all parts of the foetus' body contain characteristics of both biological parents.

The vulnerability of any component to illness depends on the condition of the other two refractions: the double and the anima.

THE DOUBLE (*uan*)  This entity is an amalgamation of souls, one for each division of the body. The double of any living human is that of a deceased person who has existed for some time as an ancestor. It becomes incarnate again by attachment to an unborn fetus in the womb of a female worshiper. Sometimes accidents occur and another woman is the vessel for rebirth.

Neither genitor nor genetrix make any contribution to the composition of their offspring's double. They merely initiate the physiological process of conception which is a precondition for incarnation.

Souls are individually detachable from the double. The unincarnated ancestors that a person worships prevent or instigate separation. The occurrence becomes evident in the dreams of anyone acquainted with the victim, who alone can identify the missing soul as his or her own, and who will inevitably incur illness unless recovery is effected.

THE ANIMA (*bo*)   This is a combination of qualities which an individual inherits from his forebears. It accounts for intelligence and stupidity, kindness or cruelty, and a host of talents and incapacities, e.g. literacy/illiteracy, linguistic facility/dumbness. More relevantly the anima determines differences in temperament between individuals and hence their compatibility with one another. Further, it provides anatomical components with innate immunity or susceptibility to sickness.

*Forebears* (ungthai) *and Ancestors* (djaafin), *Pedigree and Ancestry, Progeny and Descendants*

A Yao's forebears include every individual who features in the physiological pedigree of both his genitor and genetrix (see Figure 2). All forebears contribute to the body but some rather than others to the anima. Biological parents may transmit qualities they do not themselves manifest to their offspring. Thus an illiterate mother and father may produce a son who qualifies for the priesthood by allegedly inheriting the talent to read and write.

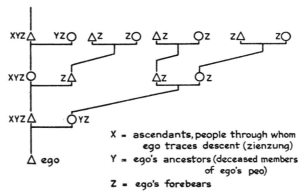

X = ascendants, people through whom ego traces descent (zienzung)

Y = ego's ancestors (deceased members of ego's peo)

Z = ego's forebears

Figure 2.   Ascendants, ancestors and forebears

Chance alone determines which attributes of what forebear become part of a person's anima. Hence, full siblings may exhibit marked differences in heredity although they have the same pedigrees and anatomies of identical composition.

The ancestors of most Pulangka Yao are the forebears through whom the individual traces descent plus the mothers of these people (see Figure 2). However, persons who become Yao by adoption from other ethnic groups are exceptional. Though they lack Yao pedigree they are deemed to possess Yao ancestry. Divination indicates that the double of an adoptee belongs to an ancestor of the fictive parent whose *tso* recruits the child; that therefore these two persons are of common descent, though the progeny of completely different forebears.

*Ancestrally Induced and Inherited Susceptibility to Illness*

At death both the double and the anima may survive the disintegration of the body as the twin refractions of a deceased human. The departed rejoins the set of ancestors from whom he or she is descended only by dying as a member of the dwelling group which worships them; i.e. as a virilocal husband, an uxorilocal wife, or premaritally. Virilocal wives enter their spouse's ancestral set in reward for the use that the *zung* has made of their bodies in the process of incarnation. Uxorilocal husbands face a different destiny which I discuss elsewhere in my treatment of shamanism.

Here I emphasize two beliefs: that all ancestors may be reborn into the *tso* of the dwelling group which worships them; and that a reincarnating ancestor relinquishes the anima of his previous existence for that of the new foetus to which he or she becomes attached.

Hence, there may be striking differences in temperament between the deceased in afterlife and their descendants. The dead express their incompatibility with a devotee by instigating the loss of one or more of the worshiper's souls, thus exposing the person to illness. No degree of inherited immunity can counteract the sickness which may result. Nor can prophylactic medicine offer any protection. *Tsiang* [ceremonial] ritual which effects the restoration of the soul to the double is the only method for avoiding the disease.

In attacking their worshipers, ancestors act with decision and full consciousness of the potential consequences. In this respect they differ greatly from forebears. No person can decide that his inherited vulnerability to sickness will pass on to posterity nor choose the progeny whom the trouble may afflict. Even though the individual may enjoy complete compatibility with the ancestors he worships, they can do nothing about his innate disability. The victim's only recourse is to compensate for the deficiencies in his anima by subjecting his body to the substitute of appropriate medical attention.

Let me summarize. All Pulangka Yao acknowledge that ancestors as well as forebears affect the health of every individual either for good or bad, that the susceptibility of any person to illness is a consequence of (1) unfortunate heredity, (2) the malevolence of the dead, or (3) a combination of both influences.

People in category 1 rely entirely on medical precautions against illness, those in category 2 use ceremonial protection only, while persons in category 3 employ both procedures. The superior popularity of medical prophylaxis in Pulangka expresses the fact that individuals in category 1 outnumber those in category 2.

I emphasize that a Yao's exclusive dependence on medical precautions has a dual meaning. It indicates to society not merely that he is a victim of unfortunate heredity but also that he is a beneficiary of ancestral grace. Concomitantly, a person who employs ceremonial procedures alone, demonstrates that, though hated by the ancestors he worships, he has inherited no vulnerabilities to sickness.

We can conclude then that Yao prophylaxis provides members of the Pulangka community both with a variety of methods for avoiding illness and with a set of symbols for distinguishing between the ancestrally blessed and cursed. The observation demands attention in any explanation for the popularity of medicine in the village. I shall now illustrate this mechanism of symbolic classification at work in the ideology of Yao social processes.


THE PRACTICE OF YAO PROPHYLAXIS

Let us consider a case study which involves the relatives of Tawla, a Pulangka priest specializing in *tsiang* rituals. Table 2 summarizes a section of a diary I kept on the prophylactic procedures these people employed during the last year of my fieldwork. The extract refers to Fam and Uantong, whose genealogical connections with other persons I shall mention are evident from Figure 3. This diagram shows that Fam (c/1) is the daughter of the priest's mother's brother, and that Uantong (e/9) is the grandson of Tawla's sister.

The outstanding contrast between the prophylactic histories of the two is that the girl (c/1) depended exclusively on medical prophylaxis up to, during, and after the period under examination (July 1 to December 31, 1967). On the other hand, the boy (e/9) had taken precautions of neither variety until September of 1967, when he was subjected to a series of six *tsiang* rituals in seven weeks. In December 1967 he became Fam's uxorilocal husband and neglected both types of protection thereafter.

I shall not describe here the preparation and application of each kind of medical treatment that the girl received in the months I am examining,

Table 2.  Prophylactic practices employed by Uantong and Fam in the period July 1 to December 31, 1967

|  | Uantong | Fam |
|---|---|---|
| July | None | Antistomachache medicine (ax3), (fx2) and (mx1)<br>Potion to avoid menstruation pains (tx1)<br>Knuckle-massage to prevent backache (qx3)<br>Antimalarial tablet |
| August | None | Technique which prevents skin complaints e.g. smallpox, acne (Kx1)<br>Anti-menstruation-pain treatment (tx1)<br>Opium treatment against coughs (nx2) |
| September | Bridge ceremony (phase 1) | Vitamin pills x6 to guard against debility during maize harvest<br>Acupuncture behind the knees to prevent sprains<br>Menstruation treatment (tx1) |
| October | Bridge ceremonies (phases 2, 3, and 4) | Chest cauterization to prevent coughs (sx1)<br>Antitetanus injection to prevent infection of wounded hand<br>Menstruation treatment (tx1) |
| November | Bridge ceremonies (phases 5 and 6) | Antiheadache treatment (0x3)<br>Vitamin pills (x15)<br>Opium treatment against coughs (nx1)<br>Antimalarial tablets |
| December | **None** | Anti-skin-complaint treatment (Kx2)<br>Another antitetanus injection<br>Cup massage to prevent backache while carrying firewood |

nor the series of bridge ceremonies held on behalf of the boy. Rather, I shall rely on photographs to illustrate these procedures and concentrate on the following question: How do the prophylactic practices of Fam and Uantong bear on their own marriage and the matrimonial transactions between their common kinfolk?

First, I draw attention to Tawla's mother, Fooeh (b/5). Premaritally, this woman lived with her own descent unit's dwelling group of which her adopted elder brother (b/3) was the head. She had inherited vulnerability to several kinds of sickness against which she regularly sought (and still takes) medical protection. Around the age of eighteen, Fooeh also began to suffer from ancestrally induced soul-loss. Her dwelling group held several *tsiang* rituals on her behalf but the costs interfered with frequent treatment. The old woman gave me these economic reasons for her elder brother's argument that she should live virilocally after marriage with Tawla's father. Betrothal negotiations confirmed that her fiancé stood in the good favor of the deceased humans his *peo* worshiped and that he had never resorted to *tsiang* ceremonies. The bride givers did not demand bride-price in the form of silver or money but accepted the receivers' written promise to pay with an adoptee or spouse at some time in the future. This contract provides the theme of the case study.

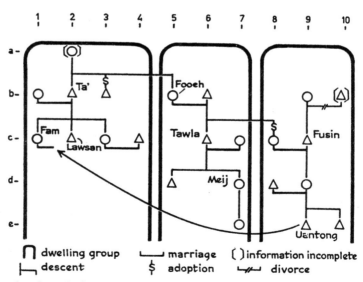

Figure 3.   Genealogical connections between Tawla's relatives

Since her wedding, Fooeh who is now aged sixty-four, has enjoyed the continuous grace of her husband's ancestors and has never sought ceremonial protection against illness.

The woman's elder brother (b/3) died a bachelor within a year of her marriage, at about which time his mother gave birth to a son in the same month that Tawla (c/6) was born. Fooeh's mother (a/2) asked to adopt Tawla but his father, a priest, was able to convince her that the infant enjoyed ancestral benevolence. Hence, there was no reason either to doubt that the child was a reincarnation of the deceased humans his father worshiped or to deprive Tawla of their grace by a residential shift. A similar obstacle prevented the grandmother from claiming the twelve-year-old girl (c/8) whom Fooeh's husband (b/6) bought from the northern Thai. Both Tawla and his adopted elder sister passed through adolescence without being subject to *tsiang* ritual but both have regularly used medical protection against inherited vulnerabilities to sickness throughout their lives.

Five years after moving to Pulangka c/8 took an uxorilocal husband called Fusin (c/9). Fooeh says there was no wedding because the girl's *peo* had exhausted all its resources on Tawla's father's funeral shortly before. Subsequently, c/8 began to incur soul-loss. This was attributed to incompatibility between the anima of the newly deceased on the one hand and that of his daughter on the other. Some people say that prior to his death, Fooeh's husband had objected to the affair with Fusin and had expressed his preference for a different lover. The initial sterility of the match was allegedly a manifestation of the father's anger. *Tsiang* rituals over a period of a year were ineffective against loss of the soul to the girl's abdomen and lower back. Medicine worked and she became pregnant but no double would attach itself to the foetus and she had a miscarriage.

Fusin (c/9) had inherited no vulnerabilities to illness. Nor had he ever experienced ancestral malevolence or used ceremonial prophylaxis. Hence there was no religious reason why the couple should not join his *peo* in an attempt to solve the problem. But because the husband was unable to pay bride-price he had to negotiate other terms for moving his wife into virilocal residence. Fooeh (b/5) agreed to the arrangement on the same conditions as had accompanied her own marriage: that some time in the future the indemnification for her daughter be settled by the bride-receivers returning either an adoptee or a spouse to the givers.

The shift to the dwelling group of Fusin's descent unit had a wondrous effect on his wife's fertility. Within six months she gave birth to a daughter (d/9) who proved to be a favorite of the paternal ancestors and was therefore deemed to be an incarnation of one of those deceased humans.

Tawla (c/6) began to study for the priesthood during adolescence. He had never incurred the anger of the dead when, at the age of twenty-seven, he married a woman (c/7) who had suffered from ancestral malevolence up to this time but ceased to do so thereafter. The couple lived virilocally after their wedding, at which bride-price was paid in silver ingots. Neither husband nor wife has resorted to ceremonial protection since that event.

When I began the diary Tawla was forty-six and had four sons between the ages of sixteen and nine years, as well as an unmarried daughter of nineteen called Meij (d/7), who was pregnant. All of his children had inherited vulnerabilities to sickness and while each took medical precautions against disease none had ever employed ceremonial protection.

The priest's sister's daughter (d/9), who was only six years his junior, used the same prophylactic procedures as his children. She had never resorted to *tsiang* and lived uxorilocally with her husband (d/8). The latter had combined ceremonial and medical prophylaxis prior to marriage but had depended exclusively on medicine thereafter. Uantong (e/9), with whom Table 2 deals, is the twenty-year-old son of this couple.

Tawla's mother's brother Ta' (b/2) had married around the age of twenty-four. He had gone through a wedding with a fully indemnified bride (b/1) and lived virilocally. This couple has a twenty-one-year-old daughter married uxorilocally (c/3), a bachelor son of nineteen years called Lawsan (c/2), and another daughter aged sixteen, who is Fam (c/1). Like their father none of these children had ever employed ceremonial prophylaxis until 1967, but each used medical protection against illness. Ta's wife and son-in-law had both combined the two procedures premaritally but used only medicine after marriage.

I shall now refocus attention on Fam and Uantong. For more than two decades the girl's father (b/2) had sought repayment for the virilocal marriage of his sister (b/5) to the priest's father (b/6). Tawla promised to redeem the debt with the first of his children who proved to be disliked by his ancestors. But he countered Ta's claim to adopt any of them in infancy or youth by citing the fact that none required *tsiang* rituals. Then towards the end of 1966, Meij, Tawla's eldest daughter (d/7) had an affair with Ta's son, Lawsan (c/2), and became pregnant.

In such circumstances a Yao genitor is under an obligation to employ a priest who determines whether ceremonial protection is necessary to avoid the prenatal illnesses which mother and child may incur. Denial of responsibility is frequent but Lawsan willingly fulfilled his duty with the enthusiastic support of his father. In March 1967 he took Meij to his mother's brother's village. There he consulted with the priest who had officiated over Tawla's initiation twenty years before and who declared that the girl was a victim of soul-loss induced by her own ancestors. Lawsan borrowed rice, pigs, chickens, and other ceremonial essentials from his matrilateral kinsman. For the first time in her life Meij went through a *tsiang* ritual.

Tawla was furious at the *fait accompli* and beat his daughter. Some people say that he had planned an uxorilocal marriage of the girl with Uantong (e/9) who, he told me, was the actual genitor. But he could not contest the diagnosis of his mentor that Meij's ancestors held her in disfavor. Within a week the priest had accepted Ta's invitation to negotiate the betrothal of their respective children as soon as the infant was born.

But two months before that event (in July, 1967) things went wrong at a routine ancestral-cult service in Ta's *peo*. The chicken sacrifice turned putrid even though the bird was killed and scalded the same morning. Whiskey mysteriously evaporated from the jug before sacramental libations could be poured. Halfway through the reading of the *peo*'s genealogy the officiating priest began to cough and sneeze. He told Ta' that the ritual would have to be postponed and then privately asked Lawsan about his recent dreams.

The youth reluctantly confirmed that during sleep he had felt the soul of his eyes leave his double. The same priest performed a successful *tsiang* ritual for the lad two days later. Lawsan's disability thereby became public knowledge. Tawla informed Ta' that he would not be proceeding with the betrothal negotiations. The boy's soul-loss had robbed him of any claim to become Meij's virilocal husband.

Between July and October, 1967, Tawla vainly tried to reestablish good relationships with his mother's brother in a number of ways. For example, he sent the man gifts of whisky and freshly killed pork. But the presents were returned. The niceties of Yao etiquette ceased to disguise Ta's hostility towards his sister's son even on formal occasions such as sittings of the village jury to which they both belonged. The headman intervened by advising Tawla to take more positive measures to mend the breach. The priest responded by exploiting his status as a matrimonial creditor of Fusin (c/9).

Until this time Tawla had never mentioned the debt which Fusin had incurred by marrying virilocally without paying bride-price. Relationships between the two men had always been warm. The priest never charged for officiating at ancestral-cult rituals in his brother-in-law's dwelling group and Fusin frequently reciprocated with free services as a shaman. During September 1967, the month of Meij's baby's birth (e/7), Tawla was performing a naming ceremony for his sister's grandson (e/10) when he encountered the same difficulties as his colleague who had conducted Ta's ancestral rite in July. On inquiry several members of the dwelling group admitted to having seen detached souls in their recent dreams. Uantong (e/9) was away planting poppy seed at the time.

When recalled home the youth confessed in private to Tawla that a week before, he had lost the soul to the left side of his head but had not yet suffered a headache. The priest performed an emergency *tsiang* ritual which took the form of a bridge ceremony. Afterward, he accused Uantong of suppressing other information about dreams. The boy then admitted the loss of his stomach's soul and, on further cross-examination, that counterparts to his arms, feet, and hands were missing.

Four *tsiang* rituals followed and decimated the dwelling-group's pig herd. Their protraction over a period of weeks was necessary because the *peo* of Uantong had to harvest the rice for the accompanying feasts. In the meantime, the patient lost the soul to the left side of the head again. Yet another recovery ritual took place for which Uantong's mother (d/9) had to borrow pigs and chickens. Note that the youth was never sick throughout this time, most of which he spent hard at work on his *peo*'s farms.

Finally, against the objections of d/9, Fusin declared that his grandson would marry out of the dwelling-group as soon as possible. He insisted that such a move was necessary not only for the boy to escape the malevolence of the dead but also for the economic welfare of the *peo*. Tawla was present when Uantong's mother tried to dissuade Fusin from this decision. The priest gave verbal support to his sister's daughter's plea, but in so doing he referred to the fact that Ta' (b/2) had a nubile daughter Fam (c/1), that she enjoyed ancestral grace, and that the girl's relatives had already accumulated the wherewithal for a wedding in preparation for Lawsan's nuptials, which were now cancelled.

Fusin asked Tawla to mediate with Fam's father. He did so by a letter to Ta', in whose house betrothal negotiations subsequently took place. The priest took a prominent role in the proceedings, reminding all present that his *peo* was owed a spouse by Fusin's. He praised Uantong's character and stated how much any man would like the boy as an uxorilocal son-in-law. However, he was prepared to revoke all claims to the youth in favor of Ta', who responded by toasting his sister's son's generosity.

In this way Tawla used his position as a priest and his rights as a matrimonial creditor to cancel his status as a matrimonial debtor without losing any personnel from his *peo*.

Meij continues to live in the dwelling group of the descent unit to which she belongs despite the malevolence of her ancestors. The girl's need to resort to ceremonial protection against illness marks her out as an individual who can never become an uxorilocal wife and who must leave the *peo* of her own *tso* at marriage. But this does not mean that she must marry. Regular performance of *tsiang* rituals justifies continuous residence in her natal group.

At present no other *peo* has a right to Meij's hand. Fam's marriage to Uantong and Lawsan's soul-loss cancelled the claim which Ta's dwelling group previously possessed. But Meij's continuous membership in her father's *peo* entails expense and inconvenience which even Tawla's status as a priest cannot altogether alleviate. Before holding any type of religious service for anyone in his own house, Tawla has to conduct a trial ceremony to ascertain whether his daughter is suffering from soul-loss. If the results are positive a ritual of recall is necessary before the main event and the sacrifice of at least one chicken is a prerequisite.

Lawsan's vulnerability to the same complaint as Meij placed much greater economic strain on Ta's *peo*. Since leaving the field I have heard that the girl's former lover married uxorilocally two years after the events described above and that he no longer takes ceremonial protection against disease.

Meij's case also warrants comparison with that of Fusin (c/9). He always enjoyed the grace of his own ancestors premaritally, but nevertheless became an uxorilocal husband when he first married. This example indicates that the benevolence of the dead toward a worshiper-by-descent provides this person with the right to stay with his own *tso*'s dwelling group at marriage but not necessarily with the obligation to do so. In contrast with descendants who incur the anger of their ancestors such a man has the right to bring his wife back to the *peo* of the dwelling group to which he belongs if economic circumstances permit.

Let me summarize. The case study shows how the prophylactic history of fourteen spouses relates to their conjugal residence and hence to the determination of which party to a marriage transmits descent. Seven of these people belong to the *tso* of the dwelling group in which they live. They consist of four virilocal husbands (b/2, b/6, c/6, and c/9) and three uxorilocal wives (c/1, c/3, and d/9). None has ever taken ceremonial precautions against the power of their own ancestors to inflict illness and with one exception (c/9) each has depended exclusively on prophylactic medicine since birth.

The other seven spouses do not belong to the *tso* of the dwelling group with which they live. They include four virilocal wives (b/1, b/5, c/7, and c/8) as well as three uxorilocal husbands (c/4, d/8, and e/9). All have incurred the anger of their own ancestors but ceased to require ceremonial protection against illness after joining their spouse's *peo*. Each of the women and two of the men (c/4 and d/8) combined both types of prophylaxis before this residential shift but have depended exclusively on medicine ever since.

Uantong (e/9), the exceptional uxorilocal husband, is like his grandfather (c/9) in that he has never used medical protection against illness. Both these shamans thus reveal a lack of inherited vulnerabilities to sickness. If they fall ill, society interprets their complaints as vocational diseases.

I return then to the nub of my inquiry. Yao ridicule the suggestion that anyone can go through life without becoming sick. They prejudge the causes of a person's diseases in terms of the type of protection the individual employs. Why is medicine the more popular of the two prophylactic practices? This question is the same as asking why most Pulangka Yao worship benevolent ancestors. The foregoing case study contributes to the answer.

The relatives of Tawla belong to one or the other of the two categories into which Pulangka community is divided. They are either blessed or cursed by their own ancestors. Each of the conjugal unions I have analyzed is between spouses of the opposite classification and has been a means by which the cursed party has become blessed. The residential shift which accompanies Yao marriage provides a resolution to the contradiction wherein people are compelled to worship deceased humans who hate them; they gain through affinity the ancestral grace ascribed to others by descent.

Let us compare the relative popularity of medical and ceremonial prophylaxis among these fourteen spouses before and after the resolution. Previously the blessed-by-descent either took medical protection against illness or used neither procedure. The cursed either combined the two types of precaution or relied on ceremony. In sum, thirteen used medicine, six ceremony and one neither.

The shift removed the need for any of these individuals to resort to *tsiang* rituals. As a result thirteen still employed medicine, none used ceremony, and two sought neither form of protection.

These observations support the following contention: that in Pulangka the popularity of medical over ceremonial methods for avoiding illness is a function of the symbolic role which Yao prophylaxis plays in the matrimonial and kinship organization of the society.

## CONCLUSION

I conclude by relating the above discussion to two anthropological issues of general theoretical interest.

There appears to be a close structural similarity between a Pulangka *peo* and the domestic unit in longhouse communities of Borneo, e.g. the Iban *bilek* (Freeman 1970), the Land Dayak household (Geddes 1954), and the Ngadju *kabali* (Miles 1972). Both local groups develop around a core of virilocal male and uxorilocal female cognates who have acquired membership by birth. Neither among the Yao nor the Borneo people does sexual identity predetermine whether a spouse leaves or remains with his or her premarital local unit after marriage. How do the Borneans justify discrimination among individuals in this respect? The answer may well be that their systems of classification have the same social function that I attribute to Yao prophylaxis. Geddes' observations (1954) about Land Dayak adoptions and name changes as disguises against evil spirits appear particularly relevant to the investigation I am suggesting.

Finally, I return to another proposition foreshadowed in the preamble to this paper: that inquiry into notions about posthumous personality among Sinitic ancestor worshipers may help to explain the discovery and use of effective medical technological by oriental societies.

Personally, I have no doubt that many of the procedures which Pulangka Yao employ to prevent sickness are at least partially successful. My discussions with Tawla's mother Fooeh are instructive in this regard. The old woman would often ridicule the prophylactic treatments her grandparents had sought for her as a child. She also described the trial-and-error processes by which she and other Pulangka people had discarded some traditional medical practices in favor of others, and whereby they had incorporated foreign products and techniques into the pharmacopoeia and medical technology of the community.

Successful trial-and-error experimentation is a means by which inquiry isolates relevant hypotheses from a range of infinite possibilities. All Pulangka adults assert that both medicine and ceremony offer protection against illness. But as I have shown, Yao who seek or are ascribed social recognition as beneficiaries of ancestral grace cannot resort to ceremonial prophylaxis.

There are two ways by which such people convince society that their susceptibility to sickness is not due to the malevolence of the dead. On the one hand they can use neither form of prophylaxis but to justify this strategy they must become shamans. For reasons I have discussed elsewhere the profession is closed to women and most men. The other method is to rely exclusively on medical protection. I have shown how a category of people who resort to the latter alternative is constantly sustained by social processes within Pulangka independently of the impact which foreign ideas have on the beliefs of the people. Such indigenous obstacles to the access the majority have to ceremonial protection against disease undoubtedly reduces the influence that chance would otherwise exercise upon their discovery of effective medical prophylaxis.

We may ask whether Pulangka Yao are unique among the Sinitic peoples who traditionally worship ancestors; whether they alone regard the dead as beings who display benignity towards some devotees but malice against others; whether only in the community I studied are variations in prophylactic practice social indicators of differences in the attitude of the deceased towards the living. I would be surprised if the answer proved to be in the affirmative.

Yet Freedman's seminal essay (1967) about posthumous personality hinges on the premise that the dead members of any ancestor-worshiping society behave in a totally consistent fashion towards their devotees; e.g. deceased Lovedu are malicious, their southeastern Chinese counterparts compassionate, etc. Yao data suggest that this assumption lacks universal validity; that Far Eastern ethnography on the subject demands revaluation along the lines suggested here, and that the indigenous development of effective medical technologies by some Oriental cultures may express the social necessity for ancestor worshipers to prove that they are blessed rather than cursed by the objects of their devotions.

## REFERENCES

FREEDMAN, M.
1967    "Ancestor worship: two facets of the Chinese case," in *Social organisation: essays presented to Raymond Firth*. Edited by M. Freedman. London: Frank Cass.
FREEMAN, D.
1970    *Report on the Iban*. London School of Economics Monographs on Social Anthropology 41. London: Athlone.

GEDDES, W. R.
1954   *The Land Dayaks of Sarawak.* London: Her Majesty's Stationery Office.
LE BAR, F. M., G. C. HICKLEY, J. K. MUSGRAVE
1964   *Ethnic groups of mainland Southeast Asia.* New Haven: Human Relations Area Files.
MILES, D.
1972   "Ngadju kinship and social change on the Upper Mentaya," in *Anthropology in Oceania.* Edited by L. Hiatt and C. Jayawardena. Sydney: Angus and Robertson.
MOSELEY, G.
1966   *The party and the national question in China.* Boston: M.I.T. Press.
NGUYEN, KHAC VIEN
1968   *Mountain regions and national minorities.* Vietnamese Studies 15. Hanoi: Xunhasaba.
UNITED NATIONS
1967   *Report of the survey team on the economic and social needs of the opium-producing areas in Thailand.* Bangkok: Government Printing Office.

# Chinese Geomancy and Ancestor Worship: A Further Discussion

YIH-YUAN LI

I. In his article on ancestor worship, Professor Maurice Freedman distinguishes two facets of the Chinese ancestor cult, i.e. *feng-shui* [geomancy], and ancestor worship:

As a set of bones an ancestor is no longer in command of his descendants; he is at their disposal. They no longer worship him; he serves their purpose (Freedman 1967: 87).

By geomancy then, men use their ancestors as media for the attainment of worldly desires. And in doing so they have ceased to worship them and begun to use them as things. . . . The authority implied in descent is ritualized in the worship of ancestor. In geomancy the tables are turned: descendants strive to force their ancestors to convey good fortune, making puppets of forbears and dominating the dominators. In ancestor worship, the ancestors are revered; in *feng-shui* they are subordinated (Freedman 1967: 88).

A Chinese would seem reluctant to accept this statement, especially the statement that geomancy is "making puppets of forbears and dominating the dominators." For Chinese anthropologists this reluctance is not a general feeling but is instead one generated by empirical evidence. Some of the materials I shall present here are based on field surveys in central Taiwan, and seem not quite in line with Freedman's argument. Dealing with the same materials, I would also like to offer my own view concerning these two facets of the Chinese ancestor cult.

II. First, let me present the "diagnosis" or explanation given by a

The author is grateful to Professor William Newell for his comments on an earlier draft of this paper and also to Mr. Richard Stamps for his help in polishing the English.

*dang-ki* [spirit medium] in dealing with his client's misfortune or illness. The activities of *dang-ki* are significant phenomena in the Chinese folk religious life in Taiwan. The *dang-ki* play quite an important role in the daily life of the Taiwanese peasants, especially when faced with disasters or difficult problems. The explanations and advice given by these religious practitioners to their clients can provide excellent materials for understanding the essence of their ritual behavior (Li 1972), particularly those explanations concerning an ancestor's or relative's spirit which clarify the relationships between living people and supernatural beings.

The data presented here are based on two field studies, both in Nan-tou *hsien* of central Taiwan. The first study is of an individual *dang-ki* performing the ritual at his family altar with the assistance of his brother, who acts as the interpreter of the spirit medium. The god who is supposed to possess the *dang-ki* is Kai-Chang-Sheng-Wang — a popular local god of the Fukienese. The altar is located in She-liau village of Chu-Shan *chen* (Li 1972: 4–5). The second study concerns a famous temple dedicated to Ti-Yeh-Kong in Sung-pei-keng of the Ming-chien *hsiang*. In this temple, as clients come from all over the island to consult the god, there is a group of about ten *dang-ki*. Sometimes a client may even invite the *dang-ki* to perform the ritual in his home, requiring the temple to maintain a large group of *dang-ki* (Chen 1972).

In the period between November 1-30, 1971, the *dang-ki* of Chu-shan *chen* was consulted by 220 clients.[1] The content of the inquiries of these 220 clients can be classified under the following three main headings: (1) psychophysical problems, 64.54 percent; (2) unfavorable or inauspicious conditions, 24.09 percent; (3) others, 11.36 percent.[2] However, of more immediate concern for us in this paper are the explanations given by the *dang-ki* in order to explain the causes of his client's misfortune.

Among the 220 recorded consultations, some clients are merely treated without further explanation. Only 148 cases involve explanations of causes of trouble. Among these 148 cases, there are 110 cases arising from a single cause, 25 cases with double causes, 11 cases with triple causes, 1 case with four causes, and 1 case with five causes. Altogether there are 202 causes. Among these 202 causes, 96 deal with misfortunes caused by the spirits of relatives either having something

[1]   These data were obtained through the help of Mr. Chuang Ying-chang, assistant Research Fellow of the Institute of Ethnology, Academia Sinica.
[2]   For a detailed description of these categories see Li (1972: 6).

to do with the ascendant's grave (*feng-shui*) or some other reasons. Table 1 gives a breakdown of the items into two categories of explanations. These explanations will be discussed below.

Table 1. Causes of trouble explained by the *dang-ki* in She-liau

| | Number of cases |
|---|---|
| (A) Misfortunes caused by problems of *feng-shui* | |
|     (1)  Caused by father's *feng-shui* | 14 |
|     (2)  Caused by mother's *feng-shui* | 6 |
|     (3)  Caused by husband's *feng-shui* | 5 |
|     (4)  Caused by wife's *feng-shui* | 2 |
|     (5)  Caused by burying parents together | 5 |
|     (6)  Caused by burying parents and grandparents in the same site | 3 |
|     Total | 35 |
| (B) Misfortunes caused by problems other than *feng-shui* | |
|     (1)  Father's spirit | 3 |
|     (2)  Stepfather's spirit | 2 |
|     (3)  Ex-husband | 5 |
|     (4)  Caused by wife's *feng-shui* | 3 |
|     (5)  Son | 3 |
|     (6)  Daughter | 10 |
|     (7)  Brother | 11 |
|     (8)  Sister | 7 |
|     (9)  Father's brother | 4 |
|     (10)  Sister- or daughter-in-law | 6 |
|     (11)  Caused by having tables of different surnames in the same house | 7 |
|     Total | 61 |

In the temple of Sung-pei-ken, one of my students, Chen Hsi-ling, recorded 40 cases of consultations which bear a total of 52 explanations. Of these, 15 are within the scope of our interest, i.e. they concern *feng-shui* issues and are involved with the spirits of relatives. These 15 explanations can be classified as shown in Table 2.

III.   From these materials we found that the victims involved with *feng-shui* issues are not uncommon. Disasters or illness brought upon descendants by their forbears are usually explained as being due to: (1) a wrong location of the grave, (2) "uncomfortable" or "unsafe" graves, (3) neglect of the grave by the descendants, and also (4) some rather peculiar cases which are due to the "dissatisfaction" of both parents, who have been buried in the same grave.

Whatever the reason may be, the *dang-ki* and their clients believe

Table 2.   Causes of trouble explained by the *dang-ki* at the temple in Sung-pei-keng

|  | Number of cases |
|---|---|
| (A) Misfortunes caused by problems of *feng-shui* | |
|    (1)  Caused by father's *feng-shui* | 3 |
|    (2)  Caused by mother's *feng-shui* | 1 |
|    (3)  Caused by grandfather's *feng-shui* | 1 |
|    Total | 5 |
| (B) Misfortunes caused by problems other than *feng-shui* | |
|    (1)  Stepfather's spirit | 1 |
|    (2)  Ex-husband | 2 |
|    (3)  Son | 1 |
|    (4)  Brother | 2 |
|    (5)  Sister | 1 |
|    (6)  Caused by tablets of different lines | 3 |
|    Total | 10 |

that the ancestors within the grave might initiate an action to cause trouble. In this light, Freedman's statement that "as a set of bones, an ancestor is no longer in command of his descendants; he is at their disposal," seems untenable, as the forbears may actually initiate the action. According to Chinese *feng-shui* theory, if a grave has been sited geomantically, it will, sooner or later, bring prosperity to the descendants of the man or woman buried in it. The descendants therefore usually try hard to find a good burial site, hoping to benefit from it. However, this is just one side of the story, at least as far as our data from central Taiwan are concerned. The ancestors in the grave are not passive; if the grave site is geomantically good, the descendants may instantly derive a benefit, but if the site is not good or the ancestor in it is not satisfied, he may cause trouble to his descendants.

It is evident that in *feng-shui* issues, a Chinese ancestor is not a puppet, he is not at all passive; if he were passive, in the case of bad *feng-shui*, good fortune would just stop, but no distasters could be initiated. Therefore, we may argue that in *feng-shui*, the relationship between ancestors and descendants is a reciprocal one rather than a dominant-subordinate one.

Although I am unable to agree with Freedman's statement concerning ancestor status in the *feng-shui* issues, I quite agree with his idea that the tombs and tablets of the ancestors represent two facets of the Chinese ancestor cult. For me, on the one hand, *feng-shui* reflects more or less the domestic or daily family relationship, while on the other hand, the aspect of tablet worship reflects the more formal descent or jural-authority relationship. The two form complementary aspects of the Chinese ancestor cult. For this point of view, I owe much to the

Africanists for their studies of African ancestor worship, and especially to the vivid analysis of the ancestor cult by Fortes (1965). But the argument is based on the Chinese evidence.

IV. In his studies of ancestor worship in the matrilineal Ashanti society, Fortes analyzes the relationships between an Ashanti son and his father and between the same man and his mother's brother. He then writes:

It stands to reason that a father will live on in his children's memory much more vividly and affectionately after his death than will a mother's brother. But it is the latter and not the former who may have a stool dedicated to him and becomes the ancestor for purposes of worship. For, though sons honour their father's memory, ancestor worship by sacrifice, libation, and prayer is a lineage cult; a cult, that is, of the basic politico-jural unit of Ashanti society, not of the domestic unit in which both parents count (1965: 129–130).

It is evident from the above quotation that, for the ancestor cult in a unilineal society, usually two relationships can be distinguished, i.e. one in politico-jural domain and one in the domestic domain. In a matrilineal society, these two relationships can be distinguished easily because they are not with the same person; one is with the mother's brother and the other with the father. However, "in a patrilineal system jural authority and parental responsibility are combined in the same persons" (Fortes 1965: 130), so it is always difficult to distinguish them. But the merging of jural authority and parental responsibility in a patrilineal setting does not mean that they are derived from the same domain — it is not even easy to distinguish them in a subtle way.

It seems to me that, in Chinese society, the aspect of the ancestral cult concerned with worshiping ancestors in the tablets belongs to Fortes' jural authority or politico-jural domain, because it "is a representation or extension of the authority component in the jural relations of successive generations" (Fortes 1965: 133). The other aspect, the issues of *feng-shui* or tombs of forbears, may be classified with Fortes' parental or domestic responsibility, as it "concerns a different sector of religious thought and behavior than does ancestor worship . . . and again the reciprocal conditions apply" (1965: 135).

In support of this argument, let me discuss the data presented above in more detail. First of all, let us examine category B of the explanations given by both groups of *dang-ki*, which deals with the misfortunes caused by the spirits of relatives. Tables 1 and 2, show that the relatives who cause trouble include quite a wide range of categories, such as parents, stepparents, exspouses, offspring, siblings, father's brothers and sisters-

or daughters-in-law. As explained by the *dang-ki*, spirits of the dead will cause trouble among their living descendants for the following reasons. The spirits (1) want to have heirs, (2) want to establish a tablet for themselves in the family shrine, or in case of unmarried female spirits, in the Buddhist or local temple,[3] (3) feel they have been neglected in regard to being worshiped. It is interesting to notice that all the ex-husbands' and ex-wives' disturbances are due to their not being satisfied with the changes of their children's surnames from their own to their stepparents' surnames.

There is also one special item which appears in both tables — the quarrels because tablets of different lines are being worshiped in the same house. Tablets of different sources or different surnames come from different lines due to adoption and varied forms of marriage. After several generations, competition for the proper worship of these different lines frequently arises. It is evident that all these troubles from the spirits of relatives are connected with the representation and extension of the authority component in the jural relation, that is, the succession and maintenance in the next life of the rights and the positions they had in this life. It cannot be doubted, therefore, that this category falls within Fortes' definition of the politico-jural domain.

I have already pointed out that the relationship between the ancestors in the tomb and their living descendants is a reciprocal one. A good grave site or *feng-shui* may benefit the descendants of the one who has been buried, but the prosperity of the descendants may in turn ensure the continuous worship of the ancestor himself, so the relationship is actually a reciprocal one. Being buried in a good site satisfies the forbears and the descendants benefit; but in the case of a bad site or improper burial, the ancestors may initiate trouble. This warns the descendants to change the situation for the welfare of the whole family, which includes the living and the dead. This kind of relationship is actually a reflection of the daily domestic relationship between parents and children in which the conduct shows affective, supportive, and rewarding-punitive relations.

Although in the realm of tablet ancestor worship the relationship between ancestors and descendants may involve protection in general, punishment and disturbance for neglect of proper ritual conduct are emphasized much more and therefore express the nature of the jural-authority relationship. This is backed by the sanctions and jurisdiction of the formal lineage system.

[3] There is no ghost marriage for unmarried girls in this part of Taiwan, as has been reported by Li and Jordan for other parts of the island (Li 1968; Jordan 1971).

We may further contrast these two aspects of the Chinese ancestor cult from the materials given by the *dang-ki*. In the first place, we found that only direct ascendants are involved with *feng-shui* issues: father, mother, grandfather, grandmother (all on the paternal side), and sometimes spouses, all of whom fall within the scope of the Chinese domestic circle. On the other hand, the relatives who are involved with issues other than *feng-shui* are much more widespread, far beyond even the loosest definition of a domestic group. More important, however, is that, as shown in the two tables, in *feng-shui* issues a mother may appear independently to cause trouble, while this would not be the case in proper ancestor worship, because in the tablet the mother is worshiped as an inseparable part of the father's tablet. It is quite clear that *feng-shui* issues are considered to be domestic affairs, different from the conduct observed in a formal descent group, and that a mother may appear as she did in ordinary family life. One further point we may emphasize is that, again as shown in the tables, in *feng-shui* sometimes the trouble may derive from the deceased father and mother, and in some cases it may include grandparents, due to the "dissatisfaction" of forbears being buried together in the same site.[4] This again, it seems to me, reflects the kind of individual expression that we see among the members of an ordinary family. This kind of expression certainly would not be allowed in the formal worship of ancestors in the tablets, where the male line is emphasized at the expense of the female's status.

Freedman has stressed the competition between brothers in *feng-shui* issues (1966: 141). Here we certainly do not have the data about sibling competition on the specific direction of a parent's grave; however, this rivalry between brothers, it seems to me, again reflects relationships between the members of the domestic group, which would not appear in tablet worship.

5. So far I have tried to argue that there are two aspects of Chinese ancestor cult which belong in different areas of the socioreligious structure: the geomancy concerning an ancestor's tomb, or *feng-shui*, falls within the realm of domestic life, while ancestor worship in the tablets reflects a more formal life concerning jural authority over the descent group. The data from Taiwan as delineated above seem quite convincing in support of this argument. However, there are further data from what may be called the ancestor-worship complex of East

---

[4] The burying together of a couple or of two generations is judged good or bad in accordance with horoscope characters of the deaths and proper timing.

Asia which also shed light on this distinction.

In the East Asian area, Japan, Korea, Vietnam, and Okinawa have all been influenced by Chinese culture. Under this influence, rituals of ancestor worship and geomancy have existed from early times to the present. However, the manifestations of these ritual complexes are not alike in these four areas. In Korea, Vietnam, and Okinawa, we find both aspects of the ancestor cult: geomancy of graves and ancestor worship in tablets going on side by side as they do in China (Osgood 1951: 149, 244; Hickey 1964: 40; Lebra 1966: 62). But in Japan the picture is somewhat different. Freedman mentioned that geomancy of graves does not appear in Japan, yet he simply ascribes this to a lack of an agnatic descent system in Japanese society without further discussion (1967: 89). For me, the picture is more complicated than that. In referring to the Japanese ancestor cult and its functioning in the social structure, Nakane says:

This point touches the essentially functional aspect of the Japanese ancestor cult. The recognition of the ancestor in Japan usually refers to the actual founder of the household (ie) in which the present occupants live. . . . It is the founders of the ie, and those who died as the members of the household, who are celebrated as ancestors (1967: 106).

And again:

The ancestor is the justifying authority for the cooperation of the living members. How an individual is related to the ancestor in terms of descent is not primarily important. The term "ancestor" which usually conveys the notion of descent, is subject to economic and local factors (1967: 107).

My colleague, Wang Sung-hsing, in his article on ancestor worship of the Chinese and Japanese, also stresses the differences between the Chinese concepts of tsu [lineage], chia [family], and chu-hsien [ancestor] and the Japanese counterparts of dōzoku, ie, and senzo (1971: 249–252). He makes it clear that the inheritance and succession of the Japanese kinship group and household are based on residential and economic factors, but not on genealogy or blood ties. In other words, they emphasize the relationship of the jural authority but neglect the domestic or family relation.

Hence, the notion of ancestor worship in Japan is only present in the worship of tablets, which belongs to the same realm of jural-authority relationship, and leaves no room for geomancy of graves which, according to our view, reflects the relationship of domestic or family life. Even other aspects of geomancy, such as the geomancy of house building, were brought from China and have been well established in Japanese society for a long time.[5]

In Korea and Vietnam, and especially in Okinawa where Japanese influence sometimes is much stronger than the Chinese, we see that the Chinese style of lineage and family has been well developed (Osgood 1951: 37–39; Hickey 1964: 88–91; Lebra 1966: 153–155). This development accounts for both the existence of ancestor worship in tablets and the geomancy of graves in these three districts. In sum, the different manifestations of ancestor cult and the social structure in these East Asian countries seem to agree with our main proposition.

From the ancestor worship complex of East Asia in general and the studies in central Taiwan specifically, it is reasonable to assert that the two aspects of Chinese ancestor cult indeed reflect different domains of socioreligious structure: the geomancy concerning the ancestor's tomb reflects the more affective, supportive and rewarding-punitive relations of domestic life, while the ancestor worship in the tablets falls into the realm of a more formal jural authority relationship derived from the descent system.

REFERENCES

CHEN, H. L.
    1972    "A case study of a spirit medium in central Taiwan." Unpublished bachelor's thesis, National Taiwan University, Taipei.
FREEDMAN, M.
    1966    *Chinese lineage and society: Fukien and Kwangtung.* London School of Economics Monographs on Social Anthropology, 33. London: Athlone.
    1967    "Ancestor worship: two facets of the Chinese case," in *Social organisation: essays presented to Raymond Firth.* Edited by M. Freedman. London: Frank Cass.
FORTES, M.
    1965    "Some reflections on ancestor worship in Africa," in *African systems of thought.* Edited by M. Fortes and G. Dieterlen. London and New York: Oxford University Press.
HICKEY, G. C.
    1964    *Village in Vietnam.* New Haven and London: Yale University Press.
JORDAN, D.
    1971    Two forms of spirit marriage in rural Taiwan. *Bijdragen tot de Taal-, Land- en Volkenkunde* 127:181–189. The Hague: Nijhoff.

[5]    In regard to the problem of geomancy in Japan, I am in debt to my colleague, Mr. Liu Chi-wan for valuable data in his unpublished paper, "Chinese traditions in Japanese folk belief" (1970).

LEBRA, W.
   1966   *Okinawan religion.* Honolulu: University of Hawaii Press.
LI, YIH-YUAN
   1968   "Ghost marriage, shamanism and kinship behavior in rural Tai-
          wan," in *Folk religion and the worldview of the southwestern
          Pacific.* A Symposium of the Eleventh Pacific Science Congress,
          Tokyo.
   1972   Shamanism in Taiwan — an anthropological inquiry. Paper pre-
          sented to the Fourth Conference on Culture and Mental Health in
          Asia and the Pacific, Honolulu.
NAKANE, CHIE
   1967   *Kinship and economic organization in rural Japan.* London School
          of Economics Monographs on Social Anthropology, 32. London.
OSGOOD, C.
   1951   *The Koreans and their culture.* New York: Ronald.
WANG, SUNG-HSING
   1971   A comparative study of ancestor worship of the Chinese and the
          Japanese (in Chinese). *Bulletin of the Institute of Ethnology,
          Academia Sinica* (31). Taipei.

# Aspects of Ancestor Worship in Northern Taiwan

ARTHUR P. WOLF

Though I have never devoted an extended period of time to the study of ancestor worship in northern Taiwan, I have recorded a good deal of information in the course of studying problems related to family organization, marriage and adoption practices, and inheritance. What impresses me most about the topic is the great variety of groups involved in ancestor worship and the complexity of the relationship between the living and the dead. I have attempted more than once to summarize my observations in an analytical fashion but have always failed to find generalizations that account for the diversity of the phenomena recorded in my notes. In this essay I can do no better than confess failure and report the stubborn facts. What follows are eight examples selected out of the forty or so described in my notes and some very tentative observations about their significance. I cannot say whether these examples are typical or not, since I have yet to find the pattern that would allow me to judge.

The people whose behavior and beliefs I describe all live either in the town of San-hsia or within a few miles of the town. They are all native speakers of Hokkien, descendants of seventeenth- and eighteenth-century immigrants from An-ch'i *hsien* in southern Fukien, and long-term residents of the area in which they now live. They are also, without exception, followers, or, in their view, "subjects," of the god Ch'ing Shui Ts'u Shih Kung, the supernatural governor of San-hsia *chen*. Whatever the source of the variation that puzzles me, it is not regional or ethnic differences, or varying historical circumstances. The people of San-hsia are all members of the same local system and share a common culture. I can prove conclusively that they have long made remarkably similar decisions about such matters as marriage, adoption, and inheritance. I am inclined to the view that ancestor worship is special because it reflects all too faithfully the full complexity of human relationships, and in so doing preserves a record of what is unique in the history of individual families as well as what is typical.

## THE CH'I-NAN LINEAGES

I begin with the case of the Ch'i-nan lineages because they appear to represent the culmination of a process that can be observed in many other groups in the San-hsia area. The source of my information is a few notes I made in 1968 and Emily Ahern's admirably detailed study entitled *The cult of the dead in a Chinese village* (1973). The reader who wants to know more about Chinese ancestor worship could do no better than to read this book. I offer only one caution. The uniformity Ahern finds in Ch'i-nan may very well reflect the fact that this is a highly integrated community in which the practices of one group exert an immediate and direct impact on the practices of the others. We will see below that one cannot generalize the details of ancestor worship in Ch'i-nan to Lin-ts'u on the edge of town or even to Liu-ts'u-p'u across the river.

Although the Ch'i-nan lineages are not so large or so old as those mainland groups that have caught the attention of anthropologists working in the New Territories of Hong Kong, there can be no question that they are in fact corporate descent groups, Morton Fried's comments on lineage organization in Taiwan notwithstanding (1970: 30–31). Three of the four own landed property; all four worship their founding ancestors in a hall specially constructed for the purpose; and all four also display a remarkable degree of what might be called pride of descent. The only distinctive feature of the Ch'i-nan lineages is that where many mainland lineages are internally segmented, the Ch'i-nan groups emphasize internal solidarity and repress all signs of segmentation. One manifestation of this is the fact that they worship the Stove God in their lineage halls. This is significant because elsewhere in San-hsia the Stove God stands for the family. The process of family division is considered complete when the parties to the division take ashes from the old stove and invite the god to their separate quarters. There is some slight comfort here for those nineteenth-century writers who treated lineages as "the family writ large." It appears that as a means of denying internal differentiation, the Ch'i-nan lineages like to present themselves as big, happy families.

This use of domestic symbols to emphasize group solidarity is also apparent in the way the Ch'i-nan lineages tend their dead. Where most mainland lineages worship their recent dead at home and reserve the lineage hall for the founding ancestor and other remote dead, the Ch'i-nan lineages place the tablets of both the recent dead and the remote dead in their halls. A man does not have to wait five or six generations to obtain a seat in the lineage hall, but is enshrined there immediately upon death. Indeed, a lineage member who is about to breathe his last is removed from his home and placed in the lineage hall, and it is here that the funeral rites are performed (Ahern 1973: 94). I hasten to add that this does not mean that Maurice Freedman's distinction between "domestic rites" and "hall rites" is irrelevant in the Ch'i-nan case (1958: 90–91). Although all of the dead are given a place in the lineage hall, the rites for the recent dead and the remote dead are not of a kind. In all four lineages the rites for the founding ancestors are paid for out of lineage funds and are conducted by its representatives; the rites for all other dead are the sole responsibility of their descendants, not the responsibility of the lineage. The only difference between the Ch'i-nan lineages and those mainland lineages that are the subject of Freedman's attention is that by putting all of their dead in the same place the Ch'i-nan groups make the distinction less obvious.

The fact that the Ch'i-nan halls are the property of corporate descent groups is most strikingly displayed by the strict rules that govern admission of the dead to the halls. Ahern notes three categories of dead to whom people in Ch'i-nan make regular offerings but whose tablets are not allowed in the hall. One is women who die before marriage but after they are socially mature (1973: 127–128). They are excluded "because girls are meant to belong to other people" and "are supposed to die in other people's houses." Some families place the tablet of an unmarried girl on a shelf in some dark corner of the house; others insist that the tablet of an unmarried girl cannot have a place anywhere on lineage property.[1] They either send the tablet to a special temple for unmarried girls or marry the girl posthumously so her tablet can be placed on her husband's altar. A second category of people excluded from the lineage halls is men who marry into Ch'i-nan families but retain their own surnames. Though they con-

---

[1] People in Ch'i-nan count as "lineage property" land held by individual families as well as land held by the lineage as corporate property. This probably reflects the fact that agnates enjoyed preemptive rights with regard to one another's land.

tribute children and labor to their wife's father's line, these men do not qualify because they are not lineage members. Also excluded are men who were born into the lineage but later married uxorilocally and agreed to allow some of their children to take their descent from their mother. As these men usually retain their own surnames and assign other of their children to their own line, one would expect them to retain lineage membership and with it the right to a place in the hall. But this is not the case. "On this issue the people of Ch'i-nan hold very strict views. Most said that if an uxorilocally married man allowed any of his children to take his wife's surname, he would lose his right to a seat in the hall. The loss of children who might have belonged to the lineage would be enough to severely weaken his status" (Ahern 1973: 124).

Other aspects of ancestor worship in Ch'i-nan will be noted in relation to the other groups I describe. At this point I want only to note that, whatever its significance, the arrangement of ancestral tablets in Ch'i-nan divides the dead into three classes. While men who marry into or out of the Ch'i-nan lineages do not qualify for a place in the hall, they are not so severely deprived as unmarried women, for they are allowed a place on lineage property. Excluded from the halls, they are worshiped on altars in the home. Thus, at one extreme, we find those dead who qualify for a place in the hall: men, and the wives of men, who are born into the lineage and contribute fully to the lineage; at the opposite extreme, dead whose tablets are denied a place on lineage property: unmarried daughters who "belong to other people"; and between the two extremes, an intermediate class of dead whose tablets do not qualify for a place in the hall but do qualify for a place on lineage property: men who contribute to the lineage but remain outsiders and men who are born into the lineage but marry into the homes of outsiders.

## THE LI LINEAGE

The anthropologist who began his study of ancestor worship in China with the Li lineage would likely arrive at very different conclusions from the one who began in Ch'i-nan, despite the fact that the old home of the Li lineage is located in Liu-ts'u-p'u not more than a mile north of Ch'i-nan. The lineage was founded by three brothers each of whom had three sons. At one time all of the members of the lineage lived in the old home in Liu-ts'u-p'u, but at present each branch has

its own home. The senior branch, the smallest and least successful of
the three, is located in Ta-p'u on the opposite side of San-hsia town;
the second branch occupies a large compound a few hundred yards
east of the old home; while the third branch resides in the old home.
In 1968 the lineage held seven *fen* of paddy land as corporate property, [2] and I was told that prior to land reform their estate was much
larger. The use of this land is rotated on an annual basis among the
nine lines headed by the sons of the three founding ancestors. The
rotation begins with the senior line of the senior branch of the lineage,
proceeds to the senior line of the second branch, moves to the senior
line of the third branch, and then returns to the second line of the
senior branch, proceeds to the second line of the second branch, and
so on.

Though the Li lineage counts as members three or four families
who have been as successful as any in Ch'i-nan, the Lis do not have
a lineage hall. Instead, they make do with a large tablet inscribed
with the names and birth and death dates of their three founding
ancestors and their wives. This tablet and responsibility for the dead
it represents rotate from branch to branch together with the use of
the lineage's property. Thus, the ancestors spend one out of every
three years in Ta-p'u and two out of every three in Liu-ts'u-p'u, one
in the home of the second branch and one in the home of the third
branch. Whether or not it is socially significant, it is a fact that where
the Ch'i-nan ancestors stand at the center of lineage communities, the
Li ancestors circulate among their scattered descendants. The arrangement reminds one of the fate of some elderly parents who spend so
many days a month with each of their married sons.

During my most recent trip to Taiwan I often stayed with a family
living in the old Li home and had an opportunity to observe the rites
performed for the dead represented on their altar. At that time there
were eleven families living in a large "U" shaped compound. Entering
the compound by way of the open end of the "U", one faced a heavy
double-leafed door that opened into a large, dark room known as the
*kong-tia:* [hall]. Here, facing the door, stood a high wooden table,
and on it, the tablets of all the recent dead worshiped by the residents
of the compound. Although all of the dead were agnatic ascendants
and their wives, I was told that the tablet of an uxorilocally married
man could be placed on this altar. "All you have to do is ask the
ancestors' permission and build a little partition on the altar. Only

[2] The primary land measure on Taiwan is the *chia* which equals 2.40 acres or
approximately one hectare. One *fen* is one tenth of a *chia*.

very strict people would put the tablet in a backroom." But while the
Lis say they would allow the tablet of a son-in-law on their altar,
they insist that this privilege could never be granted an unmarried
daughter. Their practice is to deposit the souls of unmarried daughters in a little roadside temple known as the *ko-niu-biou* [maiden's
temple]. The girl's soul then becomes part of a collectivity worshiped
by prostitutes who would "not dare" seek the assistance of the supernatural bureaucrats enshrined in the major temples.

On calendar holidays such as Ch'ing Ming Chieh and the lunar
New Year when all ancestors are worshiped, each of the eleven
families in the Li compound prepares dishes of food for the dead.
These are laid out together on a long table in front of the ancestral
altar, after which a representative of each family steps forward, bows,
and invites the dead to eat. The same procedure is followed in honoring individual ancestors on their deathdays, the only difference being
that participation is limited to those families who trace descent from
this particular person. This suggests that while responsibility for the
dead follows descent, the units involved in ancestor worship are
households. So long as they constitute an undivided domestic group,
brothers present one offering; after division, they present separate
offerings.

The role of the family in preparing and presenting offerings to the
recent dead is much the same in Ch'i-nan as in the Li compound in
Liu-ts'u-p'u. The difference is that where the Ch'i-nan lineages de-
emphasize the role of the family by worshipping the Stove God in the
lineage hall, the Lis worship the god at their individual stoves and
thereby emphasize the independence of domestic groups. A daughter-
in-law of the family I stayed with had grown up in Ch'i-nan and was
fond of comparing the customs of the two communities. She told me
that the Stove God is much more important in Liu-ts'u-p'u than in
Ch'i-nan. "Here you have to take hot charcoals from the old stove
when you divide the family and invite the god to come with you. And
people also say that you have to be very careful about what you say
around the stove. If you quarrel or say something bad, the Stove God
will punish you." My informant observed local custom as a good
daughter-in-law should, but her attitude implied something less than
complete acceptance of these customs.

Although they trace their descent to common ancestors and cooperate in providing for their souls, the residents of the Li compound
do not hold common property (except for the *kong-tia:*) and do not
act together as a group except in relation to their common ancestors.

They certainly display a greater sense of solidarity than agnates who do not see one another everyday, but this alone is not enough to put them on a par with fully corporate lineages. The fact that they worship together is largely a result of the fact that they live together. On the other hand, I am confident that if one of the eleven families were to set up an independent altar in their own quarters, the others would be offended and interpret this as symptomatic of a changed relationship. The common altar represents a community of interests albeit one that is less compelling than that created by common property.

Consequently, I feel that the type of altar found in the Li compound must be distinguished from those that serve individual families and those that are the symbolic foci of fully corporate lineages. I propose calling them "communal altars." The term "communal" seems appropriate because it suggests common residence and implies more or less voluntary cooperation. I will refer to the altars of individual families as "domestic altars," and those that serve lineages as "lineage shrines." And as long as I have raised terminological matters, I may as well note that I also feel a need for terms to replace Freedman's "domestic worship" and "hall worship." In Ch'i-nan we find domestic worship in a hall; in the Li compound, hall worship in a house. I propose the terms "domestic rites," "communal rites," and "corporate rites" to refer to worship performed by one family, by a group of agnatically related families, and by the representatives of a lineage. The terms "home" and "hall" can then be reserved to refer to the buildings in which rites are performed.

## THE TAN LINEAGE

The great majority of the members of the Tan lineage live in a rambling complex of connected apartments located a few hundred yards east of the old home of the Li lineage. Until sometime in the 1960's when the lineage dissolved as a result of a quarrel over land and use of the lineage hall, the Tans were organized in much the same fashion as the four Ch'i-nan lineages. I was told that the lineage owned one *chia* of paddy land that produced an annual rent of forty-five *shih* of rice.[3] This income financed the lineage's corporate rites and provided a small surplus that was divided on a *per stirpes* basis. As the building in which the Tans placed their ancestral tablets had fallen down a few years before my first visit, I do not know whether it was constructed

[3] One *shih* equals 47.7 gallons of husked rice.

for the purpose of ancestor worship or not. But it is clear that whatever its original purpose, the building was long used as a lineage
hall. A man whose father married into a Tan family told me that his
father's tablet was not allowed in the *kong-tia:*. The reason given him
was that the Tan ancestors would be angry and fight with anyone who
was not a Tan.

My account of the quarrel that destroyed the Tan lineage was
obtained from active participants and is undoubtedly biased. Their
story is that a man I will call Tan Bun-tua used his position in the
local government to "steal" the lineage's property. They also claim
that after the old lineage hall collapsed, Tan Bun-tua collected money
to build a new hall and then used the building as a private home. One
informant said that the breaking point came when Tan Bun-tua told
people that they could no longer lay out their dead in the hall because
the presence of corpses disturbed his sleep; another said that the
lineage was finally dissolved when Tan Bun-tua removed all of the
tablets and gave them back to their descendants. "One New Year's he
just took all of the tablets out of the *kong-tia:* and told people that
he didn't want those things in his house."

Dissolution of the Tan lineage did not result in neglect of the
remote dead. Instead, the result was a proliferation of ancestral altars
throughout the Tan settlement. Where people had formerly pooled
their resources to perform corporate rites, they now carried on individual domestic rites at altars set up in their own homes. Three families in the settlement invited me to examine the contents of the boxes
containing their ancestral tablets, probably hoping that this information would convince me that their account of Tan Bun-tua was justified. Comparison of these tablets indicates that while each of the
three worships recent dead of their own, they also make regular
offerings to a number of common ancestors. One family observes a
total of sixteen individual deathdays. They told me that only seven of
the dead represented by these tablets are the sole responsibility of
their family. Two are worshiped by five other families in the Tan
settlement, and seven are worshiped by all former members of the
Tan lineage.

The importance of this example lies in what it says about the
nature of responsibility for the dead. Certain knowledge that someone
else is making offerings to a distant ancestor does not relieve a person
from making offerings to this same man. Responsibility for the dead
falls equally and fully on all of their descendants. This is the reason
I am reluctant to view communal rites as an expression of agnatic

solidarity. The fact is that if agnates do not worship their ancestors collectively, they must worship them separately. The moral force behind these rites is not necessarily a sense of solidarity. It may be nothing more than the responsibility that each of a person's descendants has to contribute to his welfare in the other world.

## THE LIM ALTARS

The case of the Lim family altars is one of the most interesting I have encountered in the course of my fieldwork in San-hsia, partly because of the family's complicated history and partly because my informant, a woman called Song Suat, was a particularly able and willing commentator. Though seventy years old at the time I last talked to her, she was articulate and unusually frank about the history of her family. A skeleton version of the genealogy she gave me is presented in Figure 1.[4] It is important to note that Song Suat's mother and her sister, an adopted daughter, both married uxorilocally, one to a man surnamed Song and the other to a man named Lou. As Song

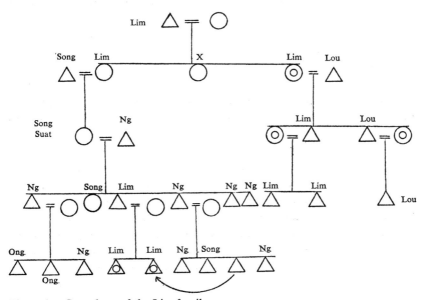

Figure 1. Genealogy of the Lim family

---

[4] The symbols △ and ⊙ indicate adoption. The status of an adopted male is essentially that of a son, but the status of an adopted female is not that of a daughter. These women, known as *sim-pua* [little daughters-in-law] are eligible to marry a son of their foster family, and this is commonly the intent of the adoption.

Suat was the only one of her parents' children to survive, she also married uxorilocally, to a man surnamed Ng. The result is that in the generation of Song Suat's children the genealogy is split between four lines of descent. Her mother's younger sister raised two sons, assigning one to the original Lim line and one to her husband's line. Their children all take their descent from their father and thus carry on the Lim and Lou lines. Song Suat named three of her sons to the Ng line, one to the Lim line, and a daughter to the Song line. The eldest son lived for a while with a woman named Ong and fathered two children who take their descent from their mother; he then married this woman and produced a third son who takes his descent from his father. Song Suat's second son married a woman who had already "bought" a son and later adopted a second son from his younger brother. These boys carry on the Lim line. Song Suat's third son bears the surname Ng but has produced children for three lines. Two of his children take their descent from him, one was given in adoption to his older brother and now bears the name Lim, and one was assigned to the Song line. This was necessary because the daughter named to this line died before marriage. Song Suat's fourth son was given out in adoption to her husband's older brother, and her fifth married out of the family and was disowned as a result.

The family formed by the marriages of Song Suat's mother and her younger sister was divided in 1919, the two women inheriting precisely equal shares of their father's estate. I do not know what happened to the share taken by Song Suat's mother except that "it was sold a long time ago," but I was told the share taken by her sister was claimed by this woman's eldest son and that his brother got nothing. As the younger brother took his descent from his father rather than from his mother, he had no right to claim land held by the Lim line. But for obvious reasons, he was not satisfied with this strict interpretation of the rules, and as a result broke away from the family and sought his own fortune. Ironically, he has been very successful and now owns a prosperous store, while his older brother is still a poor farmer. The only point to note about ancestor worship in this branch of the family is that except for his mother, the younger brother refuses to worship ancestors in the Lim line. He feels that because he did not inherit any of the Lim property, he has no responsibility for the Lim ancestors. Song Suat told me that he only makes an exception in the case of his mother "because she raised him."

The arrangements for ancestor worship in the branch of the family headed by Song Suat's mother are more interesting and far more complicated. Although Song Suat's sons have long since divided their mother's household, they still live in the old family home in a neighborhood known as Lin-ts'u [The Lim Home]. The house is a typical "U" shaped compound with a large, dark *kong-tia*: at the center and living quarters in the wings on either side. The unusual thing about the house is that the ancestral altar contains three sets of tablets arranged behind three incense burners. At stage left, in the position of honor, stand the tablets of the original Lim line; to their right, separated from them by a wooden partition, is a single tablet for Song Suat's father, the only ancestor in the Song line; and finally, at the far right, are two tablets for representatives of the Ng line, Song Suat's husband and a son who died before marriage. Song Suat told me that the Lim tablets are divided from the other tablets "because the Songs and Ngs married into the family." She also told me that "the Lims worship the Lim ancestors but not the Song and Ng ancestors, while the Songs and Ngs worship the Song and Ng ancestors but not the Lim ancestors."

It was not until my third visit to the house that I discovered two more sets of tablets located on a little shelf in one of the kitchens. Song Suat explained that these tablets could not be placed on the altar in the *kong-tia*: "because these people are outsiders who just came back here to die." Her story is that one of her mother's sisters (X in Figure 1) married a man named Ti: and bore one child, a daughter. When her parents died the daughter married a man named Tiu: who died a few years later, leaving his wife with one child, an adopted daughter, and the responsibility for the ancestral tablets of both the Ti: and Tiu: lines. At this point Song Suat adopted the adopted daughter to raise as a wife for her third son, and the girl and her mother came to live with Song Suat's family, bringing with them their ancestral tablets. The death of the adopted daughter, and shortly thereafter the death of her mother, left Song Suat's family with two sets of tablets belonging to unrelated lines. They felt they could not abandon them "because they had no children of their own," and so they put the tablets on a shelf in the kitchen where they are now cared for by Song Suat's third son.

The case illustrates as well as any I have recorded the significance of descent in ancestor worship and the less often noted fact that ancestor worship is more than a reflection of the rights and duties assigned by descent. The Lim family has always made an effort to provide all of their dead with descendants, but they have not abandoned those dead who were temporarily without descendants. They have even made a place in their home for the tablets of people to whom they are only related by tenuous links through marriage. This suggests that we must recognize a hierarchy of obligation that runs from senior members of one's own line to people who have contributed children or labor to one's line and finally to those dead whose only claim is the fact they died as dependents of the line. Where the obligation to agnatic ascendants is absolute in that one must worship them regardless of what other people do, the obligation to the dead of other lines is conditional in that one only worships them if other people do not. The fact that more is owed to people who contributed to the line than to those who died as dependents of the line is recognized in ritual as well as in the placement of their tablets. The former are always worshiped on their individual deathdays as well as on calendar holidays; the latter are only worshiped on calendar holidays.

The arrangement of ancestral tablets in Ch'i-nan and in the Lim compound reflects these three degrees of obligation. In both cases the dead are divided into three classes and their tablets arranged in positions that are more and less honored. The only difference is that the distance imposed between the three classes is greater in Ch'i-nan than in the Lim compound. Where the Ch'i-nan lineages banish the tablets of unmarried daughters and exclude those of uxorilocally married men from the lineage hall, the Lims allow "outsiders" a place in the house and only put a small wooden partition between their own tablets and those of uxorilocally married men. This difference probably reflects the fact that the Ch'i-nan altars are lineage shrines while the Lim altar is a communal altar. It makes good sociological sense to argue that strong groups emphasize the difference between members and outsiders more than weak groups.


## THE ONG ALTARS

The Ong family lives in one of the most isolated spots in San-hsia *chen*. The old family home is only accessible by way of a narow dirt road along the south bank of the Tamsui River and two miles of stone steps that climb steeply from the river's edge to the top of a mountain overlooking the Tao-yüan Plain. The twelve farm families who live along the upper reaches of the path carry all the rice they sell down to the river on their backs and have to carry back up the mountain all of their supplies, including the fertilizer they use to keep their fields productive. I mention this because it is the reason the family of my informant, a man I call Ong Hok-lai, now lives alone in a home that once housed five families. Is has been some years since Ong's four brothers tired of the hard life on the mountain and moved away to seek other livelihoods in Taipei City. This has been to Ong Hok-lai's advantage as he now farms his brothers' land as well as his own, but the strain of the work has clearly taken its toll. At sixty he is a wizened old man.

The essentials of the Ong genealogy are summarized in Figure 2. As in the case of Song Suat's branch of the Lim family, the Ong line was maintained only by uxorilocal marriages in two successive generations. Ong's grandmother "called in" a man surnamed Lim, and Ong's mother, a man named Tan. The result in the third generation is a sibling set split between three lines of descent. Ong Hok-lai is the eldest son and takes his descent from his mother and grandmother; the second and fourth sons take their descent from their father; while the third and fifth sons take their descent from their grandfather. The reader should also note that Ong has married twice and has two children, a son by his first wife and a "daughter" adopted from his second wife. The son and daughter are married and have three children not shown in Figure 2.

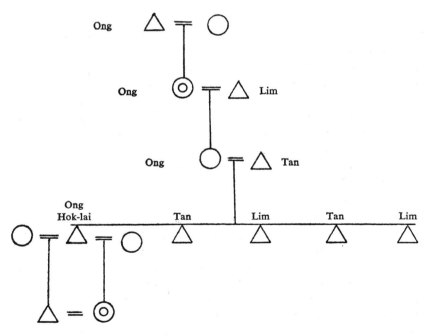

Figure 2.  Genealogy of the Ong family

The Ong family now has two ancestral altars containing four incense burners and four sets of tablets. Three of these are located on a large altar in the old *kong-tia:*, while the fourth occupies a tiny corner shelf in a storeroom next to the kitchen. The three sets of tablets on the main altar include the ancestors of the original Ong line, a set of tablets introduced by Ong Hok-lai's grandfather, and the tablets Ong's father brought with him when he married into the family. The two tablets on the shelf in the storeroom are for Ong Hok-lai's second wife's foster parents. Ong did not mention these tablets to me until his wife noted my interest in ancestor worship and pointed out the shelf in the storeroom. He insists that he has nothing to do with these tablets and that under no circumstance could they be placed on the main altar. "These people didn't marry into the family. They aren't really members of the family." It seems that where tablets brought by in-marrying men can be given a place on the main altar, those introduced by in-marrying women must be excluded because they are outsiders.

The arrangement of the tablets on the main altar is much the same as that found in the Lim compound. The Ong tablets are at the left of the altar, the Lim and Tan tablets at the right, divided from the Ong tablets by a wooden partition. But the Lim and Tan tablets are not divided from one another. Thus, again, three lines of descent are presented as representing two classes of dead. According to Ong Hok-lai, the purpose of the partition on his altar is to keep the ancestors of different lines from quarreling. Like many other people in San-hsia, Ong believes that the original occupants of an ancestral altar may resent the presence of guests. He told me that one would not dare place the tablets of another line on an established altar without first obtaining permission from its present occupants.

As is so often the case with inquiries of this kind, my questions about Ong Hok-lai's ancestors led him into a discussion of inheritance. He told me that as the only representative of the Ong line he should have inherited all of his mother's property and that this was what his grandmother had intended. Consequently, he was angry when his mother divided the land equally among her five sons and told his brothers that they now had to worship the Ong ancestors "because you have taken Ong land." He claims that his brothers ignored this obligation, and, worse yet, neglected their mother in her old age. "We agreed that each of us would give her three *shih* of rice a year, but my brothers never gave her anything." In Ong Hok-lai's view, neglect of the Ong ancestors and neglect of his mother are intimately related to one another and to rights in property. We will see below that this is not unusual. Inheritance follows from descent and involves an obligation to care for the dead as well as for elderly members of the line.

The most interesting aspect of this case is the number and variety of ancestors worshiped by Ong Hok-lai. By descent he is only obligated to his mother, his grandmother, and their ascendants in the Ong line, but he also worships ancestors in the Tan line of his father and the Lim line of his grandfather. To keep track of all the deathdays he observes, Ong has written the names of the dead and their death dates in a notebook that he keeps on the main altar. The list includes his mother and his mother's mother; this woman's parents, grandparents, and great-grandparents; a man Ong identified as his mother's mother's grandfather's younger brother's son; Ong's father; this man's father's younger brother and his wife (to whom Ong's father was given in adoption as a child); Ong's grandfather and his parents; and, finally, Ong's first wife, a total of sixteen people, not counting the tablets Ong's second wife worships in the kitchen. It is cases like this that defeat the search for simple answers. I can see why Ong Hok-lai worships his father and his grandfather: they contributed children and labor to his line and were members of his family. But why does he make deathday offerings to his father's foster parents and his grandfather's parents? And why does he worship his great-great-grandfather's younger brother's son? He told me that he ought to worship this man's parents as well but cannot because he does not know their names.


THE UI ALTAR

During one of my conversations with Ong Hok-lai I expressed surprise at the fact that the altar in his *kong-tia:* contains tablets belonging to three lines of descent. He assured me that this was not unusual and to make his point introduced me to his neighbor, Lou Thian-co, who lives in a large compound a hundred yards down the mountain. I only talked to Lou on this one occasion and did not have a chance to look for altars in backrooms, but I did see that there are ,three incense burners and three sets of tablets on the main altar in the *kong-tia:*. These are, from stage left to stage right, a large set of tablets for people surnamed Ui, an equally large set for people surnamed Lou, and a single tablet for a woman named Li. The genealogy given in Figure 3 explains the origins of these tablets. Lou Thian-co's mother married into a Ui family. When her first husband died without descen-

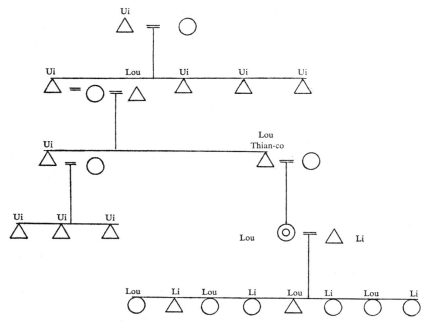

Figure 3.  Genealogy of the Ui family

dants, her father-in-law arranged a marriage for her with a man named Lou. Their eldest son was assigned to carry on the line of the first husband, while the second son, Lou Thian-co, was assigned to his father's line. The tablets at stage left represent the ancestors of the original Ui line; those at their right were brought by Lou Thian-co's father when he married into the family. Because he did not have any sons, Lou Thian-co arranged an uxorilocal marriage for his adopted daughter. The single tablet for the woman surnamed Li is her husband's mother's tablet.

I asked Lou Thian-co why his son-in-law had brought his mother's tablet but not his father's tablet. He explained that his son's-in-law mother was her husband's second wife and that this man had sons by his first wife. They told Lou's son-in-law that while he did not have to worship his father, he had to take his mother's tablet with him if he married out of the family. We should not make too much of the fact that Lou's son-in-law does not worship his father, since I suspect that his parents were not married. But the case is interesting as an example of the way tablets are moved from altar to altar. The mother's tablet spent a few years on her "husband's" altar and was then moved to the Ui altar when her son married Lou Thian-co's daughter. When

Lou dies his son-in-law will probably move out of the old house in the mountains and take both the Lou tablets and his mother's tablet with him. The Ui altar will then be the exclusive seat of the Ui ancestors. Ancestral tablets are not placed on an altar to remain there forever. The dead are as subject to the vicissitudes of life as the living.

The rites performed at the Ui altar are also interesting as evidence of the relative importance of descent and filiation. Lou Thian-co told me that "except for their own parents, the Uis worship the Uis; the Lous, the Lous; and the Lis, the Lis." I asked him if this meant that while his older brother worshiped all of the ancestors in the Ui line, he did not worship anyone in the Lou line except his father. He assured me that this was the case and noted that while he worshiped all the Lou ancestors, he did not worship any of the Uis except his own mother. This example argues that while descent and filiation operate independently, descent is the heavier obligation in that it extends to more people. The problem is that people like Ong Hok-lai worship the forebears of men who married into their family as well as the remote dead of their own line. It is hard to know where obligation leaves off and personal enthusiasm begins.


THE HONG ALTAR

What I call the Hong altar is a domestic altar located in the home of a man I will refer to as Tan Thian-lai. I asked my assistant to introduce me to Tan after he told me that the altar in Tan's home contained five sets of ancestral tablets and five incense burners. I had seen many altars with two sets of tablets and several with three sets, but I had never seen one with five sets and was curious to know how the dead of so many lines had collected in one place. It turned out that one of the five sets of tablets was a rotating lineage shrine and therefore only a temporary resident of Tan Thian-lai's altar. Tan told me that before land reform the lineage consisted of his family and six others who held two *chia* of upland as corporate property, the use of which was rotated in a regular fashion. I did not inquire further because by this time I had investigated four or five similar organizations and was convinced that they are commonplace. My interest was aroused by the other four sets of tablets. The position of honor was occupied by tablets for people surnamed Hong followed by tablets for people surnamed Ng, Yu:, and finally Tan. My assistant had told me beforehand that Tan Thian-lai's father had married into a Yu: family,

but he had not mentioned anyone named Hong or Ng and no living
member of the family bore either of these surnames.

Figure 4 outlines the story as I have it from Tan Thian-lai. A man
by the name of Hong Hue-lieng arranged an uxorilocal marriage for
his adopted daughter with a man surnamed Ng. This couple died without children and as a result a man named Yu: who had been the
"manager" of the Hong estate claimed it as his own. He then married
Tan Thian-lai's mother but died shortly thereafter without descendants.
At this point Tan Thian-lai's mother called in Tan's father who
brought with him his elderly parents. The essence of the matter is that
an estate originally owned by the Hong line passed to the Ng line and
then to the Yu: line and finally to the Tan line. Tan Thian-lai is an
inarticulate man and could not explain why this sequence of events
obliges him to worship all these people, but it is clear from what little
he did say that the obligation came with the property. Asked why he
continues to make offerings to the two Hong tablets on his altar, he
replied: "Because they once owned the whole mountain. They were
the first owners of the land."

I offer this case in support of Ahern's contention that inheritance
requires ancestor worship regardless of descent (1973: 149). I would
only have the reader note that while the Tans worship the Hong and
Ng ancestors, they have not made an effort to continue their lines.
This cannot be because these are obligations once removed. Tan

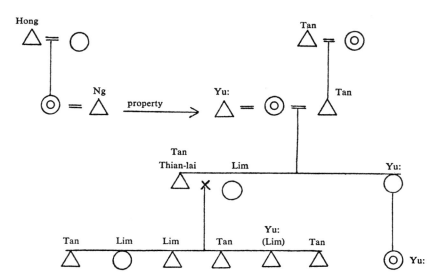

Figure 4.   Genealogy of the Hong family

Thian-lai's sister takes her descent from her mother's first husband and is therefore under the same obligation to Hong and Ng as was Yu:. It appears that while inheritance requires worship of one's benefactor, it does not require one to appoint children to continue his line. If the Tans had neglected the Hong and Ng tablets or relegated them to a backroom, one could argue that they did not assign children to these lines because they had decided to ignore their obligations. But the fact is that they make regular offerings to both the Hong and the Ng dead and have placed their tablets in the most honored positions on their altar. This argues that the debt owed to the Hong and Ng ancestors must be of a different kind than that owed to the Yu: and Tan ancestors.

The link between ancestor worship and property rights is so close that disputes over property often take the form of disputes over the possession of ancestral tablets. Although I was not aware of it at the time I interviewed Tan Thian-lai, the recent history of his family provides a dramatic case in point. Tan was a reluctant informant and I assumed that this was related to the fact that all of his children are illegitimate. In fact, his reluctance probably had more to do with his sister's daughter's marriage. Because she was the only child assigned to the Yu: line, this woman could have rightfully claimed her mother's first husband's estate. The question never arose in her lifetime because she did not marry, but it did arise when her daughter married. Encouraged by her fiancé and his mother, the daughter attempted to assert her rights as the only living representative of the Yu: line. Her mother's brother countered by assigning one of his sons to the Yu: line, insisting that if his niece were to inherit she would have to marry uxorilocally. In the realm of the dead the dispute revolved around possession of the Yu: tablets. Tan Thian-lai wanted to keep all of the tablets and was adamant in the case of his sister's tablet. His niece's fiancé's mother later told me that Tan could not allow the girl to take her mother's tablet without giving her the right to inherit Yu: property.

The dispute was finally resolved by means of an uneasy compromise. Tan Thian-lai retained the property and his sister's tablet, but agreed to forego his right to a bride price and gave his niece possession of the other Yu: tablets. The fact that Tan surrendered the majority of the Yu: tablets is significant because by this he acknowledged his niece's status as a representative of the Yu: line. Had all of the Yu: tablets remained on Tan Thian-lai's altar, her marriage would have put her in the position of a woman who has taken her share of her family's estate in the form of a dowry. The fact that she took Yu:

tablets with her and continues to worship Yu: ancestors gives the girl a chance of renewing her claims at some later date. I learned of all this when I later interviewed the niece's mother-in-law who knew that I had been talking to Tan Thian-lai. Probably because she was anxious to publicize the fact that her daughter-in-law had brought Yu: tablets with her, she allowed me to inspect the box in which the tablets were kept. We were both surprised to discover that the tablets in the box were all blank. Apparently Tan Thian-lai had decided that it would be a mistake to surrender any of the Yu: tablets and so had substituted blank slips of wood for the originals.

## THE TI: AND LIM ALTARS

I have saved the case of the Ti: and Lim altars for the last because they provide further evidence for several of my points and at the same time illustrate the difficulties involved in collecting adequate and accurate information. The genealogy in Figure 5 was given to me by Ti: Hok-hin in the course of explaining why it is that there are two sets of tablets and two incense burners on the domestic altar in his house. Ti: told me that the single tablet in the position of honor at the left was for a man surnamed Ong who had married into Ti:'s mother's foster family. The tablets at the right were identified as Ti:'s parents and his father's agnatic ascendants. What I took to be critical information was volunteered when I asked Ti: why he did not worship anyone in the Lim line. He explained that his mother had been raised to marry a son of the Lim family who was "killed by aborigines at age sixteen." Because the Lim family had only one other son, they then called in a husband for their "daughter-in-law." The agreement was that their eldest son was to take his descent from his mother, the second from his father, the third from his mother, and so on. But, according to Ti:, only the eldest son, Lim Lai-ho, was registered as a Lim and so he inherited all of the Lim property. The answer to my question appeared to be that the responsibility for the Lim tablets belonged solely to Lim Lai-ho because he had inherited. The younger brothers had been cheated and therefore refused to worship the Lims. Later the same day I visited the home of Ti: Hok-hin's older brother, Ti: Chieng-cua. His wife's account of the family genealogy was essentially the same as that I had had from Ti: Hok-hin except that she insisted that her husband's real name was Lim. I was convinced when she showed me that the *kong-tik-pun* [merit book] prepared for her

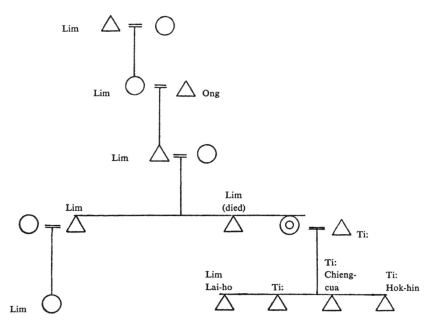

Figure 5. Genealogy of the Lim family

father's-in-law funeral lists her husband as Lim Chieng-cua. By this time I was prepared to believe the worst about Lim Lai-ho and as a result misinterpreted the fact that his altar does not contain a tablet for his father. I concluded that if a man does not take his descent from his father and has brothers who do, he is not obliged to worship his father. I knew other men in similar circumstances who did worship their fathers, but was now prepared to interpret their behavior as expressing sentiment rather than obligation. The argument I set down in my notes was premised on the assumption that Lim Lai-ho was anything but a sentimental man and this in turn on the belief that he had cheated his brothers.

It was not until I checked my field notes against the Japanese household registers that I discovered that my argument was built on quicksand. The truth is that Ti: Hok-hin's mother did marry her foster brother and that Lim Lai-ho is their son. Indeed, I later learned, quite by accident, that the Ti:s were forced to publicly acknowledge the fact that Lim Lai-ho is not Ti:'s son. To support her view that the dead are capable of inflicting misfortunes on the living, a neighbor of the Ti:s told me that when Ti: Hok-hin's father died, his sons erected a tombstone that credited him with four male children. For some reason, they counted Lim Lai-ho as well as the three Ti: brothers. When several of the Ti: children fell ill shortly thereafter, everyone agreed that the agent was Lim Lai-ho's real father who did not want his son counted as one of Ti:'s sons. The Ti:s then admitted their error by changing the inscription on the tombstone from four sons to three sons.

Though Lim Lai-ho's real father may have been killed by aborigines, this is unlikely. According to the household registers, he died in 1910 at age twenty-nine. And while Ti: Hok-hin's father may have lived with the Lims for a time, he did not marry into the family. The truth is that Ti: Hok-hin's mother divorced her first husband and married into the Ti: family. It is true that Ti: Chieng-cua did at one time bear the surname Lim, but only because he was given in adoption to a Lim family unrelated to Lim Lai-ho. The relationship between the Lim and Ti: families is confused by the fact that after divorcing a girl raised to be his wife, Lim Lai-ho married his mother's adopted daughter and went to live with the Ti: family. This may have given the Ti:s the hope that Lim Lai-ho would divide his share of the Lim estate with his half-brothers, but he was not under any obligation to do so.

I cannot explain why Ti: Hok-hin and Ti: Chieng-cua's wife gave me such a distorted account of their family's recent history. I may have misunderstood part of what I was told, but there was no mistaking Ti: Chieng-cua's wife's purpose in showing me the *kong-tik-pun*. Her point was that her husband had been assigned to the Lim line as agreed and that he had therefore had a right to inherit. There is obviously a great deal about the case that I do not understand, but it is at least clear why there are no Ti: tablets on Lim Lai-ho's altar. By Chinese reckoning, Lim's only link to the Ti: line is through his second wife. The problem is not to explain why Lim Lai-ho does not worship his father, but why he worships his mother. He is under no obligation to do so because his mother divorced his father and thereby terminated her relationship with his line. Dare I conclude that Lim Lai-ho is a sentimental man who worships his mother because he wants to? I would be inclined to do so if I could explain why Ti: Hok-hin worships a man surnamed Ong. There must be some tie other than the fact that a man named Lim is Ti:'s mother's first husband and Ong's grandson.

The data presented in this paper are too slight to serve as the basis for any firm conclusions. The paper is best viewed as a short addendum to Emily Ahern's detailed study of ancestor worship in Ch'i-nan. I will therefore conclude by briefly commenting on a few of Ahern's arguments.

On the basis of her evidence from Ch'i-nan, Ahern argues that "if X inherits property from Y, he must worship Y" (1973: 149). What makes this proposition interesting is that it appears to hold regardless of whether or not X is Y's descendant. The only link between Tan Thian-lai and the original occupants of the Hong altar is the fact that property passed from the Hongs to the Ngs to the Yu:s and finally to Tan Thian-lai's father. This case and others collected by Sung Lung-sheng argue that a person who inherits property is obligated to worship his benefactors.[5] But what then of descent and filiation? It is Ahern's view that "if X is a direct descendant of Y, he may or may not worship Y" (1973: 149). He is only obligated to worship Y if he is "Y's only descendant" or "the most obligated descendant."

To support her second proposition, Ahern notes that married women do not worship their parents if they have brothers who fulfill this duty. Evidently, she is using the term "descendant" to mean "child of." Granted this use of the term, the proposition is correct. But it may still be that descent (in the common anthropological sense of the term) creates an absolute obligation to worship the dead. The only evidence to the contrary in Ahern's book is the fact that uxorilocally married men do not always worship their ascendants. But this is equivocal evidence at best. Even when they retain their own surnames, men who marry uxorilocally are sometimes disowned on the grounds that they have deserted their parents. And occasionally uxorilocal marriages are the products of quarrels that force men out of their natal families. In either case these are exceptions that prove the rule because they involve a breach of the normal ties between a man and his ascendants.

Although the evidence is far from conclusive, I am inclined to the view that both descent and inheritance create an absolute obligation to the dead. Moreover, I think that men (but not women) are obligated to worship their parents, regardless of where they take their descent. Though Lou Thian-co's brother takes his descent from his mother's first husband, he worships his father as well as his ascendants in the Ui line. And obviously this is not because he is "the most obligated" of his father's children. Lou Thian-co takes his descent from the Lous and inherited the Lou property. It appears to me that men always worship parents who have fulfilled their duties as parents. A man does not ordinarily worship his mother if she divorces his father or marries

---

[5]   Sung Lung-sheng's material was collected as part of a detailed study of inheritance in San-hsia and Shu-lin. A preliminary report of this study will soon be available in the form of a Ph.D. dissertation submitted to the Department of Anthropology, Stanford University.

out of the family as a widow, but this is only because a woman who breaks all ties with her son's line ceases to be her son's mother.

I think Ahern is right to stress the relationship between ancestor worship and property. The case of the Hong altar argues that a man who receives property without giving compensation is obligated to worship his benefactors, and Tan Thian-lai's dispute with his sister's daughter suggests that ancestral rites also constitute a claim to property. On the other hand, I feel that Ahern's formulas make too little of descent. In my view, descent creates an even heavier obligation than inheritance. Though Tan Thian-lai's father cared for the Hong and Ng dead as well as for his own ascendants, he did not appoint any of his children to either the Hong or the Ng line. This argues that where both descent and inheritance create an obligation to care for the dead, only descent creates an obligation to perpetuate a line.

Whether or not further evidence supports Ahern's propositions, they make an important contribution by drawing a distinction between absolute and conditional obligation. If the evidence presented in this essay accomplishes nothing else, it should at least demonstrate that the obligation of ancestor worship does not follow from any one, simple principle. My guess at this point is that the great diversity of relationships involved in ancestor worship can only be accounted for by recognizing that people owe conditional obligations to a wide range of dead who are not ordinarily worshiped because they have descendants of their own. These include men who married into one's family and contributed children and labor to one's line, their ascendants, and perhaps also the ascendants of women who married into the line. Indeed, the fact that people worship dead who gave them property may best be formulated as an example of a conditional obligation. One must worship one's parents and the senior members of one's line regardless of whether or not they are worshiped by others. But if they do not have descendants or children of their own, one must also worship people who have made a substantial contribution to one's welfare.

Why then did Song Suat appoint one of her sons to care for the Ti: and Tiu: dead? And why do people commonly provide for the souls of unmarried daughters who have taken more than they have given? The answer can only be that obligation is not the only motive for ancestor worship. The belief that the dead are dependent on offerings received from the living causes people to provide for deceased dependents for the same reason they provide for living dependents. They are concerned about their welfare and do not want them to go hungry. The best evidence for this view is the fact that the tablets of dependent dead are never located on the same altar as those of people to whom one is obligated by descent. They are outsiders and are therefore relegated to an altar or a shelf in a backroom of the house. I have argued elsewhere that because they are worshiped for reasons of charity rather than out of obligation they are almost ghosts (Wolf 1974).

The arrangement of ancestral tablets in the Ch'i-nan lineage halls and in the Song and Ong compounds suggests that people also distinguish those dead to whom they owe an absolute obligation from those to whom they owe only a conditional obligation. In Ch'i-nan the tablets of men who married into the community are excluded from the lineage halls, being located instead on domestic altars in the homes into which they married. In the Lim and Ong compounds they are allowed on the main altar in the *kong-tia:*, but are separated from the tablets of the Lim and Ong lines by small wooden partitions. This, together with the fact that the tablets of dependents are never honored with a place in a *kong-tia:*, argues that all dead are sorted into three classes. At one extreme, we find those dead to whom people owe absolute obligations; at the other, those to whom they are not obligated at all.

The placement of tablets also provides some evidence for my view that there are three types of ancestral altars: domestic altars, communal altars, and lineage shrines. On all of the altars examined in this paper the tablets of each line are arranged as a set and are served by a separate incense burner. Indeed, I have never seen an altar on which which the tablets of the same line were served by different burners. But there are differences in the way in which burners and their associated tablets are arranged with respect to one another. The four lineage shrines in Ch'i-nan contain only the tablets of deceased members of the lineage, and it appears that the same was once true of the shrine of the Tan lineage in Liu-ts'u-p'u. All of the other altars discussed contain the tablets of two or more lines, but the way the tablets of host and guest lines are arranged with respect to one another varies. Where two of the three communal altars (the Lim and the Ong) divide hosts from guests by means of a partition, there are no partitions on either of the two domestic altars (the Hong and the Ti:). These differences argue that the distinctions I am making are not arbitrary. The three types of altars reflect real differences in the nature of the three types of groups they serve.

My final point concerns the fact that the Ch'i-nan lineages worship the Stove God in their halls. I think this reflects the fact that the Ch'i-nan lineages are small and exceptionally cohesive. My guess is that until lineages reach a certain size and begin to segment, they attempt to maintain internal solidarity by modeling themselves on the family. I realize that it is anthropological heresy to suggest that lineages are like families, but perhaps China is different. After all, the imperial government made good use of the family as a model. Why not lineages? Unfortunately, my hypothesis cannot be tested by looking to other lineages in the San-hsia area, since the others were either too poor to build halls or have long since abandoned them. Like many of the other hypotheses suggested in this paper, this one will have to wait for further evidence collected by fresh researchers.

## REFERENCES

AHERN, EMILY
  1973   *The cult of the dead in a Chinese village.* Stanford: Stanford University Press.
FREEDMAN, MAURICE
  1958   *Lineage organization in southeastern China.* London: Athlone Press.
FRIED, MORTON H.
  1970   Clans and lineages: how to tell them apart and why — with special reference to Chinese society. *Bulletin of the Institute of Ethnology, Academia Sinica* 29:11–36.
WOLF, ARTHUR P.
  1974   "Gods, ghosts, and ancestors," in *Religion and ritual in Chinese society.* Edited by Arthur P. Wolf. Stanford: Stanford University Press.

# Ancestors Proper and Peripheral

SUNG-HSING WANG

In the last section of a recent article, I pointed out that the Chinese and Japanese concepts of "ancestor" are clearly different (Wang 1971). The Chinese are strongly patrilineal. Every man worships his father and, in turn, is worshiped by his son or sons. The Japanese differ from the Chinese in that an individual's relation to the ancestor in terms of descent is not of primary importance. Economic and residential factors are responsible for the formation of the *dōzoku* (see Nakane 1967: 105–107). Goody, who studied the mortuary customs of the Lodagaa of West Africa, reserves the phrase "ancestor worship" for examples such as the Chinese in which the living and the dead are kin of one another (Goody 1962: 381).

It is true that the relationship of the living to the dead is much emphasized by the Chinese. According to their kinship pattern, the Chinese in Taiwan classify ancestors roughly into two categories: those who are patrilineal forebears and those who are nonpatrilineal kin. In this article I shall call the former "proper ancestors" and the latter "peripheral ancestors."

Many studies on Chinese ancestor worship have been concerned with proper ancestors and mainly in terms of lineage organization, of *feng-shui*, and jural-authority relationship. In fact, ancestor worship in Chinese society is one aspect of its emphasis on the continuity of the family line through agnatic descendants. The ancestors of a family without interruption of its line include only its patrilineal predecessors, or members sharing the surname. However, sometimes a family might have no agnatic descendants and then the continuation of the family line becomes an issue. There are several alternatives: for example, if the family has a daughter they would call in a son-in-law, or *Chao chui*; or the ancestor tablets of that interrupted family would follow their nearest kin and would be worshiped in another family. The ancestors worshiped by nonpatrilineal members are the peripheral ancestors of the family in question. Sometimes the ancestors of the natal family of a "called-in" husband are included in this category. Patrilineal and peripheral ancestral tablets are discriminated by placing the latter in less ritually important parts of a dwelling unit.

A brief description of a Taiwanese farmer's compound will explain the ritual significance of tablet location. In a dwelling with five rooms, for example, the central room is the main room or *cheng t'ing* of the family. On one side of the *cheng t'ing* is the *ta fang* or senior bedroom, which must be assigned to the eldest son and his wife. When the family increases the house is enlarged by the addition of wings at both ends, giving the dwelling a U shape (see Figure 1).

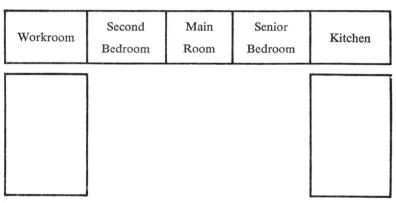

Figure 1.

The *cheng t'ing* is the most important ritual place in a dwelling. For example, when an agnatic member of the family or his spouse is dying, they are moved to the family's *cheng t'ing*. The deities and ancestors are worshiped inside this room. Upon a large, carved altar table which faces the entrance are placed the ancestor tablet or tablets, and to their left, if the family possesses one, the deity image. The *cheng t'ing* is the symbol of continuity of the family line. It is exempt from division during family partition. The family partition is mainly in terms of housing, represented by the dividing of stove and bedroom. Ritually, the *cheng t'ing* is significantly different from other parts of the dwelling.

Each family has its own ancestral tablet. When brothers divide their parents' family, some of them move out of the original dwelling and then copy and set up a tablet in a *cheng t'ing* of their own. A tablet is like a genealogical table which records the ancestors of that family line. Across the top of it is written the place of origin. In most places it is a place in southern Fukien or eastern Kwantung from where their ancestor had migrated. Down the center is written vertically: "The seats of ancestors of all generations of [surname]." At the bottom of the left side is written "dedicated to [name] by the descendants in this world forever." On a board set behind it are recorded the dates of birth and death of the ancestors. Besides these records, some families also show details of their family history.

Let us look at the tablet of a Huang family collected on the island of Kuei-shan, Taiwan. In addition to the family history the following is recorded: the paternal great-great-grandparents' names; the great-grandparents' names, with the dates of and ages at death; the grandparents' names, with the dates, times of, and ages at death; and the name of the fourth younger brother, with his birth date and time, and the death date and time. Thus the more recent generations are recorded in more detail. The kin terms on the tablet are based on the eldest living male member in the family. Ideally, only patrilineal members are included, but sometimes collateral agnatic kin without descendants are listed, as in the case of the fourth younger brother mentioned on this tablet.

The situation for a nonpatrilineal member is quite different. He is not allowed to die in the *cheng t'ing*, nor may his coffin pass through its door. His *shen chu p'ai* [tablet] if he has one, is not placed in the *cheng t'ing* but in the kitchen, or under the eaves, or at some place ritually unimportant. Most such tablets are brought in by a bride or a called-in husband, whose natal families have no descendants to worship them. Following are three examples collected in P'u Hsin of Chang-hua *hsien* in central Taiwan.[1]

Our first example (Figure 2) relates to Hsu Huang a called-in husband who adopted his wife's surname (Hsu) before his own surname

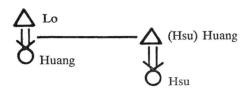

Figure 2.

[1]  I am indebted to my assistant, Chen Hsiang-hsui, of the Institute of Ethnology, Academia Sinica, for his help in collecting field data.

(Huang). In his family they worship ancestors of three different surnames, namely Hsu, Huang, and Lo. As shown in Figure 2, Hsu
Huang's father is surnamed Lo and was also a husband called into
Huang's family. Only the Hsu ancestor tablet is worshiped in the *cheng
t'ing*; the other two are worshiped in the kitchen. In the kitchen the Lo
tablet is placed to the left of the Huang tablet. This indicates that
Huang is of higher status than Lo.

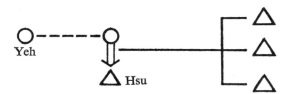

Figure 3.

Our second example (Figure 3) concerns a woman called Yeh. She
had no children and adopted a daughter, who is now Mrs. Hsu. When
Mrs. Hsu's marriage was being arranged, Yeh insisted that her adopted
daughter should marry a called-in husband; i.e. a man who was willing
to look after the Yeh family, including the living (Yeh herself) and the
dead (Yeh's ancestors). At first the Yeh tablet was placed in a room in
the wing building of the Hsu family. Later, the wing collapsed. The
family erected a small bamboo hut in the same place and worshiped
the Yeh ancestors there for about twenty years. Recently, however,
members of the Hsu family have experienced ill-luck: their children and
the housewife have been ill. They asked the deities the cause of the
sickness. The answer was that the Yeh ancestors were haunting them,
because they were displeased about being placed in the small bamboo
hut and wanted to enter the *cheng t'ing* of the Hsu family. At first
Hsu's ancestors refused to let them enter their *cheng t'ing*. Finally,
after negotiations by the deities with the Hsu ancestors, it was decided
to place them in the *cheng t'ing*. The Yeh tablet was placed on the left
of the Hsu tablet and on a lower table. However, the bad luck of the
family was not over, because the Yeh ancestors still tried to take over
the place of the Hsu ancestors in this family. The housewife threatened
the Yeh ancestors and said: "You should be satisfied with being in this
room. If you continue to haunt us, nobody will like to worship you
again." After this there was a short period of peace. But when the
housewife had her third son and suffered from serious illness, the deities
told them that the Yeh ancestors were begging for a descendant and

wanted the third son to be the Yeh family heir. The housewife did not recover from illness, though the third son was surnamed Yeh. They asked the deities again. The answer was that the Hsu ancestors had become angry about this decision. Through the negotiation by the deities on both sides, the Hsu and Yeh ancestors agreed that the third son should adopt a double surname. Incidentally, the Yeh family owns 0.2 hectares of paddy field which will be inherited by the third son.

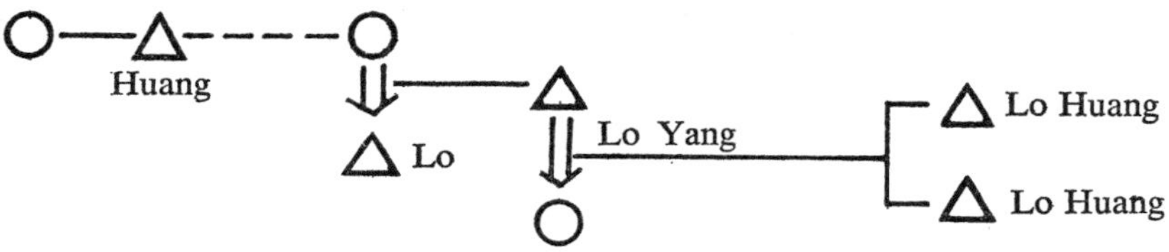

Figure 4.

Figure 4 shows our third example. Lo Yang's family has two types of ancestral tablets. One is surnamed Lo, the proper ancestor of this family, and the other is surnamed Huang, brought in by his mother. When his mother married into the Lo family, she was accompanied by her foster grandmother and a piece of land, because the Huang family had no descendant. At first, the Huang tablet was placed in the kitchen when Lo Yang was living with his brothers in the same dwelling unit. Later, Lo Yang built his new house and now has his own *cheng t'ing*. The Huang tablet then was moved to the *cheng t'ing* and is now placed on the left of the Lo tablet on a lower table. Huang's ancestors had been haunting this family until they decided to let Lo Yang's two sons succeed two family lines and adopt double family names (Lo Huang).

People believe that the peripheral ancestors will cause trouble if they are not treated well. Some peripheral ancestors even have no tablet. People tend to remember this after they have experienced ill-luck.

A woman in Lun-ya, Hua-t'an, where I conducted field work from November 1970 to March 1971, told me that her son went mad. They asked the deities why. The deities told them that a spirit haunted him. The spirit is her husband's father's wife's brother, who has no descendant. She promised to offer him some food and paper money on the first and fifteenth of each lunar month. She worshiped him outside the courtyard of the dwelling. Her son did not recover because the spirit insisted that he should have his own tablet, which should be placed inside the door. She promised she would do this only if her son had really recovered.

In his article in this volume, Li Yih-yuan mentions two tables which list the misfortunes caused by spirits of relatives. He classifies the items into two categories: misfortunes caused by problem of *feng-shui* and misfortunes caused by problems other than *feng-shui*. The former, concerning *feng-shui* issues, are those caused by spirits of proper ancestors, such as father, mother, husband, and grandfather. The latter have nothing to do with *feng-shui* and are mostly caused by peripheral ancestors (such as the spirits of stepfather, ex-husband, ex-wife, sister, and daughter) or (in Li's terms), "by having tablets of different surnames in the same house."

The peripheral ancestors are thought of as the cause of misfortunes in a family. The explanations are of many kinds: "begging for food," which means the spirits want someone to worship them; "demanding descendants," which means that they want someone to have their surname. The ultimate goal of a peripheral ancestor is to be placed in the *cheng t'ing* and to have descendants to continue his family line, such as in the second example (Figure 3) mentioned above.

So, if a girl is responsible for the care of a tablet from her natal family, which would be the peripheral ancestors of the bridegroom's family, then it is considered a disadvantage for her marriage. A tablet which is brought by a bride might be able to enter the *cheng t'ing* in the following generation, especially if the bride brought along some property as in the case of both the second and third examples. Such a case is very frequent in the fishing village of Kuei-shan Island, where almost every household has its own *cheng t'ing*. The fishermen there do this because they try to prevent troubles caused by discontented peripheral spirits. They even have multiple-surname ancestral tablets. The following, shown in Figure 5, is an example (Wang 1967: 70).

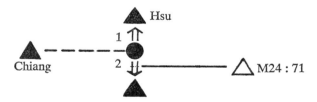

Figure 5.

M24 : 71's mother was an adopted daughter of the Chiang family. The Chiang family had no child. His mother first married a Hsu man, but they had no children. After the Hsu man's death she married M24 : 71's father, a Ch'en man. Now M24 : 71's family worships ancestors of three surnames. On a tablet is written: "Seats of the Ancestors of Ch'en

Hsu Chiang." M24 : 71 explained this is for the convenience of worship.

An excessive feeling for patrilineality sometimes also causes a family to worship more than one surname tablet such as in our first example above. Here again let me give an example from Kuei-shan Island, shown in Figure 6:

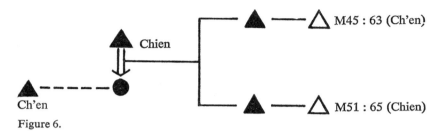

Figure 6.

There are two ancestral tablets in the *cheng t'ing* of M45 : 63. One is for the Ch'en surname and the other is Chien. M45 : 63 is surnamed Ch'en after his father. But his grandfather was surnamed Chien who married an adopted daughter of Ch'en's family as a called-in husband. According to the custom of *ch'ou chu mu sui* [to levy sow tax],[2] the eldest son of the married-in husband takes the wife's family name. So his father took Ch'en's family name and had the tablet of the Ch'en surname. However, M45 : 63 still insisted that his ancestors were surnamed Chien. So, in the *cheng t'ing* of M45 : 63 and his two brothers, besides worshiping the Ch'en ancestral tablet, they worship Chien's too. But Ch'en's tablet is placed to the left of Chien's. This means that Ch'en's are still the proper ancestors of these families. In the *cheng t'ing* of Chien's or M51 : 65's family, there is no Ch'en tablet. (Wang 1967: 71).

The appearance of peripheral ancestors in the Chinese patrilineal society might convey the wrong image of patrilineality breaking down. In fact, on the contrary, it shows that the patrilineal principle is still deeply rooted in the minds of the people. Classification into agnatic and nonagnatic ancestors, which is the central theme of this paper, is emphasized. The worship of peripheral ancestors is an alternative mode of ancestor worship in order to keep the family line from being terminated. This has received little attention by either Chinese or foreign anthropologists. As stated by Elliott (1955: 15), "it is partly due to the fact that the religions of China have received far more extensive treat-

---

[2] The girl who remains in her natal family and calls in a husband is regarded as a "sow"; the girl's family takes a son from the married couple as the fee of the sow to succeed in the family line.

ment as systems of thought than as practical expressions of popular belief."

## REFERENCES

ELLIOTT, ALAN J. A.
    1955   *Chinese spirit-medium cults in Singapore.* London School of Economics Monographs on Social Anthropology 14. London: Athlone Press.

GOODY, JACK
    1962   *Death, property and the ancestors: a study of the mortuary customs of the Lodagaa of West Africa.* London: Tavistock.

NAKANE, CHIE
    1967   *Kinship and economic organization in rural Japan.* London School of Economics Monographs on Social Anthropology 32. London: Athlone Press.

WANG, SUNG-HSING
    1967   *Kwei-shan Tao: a study of a Chinese fishing community in Formosa* (in Chinese). Monograph 13, Institute of Ethnology, Academia Sinica. Taipei.
    1971   *A comparative study of ancestor worship of the Chinese and the Japanese* (in Chinese). *Bulletin of the Institute of Ethnology Academia Sinica,* 31. Taipei.

# The Ancestors at Home: Domestic Worship in a Land-Poor Taiwanese Village

C. STEVAN HARRELL

The study of Chinese ancestor worship has been concentrated in farming communities, most of them places with some sort of lineage organization. Study in such places has produced several major findings, three of which I wish to discuss here. First, Chinese ancestor worship is two separate cults, one a series of rites which express the unity of a lineage or lineage segment (Freedman's "hall cult") and the other a group of rites which continue the acts of filial obedience to recently deceased forebears (Freedman's "domestic cult" or "cult of immediate jural superiors") (Freedman 1958: 90). Though these two cults may not be physically distinct (Ahern 1973), they are functionally distinct: agnatic solidarity is more important in the worship of distant ancestors, in which large groups of agnates ordinarily participate, while continuance of filial obligation is more important in the worship of close ancestors, which usually involves only members of one family or a small group of families.

Another finding is that ancestor worship in China is intimately connected with property inheritance: while every deceased person must receive offerings from at least one descendant to provide him with sustenance in the other world, once this obligation is fulfilled, it is not necessary for a particular living person to worship a particular ancestor unless he has inherited property, directly or indirectly, from that ancestor. He may do so because he personally feels some other obligation, but he it is not required. In particular, an ancestral tablet need be erected only to an ancestor who has transmitted property to the descendant. (Johnston 1910: 284–5; Ahern 1973: 212ff.)

A third finding is that Chinese seek to exclude from their ancestral shrines the tablets and incense burners of forebears who were members of lines of descent other than those represented in the principal tablets. Various exigencies may cause such tablets to appear on domestic altars, but they are erected only when their omission might cause some deceased person to go unworshiped altogether, and even then they are often placed in a subordinate shrine next to, and lower than, the main altar, or even on a shelf in a back room.

In light of these three findings, we can ask an interesting question: what happens to ancestor worship in a community where there are no lineages, where almost nobody owned land until recently, and where an unusually large proportion of households contains members of two or more lines of descent? Such a community is Ploughshare Village, where I did ethnographic research in 1972–73. Located on a point of land at the confluence of two streams, it contains little land suitable for rice cultivation. Because it was settled later than the surrounding areas, settlers on the plain above the village and landlords living in the neighboring market town of San-hsia had already claimed any land that was cultivable before Ploughshare itself was settled. So in the late nineteenth century, while a few villagers were tenants on other people's rice land, most of them were forced to eke a living out of the mountains surrounding Ploughshare and the nearby plains. They were unable to actually live in or close to the mountains because of the danger of aborigine raids, but they used the mountains to grow tea and to cut wood which they made into charcoal for sale. When the aborigines were "pacified" and coal mines opened up in the mountains in the early part of this century, many village men went to work as miners, and both men and women took jobs as pushers on the pushcart railway which ran from the town of Yingko into the mountains where the mines were located. As in the nineteenth century, a few (less than 25 percent) village families relied on tenant farming for part of their incomes, and most families who held mountain land continued to grow tea on it. In the Japanese period (1895–1945), only two families resident in Ploughshare ever owned rice land — one of these was the richest in the village, owning two sizeable parcels of paddy in other communities, and the other was the family of the village head, who bought a little land for security after becoming wealthy in the tea processing business.

After the land reform of the early 1950's, those villagers who had been tenant farmers became owner farmers; today 24 of 100 households in the village own some rice land. Of these 24, however, only five own enough to make farming the sole occupation of one or more household members. Until the early sixties, coal-mining, cart-pushing, and labor in distant areas continued to be the major sources of village income, supplemented by tea and later oranges grown on mountain land.

Since the early 1960's, village labor patterns have undergone another major change; industrial work opportunities have opened up in many areas. The pushcart railway was supplanted by a truck road on the other side of the San-hsia River in 1962, but the jobs it provided were more than replaced by work available in local factories, producing wood, plastics, and electronic goods and, in cottage industry, making sweaters for export on home-owned knitting machines. With the rise of these other opportunities, people have come to neglect their mountain land — the work is too hard and the return too small. But as in the Ch'ing and Japanese periods, the major source of village income is still outside of rice farming; the livelihood of most families is not dependent on scarce and heritable landholdings.[1]

In addition to being relatively landless, the villagers of Ploughshare have not developed any lineage organization. The largest group of agnatically related families contains eight households; two others have seven. None of these groups holds property in common or maintains a common ancestral altar. Families who share a surname but are not demonstrably related (there are twenty-six Ong families in the village) consider themselves no more closely related than any other villagers, and indeed it is common for older women not to know the surnames of people they see every day. In addition, affinal, matrilateral, and sworn kinship ties are often as important as, or more important than, agnatic ties. This lack of lineages is accounted for by several factors. The late date of settlement (after 1840) and the upheaval caused when the village was burned by occupying Japanese armies in 1895 both undoubtedly contributed, as did the great geographic mobility of laborers. Even in the Japanese period, many villagers went to work at coal, copper, and gold mines on the north coast of Taiwan, sugar refineries in the southern part of the island, or at other types of employment in other areas. Some returned and some did not. Mobility into the village has also been great; fourteen families who own houses and reside permanently in the village have come since 1940, and many others first arrived in the Japanese period. So unlike many Chinese villages, Ploughshare has no recognized internal divisions

---

[1]   Many villagers do, of course, own mountain land, but it is not considered in the same class with rice land as a form of property. Perhaps this is because mountain land is not scarce — more area is fallow than planted on practically any Taiwanese mountain — and because the living that can be derived from mountain land is a rather miserable one.

based on agnatic ties; the next discrete social unit above the household or perhaps group of brothers' households is the village itself, whose social structure is based on the local community and the network of dyadic ties within it, be they agnatic, affinal, sworn kinship, or simply close friendship, and not on lineage organization.

It should not be surprising that in a village which was poor, where land ownership was minimal, and where lineages never developed, marriages other than the normal virilocal types are more frequent than in other communities. There has not yet been time to analyze the data from a study of the household registration records for the Japanese period in Ploughshare Village, but a census made in the field in 1972 showed 16 percent of currently complete marriages (with both partners living in the village) to be uxorilocal, all of them first marriages for both parties. Wolf (1973: 22) found that in six neighboring districts, all richer than Ploughshare, the percentage of first marriages which were uxorilocal declined from 21.5 percent for women born 1891–95 to 9.00 percent for women born 1916–20. Since uxorilocal marriages are less stable than virilocal ones (Wolf 1973: 44), the percentage of uxorilocal marriages should be lower in a point-in-time sample than in the kind of diachronic data represented by household registration records. Instead, it is clearly higher in Ploughshare than in the other areas, a fact that fits both with Ploughshare's fluid social structure — a village which accepts outsiders who merely move in is also likely to accept them when they marry in — and with the villagers' lack of real property — a man with no land is less likely to worry about an outsider's inheriting it.

What effect does all this have on ancestor worship? First, the absence of any lineage organization means that ancestral rites in Ploughshare are reduced to the domestic cult pure and simple, with no trace of a hall or lineage cult. Freedman (1958: 84) describes the domestic cult as rites of "memorialism, in which ancestors were cared for simply as forebears and independently of their status as ancestors of the agnates of the worshippers." This description accurately portrays ancestor worship as practiced in Ploughshare. Of the eighty-five ancestral altars in the village in 1973, only four are shared by brothers who have divided their households, and none by groups of agnates of wider span than brothers. Of the four altars shared by divided brothers, one is used by two brothers, the younger of whom has no house of his own and lives in two rooms in his brother's house, and another by two brothers who live in a sprawling and rather run-down house with only one room suitable for erecting an ancestral altar. Even the other two sets of brothers who share altars have divided their property within the last six years. It is clear that the pattern in Ploughshare Village is for brothers to erect separate altars very soon after they divide their households. While I was living in Ploughshare, three new altars were set up — one a year and a half after division, one three years after division, and one by a man who, while long divided from his elder brothers, had just built a new house and for the first time had a place suitable for setting up a separate altar. Even the altar which was erected three years after division might have been put up sooner but for the fact that the division had entailed one brother and his wife's moving out and building a new house at the opposite end of the village in order to get away from a neurotic sister-in-law. All their financial resources were exhausted in building the house, and the altar was the first substantial piece of furniture which they purchased.

That the domestic cult exists in its pure form in Ploughshare is also indicated by the fact that rites and offerings get simpler, not more elaborate, as ancestors recede farther from memory. Just as the filial obligation of obedience and respect is greatest to one's own parents, just as the grief expressed in funeral ceremonies and mourning dress is greatest when the deceased is of an immediately superior generation to the mourner, the obligations of ancestral worship are felt most strongly for ancestors genealogically close to the worshiper. In Ploughshare people prepare extensive feasts for recently deceased ancestors — a group of four households, all worshiping their grandmother, dead only three years, on her deathday anniversary, spent the entire day before the celebration preparing special foods, some of which are ordinarily cooked only for major holidays. In another case, a village woman told me that now her family is well off they can have a proper feast, with two or three tables of guests, for her father's and mother's deathdays (she is uxorilocally married), though of course they would do no such thing for any more distant ancestor. I once saw this contrast in two deathday offerings prepared by the same family only a few days apart. The first was for the father-in-law of the old woman who is the senior member of the family — they invited me and several other guests to a substantial meal. A few days later, I was walking by their house and noticed that they had some offerings set out, and upon inquiry they told me, yes, they were celebrating a deathday anniversary, but it was for a distant ancestor whom none of them had ever known. The offerings were simpler and their attitude was one of bored obligation rather than enthusiastic celebration.

In this pure domestic cult, the villagers of Ploughshare do not only simplify their offerings as ancestors recede from memory, many of them also cease celebrating the deathday anniversaries of distant ones altogether, and give them combined offerings on Tiong-iong-ceq which is the ninth day of the ninth lunar month. One very knowledgeable villager told me this holiday should only be celebrated to commemorate victims of large-scale slaughters, such as those arising from the sack of a village, but the more common opinion is that Tiong-iong should be celebrated whenever the exact date of an ancestor's death is unknown. Despite even this belief, of the fifteen households where Tiong-iong was celebrated in 1972, only one family, which had been excessively poor and is still one of the poorest in Ploughshare, did not know the death dates of its ancestors. Another celebrated Tiong-iong because they had no suitable place to properly worship their ancestors.

Other villagers relegate to Tiong-iong-ceq those of their ancestors whom they consider least important. In two of these cases, the ancestors so shunted are agnatic forebears of uxorilocally married-in men whose virilocally married brothers also worship their ancestors at home on their deathday anniversaries. In all the other thirteen cases, the Tiong-iong ancestors are simply those who are more than one or two generations removed from the eldest living family members. Of these thirteen, five stated that they had celebrated deathdays for the now-shunted ancestors until a year or a few years ago, but that it was a lot less trouble to relegate them to a single day. One family, for example, had tablets for three generations of ancestors of its own surname, plus one set of parents of an uxorilocally married-in grandfather. The family head's wife told me that when her mother-in-law was alive, they had worshiped them all on deathdays, but now that she was dead and nobody still living had known any but her husband's parents and grandparents, they only celebrated deathdays for these four, and had relegated the others to Tiong-iong. Fifteen of eighty-five altars is, of course, a small percentage, but there is a definite trend in the direction of consolidating the rites of distant ancestors on Tiong-iong, and this seems a graphic illustration of the principle that obligations to ancestors weaken along with their memory. As Freedman (1958: 91) says, "people were involved with the dead whom they had known in life and towards whose happiness in the other world they could make some contribution."

A word should perhaps be said about the practice of burning or burying the tablets of remote ancestors when they cease to receive individual offerings at the domestic altar. Other observers of ancestor

worship among Chinese in Taiwan (Ahern 1973; Gallin 1966; Pasternak 1972) make no mention of the practice, and my evidence tends to
support their observations. Perhaps this departure from the customs
reported for southern China (Freedman 1958: 85) is attributable to
the physical form of the tablets found in most Taiwanese domestic
shrines. While a few altars display the traditional Chinese tablets, one
for each ancestor or married pair of ancestors, the great majority
support either Japanese-style tablet cabinets, containing wooden
strips, one for each ancestor or pair of ancestors, or large wooden
boards with all the ancestors' names written on them. Unlike the
traditional Chinese tablets, neither of these types takes up much room
on the altar — it is not necessary to remove a wooden strip from a
shrine box to add a new one, and a name-board can accomodate
several generations of ancestors before a fresh one is needed. So ancestors beyond the second or third generation removed remain on the
altar, even though their deathdays are not celebrated. But remaining
on the altar, they must be honored somehow, so people worship them
on Tiong-iong-ceq.

While the absence of lineages in Ploughshare has made ancestor
worship a purely domestic cult, the lack of land ownership has helped
to make ancestor worship much less closely connected with inheritance.
Johnston (1910) and Ahern (1973) have found that in communities
where most families own rice land, many people have no tablets for
lineal ascendants in the male line from whom they have not inherited
rice land. Carried to its logical conclusion, this principle would imply
that a great proportion of the deceased former residents of Ploughshare
would have no ancestral tablets at all erected for them. Such is almost
certainly not the case; although I only saw a few people's tablets, most
villagers assured me that there were tablets on their altars for all
ancestors in the primary line of descent. And I did examine the tablets
on the altars of two families, one of which had never held either rice
or mountain land, the other of which had only mountains — both
these sets contained tablets for all direct ancestors since the families'
arrival in Taiwan. In one case there were names written on tablets
which were completely unfamiliar to the household head, a literate
man in his sixties, who did know how many generations removed
they were, and he certainly did not celebrate their deathday anniversaries.

Another aspect of the ancestor cult in Ploughshare which is perhaps
connected with the natives' lack of property is their failure to divide
responsibility for worship of different lines of ancestors. In many com-

munities, the children of an uxorilocal marriage are divided between their two parents' lines of descent, some taking the father's surname and worshiping his ancestors; others taking the mother's surname and worshiping hers. Often those who take their descent from their father receive none of their mother's inheritance, so they feel no obligation to any of her forebears. Those who take descent from their mothers usually worship only their father in his line, as all their inheritance comes to them from their mother's line. But in Ploughshare, where there has traditionally been little property to inherit, usually the surnames are divided and that is all. The responsibility for ancestral worship remains undivided, all descendants worshiping all lines of ascent. For example, the case shown in Figure 1 is one of four similar instances in the village. C is surnamed Ong after his mother, while D bears his uxorilocally married-in father's surname, Iu:. At New Year's, 1973, when D erected an altar of his own separate from C's, he included the tablets of B's parents and grandparents as well as those of A and HIS parents and grandparents. The original altar, where C still worshipped, also retained both sets of tablets. The surnames were parcelled out among the descendants, but not the responsibilities of ancestor worship.

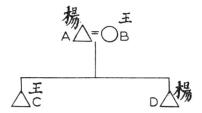

Figure 1.  Sample division of ancestor worship responsibility

To show that this divorce of ancestral worship from property inheritance in Ploughshare is related to the lack of property to be inherited, and not simply to local variation, I will illustrate with one of the few cases in the village where brothers have divided their property since acquiring it in the Land Reform (see Figure 2). A and B had no natural children, so they adopted a son and two daughters. D was never officially married, but had two sons by C, while E and F were married to each other. When A became old, he fell ill, and the parties to the case disagree about what happened concerning his care. According to F's account, she and her husband E were kind to their adopted father and spent great amounts of time and money seeing him through his illness, while C and D spent all their time playing around, as usual. According to G, F was simply a much faster talker than D and won the sick man over to her by excessive flattery. In any case, when A recovered, he arranged with a friend at the Town Office, where records were kept, to take that part of his inheritance which should have gone to D's descendants and transfer it to E and F, giving them nearly a hectare of land and leaving G and H with no property. As a consequence, E and F have a full set of ancestral tablets on their altar, while G has nothing but an incense pot for his ancestors. Because there was property to inherit, the fact that G got none of it absolved him from the responsibility of making ancestral tablets for his mother, D, or his grandparents, A and B.

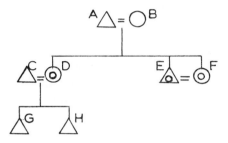

Figure 2. Sample division of ancestor worship responsibility where there has been a dispute over inheritance

The fact that the social structure of Ploughshare is based on many kinds of dyadic ties, rather than on unilineal organization, contributes to a third difference between the ancestor cult here and in other communities; the lesser extent to which ancestors of different surnames are excluded from, or separated on, domestic altars in Ploughshare. In Ch'inan, where Ahern worked, ancestor worship seems very exclusive. It is hardly surprising that in a community with strong lineage organization, no tablets for people of surnames other than that of the lineage are allowed to stand in the ancestral halls, but in Ch'inan even worship on domestic altars strongly reflects the lineage ideology of the community. Ahern states, for example, (1973: 155) that "an uxori-locally married man, WHO WOULD NORMALLY EXPECT HIS BROTHERS AT HOME TO WORSHIP HIS PARENTS, would . . . be bound to make offerings to [them] IF THERE WERE NO OTHER OFFSPRING" (Ahern 1973: 155. Emphasis added.) But in Ploughshare, where the social structure is based on dyadic ties only some of which are agnatic, people do not attempt to exclude ancestors with surnames other than that of the household's main line from their altars. When I was living in Plough-share, I collected definite information about seventeen men who had married uxorilocally into or within the village. All of these seventeen had brothers who remained at home; it is very unlikely that a man with no brothers at all will marry uxorilocally. Of these seventeen, ten had ancestral tablets for their parents on their altars, and seven of the ten worshiped their parents on deathday anniversaries. Of the three who worshiped their parents on Tiong-iong only, one had recently moved his entire altar from a prominent place at the front of his house to a shelf in a back room, in order to convert the front room to a grocery store, and had changed ALL his deathday celebrations to Tiong-iong. Of the seven uxorilocally married-in men who had no tablets for their parents on the altars in their homes in Ploughshare, four were from the mainland of China. One of these categorically refused to participate in any aspect of Taiwanese religion, one was not sure whether his parents were alive or not, a third thought it useless to worship his ancestors, since they could never cross such a wide stretch of water as the Taiwan Straits, and I have no information about the fourth. This leaves three Taiwanese men who were married uxorilocally and had no tablets for deceased parents, and of these, two specifically stated that they gave money to their brothers each year to pay for their parents' rites, which they themselves attended. The fourth had made a marriage of the type which is called *pua:-ciu-chua*, in which it is understood that the married-in husband will take his wife home with him as soon as her younger brothers are old enough to earn money, so he does not consider Ploughshare to be his permanent residence. In short, the feeling that ancestors of outside surnames should be ex-cluded from domestic altars, unless their exclusion means that nobody will worship them, is weak or absent in Ploughshare.

Not only do the villagers of Ploughshare seldom exclude ancestors of different lines or surnames from their domestic altars, but they often do not bother to separate two sets of ancestors on the same altar. Certainly there is a belief among many Taiwanese that ancestors of different surnames should not be worshiped together, and in some cases this restriction is carried so far that nonlineage ancestors are relegated to separate and subordinate altars, located in back rooms. In other instances, a subsidiary altar is built in the same room with the main one, but lower and to the stage right (junior side) of the altar containing the primary set of ancestors. Failing this, if two or more sets of tablets must inhabit the same altar, they need to be separated by a board, and people often state that placing such a board between tablets is a more convenient method, but that the proper way is to build a separate altar. In Sei-hng, another area near San-hsia where I did a summer's field work in 1970, there were eight houses which contained two lines of ancestors. One of these had the junior line on a separate altar in a back room, six had two sets on the same altar, but separated by a board, and only one had two tablet cabinets sitting next to each other undivided. People explained the fact that they separated ancestors by saying that people of different surnames might get along all right in this world, but that they certainly could not live together in the next. Ahern (1973: 130–1) describes a similar situation in Ch'inan. But in Ploughshare the feeling that unrelated ancestors must be separated is much weaker. Of eighty-five ancestral shrines in the village, forty-one contain incense burners for more than one line of ancestors. Of these forty-one, only one has the junior incense burner in a different room; all the others have all their burners on the same altar. And among these remaining forty altars, only eleven have boards separating the unrelated ancestors. In six of the remaining twenty-nine cases, the two sets of ancestors bear the same surname (this situation arises when a childless couple adopts a daughter-in-law and then takes in for her a husband of their own surname), but this still leaves twenty-three cases where people do not deem it necessary to separate ancestors of different surnames. In fact, whether the surnames of un-related ancestors are the same or different is probably immaterial, as there is one altar where two sets bear the same surname but are still separated by a board. In some cases, people go so far as to pur-chase double cabinets for their ancestral tablets — these provide spaces to insert two sets of wooden slips side by side. The two sets of an-cestors are in no sense merged, even in a double cabinet, as the in-cense burners are still separate, entailing the burning of separate in-cense sticks before the two sets of tablets. But neither is there any special effort to mark off one set of ancestors from another by the use of a conspicuous divider such as a board.

This pattern is certainly consistent with the social structure of Plough-share as a community. As mentioned before, lineages are nonexistent and surnames unimportant in community affairs; membership in the village as a whole, along with various dyadic ties, is a much more relevant consideration. The term "we" in this context does not always refer to "me and my household," or "we Ongs," but often means "I and my relatives." Twice I have had virilocally married men ask me to "Please come and be our guest," when inviting me to eat at their wives' natal homes. With so many uxorilocal marriages, even when the "we" refers to "our household," it often refers to people of more than one surname. It does not seem surprising that people who think this way about social structure among the living should think of the ancestors in the same manner.

Does all this mean that the ancestor cult is less important in Plough-share than in farming communities, that it has in a sense atrophied there because it has no basis in property and lineage organization? In a sense, it does: there is no hall cult serving as a focus for group ritual and sentiment. But what is left over, the domestic cult, is as important in Ploughshare as elsewhere. The ancestors enshrined in the home remain the focus both of lavish offerings and of much anxiety. The belief that the ancestral tablets cannot be moved without dire consequences remains very strong: even in the six days before the New Year, when ancestral spirits are supposedly no longer present in their tablets, people were unwilling to let me disturb the cabinets to examine their contents. People often expressed the belief that any slight or insult to an ancestor could bring retribution in terms of sickness or other misfortune visited upon the offending descendant, and there were misfortunes attributed to ancestors while I was in the village. In a particularly telling incident, when shamanistic seances were being held to find out if there was any supernatural cause for a young girl's arthritis, many different people tried to question the god who was possessing the shaman, and they almost all asked him if, among other possibilities, the ancestors were causing the illness. In another case, a young girl's madness was attributed partly to the discontent of a slighted ancestor. The ancestors in Ploughshare do not serve as the focus of any descent groups, but they certainly retain their importance as "immediate jural superiors."

The question remains as to whether Ploughshare is an anomaly, possessing a type of ancestor cult found only in rural communities of wage laborers, or whether we might find similar situations elsewhere. I think the latter is much more likely; in areas of China where lineage organization was weak, in villages of fishermen, loggers, or saltworkers, even in poorer communities of farmers, the order imposed on the an-cestral cult by agnatic organization and patrilineal inheritance patterns was probably considerably modified in accordance with the local situation. In urban areas, where geographic mobility was great and where affinal ties may have been very important among families of merchants, the strict patrilineal ideology might also have been weaken-ed and the ancestor cult accordingly modified. It is possible, in fact, that places like Ploughshare, where the hall cult is absent, might be better sites for the study of the domestic cult than would be communities with strong lineage organization. In Ploughshare the domestic cult develops and functions on its own, without being influenced by the strong lineage ideology which must carry over into domestic worship in places where the hall cult is highly developed. All of this is speculation; in order to verify or refute it we would need more studies of ancestor worship in nonlineage communities such as the kinds mentioned in this paragraph. When we have these, we may understand better not only the difference between ancestral cults which unite a social group and those which commemorate recently deceased forebears, but also the relationships between kinds of social groups, such as families and lineages, and the religious ceremonies in which their members participate.

## REFERENCES

AHERN, EMILY M.
  1973   *The cult of the dead in a Chinese village.* Stanford: Stanford University Press.
FREEDMAN, MAURICE
  1958   *Lineage organization in southeastern China.* London School of Economics Monograph on Social Anthropology 18. London: Athlone.
GALLIN, BERNARD
  1966   *Hsin Hsing, Taiwan: a Chinese village in change.* Berkeley and Los Angeles: University of California Press.
JOHNSTON, R. F.
  1910   *Lion and dragon in northern China.* London: J. Murray.
PASTERNAK, BURTON
  1972   *Kinship and community in two Chinese villages.* Stanford: Stanford University Press.
WOLF, ARTHUR P.
  1973   "Family organization and population processes in rural Taiwan." Unpublished research proposal.

# Biographical Notes

D. K. FIAWOO (1926–    ) received his undergraduate degree in Sociology at Cornell University and his graduate degrees at Columbia University of Edinburgh, in Anthropology and Social Anthropology respectively. He has taught Social Anthropology at the Centre of West African Studies, Birmingham University, as a Visiting Lecturer, has been a Postdoctoral Research Associate at Harvard University (one year) and a Visiting Scholar at Cambridge University for one academic year. He has published various articles on traditional and contemporary West African religion. He is currently Senior Lecturer in Sociology at the University of Ghana.

MEYER FORTES is William Wyse Professor of Social Anthropology at the University of Cambridge since 1950 and Fellow of King's College. He was originally trained as a psychologist before specializing in anthropology under the influence of C. G. Seligman and B. Malinowski. As a member of the executive council of the International African Institute he has long been a leader in African studies, especially in Ghana. As a student of religion he took an active part in supporting this symposium (of the IXth ICAES) in which active fieldworkers from East Asia combined with African scholars to lay down a common foundation for understanding the phenomenon of ancestral behavior.

STEVAN HARRELL (1947–    ) received his B.A. in Chinese and his Ph.D. in Anthropology from Stanford University. He is currently Assistant

Professor of Chinese Studies and Adjunct Assistant Professor of Anthropology at the University of Washington. He has conducted field research in rural Taiwan, and his current research interests include Chinese folk religion, the effect of economic change on the Taiwanese family, and lineage organization in premodern Chekiang.

KAREN KERNER (1942–    ) is Director of Project Evaluations for the Institute for the Study of Human Issues, Inc., in Philadelphia. After graduate work at Columbia University, she taught at Temple University. In 1972–1974, she was a principal researcher in the Philadelphia Food Survey Project, an ethnonutritional study. Her major research interest is the study of millenarian movements, particularly in Japan, and she has done extended research on Tensho-Kotai-Jingu-Kyo, a present-day Japanese movement. Among her published works are "Magical counter-spinning: an examination of Peruvian 'witching veils'" (in *Proceedings of the VIIIth ICAES*, 1968) and "Japan's new religions" (in *Changing patterns of Japanese life*, special issue of *Japan Interpreter*, 1970).

TAKIE SUGIYAMA LEBRA (1930–    ) received her B.A. from Gakushuin University, Tokyo, and her M.A. and Ph.D. from the University of Pittsburgh. Since 1967 she has been teaching at the University of Hawaii and is currently Associate Professor of Anthropology. Her specialty lies in social and psychological anthropology, religion, moral values, and behavior transformation, particularly in Japan. She has contributed numerous articles to professional journals and has coedited *Japanese culture and behavior: selected readings*.

YIH-YUAN LI (1931–    ) did his undergraduate work at the National Taiwan University and graduate studies in anthropology at Harvard University. He has been on the staff of the Institute of Ethnology, Academia Sinica, since 1955. He is now Director of the Institute and concurrently Professor of Anthropology at the National Taiwan University. His chief fields of interest have been Chinese and Southeast Asian ethnology. He is the author of two books written in Chinese: *Culture and behavior* (1966) and *An immigrant town: life in an overseas Chinese community in Southern Malaya* (1970). He is also the coeditor of a monograph *Symposium on the character of the Chinese: an interdisciplinary approach* (1972). He is Chief Editor of the *Bulletin of the Institute of Ethnology, Academia Sinica*.

TOICHI MABUCHI (1909–    ) graduated (roughly equivalent to the M.A.

in the postwar system of education) from Taihoku (= Taipei) Imperial University in 1931. Subsequently, for several years, he was a researcher with the Institute of Ethnology there, and was appointed Associate Professor at the same University in 1943. He was Professor of Social Anthropology at Toyo University, Tokyo (1951–1953), Tokyo Metropolitan University (1953–1972), and the University of the Ryukyus (1972–1975). He is a present with Nanzan University, Nagoya. His research field covers Formosa, Indonesia, and the Ryukyus and his main concern has been social anthropology. *Ethnology of the southwestern Pacific*, a volume containing about three quarters of his English articles, was issued in Taipei in March 1974, while a three-volume collection of his Japanese writings was published serially in July–September 1974.

TAKASHI MAEDA (1928–    ) did both his undergraduate and graduate work at Kyoto University. He obtained his Ph.D. from the same university. His chief fields of interest have been the sociology of religion and the sociology of the family, especially first-born succession. He is the author of *Study of ancestor worship* and *Sociological study of religious pilgrims*. He was a Research Fellow to UCLA in the year 1971–1972, and is a member of the Japan Sociological Society. Since 1972, he has been Professor of Sociology at Kansai University.

MAKIO MATSUZONO is Professor of Anthropology at Tenri University near Nara, Japan. During 1973 he was Visiting Professor at the College of Chinese Culture, Taiwan. The paper in this volume is a result of fieldwork done under the auspices of Tokyo Metropolitan University, from which university he graduated.

DOUGLAS MILES (1939–    ) received his bachelor's, master's and doctoral degrees from the University of Sydney where he is now Senior Lecturer in the Department of Anthropology. He has published several articles and has a book in press about the Ngadju Dayaks and Bandjarese Malays of Central Kalimantan, where he worked in 1959–1963. His other publications and doctoral thesis concern the Yao of Thailand, where he carried out field research in 1966–1969. He is currently working in Indonesia and Holland on the sociology of Balinese literature.

RICHARD J. MILLER (1918–    ) received his undergraduate and graduate training at the University of California, Berkeley, in the field of Japanese history. Since 1970 he has been on the faculty of the Department of History, University of California, Davis, prior to which he taught for a number of years at the International Christian University, Tokyo, and also worked as Editorial Advisor and Translator for the Center of Japanese Social and Political Studies in Tokyo. His fields of specialization are the social and cultural history of ancient Japan for the pre-Heian period, with particular reference to social structure and government organization.

WILLIAM NEWELL (1922–    ) Associate Professor of Anthropology at the University of Sydney, was formerly Head of the Department of Sociology and Anthropology at the International Christian University, Tokyo, on the faculty of the West China Union University in Szechuan and visiting Professor at the Academia Sinica, Taipei. His interests have wandered from India to Japan to China. His main East Asian books are *Treacherous River, a study of rural Teochiu Chinese in Malaya* and *The Sociology of Japanese religion* (with Marioka Kiyomi).

HERMAN OOMS (1937–    ) born in Belgium, received a candidature (B.A.) in Classics at the Facultés Universitaires Notre-Dame de la Paix, Namur, and a licentiate (M.A.) in Philosophy at the John Berchmans College, Louvain. In Japan from 1962 to 1968, he studied the Japanese language and received an M.A. in Religious Studies (Anthropology) from the University of Tokyo. Since 1968 he has been in Chicago, where in 1973 he received a Ph.D. in Japanese History from the University of Chicago, and where since 1972 he has been Assistant Professor of History at the University of Illinois at Chicago Circle. His chief interests are the social and intellectual history of Tokugawa Japan (1600–1868) and the history of Japanese religion. His publications include an article of monograph length on Japanese ancestor worship and a political biography of Matsudaira Sadanobu, a Tokugawa reformer (in press).

WALTER H. SANGREE (1926–    ) received his undergraduate degree in Philosophy from Haverford College, his M.A. in Psychology from Wesleyan University (Conn.), and his Ph.D. in Anthropology from the University of Chicago. His principal research has been among the Tiriki of Kenya and the Irigwe of Nigeria. He has taught at the University of Rochester since 1957 where he is currently Professor and Chairman of the Department of Anthropology.

JOEL S. SAVISHINSKY (1944–    ) did his undergraduate work at the City College of New York and received a doctorate in Anthropology from Cornell University. He has taught at Adelphi University and the American

Museum of Natural History, and since 1973 has been a member of the anthropology department at Ithaca College. He has done fieldwork in Turkey, the Canadian Arctic, and among Jewish ethnic groups in the United States. In addition to a book on the Arctic, *The trail of the hare*, his publications have dealt with cultural ecology, kinship, interethnic relations, psychological stress, and man-animal relationships.

GARY WORTH SEAMAN (1942– ) received his B.A. from the University of Texas in 1966 and his doctorate in Anthropology from Cornell University in 1974. He has studied in Japan and Germany and did his fieldwork for the dissertation on Taiwan. His chief interests are in the sociology of religion and ethnographic film. He has made a number of films dealing with different aspects of Chinese popular religion and culture. He has held fellowships from the Carnegie Foundation, the Ford Foundation, and the National Institute of Health. He studied at Hamburg University with a Fulbright Fellowship. In 1974–1975 he was Visiting Professor of Anthropology at Washington University in St. Louis.

ROBERT J. SMITH (1927– ) received his undergraduate degree from the University of Minnesota in 1949 and his doctorate in Anthropology from Cornell University in 1953. His major fields of interest have been social change in Japan and the relationship between history and anthropology. He is past editor of *Human Organization*, the journal of the Society for Applied Anthropology, and has served at Cornell as Chairman of the Department of Asian Studies and the Department of Anthropology. He has taught at Cornell University since 1953 and was recently named Goldwin Smith Professor of Anthropology.

CHOSHU TAKEDA (1916– ) received his undergraduate degree in Japanese Buddhist History and his doctorate in Cultural Studies from Kyoto University. He has taught at Hanazono University, Kansai University, the Kyoto Buddhist University, Hokkaido University, and Kyoto University and is currently professor in the Faculty of Letters at Doshisha University, Kyoto. His main area of study has been the historical and cultural anthropological analysis of the relationship and interaction between Japanese social structure and folk beliefs, especially ancestor worship. A few of his books in this area are: *A history of ancestor worship in Japanese folk society* (Kyoto: Heirakuji, 1947); *Japanese folk beliefs* (Osaka: Sogensha, 1957); *Folk Buddhism and ancestor worship in Japan* (Tokyo: Tokyo University Press, 1971); *Religious syncretism in Edo Period hamlet shrines and temples: a field survey of old documents* (Kyoto: Hozokan, 1972); and *Kyoto Prefecture folk customs* (volume 26 of the Japanese Folk Customs Series. Tokyo: Daiichi Hoki, 1973). From 1960 to 1964 and during 1970, he was the recipient of research and publishing grants from the Japanese Ministry of Education's Scientific Research Foundation. He is presently active on the Board of Councillors of The Folklore Society of Japan, The Japanese Society of Ethnology, and The Kyoto University Society of Historical Research. At Doshisha University he is Chairman of Family System Studies in The Institute for the Study of Humanities and Social Sciences, Chairman of The Society of Culture Studies, and on the Board of Councillors of The Institute of the Science of Cultural History.

VICTOR C. UCHENDU is Professor of Anthropology and Director of the African Studies Center, University of Illinois at Urbana-Champaign. A graduate of the University of Ibadan, Nigeria, where he distinguished himself by winning the Departmental Prize (1959/1960) and the Faculty Prize (1960/1961) of the Faculty of Economics and Social Studies, Uchendu also read Anthropology at Northwestern University, where he earned his Ph.D. Formerly Reader in Social Anthropology at Makerere University, Kampala, where he also served as the Executive Director of the Makerere Institute of Social Research, he has taught at the Food Research Institute, Stanford University, and was Research Associate, Faculty of Agriculture, University of Ghana, in 1967/1968. The author of *The Igbo of South Nigeria* (New York, 1965), he has contributed to a large number of symposia and books and has published extensively on problems of change and development in modern Africa. He studied agricultural labor migration among the Navajo Indians of the American Southwest and has also carried out field studies of agricultural change in Ghana, Uganda, Kenya, Tanzania, and Zambia.

SUNG-HSING WANG (1935–   ) did his undergraduate work at the National Taiwan University and received his M.A. and Ph.D. in Anthropology from the University of Tokyo. He has also studied at the London School of Economics and Political Science, University of London. His interest is in the comparative social organization of China and Japan and in the socioeconomic development of Taiwan. He is the author of *Kuei-shan Tao: a study of a Chinese fishing community in Formosa* (in Chinese, 1967), and coauthor of *Rice farming in Taiwan: three village studies* (1974). Since 1962, he has been affiliated with the Institute of Ethnology, Academia Sinica, and has taught at the National Taiwan University.

HOWARD WIMBERLEY (1935–    ) received his undergraduate and M.A. degrees from the University of Texas and a Ph.D. in Anthropology from Cornell University. His anthropological research has been in Japanese religion, comparative studies of social networks, and legal development. He is presently Associate Professor of Anthropology at Adelphi University.

ARTHUR P. WOLF received his Ph.D. from Cornell University in 1964 and taught there for five years. He is now Professor of Anthropology at Stanford University. His main fieldwork area is in northern Taiwan and he is at present editing a publication on Chinese religion to be published by the Stanford University Press.

SHOJI YONEMURA (1927–    ) did his undergraduate work at Kyushu University. His major fields of interest have been the kinship system, the Shintō festival system, and power structure in village Japan. He was an Assistant at Kyushu University and on the research staff of the Social Science Research Institute of the International Christian University, Tokyo. He is currently an Associate Professor of Okayama University.

# Index of Names

# Index of Subjects

Murivurivuk, Taiwan, 101

Nagasawa, Japan, 62–89
Nandi, 298
Nayar, 208, 219
New Guinea, 12
New York (city), Jews in, 241–258
Ngadju, *kabali*, 325
Nishi Ashida, Japan, 148–149
Nigeria, 264, 265, 288, 297, 300
*Nihon minzokugaku taikei* (Monographs on Japanese folklore), 61
Nuer, 20

Obora, Japan, 146, 147–148
Okinawa, 26–28, 92, 106–110, 113–117, 220, 231–240, 336–337; *buchidang*, 27–28; *bunke*, 27–28; *chōde kasabai*, 232; *fafuji*, 27; *fii no kang*, 27; *futuki*, 27; *hiki*, 27, 28; *honke*, 27; *ihee*, 27; *kami*, 27; *munchū*, 27–28, 231, 234–240; *shiji*, 234, 235, 236–237, 238; *shiji-tadashi*, 234; *tachii-majikui*, 234; *yashiki*, 27; *yuta*, 233, 236, 237
Ong, 9
"Optional descent in the sothern Ryukyus" (Mabuchi), 111–112

Ploughshare Village, Taiwan, 374–385
Polynesians, 105
Pulangka, 309–326
Punic Wars, 157, 159
Puyuma, 98–103, 105–106, 114; *karumahan* (*karuma'an*), 99

Rockefeller Foundation, 143
Rome, ancient, 20–21, 157, 159
Ryukyus, 26–28, 91–103, 105–117; *munchū*, 106, 107, 108; *mutu*, 92, 108; *mutu-ya*, 106–108; *ukudi*, 107

San-hsia, Taiwan, 339–364
*Sasa*, 286–287
*Seigō Minzoku*, 64
Seijo University, Tokyo, 96
*Sengo no Suye mura* (Postwar Suye) (Usui, ed.), 144–145
Shinohara, Japan, 146, 159
Sierra Leone, 272, 280
Sone, Japan, 34–60
Stanford University, 361
Suku, 285–286; *bambuta*, 207
Suye, Japan, 144–145, 147–148, 151

Taiwan (Formosa), 5, 8–9, 13–14, 24, 91, 98–103, 105, 114, 307, 329–337, 339–364, 365–372, 373–385; *cheng t'ing*, 366–371; Ch'ing Ming Chieh, 344; Ch'ing Shui Ts'u Shih Kung, 339; *ch'ou chu mu sui*, 371; *dang-ki*, 329–335; *feng-shui*, 330–335, 370; Hungry Ghosts, 208; *ko-niu-biou*, 344; *kongtia:*, 343, 344, 346, 349, 352, 353, 363; *kong-tik-pun*, 358–359, 360; *pua:-ciuchua*, 382; *shen chu p'ai*, 367; *sim-pua*, 347; Stove God, 340, 344, 363; *ta fang*, 366; *Tiong-iong ceq*, 378–379, 382
Takane, Japan, 34–60
Takaoka, Japan, 141
Tallensi, 1, 2, 4, 9, 22, 23, 208, 220, 266, 281
Teba Island, Japan, 145, 147–148, 155, 159
Terik, 298
Thailand, 309
Tiriki: *baguga*, 298–299, 303–304; *gugamisambwa* distinction, 303; *lusambwa*, 304; *majina gi misambwa*, 299; *misambwa*, 298–299
Tiv, 20
Togo Republic, 263–264
Tokyo University, 133
Tonga, 18
Tongu, 263, 264, 269, 271
*Totem and taboo* (Freud), 21

*Ullambana sutra*, 140
United Nations, 309
United States: National Institute of Mental Health, 205, 219; National Science Foundation, 297
University of Hawaii, 111, 219
University of Montreal, 41
University of Sydney, 139
Urukawa, Miyako Island, 94–95, 98, 113, 114, 117
Uwada, Japan, 144, 148, 419, 157–159

Vietnam, 309, 336–337

Wenner-Gren Foundation for Anthropological Research, 91, 105, 283

Yaeyama Archipelago, Ryukyus, 107, 109, 112
Yao: *be*, 313; *bo*, 313, 314; *dia*, 310–311; *djaafin*, 313, 314; *peo*, 309–310, 311, 312, 318, 321, 322, 323–325; *tsiang*,